W9-AHF-036

Marilyn Memorabilia

Putting a Price on the Priceless Performer

Clark Kidder

For Linda, Robby, and Nathan

©2002 by Clark Kidder
All rights reserved.

No portion of this publication may be reproduced or transmitted in any form or by any means, electronic or mechanical, including photocopy, recording, or any information storage and retrieval system, without permission in writing from the publisher, except by a reviewer who may quote brief passages in a critical article or review to be printed in a magazine or newspaper, or electronically transmitted on radio or television.

Published by

Please call or write for our free catalog of publications. Our toll-free number to place an order or obtain a free catalog is (800) 258-0929.

Library of Congress Catalog Number: 2001096287
ISBN: 0-87349-342-7

Cover collectibles provided by Amber Thaxton and Clark Kidder.

Photos of Marilyn Monroe collectibles contained within are from the collections of the following people: Bill Altman, Gerald Arena, Laurence Barthelemy, Mary Belzunce, Richard Chenoweth, Cheryl Downey, Liz Fisher, Tina Garland, John Harold, Norm Jensen, Clark Kidder, Marc Malfait, Mariya Matelyan, Joe Mazza, Pascal Schilling, June Smith, Amber Thaxton, Jason Thomas, and Jennifer Wooten.

Preface

Marilyn Monroe. Her very name evokes memories of a quieter, happier time in our not-so-distant past. Marilyn was a part of what we often refer to affectionately as the "fabulous '50s," the post-war boom in America. Spirits were high and the public was yearning for new, fresh ideas.

The time was never more right for a new "blonde bombshell" to sweep the cinemas. Hollywood was desperately in trouble. With the advent of television, people were staying home and not going to the movies. There was a real worry that the movie industry would collapse—a concept difficult for us to comprehend today.

Screen vamps Jean Harlow and Mae West reigned during the 1930s, and the 1940s brought Rita Hayworth and Betty Grable, but the times called for a new and more exciting presence on the screen.

Enter Marilyn Monroe.

Born Norma Jeane Baker in Los Angeles, California, on June 1, 1926, to Gladys Baker and an unknown father, presumed to be C. Stanley Gifford, little Norma Jeane had a miserable childhood. Gladys was a film cutter for the studios, but was committed to an institution for mental instability, leaving Norma Jeane to grow up in nearly a dozen foster homes and two orphanages. One foster family made her pray all day and told her it was a sin to go to a movie. Yet another family had her playing "soldiers" with empty whiskey bottles strewn across the floor.

At 16, Norma Jeane married her first husband, James Dougherty, a merchant marine and friend of the family. While Dougherty was at sea, Norma Jeane took a job assembling parachutes at a nearby factory, doing her part to aid in the war effort. One day, army photographer David Conover was sent to the factory to take photos that would help lift the morale of the troops. Norma Jeane donned a red sweater for the occasion and Conover thought her so photogenic that he encouraged her to pursue modeling—advice that she enthusiastically took.

Before long, Norma Jeane had signed with the Blue Book Modeling Agency and was on her way to a modeling career. Meanwhile, Dougherty was receiving the "Dear John" letter, along with divorce papers.

The way was cleared now for the metamorphosis to take place from Norma Jeane to Marilyn Monroe.

Between 1946 and 1952, Marilyn was given roles in a series of films for the various Hollywood studios. Her parts were generally small ones, but she was gradually earning a name for herself in Hollywood. One of her most pivotal roles career-wise was the in the1950 film, *The Asphalt Jungle*. Another equally important role was in *All About Eve*, also in 1950. This film's star was none other than Bette Davis, and it won much critical acclaim.

During this time, Marilyn supplemented her income by posing for various glamour photographers, such as Andre de Dienes and Laszlo Willinger. Many of the resulting photos found their way to the covers of magazines throughout the world and later in calendars.

After several more films in 1951 and 1952, Marilyn's career was in high gear; until, that is, the press discovered that a nude photo of Marilyn was gracing a calendar in wide circulation! Marilyn, as well as many others, thought the ensuing scandal could very well spell the end of her career. Marilyn admitted that she posed for the nude session in 1949 for photographer Tom Kelley. She was out of work at the time and needed the $50 he offered.

Luckily for Marilyn, the tide began to turn when *LIFE* magazine decided to feature her on the cover of the April 7, 1952, issue, even including the famous calendar as part of the article. The public was sympathetic with Marilyn's reasons for posing and soon people were lined up in droves to see her next film. Instead of ending her career, the nude photos had only bolstered it! And, in December 1953, one of the nude photos became the very first centerfold in the premiere issue of *Playboy* magazine. She was now truly a "star."

Marilyn found great film success in 1953. She now had top billing and was on her way to building the legendary status she would later attain. A romance soon began with baseball great Joe DiMaggio, and the couple were married in San Francisco on Jan. 14, 1954. They spent their honeymoon in Japan, where Marilyn stole the show from Joe amongst even the baseball-loving Japanese. One Japanese radio announcer referred to her as the "honorable hip-swinging blonde." Against Joe's wishes, Marilyn decided to accept an offer to entertain the troops in Korea. Braving the bitter cold, she won the admiration of thousands of battle-weary soldiers. She later called the experience the highlight of her life.

In 1955, Marilyn flew to New York to film a scene for her upcoming film, *The Seven Year Itch*. It was in this movie that the now-famous series of photos of her in the billowing white skirt were taken. During numerous retakes, husband Joe stood seething on the sidelines, appalled that his wife was baring her legs and underpants before thousands of spectators. He stormed off in a rage, and not long afterward, the two divorced. However, they remained friends until the end—even planning to remarry shortly before Marilyn's death in 1962.

By 1956, Marilyn, disgusted at Fox for casting her in nothing but "dumb blonde" roles, decided to form her own production company. Appropriately, it was called Marilyn Monroe Productions. Her partner was her well-known friend and photographer, Milton H. Greene. Never before had a star so boldly challenged the studio system. Yet, Marilyn emerged victorious, gaining critical director approval, among other things.

The next film Marilyn would do was *Bus Stop,* in which she put to use the new system of method acting she had just studied at the famed Actors Studio in New York City. Marilyn's performance in the film gained her much critical acclaim, and it would be lauded as her finest performance ever.

In 1956, a romance began to blossom between Marilyn and the famous playwright, Arthur Miller. Marilyn seemed on top of the world, and before long, the couple was married. The pair was affectionately referred to as the "egghead and the hourglass." The wedding took place first in a civil ceremony on June 29, 1956, and then in a Jewish ceremony on July 1, 1956.

But the marriage was not a happy one. Marilyn's dreams of having a child were dashed after she had several miscarriages. And Arthur, unable to live up to the expectations that Marilyn had placed upon him, realized that the marriage was slowly dissolving. Indeed, it ended in divorce in January 1961.

Before parting, however, Marilyn and Arthur flew to England in the fall of 1956 to shoot her next film, *The Prince and the Showgirl*, which would co-star Sir Lawrence Olivier. There was much tension between Marilyn and Olivier during filming, but the end result was a fine film that showcased Marilyn's tremendous comedic abilities. Released in 1957, the film is another favorite among today's Marilyn fans.

Marilyn's next film, *Some Like It Hot*, was released in 1959. Marilyn did not want to make the film, but she needed the money to help pay mounting bills. Despite her reluctance, the film, which co-starred Tony Curtis and Jack Lemmon, proved to be extremely successful at the box office.

In 1960, still under contract with Fox to do three more movies, Marilyn accepted the role in a film entitled *Let's Make Love*. Her costar was French actor Yves Montand, with whom Marilyn had an affair both on-screen and off. Unfortunately, the film proved to be a flop and prompted critics and industry officials to predict the end of Marilyn's reign at the top of the box office.

Sadly, Marilyn would complete only one more film, *The Misfits*, in 1961. It co-starred Montgomery Clift and Clark Gable, and its screenplay was written for Marilyn as a gift from then-husband Miller. It was only a marginal success at the box office, but it proved that Marilyn could handle playing more serious roles.

Marilyn became increasingly fragile during filming of *The Misfits* in the hot desert surrounding Reno, Nevada. To complicate things further, her marriage to Miller was falling apart during filming and the two went their separate ways after completing it.

Marilyn struggled through 1961, and in 1962, she began work on her next film for Fox, *Something's Got To Give*, which co-starred her good friend, Dean Martin. The studio was infuriated when Marilyn accepted an invitation to sing "Happy Birthday" to President Kennedy in Washington instead of continuing work on the film. To add to the fire, not long after shooting began, Marilyn came down with a serious sinus infection and was absent so often that it angered Fox enough to actually fire her and file a lawsuit.

In a matter of weeks, Fox rehired Marilyn, but her downhill spiral continued. She drank heavily, took pills to fall asleep, and then took even more to wake up. Everything came to a head on the evening of Aug. 4, 1962. Alone on a Saturday night, the greatest—yet loneliest—star in the world retired to her bedroom, and within hours, was dead of an overdose. Whether by her own hand, accident, or, as some have suggested, by the hands of others, an American legend was gone.

Although Marilyn Monroe was with us for only a brief moment in time, she left such an indelible impression on the world that she will be remembered for an eternity.

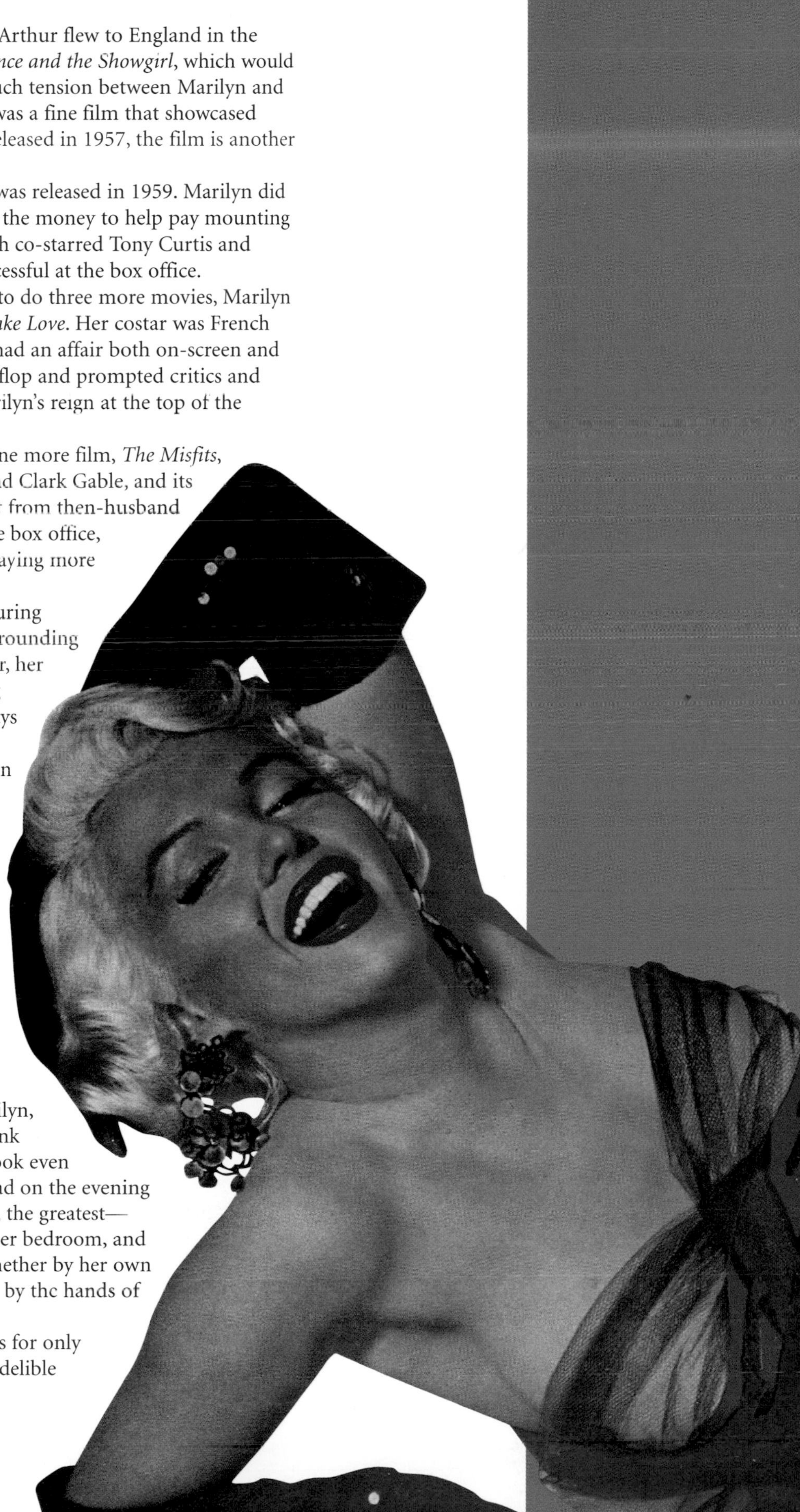

Table of Contents

Acknowledgments

I would like to thank all of those people who helped make this book possible.

For contributing materials for use in this book, as well as their knowledge and photography skills, I would like to extend a very special thanks to: Frederic Cabanas, Amber Thaxton, Liz Fisher, Cheryl Downey, Ken Mikkelson, Don and Pat Smith, Jason Thomas, Scott Anderson, Tina Garland, Joe Mazza, Gerald Arena, Jennifer Wooten, Richard Chenoweth, June Smith, Mariya Matelyan, Bill Altman, Pat Austin, John Harold, Skip Drew, Laurence Barthelemy, Pascal Schilling, Mary Belzunce, David Acevedo, Thomas Stack, Norm Jensen, and Marc Malfait.

Thanks as well to Maria Turner, my editor at Krause Publications, for her expert assistance. And to page designer Jamie Martin for her hard work in making these pages come to life.

I'm also very grateful to Paul Kennedy at Krause for believing in this book.

Introduction

The need for a comprehensive price guide covering Marilyn Monroe collectibles has been long overdue.

Why?

Ask any paper dealer who its fastest-selling star is and the answer will be Marilyn Monroe every time.

Marilyn's career spanned just 16 years, but it was long enough to create a myriad of collectible items. In fact, new Monroe collectibles are being made at a feverish pace to this day, nearly 40 years after her untimely death in August 1962. At auction houses around the world, Marilyn memorabilia is fetching record prices. One of the dresses she wore in *There's No Business Like Show Business* recently brought $57,000 at a Christie's auction.

Owning a piece of vintage Americana is something of a fad these days, both in the United States and abroad. Marilyn Monroe is about as close as you can get to true Americana. She's right up there with baseball, hot dogs, and apple pie.

In writing this book, I have attempted to be as comprehensive as possible in my coverage of the vast array of Monroe collectibles that were produced both during and after her lifetime—not only in the U.S., but in foreign countries as well. You'll find chapters on how a beginning collector gets started, and tips on dealing with foreign countries and storing your valuable collectibles, as well as on trading with fellow collectors. In addition, detailed information and price ranges (which are for items in very good to near-mint condition) are given for many of the hundreds of Monroe collectibles listed within, such as sheet music, movie posters, books, magazine covers, calendars, autographs, and much more. Such information will allow you to be better informed when purchasing or selling such items.

Whether you inherit an attic full of goodies from your great uncle, or stumble onto a Marilyn Monroe collectible at a local flea market, or even if you are a veteran collector of Monroe, you'll find informative and interesting information within.

Interest in Marilyn Monroe is universal, which you'll see as you scan the following pages. There are currently fan clubs located in Germany, England, Australia, and France. With access to millions via the Internet, the ability to connect with other Monroe collectors around the world is at an all-time high. The sky is the limit!

Chapter 1

The Beginning Collector

Nearly all of us have collected something in our lifetime. Remember that baseball card or stamp collection you had as a child? Sooner or later such collections got tucked away in the attic, sold in a rummage sale, or simply (and sadly) tossed in the trash. It really takes a special sort of person to be a collector. You might say you have to be bitten by the "collecting bug."

Quite often, collections are started on a very small scale and at a slow pace. There are, of course, exceptions to this rule. Some people collect for monetary reasons exclusively—for investment purposes.

There is certainly nothing wrong with collecting for investment purposes, and it makes great sense from a business standpoint. However, a true dyed-in-the-wool collector is one who cares little about the investment potential, but instead derives an extreme amount of pleasure from the pursuit of collecting itself.

I tend to fall somewhere in the middle. There is the businessman in me who really cares about the long-term investment potential of my collection. However, I also derive great pleasure from my Marilyn collectibles; to me, that is the true meaning of collecting.

I began my Marilyn collection at a snail's pace in the early 1980s. My first purchases were a framed photo from Kmart and a couple books that had just been published on Marilyn.

After spying the *LIFE* magazine article on Marilyn collector George Zeno in the October 1981 issue, which featured a two-page spread on George's wall of Marilyn magazine covers, I was hooked!

From then on, I hunted at a more feverish pace for vintage Monroe items—primarily magazine covers.

My first finds were at local auctions, garage sales, and antique shops. They consisted mainly of Marilyn's 1950s and '60s magazine cover appearances on *LIFE* and *Look* magazines.

I was soon extracting the names and addresses of people who dealt in old magazines, or Hollywood memorabilia in general, from the classifieds of collecting-related periodicals.

From there, my collection really took off via mail-order. The sky was the limit, and I soon found myself dealing with foreign sellers and trading with foreign collectors who had also advertised in the United States. (A list of such periodicals can be found elsewhere in this book.)

It's best to stick to a budget as closely as you can when amassing your collection. It's very easy and tempting to purchase every item that comes your way. Set some realistic goals and stick to them. Perhaps you'll wish to specialize in movie posters, books, or magazine covers. Stay focused, whatever your collecting objective may be, and you'll be just fine.

Consider such things as how much space you have to store or display your collection safely and effectively.

Visit your library. Surf the Internet! Read up and ask as many questions as you can from experienced collectors. The better informed you are from the start, the better your entire collecting experience will be.

Most important of all, enjoy yourself along the way!

Storing Paper Collectibles

After going to the trouble of hunting down a valuable and fragile Marilyn paper collectible, it is a very good idea to take some precautions to preserve it.

One good rule of thumb is to never store magazines in deep stacks, as this can crush the already fragile spines.

Ideally, one should secure acid-free backing boards and plastic sleeves to store and encase your paper collectibles. It's best to wear a pair of plastic gloves when you handle an item, as this will prevent the damaging oils and acids on your skin from blemishing its surface.

Always store your paper collectibles in an environment that is fairly dry, but not overly dry. Avoid placing the items in the direct path of sunlight, or near registers and water pipes that can also damage them. It only takes exposure to a half-hour of sunlight per day to badly damage an item. Use a common sense approach, and you'll be fine.

Some collectors prefer to display their items, which allows them to enjoy their collectibles every day. If you choose to frame the pieces for display, it's always a good idea to use acid-free matting material. Some folks choose to shrink-wrap their items, which is fine, as long as they don't forget to punch the occasional hole in the plastic so that the article can "breathe."

Ideally, collectible paper items should be stored in a temperature-controlled room. Short of this, one can utilize an air-conditioning system during the humid summer months and a humidifier during the super dry months of winter. It's not uncommon for humidity levels in a home to dive to 13 percent during the winter.

Insuring Your Collection

It's a great idea to insure your collectibles, because before you know it you may have a considerable investment. Usually, you can just simply contact the company you have your household insurance with and they will accommodate you. If this fails, ask your insurance agent to recommend someone who will insure your collectibles.

I have found that the cost is minimal and, in my case, it costs just 40 cents to insure each $100 worth of collectibles per year.

Usually the insurance company requires an inventory list, and it's a good idea to go a step further and make a videotape of all of the insured items as well. Place a copy of the tape with your insurance company and put one in your safe-deposit box at the bank.

Here's a cautionary example: I have a friend with a sizeable Marilyn collection who woke up one morning to discover that a water pipe had ruptured in the bathroom situated directly above his collectibles. The result was disastrous. Luckily, he had insurance and was reimbursed for his loss, although the loss of such cherished items was very upsetting.

Don't procrastinate! Get that insurance today!

Restoring Paper Collectibles

The thought of restoring collectible paper items tends to intimidate most of us, and justifiably so. However, one should not be afraid to consider either sending a certain item to a professional restorer or doing a little home restoration on a piece that has minimal problems. Restoration of such items as movie posters, lobby cards, etc. can actually increase their value substantially. With the passing of time, the collecting community is becoming more comfortable with the idea of purchasing restored pieces for their collections. After all, there are only so many of these items, and there are more collectors born every day!

In the case of minor scratches and creases on the surface of your paper collectible, you can fill crevices with good results by using pastel chalks. Watercolors are another option, though it's best to let a professional artist or restorer use these. Quite often a local artist will do the work for a fee. One should never use oil-based products for the restoration of paper items since they permeate the paper and are nearly impossible to remove if one desires to do so at a later date. In addition, collectors of movie posters often choose to have their posters either linen backed or backed with special removable and acid-free paper to help reinforce the item. You can also do this with old calendars.

To perfect your technique it is best to experiment first on old magazines or other items of no value. It takes time to get the hang of it, but like anything, practice makes perfect! You'll be amazed at the wonderful results you can achieve, and, at the same time you'll be increasing the value of your collection.

Buying From Foreign Countries

I have amassed nearly half of my paper collection by dealing with foreign dealers and collectors. The rules are not much different than those for ordering from U.S. sources.

Sources for foreign Monroe material can be found on the Internet or in trade publications. It generally takes one week for a letter to reach a foreign destination and/or to receive one. If the items are not priced in U.S. dollars, you can call your local bank or the Internet to get the current exchange rate for the specific currency you are dealing with. You may also request that the seller quote you the items in U.S. dollars. The method of payment is usually an international money order, which you can secure from your post office. You make the money order out for the U.S. dollar amount due the seller, and the post office converts it to the specified currency. Sending cash through the mail is, of course, a definite no-no, but something that is done quite often nonetheless. Some foreign sellers are able to take personal checks, but there will be a conversion charge you will be asked to pay in most cases.

You must instruct the seller to ship the items either via surface or airmail. There is an intermediate service available from certain countries that costs more than the surface rate but less than the air mail rate. Surface mail will take from one and one-half to three months, while airmail will take about one week. The price difference in postage is substantial, and you must decide which way you want to go. Instruct the shipper to sandwich the flat-paper items between two pieces of stiff cardboard and otherwise pack well, and you'll receive your precious collectibles in good shape.

Trading With Other Collectors

Just as sports card collectors do, collectors of Marilyn memorabilia often trade amongst themselves. This is usually done between friends who have established a rapport over a period of time. Trading is fun and is a win-win situation for both parties involved, allowing them to trade duplicates in their collection for items they don't have.

I have traded for years with many U.S. and foreign Marilyn collectors. Problems have only arisen when an item offered for trade is not fully and honestly described. It is best to make either a black-and-white or color copy of the item offered for trade, so that the other person involved has an accurate idea of the condition of at least the outside cover of the item. Be sure to describe any damage to the interior of the item, such as articles that have been clipped, or writing on the pages, or pages that are missing.

Honesty is the best policy, and for it, you will be rewarded with success.

Mail-Order Buying

Without mail-order, my collection would be tiny. It has opened doors that would otherwise have been closed and has given me access to exciting items the world over. After seventeen years of collecting, I have had only one bad experience in the hundreds of transactions I have made.

Certain precautions must, of course, be taken. When first dealing with a new person, you should purchase a lower-priced item on the list in order to get a feel for the kind of service the seller will give you. If the seller has a return policy, all the better. In fact, try to purchase only from those that are willing to provide this return policy, as it is a common courtesy. It's not a bad idea to request a photocopy of the item(s) you are interested in buying. It's also courteous to offer to pay for this service.

Discuss who is going to pay for postage, especially if the items need to be returned. Explain to the seller that you want your merchandise insured and packaged very well. Insurance costs little and gives you peace of mind.

Magazines should always be sandwiched between two pieces of stiff cardboard, and posters or calendars should be rolled and placed in mailing tubes. Fragile collectible items should be carefully wrapped in Bubble Wrap with thick layers of newspaper placed around them to avoid breakage. Don't allow newspaper to come in direct contact with the collectible, however, as the newsprint can be transferred to the surface of your valuable item, tarnishing it.

It is a very good idea to pay with a credit card if you can. Some credit card companies do things such as reverse the charges on unsatisfactory purchases or offer a refund if you find lower prices elsewhere. Call your credit card issuer and ask what its policy is in this area. If the items are paid for with a personal check, the seller may opt to wait a few weeks before shipping the item to you to be sure that your check clears. Money orders or transfers will allow the seller to expedite your shipment.

Another good idea is to keep a record of your phone calls and correspondence regarding the order, so in the case of any questions or discrepancies, you can refer back to the notes to clear up any confusion. If you are answering someone's ad, be aware of the time difference when calling, and if you write, it's common courtesy to include a self-addressed stamped envelope (SASE).

These rules also apply to any dealings over the Internet. If these tips are followed, you will greatly reduce the risk of having a bad experience with mail-order.

Chapter 2

Autograph Values

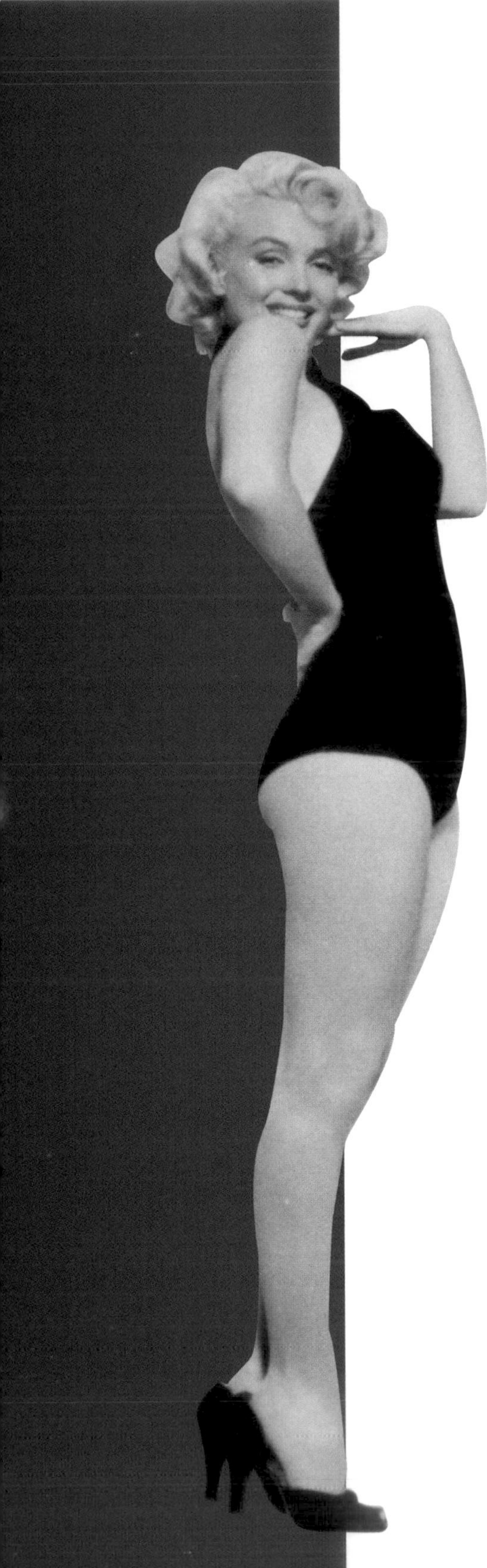

Autographs of famous people have been highly collectible for a long time. Certain signed documents can fetch many thousands of dollars. From presidents to dictators to glamorous movie stars and persecuted Native American chiefs, we find a myriad of potentially collectible autographs.

Of all the movie stars that have come and gone since the beginning of motion pictures, Marilyn Monroe commands the highest prices of any in the area of autographs. Marilyn was known to sign many autographs early on in her career. After becoming famous in 1952, due to her "exposure" as a nude model that graced the tops of calendars, Marilyn had less time to sign autographs. The job then fell on studio secretaries. However, several photos are extant of Marilyn after her sudden rise to stardom, signing autographs during public appearances. She gave particular attention to young children. During her tour of Korea to entertain the troops, she was known to sign photos, posters, and even casts for the soldiers.

There are certain things to look for when attempting to authenticate a Monroe autograph. Some tips are listed below to aid you in doing so.

1. Marilyn's signatures have a look of rapidity to them. She always signed with a definite slant to the right and overemphasized the capital letters in her name and those of the inscriptions.

2. "Monroe" is always the more legible half of her name.

3. Marilyn tended to bring the dot in her first name back over the top of the "a."

4. In nearly every example of her signature her first name is broken into two parts: "Mar" and "ilyn." The "ily" in "ilyn" is written quickly and is not formed well, appearing like a figure eight or a script like "S."

5. The "M-a" in Marilyn and the "M-o" in Monroe are always connected, and there is a sharp angle where "M" meets the following letter.

6. In Marilyn's inscribed signatures (and most of them were), there is a great uniformity in the word "To" in every example. Marilyn often used "Warmest Regards" or "Love and Kisses" in these inscriptions. Inscriptions to friends or co-workers would often include a personal reference as well.

7. Marilyn nearly always signed her name on the same line.

Note: Marilyn began writing in the above style in about 1950. Prior to this time, she wrote much more legibly, but still had a distinctive right slant to her signature. There was no break between letters in "Marilyn" or "Monroe" either.

Secretarial signature on an 8 x 10 photo (circa 1950), $150-$300.

Secretarial and Forgery Signatures

A great many secretarial signatures were done to appease the droves of Marilyn fans writing to acquire one of her signed photos. These signatures are always slower and more legible than Marilyn's own. The other "footprints" of an authentic Marilyn autograph are always missing, namely the unique formation of the "ily." The "M" in Marilyn and Monroe are more erect and legible, lacking the distinctive right slant and rapidity of an authentic Monroe signature.

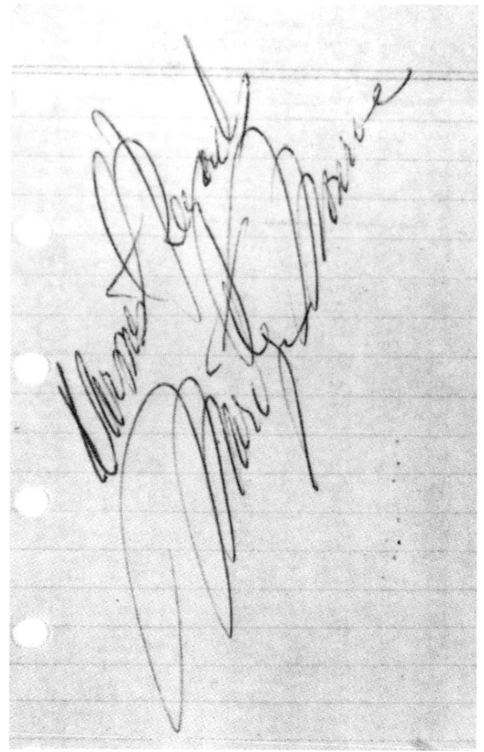

Authentic Marilyn Monroe signature, $1,500-$2,000.

Authentic Marilyn Autographs

- Marilyn Monroe signed black and white 5 x 7 photo (1950s-'60s) ....$1,500-$3,000
- Marilyn Monroe signed color 5 x 7 photo (1950s-'60s)....................$1,500-$3,000
- Marilyn Monroe signed black and white 8 x 10 photo (1950s-'60s) ..$3,000-$4,000
- Marilyn Monroe signed black and white 8 x 10 photo (1940s) ....$5,000-$7,000
- Marilyn Monroe signed color 8 x 10 photo (1940s-'60s)...................$3,500-$4,500
- Marilyn Monroe signed black and white 11 x 14 photo (1950s-'60s). ....$5,000-$10,000
- Marilyn Monroe signed color 11 x 14 photo (1950s-'60s)...............$5,000-$10,000
- Marilyn Monroe signed and cancelled check (Note: The more desirable checks are those with no bank stamps over the actual signature)....................$1,500-$2,500
- Marilyn Monroe signed studio contract (1940s-'60s) ....$4,000-$9,000
- Marilyn Monroe signed album page (about 4 x 5) ....$1,500-$2,000
- Marilyn Monroe signed typed legal document...................................$3,000-$4,000
- Marilyn Monroe signed typed letter (1950s-'60s) ....$2,000-$3,000
- Norma Jeane signed personal letter (1940s)...................................$8,000-$12,000
- Marilyn Monroe signed record album sleeve (1950s-'60s) ....$3,000-$4,000
- Marilyn Monroe signed one-sheet movie poster (1940s-'60s)...........$4,000-$5,000

Authentic Marilyn Monroe signature on album page, $1,500-$2,000.

Authentic signature on album page, $1,500-$2,000.

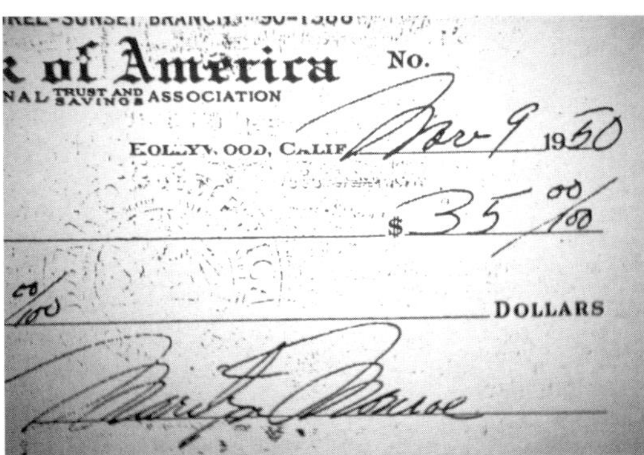

of America No.
NAL TRUST AND SAVINGS ASSOCIATION
HOLLYWOOD, CALIF. Nov 9 1950
$ 35 00/100
DOLLARS

1950 signed check, $1,500-$2,500.

luction of $200.00 weekly shall commence
from Twentieth Century-Fox Film Corpor-
5, 1951.

Very truly yours,

Marilyn Monroe

he $1,800. due me from Natasha Lytess, as
of any and all claims I may have against

Signed contract, 1951, $4,000-$9,000.

Secretarial Signatures

Marilyn Monroe secretarial signatures are worth $150 to $300 per signed 8 x 10 photo and $100 to $200 per signed photo in smaller sizes. The original photos themselves are appealing to collectors because of their sharpness, due to being first generation prints.

Secretarial signature on 8 x 10 photo (circa 1953), $150-$300.

Buyers Beware!

I have seen a great many forged Monroe signatures selling at high prices on various Internet auction sites. Many faked certificates of authenticity are giving people a false scnse of security. Many times the fake signatures are elaborately framed and matted to add to the confusion. If you are familiar with the official Marilyn Monroe signature used by her estate (most modern MM products feature a facsimile of the signature on them), you will note that this signature in particular is used fairly often when producing a fake. Some people have plainly laid a piece of paper over such signature to produce their counterfeit.

A popular misconception, due primarily to misinformation given on a well-known television show about antiques, is that Marilyn Monroe signed exclusively in red ink. The opposite is actually true. She rarely signed in red ink, though the studio secretaries were known to do so.

Authentic signature on 8 x 10 photo (1948), $5,000-$9,000.

Authentic 1951 Marilyn signature on 8 x 10 photo, $3,000-$4,000.

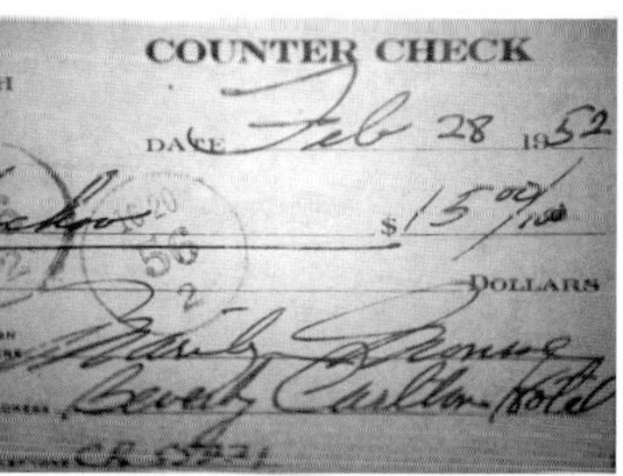

Signed check, 1952, $1,500-$2,500.

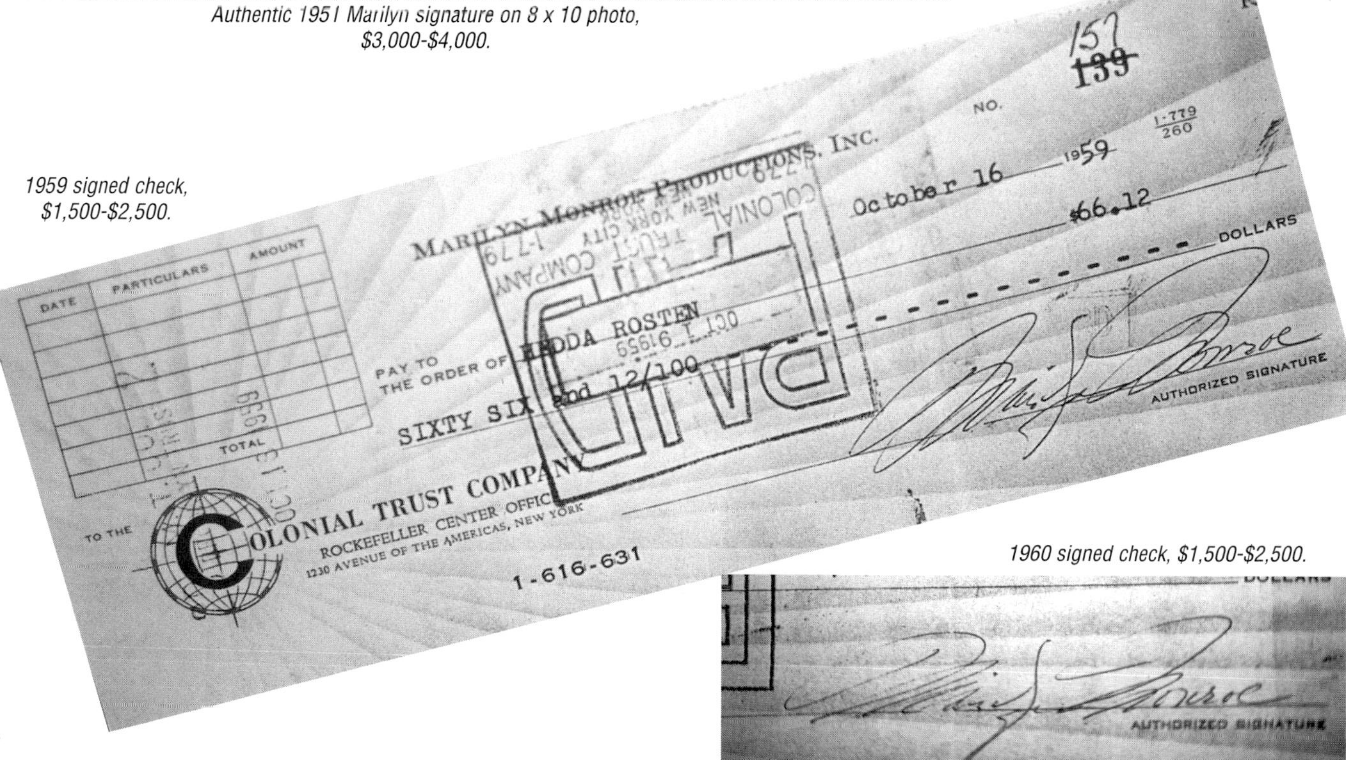

1959 signed check, $1,500-$2,500.

1960 signed check, $1,500-$2,500.

Chapter 3

Books

Marilyn Monroe is undoubtedly the most written-about star ever. Hundreds of books exist on her in every language imaginable. Authors in countries around the world began writing books about Marilyn in unison with the first American books published about the star.

The first, which were published in 1953, featured a selection of studio photographs of Marilyn and chronicled her rise to stardom. The early 1960s brought a biography or two, but the greatest number of works were published after her death in 1962.

A few of the books published in the late-1960s speculated about the circumstances of Marilyn's death and the possibility that it hadn't been an accident. From the early 1970s on, just about anyone who had ever even brushed shoulders with Marilyn Monroe began writing books about her. Some of the finest publications came in the 1980s and '90s and consisted of photos taken by the world's leading photographers who had photographed Marilyn extensively and quite beautifully. These are the most treasured books by Marilyn fans. As in most cases, there are also a certain number of books that fall into the "trash" category, but they are the minority, thank goodness.

It's inevitable that the flow of books will continue on Marilyn, as "lost" photos and new murder theories continue to arise and new generations discover the mystery and intrigue that will forever surround our all-American icon, Marilyn Monroe.

What follows is an exhaustive listing of nearly all of the books ever written on or with a reference to Marilyn Monroe. They are arranged alphabetically by the author's name, followed by the book's title; the estimated current value in U.S. dollars; the publisher; the year it was published; the edition number or number of reprints; cover type (hardcover, softcover, or paperback); number of pages; original price, if available; International Standard Book Number; and country of origin code. (Codes and abbreviations are listed in the colored box in the right margin on the next page.)

International Books on Marilyn Monroe

Abbreviations
ed.=number of edition
re.=number of reprint
pgs.=number of pages
ISBN=International Standard Book Number

Country Codes
ARG-Argentina
AUS-Australia
BEL-Belgium
BRA-Brazil
CAN-Canada
CAT-Catalunya
CHI-Chile
DEN-Denmark
SPA-Spain
FIN-Finland
FRA-France
GER-Germany
ITA-Italy
MEX-Mexico
SAM-South America
SWE-Sweden
SWI-Switzerland
UK-United Kingdom
USA-United States of America

Gailyn ADDIS
- *Be Marilyn* .... $5-$10
  Sourcebooks Trade, 2000. 128 pgs. ISBN-1570715572 (USA)

Anitti ALANEN
- *Marilyn. Alaston naamio. Marilyn Monoen elokuvat* .... $50-$75
  Valtion painatuskeskus, 1982. Softcover. 218 pgs. ISBN-951-859-284-5 (FIN)

Alfanso ALCADE
- *Marilyn Monroe que est'as en el cielo* .... $50-$70
  University Ed., 1972. Softcover. Inscription no. 39.948 (CHI)

Jack ALLEN
- *Marilyn By Moonlight* .... $50-$90
  Barclay House, 1996. 1st ed. Hardcover. 133 pgs. ISBN-0-935016-45-7 (USA)

Janice ANDERSON
- *Marilyn Monroe* .... $40-$60
  Crescent Books, 1993. 1st ed. Hardcover. 192 pgs. ISBN-0-517-41476-7 (USA)
- *Marilyn Monroe* .... $40-$60
  Optimum Books, 1993. 1st ed. Hardcover. 192 pgs. ISBN-0-603-03099-8 (UK)
- *Marilyn Monroe* .... $40-$60
  W.H. Smith, 1987. 4th re. Softcover. 192 pgs. ISBN-0-603-03125-0 (UK)
- *Marilyn Monroe—Quote UnQuote* .... $15-$20
  Crescent, 1995. 1st ed. Hardcover. 80 pgs. ISBN-1-85813-831-0 (USA)

ANONYMOUS
- *Violations of the Child—Marilyn Monroe by her psychiatrist friend* .... $75-$125
  Bridgehead Books, 1962. 1st ed. Hardcover. 159 pgs. (USA)
- *Marilyn Monroe—Collection Cinema pour tous* .... $30-$50
  Anagramme (Ariel Camacho), 1985. 1st ed. Hardcover. 62 pgs. ISBN-2-85199-364-X (FRA)
- *Marilyn Monroe—Album Souvenir Cine Revue* .... $30-$50
  Ciné-Revue, 1987. 1st ed. No. 1. Softcover. 78 pgs. ISBN-000-0272395-19 (BEL)
- *Marilyn Monroe—Grandes reportajes de crisis* .... $50-$70
  Ed. de Crisis (Julia Constenla), 1974. 1st ed. Softcover. 141 pgs. (ARG)

Serge ANTIBI
- *Album Photos, Marilyn Monroe* .... $40-$60
  Pac, 1984 . 1st ed. Hardcover. 139 pgs. (195*f*) (FRA)
- *Marilyn Monroe, Revelations et passion* .... $40-$55
  Favre, 1988. 1st ed. Softcover. 313 pgs. (110*f*) ISBN-2-8289-0364-8 (FRA)

Eve ARNOLD
- *Marilyn Monroe, An Appreciation by Eve Arnold* .... $40-$60
  Alfred A. Knopf, 1987. 1st ed. Hardcover. 141 pgs. ($30) ISBN-0-394-55672-0 (USA)
- *Marilyn Monroe, An Appreciation by Eve Arnold* .... $40-$60
  Hamish Hamilton, 1987. 1st ed. Hardcover. 141 pgs. ISBN-0-241-12381-X (UK)
- *Marilyn Monroe, An Appreciation by Eve Arnold* .... $40-$60
  Pan Books Ltd., 1987. 1 re. Softcover. 141 pgs. (£9.99) ISBN-0-330-30991-9 (UK)
- *Marilyn, For Ever* .... $40-$55
  Albin Michel, 1987. 1st ed. Hardcover. 141 pgs. ISBN-2-226-03021-2 (FRA)
- *Marilyn Monroe. Un homenaje de Eve Arnold* .... $40-$55
  Mondadori Espana S. A., 1987. 1st ed. Hardcover. 141 pgs. ISBN-84-397-1122-0 (SPA)
- *Omaggio a Marilyn* .... $40-$55
  Arnoldo Mondadori L., 1987. Hardcover. 143 pgs. ISBN-88-04-30523-1 (ITA)

Marilyn Monroe by Anderson. U.S. hardcover, $40-$60

Marilyn Monroe—An Appreciation by Arnold. British softcover, $40-$60.

Marilyn Monroe by Cabanas. Spanish softcover, $30-$50.

Stars, Mythen, and Legenden by Cahill. German hardcover, $35-$50.

Marilyn Monroe—A Life of the Actress by Rollyson. U.S. hardcover, $25-$40.

Francoise ARNOULD and F. GERBER
- *Marilyn Monroe* .... $40-$60
  Pac, 1982. 1st ed. Softcover. 185 pgs. (FRA)

Erica AROSIO
- *Marilyn Monroe* (In folding box with cassette) .... $40-$60
  Multiplo Edizioni, 1989. Softcover. 170 pgs. (Lit. 35.000) (ITA)

Renzo BAILINI
- *Marilyn Monroe: Un mistero all'americana* (Vita and Memoria No. 11) .... $40-$60
  Book Editore, 1988. 1st ed. Softcover. 158 pgs. (Lit. 19.000) (ITA)

Bernice BAKER and Mona Rae MIRACLE
- *Marilyn, ma soeur* .... $20-$30
  AJ, 1994. 285 pgs. ISBN-2-84157-000-2 (FRA)

Roger BAKER
- *Marilyn Monroe United Press International/Bettmann* .... $40-$60
  Portland House, 1990. 1st ed. Hardcover. 176 pgs. ISBN-0-517-69326-7 (UK)
- *Marilyn Monroe United Press International/Bettmann* .... $40-$60
  Soline, 1991. 1st ed. Hardcover. 176 pgs. ISBN-2-87677-104-7 (FRA)
- *Marilyn Monroe Eine Biographische Fotodokumentation O. Verlag* .... $40-$60
  Orbis Verlag, 1991. Hardcover. 176 pgs. (28,80 DM) ISBN-3-572-00508-6 (GER)
- *Marilyn Monroe* .... $20-$40
  Grange Books, 1994. Hardcover. (UK)

George BARRIS
- *Marilyn—Her Life in Her Own Words* .... $30-$50
  Birch Lane, 1995. 1st ed. Hardcover. 166 pgs. ($24.95) ISBN-1-55972-306-8 (USA)
- *Marilyn—Her Life in Her Own Words* .... $15-$20
  Citadel Press, 2001. Hardcover. 176 pgs. ISBN-0806522402 (USA)

Carlo BASSI
- *Che Fine Ha Fa Ho Norma Jeane?* .... $30-$50
  Skema, 1992. Softcover. (ITA)

S. Paige BATY
- *American Monroe: The Making of a Body Politic* .... $15-$20
  University California Press, 1995. Paperback. 197 pgs. ISBN-052088069 (USA)

Marsha BELLAVANCE-JOHNSON
- *Marilyn Monroe in Hollywood: A Guide* .... $3-$5
  Computer Lab, 1992. Paperback. 40 pgs. ISBN-0929709101 (USA)

Georges BELMONT and Jane RUSSELL
- *Marilyn Monroe and the Camera* .... $40-$60
  Schirmer Arts Book, 1989. 245 pgs. ISBN-3-88814-481-7 (UK)
- *Marilyn Monroe and the Camera* .... $20-$25
  Neues, 2000. Hardcover. 245 pgs. ISBN-3823854674 (USA)

Bruno BERNARD
- *Requium for Marilyn by Bernard of Hollywood* .... $70-$125
  Kensal Press, 1996. 1st ed. Hardcover. 207 pgs. (£12.50) ISBN-0-946041-52-0 (UK)

Susan BERNARD
- *Bernard of Hollywood's Marilyn* .... $30-$50
  St. Martin's, 1993. Hardcover. 122 pgs. ($29.95) ISBN-0-312-08882-5 (USA)
- *Bernard of Hollywood's Marilyn (Ed. du collectioneur)* .... $80-$90
  Boxtree, 1993. Hardcover. 122 pgs. ISBN-1-85283-856-6 (FRA)

Herb BOYD
- *Seductive Sayings—Marilyn Monroe* .... $30-$50
  Longmeadow, 1994. 1st ed. Hardcover. 60 pgs. ISBN-0-681-45364-8 (USA)

Pierre BROUSSEAU
- *Marilyn et ses amants celebres—Sa vie secrete* .... $40-$60
  Quebecor Inc., 1983. 1st ed. Softcover. 156 pgs. ISBN-2-89089-197-6 (CAN)

Peter Harry BROWN and Patte BARHAM
- *Marilyn Monroe—The Last Take* .... $25-$35
  Dutton, 1992. Hardcover. 452 pgs. ($23) ISBN-0-525-93485-5 (USA)
- *Marilyn Monroe-The Last Take* .... $8-$12
  Signet, 1993. 1st ed. Paperback. 549 pgs. ($6.50) ISBN-0451-40420-3 (USA)
- *Marilyn Das Ende, wie es wirklich War* .... $20-$30
  Droemer Knaur, 1992. Hardcover. 447 pgs. ISBN-3-425-26567-2 (GER)
- *Marilyn Histoire d'un assassinat* .... $20-$30
  Plon, 1992. 416 pgs. ISBN-2-259-02498-X (FRA)

Richard BUSKIN
- *The Films of Marilyn Monroe* .... $20-$40
  Publications Int'l Unlimited, 1992. Hardcover. 96 pgs.
  ISBN-1-56173 277 X (USA)
- *Blonde Heat: The Sizzling Screen Career of Marilyn Monroe* .... $30-$35
  Watson-Guptill Publishing, 2001. Hardcover. 256 pgs. ISBN-0823084140 (USA)

Frederic CABANAS
- *Marilyn Monroe—A Bibliography* .... $30-$50
  Ixia Llibres, 1992. 1st ed. Softcover. 121 pgs. ISBN- 84-87530-18-4 (SPA)

Marie CAHILL
- *Forever Marilyn* .... $35-$50
  Binson Group, 1991. 1st ed. Hardcover. 64 pgs. ISBN-0-86124-819-8 (UK)
- *Forever Marilyn* .... $30-$45
  Smithmark, 1992. Hardcover. 64 pgs. ISBN-0-8317-3470-1(USA)
- *Marilyn* .... $30-$45
  Publisher unknown, 1994. Hardcover. ISBN-157215-0319 (USA)
- *Stars, Mythen and Legend—Marilyn* .... $35-$50
  Lechner, 1992. Hardcover. 64 pgs. ISBN-3-85049-098-X (GER)
- *Marilyn* .... $30-$40
  Libsa, 1993. Hardcover. (SPA)

Domenico CAMMAROTA
- *Il cinema di Marilyn Monro—Futuro saggi vol. XVII* .... $40-$60
  Fanucci, 1988. 1st ed. 275 pgs. (Lit. 22.000) ISBN-88-347-0301-4 (ITA)

Francesco CAMPANESE
- *Lo Marilyn—No. 3* .... $40-$60
  D.N. - Milano, 1977. 1st ed. Softcover. 122 pgs. (ITA)

Frank A. CAPELL
- *The Strange Death of Marilyn Monroe* .... $60-$125
  Herald of Freedom, 1994. 1st ed. Softcover. 79 pgs. ($2) (USA)

Truman CAPOTE
- *Marilyn Monroe: Photographies 1945-1962—Bibliotheque Visuelle* .... $40-$60
  Schirmer/Mosel, 1991. 1st ed. Paperback. 119 pgs. ISBN-3-88814-577-5 (FRA)
- *Marilyn Monroe: Photographien 1945-1962* .... $40-$60
  Schirmer/Mosel, 1991. 1st ed. Paperback. 119 pgs. ISBN-3-88814-385-3 (GER)
- *Marilyn Monroe Photographs 1945-1962* .... $20-$40
  Norton Schirmer's Visual Library, 1994. Softcover. (UK)

Marilyn Monroe Photographien by Capote. German softcover, $40-$60.

Marilyn Monroe Confidential by Pepitone and Stadiem. U.S. hardcover, $20-$40.

Marilyn—The Tragic Venus by Hoyt. U.S. hardcover (1965), $70-$125.

Marilyn Monroe "Her Own Story" by Carpozi. U.S. paperback, $60-$90.

Marilyn Monroe: Crypt 33 by Gregory and Speriglio. U.S. hardcover, $25-$35.

Why Norma Jean Killed Marilyn Monroe by Freeman. U.S. hardcover, $10-$15.

Ernesto CARDENAL
- *Marilyn Monroe and Other Poems* (with only one poem about MM) ....$20-$30
  Search Press London, 1975. 2nd re. Softcover. 136 pgs.
  ISBN-0-85532-358-2 (UK)

Ernesto CARDENAL and Dorothee SOLLE
- *Gebet fur Marilyn Monroe—Meditationen* ....$30-$50
  Jugenddienst-Verlag, 1984. 1st ed. Softcover. 64 pgs.
  ISBN-3-7795-7385-7 (GER)

George CARPOZI, Jr.
- *Marilyn Monroe—"Her Own Story"* ....$60-$90
  Belmont Books, 1961. 1st ed. Paperback. 222 pgs. (USA)
- *Marilyn Monroe—"Her Own Story"* ....$15-$25
  Universal Award House Inc., 1973. 1st ed. Softcover. 112 pgs. ($1.50) (USA)
- *The Agony of Marilyn Monroe* ....$80-$125
  Consul Books/World D., 1962. 1st ed. Paperback. 187 pgs. (UK)
- *Marilyn Monroe su Propia Historia* ....$80-$125
  Ibero Mundial Ed., 1962. 1st ed. Paperback. 211 pgs. (SPA)

- *Marilyn Monroe Historia de su Vida* ....$80-$125
  Malinca Pocket, 1963. 1st ed. Paperback. 186 pgs. (ARG)

Jock CARROLL
- *Falling For Marilyn* ....$30-$50
  Friedman/Fairfax, 1996. Hardcover. 101 pgs. ($25)
  ISBN-1-56799-411-3 (USA)
- *Falling For Marilyn* ....$15-$20
  Metro Books, 1997. Hardcover. 112 pgs. ISBN-1567994113 (USA)

David CONOVER
- *Finding Marilyn—A Romance by David Conover* ....$50-$75
  Grosset and Dunlap, 1981. 1st ed. 199 pgs. ($14.95)
  ISBN-0-448-12020-8 (USA)
- *Norma Jean/Marilyn Monroe: The Discovery Photographs—1945* ....$30-$45
  A Moment in Time Gallery, 1990. Softcover Brochure.
  ISBN-0-9695079-0-9 (CAN)

Michael CONWAY and Mark RICCI
- *The Films of Marilyn Monroe* ....$40-$60
  Bonanza and Citadel, 1964. 1st ed. Hardcover. 160 pgs. (USA)
- *The Films of Marilyn Monroe* ....$40-$60
  The Citadel Press, 1964. Softcover. 160 pgs. ($7.95)
  ISBN-0-8065-0145-6 (USA)
- *The Complete Films of Marilyn Monroe* (different cover) ....$40-$60
  The Citadel Press, 1964. Softcover. 160 pgs. ($12.95)
  ISBN-0-8065-1016-1 (USA)
- *The Films of Marilyn Monroe* ....$40-$50
  The Citadel Press (C-265), 1974. 7th re. Softcover. 160 pgs.
  ISBN-0-8065-0145-6 (USA)
- *The Films of Marilyn Monroe* ....$40-$50
  Cadillac and Citadel, 1964. 9th re. Hardcover. 160 pgs. (USA)
- *Marilyn Monroe* ....$40-$50
  Artefact, 1974. 160 pgs. ISBN-9-782851994004 (FRA)
- *Marilyn Monroe* ....$30-$40
  Henry Veyrier, 1983. 160 pgs. ISBN-2-85199-286-4 (FRA)
- *The Complete Films of Marilyn Monroe* ....$25-$35
  Citadel/Carol Press, 1990. 1st ed. 160 pgs. ($14.95) ISBN-0-8065-1016-1 (USA)
- *Todas Las Peliculas De Marilyn Monroe* ....$40-$50
  Odin, 1993. Softcover. (SPA)

CONWAY, RICCI, and Enrico MAGRELLI

- *Marilyn Monroe* .... $30-$40
  Gremese Editore, 1992. Hardcover. (ITA)
- *Marilyn Monroe* .... $30-$50
  Henri Veyrier, 1990. Softcover. 160 pgs. ISBN-2-85199-209-0 (FRA)
- *Marilyn Monroe* .... $30-$50
  Henri Veyrier, 1990. Softcover. 160 pgs. (68*f*) ISBN-2-85199-219-8 (FRA)
- *Marilyn Monroe* .... $30-$50
  Henri Veyrier, 1983. Softcover. 160 pgs. (78*f*) ISBN-2-85199-286-4 (FRA)
- *Marilyn Monroe* .... $30-$50
  Artefact, 1986. Softcover. 160 pgs. (FRA)
- *Marilyn Monroe und ihre filme* .... $30-$50
  Goldmann Magnum/Citadel, 1980. Softcover. 174 pgs.
  ISBN-3-442-10208-1 (GER)
- *Marilyn Monroe—Le Stelle Filanti, 10* .... $30-$50
  Gremese Ed., 1981. 1st ed. Hardcover. 156 pgs. (Lit. 20.000)
  ISBN-88-7605-028-0 (ITA)

Lawrence CROWN

- *Marilyn at Twentieth Century Fox* .... $20-$35
  Comet, 1987. 1st ed. Hardcover. 213 pgs. ISBN-1-85227-025-X (USA)
- *Marilyn at Twentieth Century Fox* .... $25-$45
  Planet Books, 1987. 1st ed. Hardcover. 213 pgs. (£14.95)
  ISBN-1-85527-025-X (UK)
- *Marilyn at Twentieth Century Fox* .... $20-$40
  W. H. Allen/Planet, 1987. Softcover. 213 pgs. (£8.99)
  ISBN-1-855227-002-0 (UK)

Ernest CUNNINGHAM

- *The Ultimate Marilyn* .... $10-$15
  Audio Renaissance, 1998. Paperback. 384 pgs. ISBN-1580630030 (USA)

Peter DAINTY

- *Marilyn Monroe* .... $20-$35
  Collins ELT, 1986. 1st ed. Paperback. 69 pgs. ISBN-0-00-370170-0 (UK)
- *Marilyn Monroe* .... $20-$35
  Collins ELT, 1991. 5th re. Paperback. 69 pgs. ISBN-0-00 370170-0 (UK)

James KOTSIBILAS-DAVIS

- *Milton's Marilyn* .... $35-$45
  Schirmer/Mosel, 1994. Hardcover. 220 pgs. ISBN-3-88814-610-0 (FRA)

Oliver DAZAT

- *Marilyn Monroe—Les Noms duCinema 'M' Le Club des Stars* .... $40-$60
  Seghers (Phillippe), 1989. 1st ed. 189 pgs. Softcover. (82*f*)
  ISBN-2-232-10190-8 (FRA)

Kathy ROOKS-DENES

- *Marilyn* .... $30-$40
  Grange, 1993. Hardcover. 176 pgs. ISBN-185627-289-3 (UK)

André DE DIENES

- *Marilyn Mon Amour—The Private Album* .... $40-$60
  St. Martin's, 1985. 1st ed. Hardcover. 155 pgs. ($24.95)
  ISBN-0-312-51504-9 (USA)
- *Marilyn Mon Amour—The Private Album* .... $40-$60
  Sidgwick and Jackson, 1986. Hardcover. 155 pgs. (£13.00)
  ISBN-0-283-99337-5 (UK)
- *Marilyn Mon Amour—The Private Album* .... $40-$60
  Sidgwick and Jackson, 1989. Softcover. 155 pgs. (£10.99)
  ISBN-0-283-99533-5 (UK)

The Agony of Marilyn Monroe by Carpozi. British paperback, $80-$125.

Finding Marilyn by Conover. U.S. hardcover, $50-$75

Goddess—The Secret Lives of Marilyn Monroe by Summers. U.S. Hardcover, $25-$45.

Marilyn at Twentieth Century Fox by Crown. U.S. hardcover, $20-$35.

Marilyn and Me by Strasburg. U.S. hardcover, $25-$35.

The Return of Marilyn Monroe by Staggs. U.S. paperback, $10-$15.

André DE DIENES (continued)

- *Marilyn Mon Amour—L'album intime* .... $40-$60
  Filipacchi, 1985. 1st ed. Hardcover. 155 pgs. (199*f*)
  ISBN-2-85018-595-7 (FRA)
- *Marilyn Mon Amour* .... $40-$60
  Schirmer/Mosel, 1986. Softcover. 155 pgs. ISBN-3-88814-189-3 (GER)
- *Marilyn Mon Amour* .... $20-$30
  Bracken, 1993. Softcover. (UK)

Michael DEL MAR

- *Marilyn Cherie* .... $40-$60
  Ige Michel Lafon, 1982. 1st ed. Hardcover. 144 pgs. (100*f*)
  ISBN-2-902259-04-2 (FRA)
- *Marilyn Cherie—Collection MA VIE No. 3* .... $40-$60
  Ige Michel Lafon, 1982. Softcover. 144 pgs. (49*f*) ISBN-2-902259-04-2 (FRA)

Susan DOLL

- *Marilyn—Her Life and Legend* .... $40-$60
  Omnibus Press, 1990. 1st ed. Hardcover. 256 pgs. ISBN-0-7119-2421-X (GER)
- *Marilyn—Her Life and Legend* .... $40-$60
  Beekman House, 1990. Hardcover. 256 pgs. ISBN-0-517-03069-1 (USA)
- *Marilyn—Vie & Legende* .... $40-$60
  Karl Muller Verlag, 1991. 1st ed. Hardcover. 256 pgs. (GER)
- *Marilyn—Leben und Legende* .... $40-$60
  Karl Muller Verlag, 1991. 1st ed. Hardcover. 256 pgs. (GER)
- *Marilyn Vie et Leg* .... $40-$60
  Ramsay Cinema, 1991. 256 pgs. ISBN-2-85956-942-1 (FRA)

Paul DONNELLY

- *Marilyn Monroe* .... $3-$6
  Trafalgar Square, 2000. ISBN-1903047315 (USA)

James E. DOUGHERTY

- *The secret happiness of Marilyn Monroe* .... $35-$55
  Playboy Press, 1976. 1st ed. Paperback. 150 pgs. ($1.95) (USA)
- *El amor secreto de Marilyn Monroe* .... $35-$55
  Dopesa/Espectaculo, 1st ed. Paperback. 192 pgs. 1976 (SPA)
- *To Norma Jeane With Love, Jimmie* .... $15-$20
  Science and Humanities Press, 2001. Paperback. 220 pgs.
  ISBN-1888725516 (USA)

Carole Nelson DOUGLAS

- *Marilyn—Shades of Blonde* .... $20-$25
  Forge, 1997. Hardcover. ISBN-0312857373 (USA)

Claude DUFFAU

- *La femme poete-Un portrait de Marilyn Monroe dans son miroir* .... $45-$55
  Jean-Claude Simoen, 1978. 1st ed. Softcover. 189 pgs. (FRA)

Richard DYER

- *Marilyn Monroe Star Dossier One (The Images of Marilyn Monroe)* .... $60-$80
  bfi education, 1980. 1st ed. Softcover. 46 pgs. (UK)

Ed FEINGERSH and Bob LABRASCA

- *Marilyn—March 1955* .... $30-$50
  Delta/Bantam Books, 1990. 1st ed. Softcover. ($12.95)
  ISBN-0-385-30119-7 (USA)
- *Marilyn—Fifty-Five* .... $30-$50
  Bloomsbury, 1990. 1st ed. Hardcover. ISBN-0-7475-0746-5 (UK)
- *Marilyn* .... $40-$50
  Nathan Image, 1990. 1st ed. Hardcover. ISBN-2-09-240072-X (FRA)

- *Marilyn* ....$20-$30
  Editions de la Martiniere, 1996. 99 pgs. ISBN-2-7324-2188-X (FRA)

Ed FEINGERSH and Michael OCHS
- *Marilyn in New York* (aus dem Michael Ochs Archives) ....$40-$55
  Schirmer/Mosel, 1991. 1st ed. Hardcover. ISBN-3-88814-445-0 (GER)

Piergiorgio FIRINU
- *Marilyn Monroe—Immagini di un mito* ....$40-$50
  Studio 46, 1980. 1st ed. Softcover. 111 pgs. (ITA)

Mogens FONSS
- *Marilyn Monroe—Samlerens Filmboger-2* ....$65-$125
  Samlerens Forlag Kr., 1958. 1st ed. Softcover. 55 pgs. (5,85) (DEN)

Joe FRANKLIN and Laurie PALMER
- *The Marilyn Monroe Story*...$500-$800
  Rudolph Field Co., 1953. 1st ed. Hardcover. 63 pgs. (USA)
- *The Marilyn Monroe Story—The Intimate Inside Story of…* ....$500-$800
  Rudolph Field Co., 1953. 1st ed. Softcover. 63 pgs. (USA)

Lucy FREEMAN
- *Why Norma Jeane Killed Marilyn Monroe* ....$10-$15
  Global Rights Ltd., 1992. Hardcover. 191 pgs. ISBN-1-880141-13-2 (USA)
- *Pourquoi Norma Jeane tue Marilyn Monroe*...$20-$30
  Zelie, 1993. 257 pgs. ISBN-2-84069-044-6 (FRA)

Lluis GASCA
- *Marilyn Monroe: Toda la verdad*...$35-$55
  Plaza and Janes, 1987. 1st ed. Hardcover. 191 pgs. ISBN-84-0137281-X (SPA)
- *Marilyn Monroe La Diosa Del Deseo* ....$30-$40
  Mascara, 1994. Paperback. (SPA)

Ruth Esther GEIGER
- *Marilyn Monroe*..$8-$12
  Rororo, 1995. Paperback. (GER)

Nicki GILES
- *The Marilyn Album* ....$35-$55
  Gallery Books, 1991. 1st ed. Hardcover. 303 pgs. ISBN-0-8317-5743-4 (USA)
- *The Marilyn Album* ....$35-$55
  Binson Group, 1991. 1st ed. Hardcover. 303 pgs. ISBN-0-86124-842-2 (UK)
- *Marilyn Photobiographie* ....$30-$40
  Presses de la Cite Hors Collection, 1992. 304 pgs. ISBN-2-258-03579-1 (FRA)

Rene GILSON
- *Marilyn Monroe—Anyhologie du cinema* ....$45-$60
  Avant-Scene Mars, 1969. 1st ed., no. 43. Paperback. (FRA)

Jonio GONZALEZ
- *Marilyn Monroe*...$25-$35
  Mitografias, 1993. Paperback. (SPA)

Jacky GOUPIL
- *Marilyn je t'aime*...$40-$60
  Vents d'Quest, year unknown. 1st ed. 96 pgs. (129*f*) ISBN-2-86967-016-8
- *Marilyn en images bandes dessinees*..$20-$30
  Vents d'Quest, 1998. 102 pgs. ISBN-2-86967-616-9 (FRA)

Neil GRANT
- *Marilyn in Her Own Words*..$30-$50
  Crescent, 1991. 1st ed. Hardcover. 64 pgs. ISBN-0-517-06103-1 (USA)

Marilyn Mon Amour by de Dienes. U.S. hardcover, $40-$60.

The Marilyn Monroe Story by Franklin and Palmer. U.S. softcover, $500-$800.

Requiem for Marilyn by Bernard. British hardcover, $70-$125.

Norma Jean by Guiles. U.S. hardcover, $50-$75.

My Sister Marilyn by the Miracles. U.S. hardcover, $30-$40.

The Life and Curious Death of Marilyn Monroe by Slatzer. British hardcover, $50-$65.

Neil GRANT (continued)

- *Marilyn in Her Own Words*..........$30-$50
  Hamlyn, 1991. 1st ed. Hardcover. 64 pgs. ISBN-0-600-57205-6 (UK)
- *Marilyn in Her Own Words*..........$30-$50
  Pyramid Books, 1991. 1st ed. Hardcover. 64 pgs. ISBN-1-85510-073-8 (UK)
- *Marilyn par elle-meme*..........$30-$50
  Grund, 1991. 1st ed. Hardcover. 64 pgs. ISBN-2-7000-6610-3 (FRA)

Adela GREGORY and Milo SPERIGLIO

- *Crypt 33*..........$25-$35
  Birch Lane Press, 1993. Hardcover. 310 pgs. ($21.95)
  ISBN-1-55972-125-1 (USA)

Fred Lawrence GUILES

- *Norma Jean by Fred Lawrence Guiles*..........$50-$75
  McGraw-Hill, 1969. 1st ed. Hardcover. 373 pgs. (USA)
- *Norma Jean—The Life of Marilyn Monroe*..........$40-$60
  Bantam Books, 1970. 1st ed. Paperback. 406 pgs. (USA)
- *Norma Jean—The Life of Marilyn Monroe*..........$40-$60
  Bantam Books, 1970. 6th re. Paperback. 406 pgs. (USA)
- *Norma Jean—The Life of Marilyn Monroe*..........$50-$75
  W. H. Allen, 1969. 1st ed. Hardcover. 341 pgs. (UK)
- *Norma Jean—The Tragedy of Marilyn Monroe*..........$40-$60
  Mayflower, 1971. 1st ed. Paperback. 351 pgs. (£ .40) (UK)
- *Norma Jean: F.L. Guiles Biography of Marilyn Monroe*..........$40-$60
  Mayflower/Granada, 1973. 1 re. Paperback. 351 pgs. (£ .50)
  ISBN-0-583-11834-8 (UK)
- *Norma Jean: F.L. Guiles Biography of Marilyn Monroe*..........$40-$60
  Mayflower/Granada, 1975. 3rd re. Paperback. 351 pgs. (£ .75)
  ISBN-0-583-11834-8 (UK)
- *Norma Jean: F.L. Guiles Biography of Marilyn Monroe*..........$20-$40
  Granada, 1982. 7th re. Paperback. 351 pgs. (£1.95) ISBN-0-583-11834-8 (UK)
- *Norma Jean: F.L. Guiles' Biography of Marilyn Monroe*..........$20-$40
  Granada/Panther, 1985. 9th re. Paperback. 351 pgs. (£2.50)
  ISBN-0-583-11834-8 (UK)
- *Norma Jaen vida de Marilyn Monroe*..........$40-$60
  Lumen, 1970. 1st ed. no. 72. Paperback. 450 pgs. (SPA)
- *Legend—The Life and Death of Marilyn Monroe*..........$30-$50
  Stein and Day, 1984. 1st ed. Hardcover. 501 pgs. ISBN-0-8182-2983-2 (USA)
- *Legend—The Life and Death of Marilyn Monroe*..........$30-$50
  Scarborough House, 1991. 1st ed. Softcover. 501 pgs. ($16.95)
  ISBN-0-8128-8525-2 (USA)
- *Norma Jeane—The Life and Death of Marilyn Monroe*..........$30-$50
  Granada, 1985. 2nd ed. Hardcover. 377 pgs. (£12.95) ISBN-0-246-12307-9 (UK)
- *Norma Jeane—The Life and Death of Marilyn Monroe*..........$30-$50
  Grafton Books, 1986. 1 re. Paperback. 528 pgs. (£3.95)
  ISBN-0-586-06246-7 (UK)
- *Norma Jean—The Life and Death of Marilyn Monroe*..........$20-$35
  Grafton Books, 1988. 2nd re. Paperback. 528 pgs. (£3.95)
  ISBN-0-586-06246-7 (UK)
- *Marilyn*..........$25-$35
  Solar, 1993. 192 pgs. ISBN-2-263-02052-7 (FRA)

Diane KARANIKAS HARVEY

- *Marilyn: A Life in Pictures*..........$5-$10
  Metro Books, 1999. Hardcover. 96 pgs. ISBN-1567997740 (USA)

James HASPIEL

- *Marilyn—The Ultimate Look at the Legend*..........$50-$60
  Henry Holt, 1991. 1st ed. Hardcover. 207 pgs. ($45) ISBN-0-8050-1856-5 (USA)

- *Marilyn—The Ultimate Look at the Legend* .... $50-$60
  Smith Gryphon, 1991. 1st ed. Hardcover. 207 pgs. ISBN-1-85685-007-2 (UK)
- *Young Marilyn—Becoming the Legend* .... $35-$45
  Hyperion, 1994. Hardcover. 168 pgs. ($34.95) ISBN-0-7868-6077-4 (USA)
- *Young Marilyn—Becoming the Legend* .... $35-$45
  Smith Gryphon Ltd., 1994. Hardcover. (UK)

Joe HEMBUS
- *Marilyn—The Destruction of an American Dream* .... $70-$100
  Tandem, 1973. 1st ed. Paperback. 112 pgs. (£ .35) ISBN-426-13362-5 (UK)
- *Marilyn Monroe—Glanz und Tragik Eines Idols* .... $70-$100
  Heyne Verlag, 1973. 1st ed. Paperback. 127 pgs. (4,80 DM) ISBN-3-453-01120-1 (GER)

Iris HOWDEN
- *Marilyn Monroe—Real Lives Series* .... $25-$35
  Publisher unknown, 1994. Softcover. (UK)

Edwin P. HOYT
- *Marilyn—The Tragic Venus* .... $70-$125
  Duel Sloan and Pierce, 1965. 1st ed. Hardcover. 279 pgs. (USA)
- *Marilyn—The Tragic Venus* .... $60-$80
  Chilton Books, 1973. New ed. Hardcover. 279 pgs. ($6.95) ISBN-0-8019-5915-2 (USA)
- *Marilyn—The Tragic Venus* .... $70-$125
  Robert Hale, 1967. 1st ed. Hardcover. 256 pgs. (UK)

James A. HUDSON
- *The Mysterious Death of Marilyn Monroe—Suicide? Accident?* .... $60-$90
  Volitant, 1968. 1st ed. Paperback. 112 pgs. (USA)

Tom HUTCHINSON
- *The Screen Greats—Marilyn Monroe* .... $40-$60
  Optimum, 1982. 1st ed. Hardcover. 80 pgs. ISBN-0-600-37789-X (USA)
- *The Screen Greats—Marilyn Monroe* .... $40-$60
  Gallery Press, 1982. 1st ed. Hardcover. 80 pgs. ISBN-0-861-36965-3 (UK)

Kathleen IRVING
- *Les plus belles Histoires d'amour de Hollywood Marilyn Monroe* .... $40-$60
  Balland, 1981. 1st ed. Softcover. 216 pgs. ISBN-2-7158-0304-4 (FRA)

Elton JOHN and Bernie TAUPIN
- *Candle in the Wind* .... $20-$40
  Hyperion, 1993. 1st ed. Hardcover. 45 pgs. ISBN-0-7868-6000-6 (USA)
- *Candle in the Wind* .... $20-$40
  Pavilion, 1993. Hardcover. (UK)

Ted JORDAN
- *Norma Jean—My Secret Life with Marilyn Monroe* .... $20-$35
  Morrow & Co., 1989. 1st ed. Hardcover. 255 pgs. ($18.95) ISBN-0-688-09118-0 (USA)
- *Norma Jean—My Secret Life with Marilyn Monroe* .... $8-$12
  Signet, 1991. 1st ed. Paperback. 285 pgs. ($4.99) ISBN-0-451-16912-3 (USA)
- *Norma Jean—A Hollywood Love Story* .... $20-$35
  Sidgwick & Jackson, 1989. Hardcover. 234 pgs. (£13.95) ISBN-0-28-99879-2 (UK)
- *Norma Jean—A Hollywood Love Story* .... $8-$15
  Pan, 1990. 1st ed. Paperback. 358 pgs. (£3.99) ISBN-0-330-31396-7 (UK)

Roger KAHN
- *Joe & Marilyn—A Memory of Love* .... $20-$40
  Morrow & Co., 1986. 1st ed. Hardcover. 269 pgs. ISBN-0-688-02517-X (USA)

Norma Jeane by Guiles. British paperback, $40-$60.

Marilyn by Hembus. British paperback, $70-$150.

Marilyn Das Ende (The Last Take) by Brown and Barham. German hardcover, $20-$30.

Marilyn Monroe Cover To Cover by Kidder. U.S. softcover, $20-$30.

Marilyn Memorabilia by Kidder. U.S. softcover, $25-$30.

Marilyn Monroe by Hutchinson. British hardcover, $40-$60.

Roger KAHN (continued)
- *Joe & Marilyn—the Hero Athlete, the Sex Goddess*.... $20-$40
  Avon Books, 1988. 1st ed. Paperback. 295 pgs. ($4.95)
  ISBN-0-380-70462-5 (USA)
- *Joe & Marilyn—A Memory of Love*.... $40-$60
  Sidgwick & Jackson, 1987. Hardcover. 269 pgs. (£10.95)
  ISBN-0-283-99427-4 (UK)

Clark KIDDER
- *Marilyn Monroe UnCovers*.... $150-$250
  Quon Editions, 1994. 1st ed. Softcover. 160 pgs. ($19.95)
  ISBN-0-9695539-7-8 (CAN)
- *Marilyn Monroe Cover To Cover*.... $20-$30
  Krause Publications, 1999. Softcover. 159 pgs. ($24.95)
  ISBN-0-87341-740-2 (USA)
- *Marilyn Monroe Collectibles: A Guide to the Memorabilia...* .... $8-$15
  Avon, 1999. Paperback. 320 pgs. ($15) ISBN-0-380-79909-X (USA)
- *Marilyn Memorabilia: Putting a Price on the Priceless Performer*.... $25-$30
  Krause Publications, 2002. Softcover. 224 pgs. ($24.95)
  ISBN-0-87349-342-7 (USA)

John KOBAL and David ROBINSON
- *Marilyn Monroe—A Life of Film*.... $40-$60
  Hamlyn, 1974. 1st ed. Hardcover. 176 pgs. ISBN-0-600-36172-1 (UK)
- *Marilyn Monroe—A Life of Film*.... $30-$50
  Gondola/Hamlyn, 1983. 1st ed. Softcover. 176 pgs. (£4.99)
  ISBN-0-600-37310-X (UK)
- *Marilyn Monroe—A Life of Film*.... $20-$40
  Hamlyn, 1987. Softcover. 176 pgs. (£4.99) ISBN-0-600-37310-X (UK)
- *Marilyn Monroe*.... $30-$50
  Henri Veyrier, 1984. 1st ed. Softcover. 174 pgs. (148*f*)
  ISBN-2-85199-319-4 (FRA)
- *Marilyn Monroe*.... $30-$50
  Taco, 1986. Softcover. 176 pgs. ISBN-3-8228-0014-7 (GER)
- *Marilyn Monroe*.... $40-$60
  Taco, 1989. Hardcover. 176 pgs. ISBN-3-89268-092-2 (GER)

Michael KORDA
- *Les Immortels*.... $20-$40
  Belfond, 1993. 554 pgs. ISBN-2-71443104-6 (FRA)

Ado KYROU
- *Marilyn Monroe—Collection Etoiles*.... $50-$70
  E. P. Denoel, 1972. 1st ed. Paperback. 239 pgs. (FRA)

Michael LACLOS
- *Marilyn Monroe—Vedettes du Cinema—Col. dirigee J. P. Castelnau*.... $50-$80
  Jean-Jacques Pauvert, 1962. 1st ed. Softcover. 41 pgs. (FRA)

Barbara LEAMING
- *Marilyn Monroe*.... $10-$15
  Three Rivers Press, 2000. Hardcover. 468 pgs. ISBN-0-60980-553-3 (USA)

Frances LEFKOWITZ
- *Marilyn Monroe*.... $15-$20
  Econo-Clad Books, 1999. Hardcover. ISBN-0-78577-114-X (USA)

Hans Jorgen LEMBOURN
- *Diary of a Lover of Marilyn Monroe*.... $20-$30
  Arbor House, 1979. Hardcover. 214 pgs. ($8.95) ISBN-0-87795-216-7 (USA)
- *Diary of a Lover of Marilyn Monroe—A Forty-Night Love Affair*.... $10-$15
  Bantam Books, 1979. Paperback. 214 pgs. ($2.25) ISBN-0-553-13123-0 (USA)

- *Forty Days with Marilyn*....................$20-$30
  Hutchinson, 1979. 1st ed. Hardcover. 214 pgs. ISBN-0-09-139010-9 (UK)
- *40 Days with Marilyn*....................$10-$15
  Arrow Books, 1980. Paperback. 214 pgs. (£1.25) ISBN-0-09-922690-1 (UK)
- *Quarante jours et Marilyn*....................$20-$30
  Robert Laffont, 1980. Softcover. 240 pgs. ISBN-2-221-00454-X (FRA)
- *40 dias con Marilyn-Cuarenta dias con Marilyn*....................$20-$35
  Brugera, 1979. 1st ed. Hardcover. 221 pgs. ISBN-84-02-06190-7 (SPA)
- *40 dage med Marilyn*....................$20-$35
  Schonberg, 1977. 1st ed. Softcover. 190 pgs. ISBN-87-570-0960-0 (DEN)
- *40 dage med Marilyn*....................$10-$20
  Spaendende boger Forum, 1977. Paperback. 190 pgs. ISBN-87-553-0651-9 (DEN)
- *40 Noites com Marilyn Monroe*....................$20-$35
  Ricord, 1979. Softcover. 178 pgs. (BRA)

Lyn LIFSHIN
- *Marilyn Monroe—Poems*....................$15-$20
  Quiet Lion Press, 1994. Softcover. (USA)

Guus LUIJTERS
- *Marilyn—A Never-Ending Dream*....................$40-$60
  St. Martin's Press, 1987. 1st ed. Hardcover. 171 pgs. ($22.95) ISBN-0-312-01148-2 (USA)
- *Marilyn—A Never-Ending Dream*....................$40-$50
  Plexus, 1986. Softcover. 171 pgs. (£6.95) ISBN-0-85965-145-2 (UK)
- *Marilyn, un Reve sans Fin*....................$40-$50
  ArteFact, 1985. Softcover. 171 pgs. (75*f*) ISBN-2-86697-082-9 (FRA)
- *Marilyn Monroe—In Her Own Words*....................$40-$50
  Omnibus Press, 1991. Softcover. 128 pgs. ISBN-0-7119-2302-7 (UK)
- *Marilyn Monroe*....................$40-$50
  Moewig, 1991. Softcover. 112 pgs. (16,80 DM) ISBN-3-8118-3080-5 (GER)
- *Marilyn Monroe—In Her Own Words*....................$45-$65
  Uplink, 1992. Softcover. 146 pgs. ISBN-4-309-90097-6 (JPN)
- *Marilyn Monroe Compleet*....................$40-$60
  Loeb, 1988. Softcover. 295 pgs. ISBN-90-6213-795-4 (HOL)

Ann LLOYD
- *Marilyn—A Hollywood Life*....................$40-$50
  Mallard Press, 1989. 1st ed., Hardcover. 118 pgs. ISBN-0-792-45088-4 (USA)
- *Marilyn—A Hollywood Life*....................$40-$50
  W. H. Smith, 1989. Hardcover. 118 pgs. ISBN-0-86124-541-5 (UK)
- *Marilyn—A Hollywood Life*....................$40-$50
  Park Lane, 1989. Hardcover. 118 pgs. ISBN-0-9509620-9-0 (UK)
- *Marilyn—Une vie d'Hollywood*....................$40-$50
  Minerva, 1990. Hardcover. 118 pgs. (120*f*) ISBN-2-8303-0079-1 (FRA)

Kai Berg MADSEN
- *En amerikansk Sukces-Historien om Marilyn Monroe*....................$200-$400
  Kobenhavn, 1953. 1st ed. Softcover. 32 pgs. (DEN)

Christa MAERKER
- *Marilyn Monroe—Arthur Miller*....................$20-$40
  Rowohlt, 1997. Hardcover. (GER)

Norman MAILER
- *Marilyn—Limited Signed Edition*....................$70-120
  Grosset and Dunlap, 1973. 1st ed. Hardcover. 270 pgs. ISBN-0-448-01029-1 (USA)

Marilyn Monroe Compleet by Luijters. Dutch softcover, $40-$60.

The Films of Marilyn Monroe by Buskin. U.S. hardcover, $20-$40.

Marilyn Monroe by Kobal and Robinson. British hardcover, $20-$40.

Marilyn— A Biography... by Mailer. U.S. paperback, $50-$75.

Marilyn by Sinyard. British softcover, $20-$35.

Marilyn Monroe by Kobal. German hardcover, $40-$60.

Norman MAILER (continued)

- *Marilyn—A Biography by Norman Mailer*......$50-$70
  Grosset and Dunlap, 1973. 1st ed. Hardcover. 270 pgs.
  ISBN-0-448-01029-1 (USA)
- *Marilyn—A Biography by Norman Mailer*......$50-$70
  Grosset and Dunlap, 1974. 1st ed. Softcover. 270 pgs.
  ISBN-0-448-11813-0 (USA)
- *Marilyn—A Biography by Norman Mailer, Pictures by the World's...* ......$20-$30
  Warner Books, 1975. 1st ed. Paperback. 381 pgs. ($3.50)
  ISBN-0-446-96747-5 (USA)
- *Marilyn—A Biography by Norman Mailer, Super Bestseller...* ......$20-$30
  Warner Pub.Library, 1975. Paperback. 381 pgs. ($2.50)
  ISBN-0-446-71850-5 (USA)
- *Marilyn—A Biography by Norman Mailer*......$50-75
  Holdder/Stoughton, 1973. 1st ed. Hardcover. 270 pgs. (£4.95)
  ISBN-0-340-18104-4 (UK)
- *Marilyn—A Biography by Norman Mailer, Pictures by...* ......$45-$65
  Coronet Books, 1974. Softcover. 270 pgs. (£2.50) ISBN-0-340-18828-6 (UK)
- *Marilyn—A Biography by Norman Mailer, Pictures by...* ......$40-$60
  Spring Books, 1988. 1st ed. Hardcover. 270 pgs. (£8.95)
  ISBN-0-600-55726-X (UK)
- *Marilyn—A Biography by Norman Mailer, Pictures by...* ......$40-$60
  Spring Books, 1989. 2nd re. Hardcover. 270 pgs. ISBN-0-600-55726-X (UK)
- *Marilyn—Une Biographie par Norman Mailer* ......$45-$65
  Stock/Albin Michel, 1974. 1st ed. Softcover. 270 pgs. (FRA)
- *Marilyn—Une Biographie par Norman Mailer* ......$35-$55
  Ramsay/Stock Albin Michel, 1985. Softcover. 270 pgs.
  ISBN-2-85956-437-3 (FRA)
- *Marilyn—Une Biographie par Norman Mailer* ......$35-$55
  Ramsay/Stock Albin Michel, 1986. Softcover. 270 pgs.
  ISBN-2-85956-437-3 (FRA)
- *Marilyn—Una Biografia...* ......$60-$80
  Lumen, 1974. 1st ed. Hardcover. 270 pgs. ISBN-84-264-2510-0 (SPA)
- *Marilyn—Una Biografia....* ......$45-$55
  Lumen, 1974. Softcover. 270 pgs. ISBN-84-264-2510-0 (SPA)
- *Marilyn—Una Biografia...* ......$40-$60
  Lumen/Circulo de Lectores, 1987. Hardcover. 270 pgs.
  ISBN-84-264-2510-0 (SPA)
- *Marilyn Monroe—Eine Biographie von Norman Mailer*......$30-$45
  Knaur, 1976. no. 429. Paperback. 391 pgs. (9,80 DM)
  ISBN-3-426-00424-0 (GER)
- *Marilyn—Biografia di Norman Mailer*......$40-$60
  Arnoldo Mondadori, 1982. 2nd ed. Hardcover. 261 pgs. (Lit. 35.000) (ITA)
- *Marilyn—en Biografi av Norman Mailer*......$50-75
  Bonniers/Manadens Books, 1973. Hardcover. 292 pgs.
  ISBN-91-0-038841-6 (SWE)
- *Marilyn—Eine Biographie*......$10-$20
  Knaur, 1993. Paperback. (GER)
- *Marilyn—The Classic by Norman Mailer*......$30-$45
  Galahad, 1993. Hardcover. 271 pgs. ISBN-0-88365-731-7 (USA)
- *Memories imaginaires de Marilyn (Of Women & Their Elegance)*......$40-$60
  Robert Laffont, 1982. 1st ed. Softcover. 193 pgs. (30*f*)
  ISBN-2-221-00812-X (FRA)

MARC'O

- *L'impossible, et pourtant-di MARC'O con Marilyn e Federica*......$40-$60
  Edizioni Nuovi Strumenti (Cavellini, Bertelli), 1984. Softcover. (ITA)

Julie MARS

- *Marilyn Monroe*......$10-$15
  Ariel, 1995. 1st ed. Hardcover. 79 pgs. ($4.95) ISBN-0-8362-3115-5 (USA)

Pete MARTIN

- *Will Acting Spoil Marilyn Monroe?* .... $125-$200
  Doubleday & Co., 1956. 1st ed. Hardcover. 128 pgs. ($2.95) (USA)
- *Will Acting Spoil Marilyn Monroe?* .... $60-$100
  Pocket Books/Cardinal, 1957. Paperback. 128 pgs. (35¢) (USA)
- *Will Acting Spoil Marilyn Monroe?* .... $200-$250
  Frederick Muller Ltd. London, 1956. Hardcover. 110 pgs. (UK)
- *Mi Sento Tutta Bionda* .... $150-$225
  1957. Paperback. 168 pgs. (ITA)

Dorothea KUHL-MARTINE

- *Marilyn an pabst Johannes* .... $20-$40
  Patmos, 1997. Hardcover. (GER)

Graham McCANN

- *Marilyn Monroe* .... $40-$60
  Rutgers University Press, 1988. 1st ed. Hardcover. 241 pgs.
  ISBN-0-8135-1302-2 (USA)
- *Marilyn Monroe* .... $40-$55
  Rutgers University Press, 1988. 1st ed. 241 pgs. Softcover.
  ISBN-0-8135-1303-0 (USA)
- *Marilyn Monroe* .... $40-$60
  Polity Press, 1988. 1st ed. Hardcover. 241 pgs. (£35.00)
  ISBN-0-7456-0378-5 (UK)
- *Marilyn Monroe—The Body in the Library* .... $40-$55
  Polity Press, 1988. 1st ed. Softcover. 241 pgs. (£7.95)
  ISBN-0-7456-0379-3 (UK)

Joan MELLEN

- *Marilyn Monroe—The Pictorial Treasury of Film Stars* .... $40-$60
  Galahad Books, 1973. Hardcover. 157 pgs. ($4.95) ISBN-0-88365-165-3 (USA)
- *Marilyn Monroe—Pyramid Illustrated History of The Movies* .... $30-$40
  Pyramid Books, 1973. Paperback. 157 pgs. ($1.45) ISBN-0-515-03129-1 (USA)
- *Marilyn Monroe—Pyramid Illustrated History of The Movies* .... $30-$40
  Pyramid Books, 1976. Paperback. 157 pgs. ($1.75) ISBN-0-515-03129-1 (USA)
- *Marilyn Monroe—Pyramid Illustrated History of The Movies* .... $30-$40
  Star Book/W. Allen, 1973. Paperback. 157 pgs. (£ .70)
  ISBN-0-352-30059-0 (UK)
- *Marilyn Monroe—Historia Illustrada del Cine* .... $30-$40
  Iesa, 1977. 1st ed. No. 3. Paperback. 152 pgs. ISBN-84-7311-017-X (SPA)
- *Marilyn Monroe—Storia Illustrata del Cinema* .... $30-$40
  Milano Libri E., 1975. 1st ed. Paperback. 157 pgs. (ITA)
- *Marilyn Monroe—Ihre Filme-Ihr Leben* .... $20-$35
  Heyne Film Bibliothek, 1992. Paperback. (GER)
- *Marilyn Das M. M. Kultbuch—Heyne Mini* .... $20-$35
  W. Heyne Verlag, 1986. 1st ed. No. 33/26. Paperback. 121 pgs. (3 DM)
  ISBN-3-453-35372-2 (GER)

Gianni MERCURIO and Stephano PETRICCA

- *Marilyn Monroe—La Vita Il Mito* .... $50-$65
  Rizzoli, 1995. Softcover. 319 pgs. (Lit. 75.000) ISBN-88-17-24824-X (ITA)
- *Marilyn—The Life and Myth* .... $50-$70
  Rizzoli, 1996. 1st ed. Hardcover. 319 pgs. ($60) ISBN-0-8478-1960-4 (USA)

Arthur MILLER and Serge TOUBIANA

- *The Misfits—Chroniques d' un tournage par les photographes* .... $20-$30
  Les chahiers du cine, 1999. 189 pgs. ISBN-2-86642-207-4 (FRA)

Will Acting Spoil Marilyn Monroe? by Martin. Italian paperback, $150-$225.

An American Success by Madsen. Danish softcover, $200-$300.

Marilyn Monroe Star Dossier One by Dyer. British softcover, $60-$80.

Will Acting Spoil Marilyn Monroe? by Martin. U.S. hardcover, $125-$200.

Will Acting Spoil Marilyn Monroe? by Martin. U.S. paperback, $60-$100.

Marilyn A Never Ending Dream by Luijters. U.S. hardcover, $40-$60.

Bart MILLS
- *Marilyn On Location* .... $40-$60
  Sidgwick & Jackson, 1989. Hardcover. 160 pgs. (£13.95)
  ISBN-0-283-99766-4 (UK)
- *Marilyn On Location* .... $30-$50
  Pan, 1990. Softcover. 160 pgs. (£9.99) ISBN-0-330-31841-1 (UK)

Bernice Baker MIRACLE and Mona Rae MIRACLE
- *My Sister Marilyn* .... $30-$40
  Algonquin, 1994. 1st ed. Hardcover. 238 pgs. ($19.95)
  ISBN-1-56512-070-1 (USA)
- *Mijn zus Marilyn* .... $30-$40
  de Kern, 1994. Softcover. (HOL)

Vincenzo MOLLICA
- *Dedicato a Marilyn* (boxed with two compact discs) .... $30-$40
  Ed. del Grifo, 1990. Softcover. (ITA)

Marilyn MONROE
- *My Story by Marilyn Monroe* .... $45-$60
  Stein and Day, 1974. 1st ed. Hardcover. 143 pgs. ($5.95)
  ISBN-0-8128-1707-9 (USA)
- *My Story by Marilyn Monroe* .... $20-$40
  Stein and Day, 1976. 1st ed. Paperback. 143 pgs. ($1.75)
  ISBN-0-8128-2112-X (USA)
- *My Story by Marilyn Monroe* .... $10-$15
  Stein and Day, 1986. 2nd re. Paperback. 239 pgs. ($3.50)
  ISBN-0-8128-8283-0 (USA)
- *My Story by Marilyn Monroe—Never before published* .... $45-$65
  W. H. Allen, 1975. 1st ed. Hardcover. 143 pgs. ISBN-0-491-01754-5 (UK)
- *Marilyn Monroe—Confession Inachevee* .... $25-$45
  Robert Laffont, 1974. Paperback. 233 pgs. (FRA)
- *Recuerdos de mi vida-Marilyn Monroe—Coll. Personae, 8* .... $45-$65
  Euros/Club de Vanguardia, 1975. No. 565. Hardcover. 232 pgs.
  ISBN-84-7364-041-1 (SPA)
- *Marilyn Monroe—Meine Story* .... $15-$25
  Fischer Taschenbucher, 1980. Paperback. 156 pgs. ISBN-3-596-23663-0 (GER)
- *Nuorunteni* .... $45-$65
  Otava, 1975. 1st ed. Softcover. 156 pgs. ISBN-951-1-01972-4 (FIN)
- *My Story* .... $15-$20
  Cooper Square Press, 2000. Hardcover. 152 pgs. ISBN-0815411022 (USA)

Robin MOORE
- *Marilyn & Joe DiMaggio* .... $30-$50
  Manor Books, 1977. 1st ed. Paperback. 298 pgs. ($1.95)
  ISBN-0-532-19132-8 (USA)

Richard S. MOORE
- *Marilyn Monroe—Su vida-sus amores-su muerte* .... $50-$80
  Petronio, 1973. 1st ed. Hardcover. 245 pgs. (250 pta.)
  ISBN-84-365-0196-9 (SPA)
- *Marilyn Monroe—Su vida-sus-amores-su muerte* .... $50-$80
  Petronio, 1973. 2nd re. Hardcover. 245 pgs. (250 pta.)
  ISBN-84-365-0196-9 (SPA)
- *Marilyn Monroe—Su vida-sus-amores-su muerte* .... $40-$55
  Gaviota, 1987. Softcover. 245 pgs. (700 pta.) ISBN-84-7693-066-6 (SPA)

Sheridan MORLEY and Ruth LEON
- *Marilyn Monroe* .... $5-$10
  Sutton Publishing, 1998. Paperback. 128 pgs. ISBN-0750915102 (USA)

Eunice MURRAY and Rose SHADE

- *Marilyn: The Last Months—Intimate Facts Never Before Revealed*.............$35-$45
  Pyramid Books, 1975. 1st ed. Paperback. 157 pgs. ($1.75)
  ISBN-0-515-03787-7 (USA)

Joel OPPENHEIMER

- *Marilyn Lives! by Joel Oppenheimer*...$40-$60
  Delilah Books, 1981. 1st ed. Softcover. 123 pgs. ($8.95)
  ISBN-0-933328-02-8 (USA)
- *Marilyn Lives! by Joel Oppenheimer*...$40-$60
  Pipeline Books, 1981. 1st ed. Softcover. 123 pgs. (£5.95)
  ISBN-0-933328-02-8 (UK)

Mary Jo PACE

- *Marilyn Monroe—Una donna bruciata-I magnifici di Hollywood*.................$20-$40
  Alberto, 1981. 1st ed. No. 10. Paperback. 66 pgs. (Lit. 500.000) (ITA)

Ulises PARAMO

- *Marilyn Suicidio o Asesinato?* . . . . $60-$80
  Esamex, 1993. Softcover. (MEX)

Lena PEPITONE and William STADIEM

- *Marilyn Monroe Confidential—An Intimate Personal Account*. . . . . $20-$40
  Simon & Shuster, 1979. 1st ed. Hardcover. 251 pgs. ($9.95)
  ISBN-0-671-24289-X (USA)
- *Marilyn Monroe Confidential—An Intimate Personal Account*. . . . . $30-$45
  Simon & Shuster, 1979. 1st ed./Book Club ed. Hardcover. 222 pgs. (USA)
- *Marilyn Monroe Confidential* (blue cover). . . . . $10-$15
  Pocket Books, 1980. 1st ed. Paperback. 223 pgs. ($2.50)
  ISBN-0-671-83038-4 (USA)
- *Marilyn Monroe Confidential—The Whole World Knows Her* (pink cover) ..$10-$15
  Pocket Books, 1980. 1st ed. Paperback. 223 pgs. ($2.50)
  ISBN-0-671-83038-4 (USA)
- *Marilyn Monroe Confidential—An Intimate Personal Account*.....................$25-$45
  Sidgwick & Jackson, 1979. 1st ed. Hardcover. 251 pgs.
  ISBN-0-283-98537-2 (UK)
- *Marilyn Monroe Confidential—An Intimate Personal Account*.....................$15-$20
  New English Library, 1980. 1st ed. Paperback. 221 pgs. (£1.25)
  ISBN-0-450-04765-2 (UK)
- *Marilyn Monroe Secrete—Les Bouleversantes Revelations*... ....$35-$45
  Pygmalion/G. Watelet, 1979. Softcover. 253 pgs. ISBN-2-85704-052-0 (FRA)
- *Marilyn Monroe Secrete—Les Bouleversantes Revelations*... ....$35-$45
  Pygmalion/G. Watelet, 1979. Softcover. 253 pgs. ISBN-2-85704-052-0 (FRA)
- *Marilyn Secrete*..$35-$45
  Pygmalion/G. Watelet, 1986. Softcover. 248 pgs. ISBN-2-85704-206-X (FRA)
- *Marilyn Monroe Intim*...$15-$25
  Heyne Verlag, 1979. 1st ed. Paperback. 189 pgs. (5,80 DM)
  ISBN-3-453-01045-0 (GER)
- *Marilyn Monroe Confidencial Confidencialmente*...$15-$25
  Crea, 1980. 2nd ed. Paperback. 149 pgs. (ARG)
- *Farval Lammunge Marilyn Monroe in pa skinnet*...$40-$60
  Corona, 1979. 1st ed. Hardcover. 180 pgs. ISBN-91-564-0990-7 (SWE)

Maurice PERISSET

- *Marilyn Monroe—Sa vie, ses films et son mystere*......................................$15-$20
  Garanciere, 1985. 1st ed. Paperback. 195 pgs. (48*f*) ISBN-2-7340-0087-3 (FRA)

Anna PRADERIO

- *Marilyn Monroe—Ciakintasca No. 1* (supplement to Ciak Mag. No. 6)........$15-$25
  Silvio Berlusconi/Ciak, 1989. 1st ed. Paperback. 126 pgs. (ITA)

My Story by Monroe. U.S. hardcover, $45-$60.

Bernard of Hollywood's Marilyn by Bernard. U.S. hardcover, $30-$50.

Marilyn Lives! by Oppenheimer. U.S. softcover, $40-$60.

Marilyn Monroe as The Girl by Shaw. U.S. paperback, $60-$100.

Marilyn Monroe—An Appreciation by Arnold. U.S. hardcover, $40-$60.

Marilyn by Rooks-Denes. British hardcover, $30-$40.

Silvain REINER
- *La Tragedie de Marilyn Monroe—victime de l'usine a idoles* ....$70-$100
  Presses Pocket, 1966. Paperback. 309 pgs. (FRA)
- *De Tragedie Van Marilyn Monroe*
  Uitgeverij Heideland, Hasselt, 1969. Hardcover. 276 pgs. (BEL) ....$70-$100
- *La Tragedia de Marilyn Monroe—Coll.'Fifuras del Cine No. 2* ....$70-$100
  Grigalbo, 1972. 1st ed. Paperback. 277 pgs. (UNKNOWN ORIGIN)
- *Marilyn Monroe* ....$20-$30
  Le Castor Astral, 1997. 247 pgs. ISBN-2-85920-320-6 (FRA)

Tony RICHARDSON
- *La vida privada de Marilyn Monroe—Coll. 'Rosa' No. 1* .... $30-$40
  Tarquimia, 1980. 1st ed. Paperback. 63 pgs.
  ISBN-84-300-2501-4 (SPA)

Randall RIESE and Neil HITCHENS
- *The Unabridged Marilyn—Her Life from A to Z*...$30-$40
  Congdon & Weed, 1987. 1st ed. Hardcover. 578 pgs. ($25)
  ISBN-0-86553-176-5 (USA)
- *The Unabridged Marilyn—Her Life from A to Z*...$30-$40
  Congdon & Weed, 1987. Softcover. 578 pgs. ($14.95)
  ISBN-0-86553-167-6 (USA)
- *The Unabridged Marilyn—Her Life from A to Z*...$30-$40
  Bonanza Books, 1990. Hardcover. 578 pgs. ($25)
  ISBN-0-517-69619-3 (USA)
- *The Unabridged Marilyn—The Definitive, Illustrated A-Z...* ....$20-$30
  Corgi, 1988. Softcover. 587 pgs. (£9.95) ISBN-0-552-99308-5 (UK)

Gary VITACCO-ROBLES
- *Cursum Perficio: Marilyn Monroe Brentwood Hacienda: The Story of...* ....$5-$10
  Club Ltd., 2000. Paperback. 176 pgs. ISBN-0595010822 (USA)

P. RODELLAR (Helmuth Von Soegl)
- *Marilyn Monroe—Inedita*..$40-$65
  Prod. Editoriales, 1976. 1st ed. Softcover. 95 pgs. (150 pta.)
  ISBN-84-365-0951-X (SPA)

Carl E. ROLLYSON, Jr.
- *Marilyn Monroe—A Life of the Actress* ....$25-$40
  U.M.I. Research Press, 1986. Hardcover. 255 pgs. ($16.95)
  ISBN-0-8357-1771-2 (USA)
- *Marilyn Monroe—A Life of the Actress* ....$25-$40
  Souvenir Press, 1986. 1st ed. Hardcover. 255 pgs.
  ISBN-0-285-62827-5 (UK)
- *Marilyn Monroe—A Life of the Actress* ....$10-$15
  New English Library, 1990. 1st ed. Paperback. 306 pgs. (£4.50)
  ISBN-0-450-53720-X (UK)

Norman ROSTEN
- *Marilyn: An Untold Story—An Intimate Close-Up...* ....$25-$40
  Signet/New American Library, 1973. 1st ed. Paperback. 125 pgs. ($1.50)
  ISBN-0-451-08880-8 (USA)
- *Marilyn—A Very Personal Story by Norm Rosten*.......................................$45-$65
  Millington, 1974. 1st ed. Hardcover. 125 pgs. ISBN-0-86000-001-X (UK)
- *Marilyn—A Very Personal Story by Norm Rosten*.......................................$20-$30
  Millington, 1980. Paperback. 114 pgs. ISBN-0-86000-118-0 (UK)
- *Marilyn un relato inedito*...$20-$35
  Grijalbo, 1980. 2nd ed. Paperback. 144 pgs. ISBN-84-253-0461-X (UK)
- *Marilyn: A unica estoria nao revelada*..$25-$45
  Nova Epoca, year unknown. Softcover. 111 pgs. (BRA)
- *Marilyn Monroe un autre regard-et Marilyn Monroe par elle-meme*............$40-$50
  Lherminier, 1984. 1st ed. Softcover. 189 pgs. (136*f*) ISBN-2-86244-029-9 (FRA)

Jeannie SAKOL and Joseph JASGUR

- *The Birth of Marilyn—The Lost Photographs of Norma Jean* .... $30-$40
  St. Martin's Press, 1991. 1st ed. Hardcover. 93 pgs. ISBN-0-312-06770-4 (USA)
- *The Birth of Marilyn—The Lost Photographs of Norma Jean* .... $30-$40
  Sidgwick & Jackson, 1991. 1st ed. Hardcover. 93 pgs. (£17.50)
  ISBN-0-283-99852-0 (UK)

Lothar SCHIRMER

- *Marilyn Monroe and the Camera* (with Jane Russell and G. Belmont) .... $50-$70
  Bloomsbury, 1989. 1st ed. Hardcover. 245 pgs. (£40.00)
  ISBN-0-7475-0490-3 (UK)
- *Marilyn Monroe et les Cameras* (with Jane Russell and G. Belmont) .... $50-$70
  Schirmer/Mosel, 1989. 1st ed. Hardcover. 248 pgs. ISBN-3-88814-538-4 (FRA)
- *Marilyn Monroe und die Kamera* (with Jane Russell and G. Belmont) .... $50-$70
  Schirmer/Mosel, 1989. 1st ed. Hardcover. 248 pgs. ISBN-3-88814-334-9 (GER)
- *Marilyn Monroe immagini di un mito* (with Russell and Belmont) .... $50-$70
  RCS Rizzoli, 1989. 1st ed. Hardcover. 248 pgs. ISBN-88-17-24244-6 (ITA)
- *Marilyn Monroe and the Camera* .... $60-$80
  New Art Seibu, 1989. 1st ed. Hardcover. 245 pgs. ISBN-4-8457-0464-1 (JPN)

Tony SCIACCA

- *Who Killed Marilyn? And Did the Kennedys Know?* .... $20-$30
  Manor Book, 1976. 1st ed. Paperback. 222 pgs. ($1.75)
  ISBN-532-17124-175 (USA)
- *Quien Mato a Marilyn? y...Lo sabian los Kennedy?* .... $25-$35
  Novarro, 1977. 1st ed. Softcover. 182 pgs. (MEX)

Esther SELSDON

- *They Died Too Young—Marilyn Monroe* .... $15-$25
  Parragon Mini Book, 1995. Hardcover. (UK)

Sam SHAW

- *Marilyn Monroe as The Girl* (based on *The Seven Year Itch*) .... $60-$100
  Ballantine Books, 1955. 1st ed. Paperback. 123 pgs. (35¢) (USA)
- *The Joy of Marilyn—In the Camera Eye* .... $45-$60
  Exeter Books, 1979. 1st ed. Hardcover. 160 pgs. ISBN-0-89673-030-1 (USA)
- *Marilyn—In the Camera Eye* .... $45-$60
  Hamlyn, 1979. 1st ed. Hardcover. 160 pgs. (£4.95) ISBN-0-600-34156-9 (UK)
- *Marilyn-Dans l'objectif* .... $45-$60
  L. Champs-Elysees, 1979. 1st ed. Hardcover. 160 pgs.
  ISBN-2-7024-0972-5 (FRA)

Sam SHAW and Norm ROSTEN

- *Marilyn Among Friends* .... $40-$60
  Henry Holt, 1987. 1st ed. Hardcover. 192 pgs. ISBN-0-8050-0843-8 (USA)
- *Marilyn Among Friends* .... $40-$60
  Bloomsbury, 1987. 1st ed. Hardcover. 192 pgs. (£14.95)
  ISBN-0-7475-0012-6 (UK)
- *Marilyn Among Friends* .... $40-$60
  Bloomsbury, 1988. Softcover. 192 pgs. (£9.95) ISBN-0-7475-0172-6 (UK)
- *Marilyn Among Friends* .... $40-$60
  Bloomsbury, 1989. 2nd re. Softcover. 192 pgs. (£6.99)
  ISBN-0-7475-0629-9 (UK)
- *Marilyn et ses amis* .... $40-$60
  Ramsay, 1988. 1st ed. Hardcover. 192 pgs. (250*f*) ISBN-2-85956-678-3 (FRA)
- *Marilyn ganz privat* .... $40-$60
  Heyne Verlag, 1987. 1st ed. Hardcover. 192 pgs. ISBN-3-453-02498-2 (GER)
- *Marilyn fra i suoi amice* .... $40-$60
  A. Vallardi, 1988. 1st ed. Hardcover. 192 pgs. (Lit. 50.000)
  ISBN-88-11-95291-3 (ITA)
- *Marilyn Among Friends* .... $60-$80
  Bungeishunju, 1989. 1st ed. Hardcover. 192 pgs. ISBN-4-16-380310-6 (JPN)

Marilyn-Norma Jeane by Steinem and Barris. U.S. paperback, $10-$15.

Marilyn Book No. 2, Japanese softcover, $60-$80.

The Strange Death of Marilyn Monroe by Capell. U.S. softcover, $60-$125.

Marilyn Book No. 1, Japanese softcover, $60-$80.

Marilyn's Men by Wayne. U.S. paperback, $5-$10.

Marilyn Monroe An Uncensored Biography by Zolotow. U.S. paperback, $35-$45.

Sandra SHEVEY

- *The Marilyn Scandal: Her True Life Revealed By Those Who Knew...* ....$20-$35
  W. Morrow & Co., 1988. 1st ed. Hardcover. 326 pgs. ($18.95)
  ISBN-0-688-08219-X (USA)
- *The Marilyn Scandal: Her True Life Revealed By Those Who Knew*..............$10-$15
  Jove Books, 1990. Paperback. 341 pgs. ($4.95) ISBN-0-515-10238-5 (USA)
- *The Marilyn Scandal: Her True Life Revealed By Those Who Knew...* ....$20-$35
  Sidgwick & Jackson, 1987. Hardcover. 326 pgs. (£12.95)
  ISBN-0-283-99456-8 (UK)
- *The Marilyn Scandal: TheTrue Story*..$10-$15
  Arrow, 1989. Paperback. 434 pgs. (£3.99) ISBN-0-09-960760-3 (UK)
- *Le Scandale Marilyn* ....$20-$35
  Press Renaissance, 1989. Softcover. 342 pgs. (120*f*)
  ISBN-2-85616-526-5 (FRA)

Neil SINYARD

- *Marilyn* ....$20-$35
  Gallery Books, 1989. 1st ed. Hardcover. 109 pgs.
  ISBN-0-8317-5753-1 (USA)
- *Marilyn* ....$20-$35
  Magna Books, 1989. 1st ed. Hardcover. 109 pgs.
  ISBN-1-85422-020-9 (UK)

Robert F. SLATZER

- *The Life and Curious Death of Marilyn Monroe*...$50-$65
  Pinnacle House, 1974. 1st ed. Hardcover. 348 pgs. ISBN-0-8467-001-8 (USA)
- *The Life and Curious Death of Marilyn Monroe*...$50-$65
  Pinnacle House, 1974. 2nd ed. Hardcover. 348 pgs. ISBN-0-8467-001-8 (USA)
- *The Curious Death of Marilyn Monroe*...$25-$35
  Pinnacle Books, 1975. 1st ed. Paperback. 417 pgs. ($1.95)
  ISBN-0-523-00575-3 (USA)
- *Enquete sur une mort suspecte: Marilyn Monroe*...$50-$65
  Julliard, 1974. 1st ed. Softcover. 346 pgs. (FRA)
- *Enquete sur une mort suspecte: Marilyn Monroe*...$35-$45
  Presses Pocket, 1976. Paperback. 409 pgs.
  ISBN-2-266-00021-7 (FRA)
- *The Marilyn Files* ....$10-$15
  SPI Books, 1992. Paperback. (USA)

Matteo SOCCIO

- *Marilyn in cartellone*..$30-$40
  Bastogi di Angelo Manuali, 1983. Softcover. (Lit. 7.000) (ITA)

James SPADA and George ZENO

- *Monroe—Her Life in Pictures*...$30-$50
  Doubleday & Co., 1982. 1st ed. Hardcover. 194 pgs. ($24.95)
  ISBN-0-385-17941-3 (USA)
- *Monroe—Her Life in Pictures*...$30-$50
  Doubleday/Dolphin, 1982. 1st ed. Softcover. 194 pgs. ($14.95)
  ISBN-0-385-17940-5 (USA)
- *Monroe—Her Life in Pictures*...$30-$50
  Sidgwick & Jackson, 1982. 1st ed. Hardcover. 194 pgs. (£8.95)
  ISBN-0-283-98871-1 (UK)
- *Monroe—Her Life in Pictures*...$30-$50
  Sidgwick & Jackson, 1987. 6th re. Softcover. 194 pgs. (£9.95)
  ISBN-0-283-98998-X (UK)
- *Marilyn Monroe—Sa vie en images* ....$30-$50
  Jai lu-Cinema, 1988. 1st ed. Paperback. 143 pgs. (3*f*)
  ISBN-2-277-37003-7 (FRA)
- *Marilyn Monroe—Ihr Leben in Bildern*..$35-$55
  Bussesche, 1983. Hardcover. 193 pgs. ISBN-3-87120-813-2 (GER)

- *Marilyn: sa vie en images* ....$20-$30
  Succes du livre, 1989. 208 pgs. ISBN-2-73-820247-0 (FRA)

Milo SPERIGLIO
- *Marilyn Monroe—Murder Cover-up* ....$20-$40
  Seville, 1982. 1st ed. Softcover. 269 pgs. ($7.95) ISBN-0-930990-77-3 (USA)
- *The Marilyn Conspiracy...* ....$10-$15
  Pocket Nonfiction, 1986. 1st ed. Paperback. 221 pgs. ($3.50)
  ISBN-0-671-62612-4 (USA)
- *The Marilyn Conspiracy—Suicide? Accidental Death? Murder?...* ....$10-$15
  Corgi Books, 1987. 1st ed. Paperback. 173 pgs. (£2.50)
  ISBN-0-552-13058-3 (UK)
- *The Marilyn Conspiracy—Suicide? Accidental Death? Murder?...* ....$10-$15
  Corgi Books, 1988. 4th re. Paperback. 173 pgs. (£2.99)
  ISBN-0-552-13058-3 (UK)
- *A Conspiracao Marilyn* ....$20-$40
  Imago,1987. 1st ed. Softcover. 137 pgs. (BRA)

Donald SPOTO
- *Marilyn Monroe—The Biography* ....$25-$35
  Harper-Collins, 1993. Hardcover. 698 pgs. ($25) ISBN-0-06-017987-2 (USA)
- *Marilyn Monroe—The Biography* .... $8-$10
  Harper-Collins, 1994. 1st ed. Paperback. 841 pgs. ($6.99)
  ISBN-0-06-109166-9 (USA)
- *Marilyn La Biografia* ....$20-$30
  Anagrama, 1993. Paperback. (SPA)
- *Marilyn Finalmente La Verita* ....$20-$30
  Sperling and Kupfer, 1993. Hardcover. (ITA)
- *Marilyn Monroe La biographie* ....$20-$30
  Presses de la Cite, 1993. 575 pgs. ISBN-2-258-036003 (FRA)
- *Marilyn Monroe—The Biography* ....$15-$20
  Cooper Square, 2001. 2nd ed. Paperback. 752 pgs. ISBN-0815411839 (USA)

Roger ST. PIERRE
- *Marilyn Monroe—An Independent Story in Words and Pictures* ....$20-$35
  Anabas Look Book Series, 1985. 1st ed. Softcover. 27 pgs.
  ISBN-1-85099-013-1 (UK)

Gloria STEINEM and George BARRIS
- *Marilyn-Norma Jeane* ....$30-$50
  Henry Holt & Co., 1986. 1st ed. Hardcover. 182 pgs. ($24.95)
  ISBN-0-8050-0060-7 (USA)
- *Marilyn—The Nationwide Bestseller!* ....$30-$50
  Plume/N.A.L., 1987. 1st ed. Softcover. 182 pgs. ($14.95)
  ISBN-0-452-2598-7 (USA)
- *Marilyn-Norma Jeane—The Nationwide Bestseller!* ....$10-$15
  Signet Book/N.A.L., 1988. 1st ed. Paperback. 220 pgs. ($4.95)
  ISBN-0-451-15596-3 (USA)
- *Marilyn-Norma Jeane* ....$30-$50
  Victor Gollancz, 1987. 2nd re. Hardcover. 182 pgs. (£12.95)
  ISBN-0-575-03945-0 (UK)
- *Marilyn Inconnue* ....$30-$50
  Sylvie Messinger, 1987. 1st ed. Hardcover. 182 pgs. (195*f*)
  ISBN-2-86583-080-2 (FRA)
- *Marilyn—Un ritratto tenero e realistico...* ....$30-$50
  Armenia Editore, 1987. 1st ed. Hardcover. 268 pgs. (Lit. 24.000)
  ISBN-88-344-0243-X (ITA)
- *Marilyn-Norma Jeane* ....$30-$50
  Informations Forlag, 1987. 1st ed. Hardcover. 192 pgs.
  ISBN-87-7514-0071 (DEN)

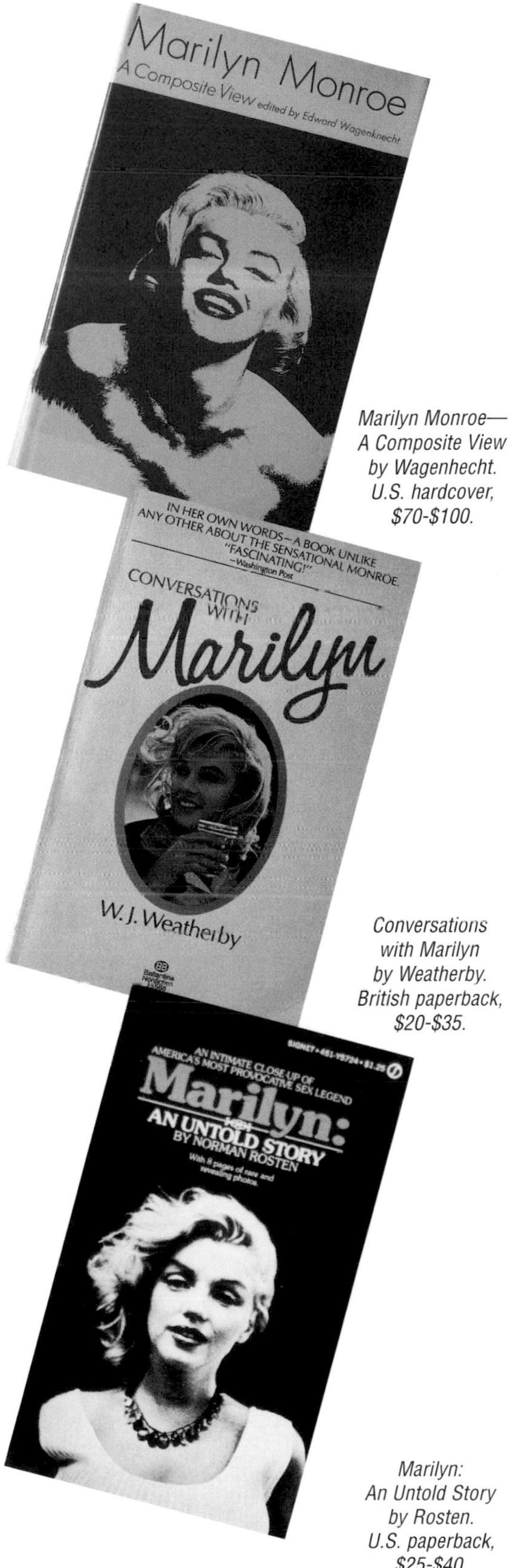

Marilyn Monroe—A Composite View by Wagenhecht. U.S. hardcover, $70-$100.

Conversations with Marilyn by Weatherby. British paperback, $20-$35.

Marilyn: An Untold Story by Rosten. U.S. paperback, $25-$40.

Marilyn Monroe by Zolotow. Spanish paperback, $35-$50.

How to Shoot for Glamour by Bakal. U.S. hardcover, $50-$75.

The Marilyn Conspiracy by Speriglio. U.S. paperback, $10-$15.

Gloria STEINEM and George BARRIS (continued)

- *Marilyn-Norma Jeane* .... $30-$50
  Wahlstrom and Widstrand, 1987. 1st ed. Hardcover. 190 pgs. ISBN-91-46-15522-8 (SWE)

Bert STERN

- *Marilyn Monroe* (slipcased/edit. de luxe/limitee a 1,000) No. 00578 ....$200-$300
  Chene/Hachette, 1982. 1st ed. Hardcover. 463 pgs. (790*f*) ISBN-2-85108-3090 (FRA)
- *Marilyn Monroe—The Complete Last Sitting* (slipcased) .... $200-$300
  Schirmer/Mosel, 1982. 1st ed. Hardcover. 463 pgs. ISBN-3-88814-103-6 (GER)
- *Marilyn Monroe—The Complete Last Sitting* .... $100-$115
  Schirmer/Mosel Verlag, 2000. Hardcover. 464 pgs. ISBN-3-82385-483-6 (GER)
- *The Last Sitting* .... $40-$60
  W. Morrow & Co., 1982. 1st ed. Hardcover. 188 pgs. ISBN-0-688-01173-X (USA)
- *The Last Sitting* .... $40-$60
  Black Cat, 1982. 1 re. Hardcover. 188 pgs. (£13.95) ISBN-0-7481-0107-1 (UK)
- *Marilyn—Sa Derniere Seance par Bert Stern* .... $40-$60
  Filipacchi, 1982. 1 re. Hardcover. 188 pgs. (195*f*) ISBN-2-85018-427-6 (FRA)
- *Marilyn's Last Sitting* .... $10-$15
  Knaur/Biographie, 1982. Paperback. 242 pgs. (17,80 DM) ISBN-3-426-02328-8 (GER)
- *Marilyn—Haar laatste fotosessie* .... $40-$60
  van holkema en warendorf, 1982. Softcover. (HOL)
- *Marilyn Monroe—The Last Sitting* .... $30-$40
  Schirmer/Mosel, 1994. 111 pgs. ISBN-3-88814-631-3 (FRA)

Bert STERN and Ann GOTTLIEB

- *Marilyn viva* .... $40-$60
  Frassinelli, 1982. Hardcover. ISBN-88-200-0271-X (ITA)

Susan STRASBERG

- *Marilyn and Me* .... $25-$35
  Warner, 1992. 1st ed. Hardcover. 282 pgs. ($21.95) ISBN-0-446-51592-2 (USA)
- *Marilyn and Me* .... $10-$15
  Warner, 1993. 1st ed. Paperback. 254 pgs. ($5.99) ISBN-0-446-36425-8 (USA)
- *Marilyn Et Moi* .... $20-$30
  J'ai lu, 1992. Paperback. (FRA)

Anthony SUMMERS

- *Goddess—The Secret Lives of Marilyn Monroe* .... $25-$45
  MacMillan, 1985. 1st ed. Hardcover. 415 pgs. ($18.95) ISBN-0-02-615460-9 (USA)
- *Goddess—The Secret Lives of Marilyn Monroe* .... $25-$45
  MacMillan, 1985. Book Club ed. Hardcover. 430 pgs. (USA)
- *Goddess—The Secret Lives of Marilyn Monroe* .... $10-$15
  Onyx Book/N.A.L. , 1986. 1st ed. Paperback. 526 pgs. ($18.95) ISBN-0-451-40014-3 (USA)
- *Goddess—The Secret Lives of Marilyn Monroe* .... $25-$45
  Gollancz, 1985. 1st ed. Hardcover. 414 pgs. (£12.95) ISBN-0-575-03641-9 (UK)
- *Goddess—The Secret Lives of Marilyn Monroe* .... $10-$15
  Sphere, 1986. 1st ed. Paperback. 619 pgs. (£3.95) ISBN-0-7221-8284-8 (UK)
- *Les vies secretes de Marilyn Monroe* .... $25-$45
  Pre. de la renaissance, 1986. Softcover. 522 pgs. ISBN-2-35616-370-X (FRA)
- *Les vies secretes de Marilyn Monroe* .... $25-$45
  Ed. Club France Loisirs, 1987. 1st ed. Paperback. 522 pgs. ISBN-2-277-22282-8 (FRA)
- *Les vies secretes de Marilyn Monroe* .... $10-$15
  Jai lu, 1987. 1st ed. Paperback. 568 pgs. ISBN-2-277-22282-8 (FRA)

- *Las vidas secretas de Marilyn Monroe* .... $25-$45
  Planeta, 1986. 1st ed. Softcover. 349 pgs. (1400 pta.)
  ISBN-84-320-4769-4 (SPA)
- *Marilyn Monroe—Die Wahrhelt uber ihr Leben und Sterben* .... $10-$15
  Fischer, 1990. 1st ed. Paperback. 519 pgs. (16,8 DM)
  ISBN-3-596-25679-8 (GER)
- *Marilyn Monroe Le vite segrete di una diva* .... $25-$45
  Tascabili sonzogno, 1988. 1st ed. Softcover. 425 pgs. (Lit. 8.000) (ITA)
- *De Geheime Levens van Marilyn Monroe* .... $25-$45
  De Bezige Bij, 1986. 1st ed. Softcover. 526 pgs. ISBN-90-234-5297-6 (HOL)
- *Gudinnan Marilyn Monroes Hemliga Liv* .... $25-$45
  Forum, 1986. 1st ed. Hardcover. 516 pgs. ISBN-91-37-09126-3 (SWE)
- *Den nogne gudinde-Sandheden om Marilyn Monroe* .... $25-$45
  Chr. Erichsen, 1986. Softcover. 424 pgs. ISBN-87-555-1069-8 (DEN)
- *A Deusa as vidas secretas de Marilyn Monroe* .... $25-$45
  Best Seller, 1987. 1st ed. Softcover. 523 pgs. ISBN-85-85091-52-5 (BRA)
- *Marilyn* .... $25-$40
  Sonzogno, 1992. Hardcover. (ITA)

Roger TAYLOR
- *Marilyn Monroe In Her Own Words* .... $40-$60
  Delilah/Putnam, 1983. 1st ed. Softcover. 122 pgs. ($5.95)
  ISBN-0-399-41011-7 (USA)
- *Marilyn on Marilyn* .... $40-$60
  Zachary Kwintner Books, 1983. 1st ed. Hardcover. 122 pgs.
  ISBN-1-872532-01-2 (UK)
- *Marilyn on Marilyn* .... $40-$50
  Comet Book, 1985. 1 re. Softcover. 122 pgs. (£4.95)
  ISBN-0-86379-080-1 (UK)
- *Marilyn in Art* .... $40-$60
  Salem House, 1984. 1st ed. Softcover. ($12.95) ISBN-0-88162-169-2 (USA)
- *Marilyn in Art* .... $40-$60
  Elm Tree Books, 1984. 1st ed. Hardcover. (£10.00) ISBN-0-241-11326-1 (UK)

William C. TAYLOR
- *Marilyn Monroe* .... $50-$60
  Ultramar, 1995. Hardcover. (SPA)

Wolfgang TUMLER
- *Marilyn Monroe* .... $40-$60
  Dressler/Menschen, 1978. Softcover. 172 pgs. (12,80 DM)
  ISBN-3-7915-5009-8 (GER)

UNKNOWN AUTHOR
- *Marilyn Monroe No. 1-1945-1958* .... $60-$85
  G.I.P. Tokyo, 1983. Paperback. 238 pgs. ISBN-4-10-219701-X (JPN)
- *Marilyn Monroe No. 2* .... $60-$80
  Publisher unknown, 1987. Softcover. 238 pgs. ISBN-4-8261-0001-9 (JPN)
- *Marilyn Monroe No. 3* .... $60-$80
  Publisher unknown, 1987. Softcover. 158 pgs. ISBN-4-8261-0505-3 (JPN)
- *Marilyn Monroe—Best Collection 1926-1962* .... $35-$45
  Flix, 1991. Softcover. ISBN-89389-042-5 (JPN)
- *Joe DiMaggio and Marilyn Monroe* .... $40-$50
  Kazuo Sayama, 1995. Hardcover. 261 pgs. ISBN-4-309-010-27-X (JPN)

Michael VENTURA and Earl LEAF
- *Marilyn Monroe—From Beginning to End* .... $25-$40
  Blandford, 1997. Hardcover. 220 pgs. ISBN-09646873-3-X (UK)

Orbis VERLAG
- *Marilyn Monroe—The Story of Her Life* .... $30-$50
  Colour Library Books Ltd., 1992. Hardcover. (GER)

The Casting Couch by Ford. British paperback, $10-$15.

The Marilyn Files by Slatzer. U.S. paperback, $10-$15.

Who Killed Marilyn? by Sciacca. U.S. paperback, $20-$30.

Who Killed Marilyn Monroe? by Hamblett. Dutch softcover, $40-$60.

Marilyn Monroe by Zolotow. Finnish paperback, $35-$50.

Goddess—The Secret Lives of Marilyn Monroe by Summers. U.S. paperback, $10-$15.

Adam VICTOR
- *The Marilyn Encyclopedia*..........$30-$40
  Overlook Press, 1999. Hardcover. ISBN-0-87951-718-2 (USA)

Ricardo VOLTOLINI
- *Marilyn Monroe por ela mesma-Colecao 'O autor por ele mesmo'*..........$30-$50
  Martin Claret, 1991. 1st ed. Softcover. 158 pgs. (BRA)

Edward WAGENKNECHT
- *Marilyn Monroe—A Composite View*..........$70-$100
  Chilton Book Co., 1969. 1st ed. Hardcover. 200 pgs. ($5.95) (USA)

Jane Ellen WAYNE
- *Marilyn's Men—The Private Life of Marilyn Monroe*..........$25-$40
  Robson Books, 1992. 1st ed. Hardcover. 241pgs. ISBN-0-86051-792-6 (UK)
- *Marilyn's Men*..........$5-$10
  St. Martin's, 1993. Paperback. 241 pgs. ($4.50) ISBN-0-312-92943-9 (USA)
- *Marilyn's Men*..........$10-$15
  Knauer, 1994. Paperback. (GER)
- *Marilyn's Men—The Private Life of Marilyn Monroe*..........$10-$15
  Warnerbooks, 1993. Paperback. (UK)

W. J. WEATHERBY
- *Conversations With Marilyn*..........$40-$70
  Manson/Charter, 1976. 1st ed. Hardcover. 229 pgs. ($7.95)
  ISBN-0-88405-148-X (USA)
- *Conversations With Marilyn*..........$40-$70
  Manson/Charter, 1976. 2nd re. Hardcover. 229 pgs. ($7.95)
  ISBN-0-88405-148-X (USA)
- *Conversations With Marilyn*..........$20-$35
  Ballantine Nonfiction, 1977. 1st ed. Paperback. 178 pgs.
  ISBN-345-25568-2-175 (USA)
- *Conversations With Marilyn*..........$40-$70
  Robson Books, 1976. 1st ed. Hardcover. 229 pgs. ISBN-0-903895-68-4 (UK)
- *Conversations With Marilyn*..........$20-$35
  Sphere Books, 1977. 1st ed. Paperback. 229 pgs. (£ .95)
  ISBN-0-7221-8982-6 (UK)
- *Conversations With Marilyn*..........$20-$30
  Sphere Books, 1987. 1 re. Paperback. 229 pgs. (£2.99)
  ISBN-0-7221-8982-6 (UK)
- *Conversaciones con Marilyn*..........$20-$30
  Gedisa, 1978. 1st ed. No. 7. Paperback. 269 pgs. (990 pta.)
  ISBN-84-7432-051-8 (SPA)
- *Conversations With Marilyn*..........$15-$20
  Paragon, 1992. Softcover. 229 pgs. ($12.95) ISBN-1-55778-512-0 (USA)

Leigh WIERNER
- *Marilyn—A Hollywood Farewell*..........$70-$100
  Leigh Wierner, 1990. 1st ed. Hardcover. 93 pgs. ISBN-0-9619146-3-7 (USA)

Corrina WINTER
- *Marilyn Super-Star Der Funfziger Jahre*..........$30-$45
  Quadro, 1992. Hardcover. (ITA)

Donald WOLFE
- *Marilyn Monroe Enquete sur un assassinat*..........$60-$70
  Albin Michel, 1998. 587 pgs. ISBN-2-226-10521-2 (FRA)
- *The Last Days of Marilyn Monroe*..........$15-$20
  William Morrow, 1998. Hardcover. 560 pgs. (USA)

Adam WOOG
- *Marilyn Monroe—Mysterious Deaths*..........$20-$25
  Lucent Books, 1997. 96 pgs. ISBN-1560062657 (USA)

Maurice ZOLOTOW

- *Marilyn Monroe—A Biography*.......................................$60-$90
  Harcourt Brace, 1960. 1st ed. Hardcover. 340 pgs. ($5.75) (USA)
- *Marilyn Monroe—An Uncensored Biography*.......................................$35-$45
  Bantam Books, 1961. Paperback. 338 pgs. (75¢) (USA)
- *Marilyn Monroe—Revised, Updated and Expanded Edition*.. ....$25-$40
  Perennial Library, 1990. 1st ed. Softcover. 359 pgs. ($9.95)
  ISBN-0-06-097196-7 (USA)
- *Marilyn Monroe—A Biography*.......................................$60-$100
  W. H. Allen, 1961. 1st ed. Hardcover. 333 pgs. (£ .25) (UK)
- *Marilyn Monroe—An Uncensored Biography*.......................................$35-$50
  Panther Books, 1962. 1st ed. Paperback. 287 pgs. (UK)
- *Marilyn Monroe—par Maurice Zolotow-L'air du tepms*...............................$60-$85
  Gallimard, 1961. 1st ed. Softcover. 416 pgs. (16.50*f*) (FRA)
- *Marilyn Monroe*.......................................$35-$50
  Plaza and Janes, 1965. 1st ed. Paperback. 318 pgs. (50 pta.) (SPA)
- *Marilyn Monroen elama*.......................................$35-$50
  Otava-Kompassikirja, 1964. 1st ed. Paperback. 422 pgs. (FIN)

SEVERAL AUTHORS

- *Marilyn Sings—The Marilyn Monroe Songbook*.......................................$25-$40
  Wise Publications, 1991. 1st ed. Softcover. 47 pgs. ISBN-0-7119-2712-X (UK)
- *Marilyn Monroe*.......................................$50-$70
  Film Editions (Pierre Lherminier), 1975. 1st ed. No. 1.
  Softcover. 116 pgs. (15*f*) (FRA)
- *Marilyn Monroe*.......................................$50-$70
  Sedmay Ediciones, 1976. 1st ed. Softcover. 222 pgs. (250 pta.)
  ISBN-84-7380-122-09 (SPA)
- *Marilyn Monroe*.......................................$30-$45
  Editions Cinemania (Solange Devilles), 1978. 1st ed. No. 2.
  Softcover. 45 pgs. (12*f*) (FRA)
- *Marilyn Revisitada*.......................................$35-$45
  Editorial Anagrama (Joaquin Jorda), 1971. 1st ed. No. 20.
  Paperback. 95 pgs. (SPA)

Books With References to Marilyn

Many of these books feature Marilyn on the front cover.

Patrick AGAN

- *The Decline and Fall of the Love Goddesses*.......................................$20-$30
  Pinnacle Books, 1979. 1st ed. Hardcover. 286 pgs. ($20)
  ISBN-0-523-40623-1 (USA)

ANONYMOUS

- *The Pocket Playboy*.......................................$20-$40
  Playboy Press, 1974. 1st ed. Paperback. 224 pgs. ($1.75) (USA)
- *Movie Trivia Quiz Book*.......................................$15-$25
  Ventura Associates, 1982. Paperback. ($3.95) (USA)
- *500 biografias de personajes celebres*....................................... $5-$10
  Planeta, 1983. 1st ed. Paperback. 249 pgs. ISBN-84-320-6540-4 (SPA)
- *Wedding book*.......................................$20-$35
  Libro Port, 1990. Paperback. 32 pgs. ISBN-8457-0517-6 (JPN)

Zinn ARTHUR

- *Shooting Superstars—Me, My Camera, and the Showbiz Legends*............$30-$40
  Artique Press, 1990. 1st ed. Hardcover. 240 pgs. ($29.95)
  ISBN-0-9623788-0-1 (USA)

The Models Blue Book by Snively. U.S. softcover, $200-$300.

Conversations With Marilyn by Weatherby. U.S. hardcover, $40-$70.

Marilyn Monroe—The Biography by Spoto. U.S. paperback, $8-$10.

Japanese softcover, $60-$80.

Marilyn Monroe Book of 30 Postcards, 1992 Magna, $15-$25.

The Unabridged Marilyn—Her Life From A to Z by Riese and Hitchens. U.S. hardcover, $30-$40.

Carl BAKAL
- *How To Shoot For Glamour* .... $50-$75
  Ziff-Davis, 1961. 2nd re. Hardcover. 128 pgs. (USA)

David BARRACLOUGH
- *Hollywood Heaven—The Apple Press* .... $10-$15
  Quintet Publishers, 1991. 1st ed. Hardcover. 95 pgs. ($8.95)
  ISBN-1-85076-298-8 (UK)

Cecil BEATON
- *Cecil Beaton (Preface de Jean Sagne)* .... $25-$35
  Chene/Paris Audiovisuel, 1989. 1st ed. Paperback. (185*f*)
  ISBN-2-264-01372-9 (FRA)

Robert BLOCH
- *Le crepuscule des stars* .... $5-$10
  Christian Bougois, 1989. No. 2017. Paperback. 279 pgs.
  ISBN-2-264-01372-9 (FRA)

Claude BONNEFOY
- *Le cinema et ses mythes* .... $15-$20
  Hachette, 1965. 1st ed. No. 14. Paperback. 126 pgs. (370*f*) (FRA)

Douglas BRODE
- *The Films of the Fifties* .... $20-$30
  The Citadel Press, 1976. 1st ed. Hardcover. 288 pgs. ISBN-0-8065-0510-9 (USA)

Giovanni CALENDOLI
- *Maschere* .... $20-$30
  Ribalta Maschere, 1962. 1st ed. Softcover. 158 pgs. (Lit. 300) (ITA)

Jock CARROLL
- *Down the Road* .... $5-$10
  Pocket Books, 1974. Paperback. ($1.50) ISBN-671-78739-X (CAN)

Colin CLEMENTS
- *Bluff Your Way in Hollywood* .... $5-$10
  Ravette London, 1987. 1st ed. Paperback. 63 pgs. (£1.00)
  ISBN-0-948456-42-6 (UK)

Daniel and Susan COHEN
- *Screen Godesses* .... $20-$30
  Hamlyn Bison, 1984. 1st ed. Hardcover. 128 pgs. ISBN-0-600-34738-9 (UK)

Gilles COLPART
- *Billy Wilder* .... $15-$25
  Edilig, year unknown. 1st ed. Softcover. 126 pgs. ISBN-2-85601-040-7 (FRA)

Kirk CRIVELLO
- *Fallen Angels—The Lives & Untimely Deaths of 14 Hollywood...* .... $5-$20
  Futura, 1990. 1st ed. Paperback. 282 pgs. (£3.99) ISBN-0-7088-4836-2 (UK)
- *Angels caiguts—La vida i la mort tragica de set gransestrelles* .... $5-$10
  Ixia Fahrenheit, 1991. 1st ed. Paperback. 199 pgs. (451,5)
  ISBN-84-87530-07-9 (CAT)

Robin CROSS
- *2000 Movies of the 1950's* .... $20-$30
  Arlington House, 1989. 1st ed. Hardcover. 255 pgs. ISBN-0-517-67973-6 (USA)

Anthony CURTIS
- *The Rise and Fall of the Matinee Idol*...$20-$30
  New English Library, 1976. 1st ed. Softcover. 215 pgs. (£1.95) ISBN-450-02662-0 (UK)

Lo DUCA
- *L'erotisme au cinema*..........................$30-$40
  J. Pauvert, 1958. 1st ed. Paperback. 218 pgs. (FRA)
- *L'erotisme au cinema*..........................$25-$35
  J. Pauvert, 1962. No. 1. Paperback. 220 pgs. (FRA)

William A. EWING
- *Flora Photographica*............................$20-$30
  Vilo, 1991. 1st ed. Hardcover. 224 pgs. ISBN-2-7191-0287-3 (FRA)

Xavier FAUCHE and Christiane NOETZLIN
- *Al bacio—Casto, perverso, rubato, mistico.* ....$20-$30
  Sugarco Ed., 1987. 1st ed. Softcover. 269 pgs. (Lit. 22.000) (ITA)

Marilyn Monroe—Classic Postcard Collection, 1990 Pyramid, $15-$20.

Joel W. FINLER
- *El gran libro del cine*..........................$20-$30
  Editorial HMB, 1979. 1st ed. Hardcover. 171 pgs. ISBN-84-85123-74-3 (SPA)

Selwyn FORD
- *The Casting Couch—Making it in Hollywood*..........................$10-$15
  Grafton Books, 1990. 1st ed. Paperback. 229 pgs. (£3.99) ISBN-0-586-20386-9 (UK)

James GOODE
- *The Story of The Misfits*..........................$45-$65
  Bobbs-Merrill, 1963. 1st ed. Hardcover. 331 pgs. ($5) (USA)
- *The Making of The Misfits*..........................$15-$25
  Limelight Ed., 1986. 1st ed. Softcover. 331 pgs. ($9.95) ISBN-0-87910-065-6 (USA)

Leslie HALLIWELL
- *Halliwell's Film Guide, 7th Edition*..........................$20-$30
  Paladin, 1989. 7th ed. Softcover. 1,171 pgs. (£12.99) ISBN-0-586-08894-6 (UK)

Charles HAMBLETT
- *Who Killed Marilyn Monroe (or cage to catch our dreams)*..........................$40-$60
  Leslie Frewin, 1966. 1st ed. Hardcover. 175 pgs. (UK)
- *Wie Vermoordde Marilyn Monroe?*..........................$40-$60
  Flamingo, 1966. Softcover. 211 pgs. (HOL)
- *The Hollywood Cage*..........................$30-$40
  Hart, 1969. 1st ed. Hardcover. 437 pgs. (USA)
- *The Hollywood Cage*..........................$30-$40
  Hart, 1969. 1st ed. Softcover. 437 pgs. (USA)

Suzanne LLOYD HAYES
- *3-D Hollywood*..........................$35-$50
  Simon and Schuster, 1992. Hardcover. 95 pgs. ISBN-0-671-76948-0 (USA)

Joe HEMBUS
- *Tillustriecte Film-Buhne—50 Hollywood-filme*..........................$20-$30
Monika Nuchtern, 1976. 1st ed. Softcover. (GER)

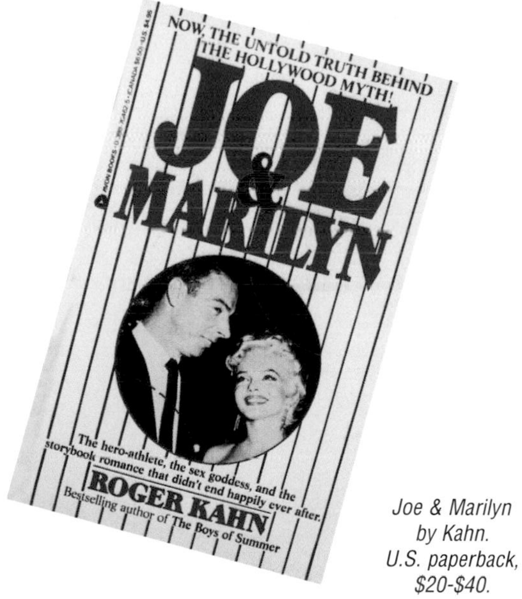

Joe & Marilyn by Kahn. U.S. paperback, $20-$40.

Marilyn: Portraits of a Goddess, Running Press postcard book, $15-$20.

Danielle HEMMERT and Alex ROUDENE
- *TLes Amazones—Hitler et Eva Braun-Marilyn Monroe* .... $20-$30
Rombaldi, 1974. 1st ed. Hardcover. 292 pgs. (FRA)

Tom HUTCHINSON
- *TDeesses de L' Ecran* .... $20-$30
Edilig, 1985. 1st ed. Hardcover. 195 pgs. ISBN-2-85601-122-5 (FRA)

Rodolfo IZAGUIRRE
- *Historia sentimental del cine norteamericano* .... $5-$10
Rodolfo Alonso, 1971. 1st ed. Paperback. 119 pgs. (ARG)

Rene JEANNE and Charles FORD
- *Historia ilustrada del cine 3* .... $5-$10
Alianza, 1988. 4th re. Paperback. 436 pgs. 84-206-1512-9 (SPA)

Jean-Claude JITROIS
- *Parfums de Stars* .... $20-$30
  Filipacchi, 1990. 1st ed. Hardcover. (230*f*) (FRA)

John KOBAL
- *Film-Star Portraits of The Fifties* .... $20-$30
  Dover, 1980. 1st ed. Softcover. 163 pgs. ISBN-0-486-24008-8 (USA)
- *Hollywood Colour Portraits* .... $20-$30
  Aurum, 1985. 1st ed. Softcover. 159 pgs. (£6.95) ISBN-0-906053-83-8 (UK)
- *Hollywood Couleur* .... $20-$30
  Henri Veyrier, 1983. 1st ed. Hardcover. 156 pgs. (150*f*)
  ISBN-2-85199-295-3 (FRA)

Madison S. LACY and Don MORGAN
- *Hollywood Cheesecake—Sixty Years of America's Favorite Pinups* .... $20-$30
  Citadel Press, 1991. 1st ed. Softcover. 286 pgs. ($19.95)
  ISBN-0-8065-0830-2 (USA)

Joshua LOGAN
- *Movie Stars, Real People, and Me* .... $20-$30
  Delacorte Press, 1978. 1st ed. Hardcover. 346 pgs. (USA)

Elizabeth MACAVOY and Susan ISRAELSON
- *Lovesick—The Marilyn Syndrome* .... $20-$30
  Donald I. Fine, 1991. 1st ed. Hardcover. 248 pgs. ($18.95)
  ISBN-1-55611-220-3 (USA)

Enrico MAGRELLI
- *Hollywood-Party—Quaderni di Filmcritica, 8* .... $15-$20
  Bulzoni, 1979. Paperback. 303 pgs. (ITA)

Daily MAIL
- *Films* .... $20-$25
  Morrison and Gibb, 1957. 1st ed. No. 6. Paperback. 160 pgs. (UK)

Norman MAILER and Milton H. GREENE
- *Of Women and Their Elegance* .... $30-$40
  Simon & Schuster, 1980. 1st ed. Hardcover. 288 pgs. ($29.95)
  ISBN-0-671-24020-X (USA)
- *Of Women and Their Elegance* .... $10-$15
  Tor, 1981. 1st ed. Paperback. 286 pgs. ($3.50) ISBN-0-523-48015-6 (USA)
- *Of Women and Their Elegance* .... $30-$40
  Hodder and Stoughton, 1980. 1st ed. Hardcover. 288 pgs.
  ISBN-0-340-23920-4 (UK)

Marilyn Monroe—In Her Own Words by Taylor. U.S. softcover, $40-$60.

Milton's Marilyn by Kotsilibas-Davis. German hardcover, $60-$70.

Tom MALONEY
- *U.S. Camera Annual 1964* ....$30-$50
  U.S. Camera-Duell, Sloan and Pearce, 1963. 1st ed. Hardcover. 231 pgs. (USA)

Dirk MANTHEY
- *Gottinnen des Erotischen Films* ....$20-$30
  Redaktion cinema, 1985. 1st ed. Softcover. 162 pgs. ISBN-3-88724-012-X (GER)

Doug McCLELLAND
- *Star Speak—Hollywood on Everything* ....$20-$30
  Faber and Faber, 1987. 1st ed. Softcover. 337 pgs. ($14.95)
  ISBN-0-571-12981-1 (USA)

Nellie McCLUNG
- *My Sex is Ice Cream* ....$5-$10
  Ekstasis Editions, 1996. 96 pgs. ISBN-0-921-21595-9 (UNKNOWN ORIGIN)

Terence MOIX
- *Hollywood Stories* ....$10-$15
  Lumen, 1971. 1st ed. No. 8. Paperback. 302 pgs. (SPA)

Edgar MORIN
- *The Stars by Edgar Morin—An Account of the Star System* .... $5-$10
  Profile Books/Grove Press, 1960. Paperback. 189 pgs. ($1.35) (USA)
- *Les Stars—Le temps qui court* ....$10-$15
  Ed. du Seuil, 1957. 1st ed. Paperback. 192 pgs. (FRA)
- *Les Stars—Points No. 34* .... $5-$10
  Ed. du Seuil, 1972. Paperback. 188 pgs. (FRA)
- *Las Stars—Servidumbres y mitos: Marilyn, Charlot, James Dean* .... $5-$10
  Dopesa-col. Espectaculo 4/cine, 1972. 1st ed. Paperback. 166 pgs. (SPA)

Michael MUNN
- *The Hollywood Murder Casebook* ....$20-$30
  Robson Books, 1987. 1st ed. Hardcover. 192 pgs. ISBN-0-86051-414-5 (UK)
- *The Hollywood Murder Casebook* .... $5-$10
  Headline, 1989. 1st ed. Paperback. 192 pgs. (£3.99) ISBN-0-7472-3112-5 (UK)

Jean NEGULESCO
- *Things I Did...and Things I Think I Did* ....$20-$30
  Linden Press/Simon and Schuster, 1984. Hardcover. 317 pgs. ($18.95)
  ISBN-0-671-50734-6 (USA)

Thomas NOGUCHI
- *Les dossiers secrets du medecin legiste de Hollywood Coroner* .... $5-$10
  France Loisirs, 1985. Hardcover. 211 pgs. ISBN-2-7242-2034-X (FRA)
- *Coroner* .... $5-$10
  Pocket Books, 1983. Paperback. 252 pgs. ($3.50)ISBN-0-671-54088-2 (USA)

Charles NUETZEL
- *Whodunit? Hollywood Style* ....$10-$15
  Book Co. of America, 1965. 1st ed. Paperback. 169 pgs. (75¢) (USA)

Tilman OSTERWOLD
- *Pop Art* ....$20-$30
  Benedikt Taschen, 1992. 1st ed. Softcover. 239 pgs. ISBN-3-8228-0667-6 (SPA)

Toy PICKARD
- *Hollywood's Fallen Idols* ....$20-$30
  Batsford Ltd., 1989. 1st ed. Softcover. 192 pgs. ISBN-0-7134-6152-7 (UK)

Monroe—A Portfolio of 6 Classic Athena Postcards, $15-$25.

Marilyn Monroe #11 postcard book, $20-$30.

Marilyn—Her Life In Her Own Words by Barris. U.S. hardcover, $30-$50.

Marilyn Monroe: A Postcard Book, 1989 Running Press, $15-$25.

R. POMARES et all
- *Churchil/Marilyn Monroe/M. Hernandez—Los revolucionarios siglo*...........$25-$35
  Club International Libro, 1978. tomo 11. Hardcover. 319 pgs.
  ISBN-84-7461-093-1 (SPA)

Dilys POWELL
- *The Golden Screen—Fifty years of films*..$20-$30
  Pavilion, 1989. Hardcover. 302 pgs. (£15.95) ISBN-1-85145-342-3 (UK)

Tom PRIDEAUX
- *Life Goes to the Movies*...$25-$35
  Time-Life Books, 1987. Hardcover. 304 pgs. ISBN-0-517-62585-7 (USA)

David ROBINSON
- *Panorama du cinema mondial 2—De 1947 anos jours*................................. $5-$10
  Denoel/Gonthier, 1980. 1st ed. Paperback. 667 pgs. (FRA)

Eve RUGGIERI
- *Raconte...quelque femmes remmarquables* ....$15-$25
  Menges, 1980. 1st ed. Softcover. 410 pgs. ISBN-2-85620-093 (FRA)
- *Raconte...quelque femmes remmarquables* ....$15-$25
  France Loisirs, 1980. 1st ed. Hardcover. 410 pgs. ISBN-2-7242-0797-1 (FRA)

Enrique SALGADO
- *El libro de la vida y la muerte*...$20-$30
  Nauta, 1974. 1st ed. Softcover. 218 pgs. ISBN-84-278-0360-5 (FRA)

Ken SCHESSLER
- *This is Hollywood—An Unusual Movieland Guide*.......................................$10-$20
  Ken Schessler, 1987. 6th re. Softcover. 85 pgs. ISBN-0-915633-00-0 (USA)

Georg SEEBLEN
- *Unterhaltung 2—Lexikon zur poplaren kultur—Ro ro ro 6210*....................$10-$15
  Rowohlt, 1977. 1st ed. Paperback. 327 pgs. ISBN-3-499-16210-5 (GER)

Claudius SEIDL
- *Billy Wilder*.. $5-$10
  Catedra, 1991. 1st ed. No. 8. Paperback. 287 pgs. ISBN-84-376-1023-0 (SPA)

SESAR
- *Hollywood, Hollywood—Glamour Star 3*...$20-$30
  Glamour International, 1986. Supplement No. 7. Softcover. 48 pgs. (ITA)

Eric SHANES
- *Warhol—The Masterworks*...$20-$30
  Portland House, 1991. Hardcover. (USA)

Patricia FOX-SHEINWOLD
- *Too Young To Die—The Stars the World Tragically Lost*..............................$20-$30
  Cathay Books, 1979. 1st ed. Softcover. 353 pgs. ISBN-0-86178-051-5 (UK)

Marianne SINCLAIR
- *Those Who Died Young—Cult Heroes of the Twentieth Century*........ $20-$30
  Plexus, 1979. 1st ed. Softcover. 192 pgs. (£8.95) ISBN-0-85965-023-5 (UK)

Emmeline SNIVELY
- *The Models Blue Book*.. $200-$300
  Snively, 1947-48. Softcover. 128 pgs. ($1) (USA)

Penny STALLINGS and H. MANDELBAUM
- *Flesh & Fantasy—The Truth Behind the Fantasy*... ....$20-$30
  Perrenial Library, 1989. Softcover. 285 pgs. ($15.95)
  ISBN-0-06-096343-3 (USA)

Bert STERN
- *Eros*... ....$40-$60
  Eros (Ralph Ginzburg), 1962. 1st ed. Hardcover. 96 pgs. (USA)

Ray STUART
- *Immortals of the Screen*...$30-$40
  Bonanza Books, 1965. 1st ed. Hardcover. 224 pgs. (USA)

Holmero ALSINA THEVENET
- *Cronicas de cine*.. $5-$10
  Ed. de la Flor, 1973. 1st ed. Paperback. 330 pgs. (ARG)

Peter UNDERWOOD
- *Death—In Hollywood* ....$20-$25
  Piatkus, 1992. Hardcover. 279 pgs. (£13.95) ISBN-0-7499-1087-9 (UK)

UNKNOWN AUTHOR
- *Marilyn 1962-1982*...$50-$70
  1982. Softcover. 175 pgs. (GRE)
- *Marilyn Monroe*...$50-$70
  1988. Softcover. 124 pgs. (GRE)

Edward WAGENKNECHT
- *Seven Daughters of the Theater*..$20-$25
  Da Capo Press, 1976. 1st ed. Softcover. 234 pgs. ($7.95)
  ISBN-0-306-80153-1 (USA)

The Misfits by Miller. German paperback, $30-$40.

The Prince and the Showgirl by Rattigan. U.S. paperback, $30-$50.

The Curious Death of Marilyn Monroe by Slatzer. U.S. paperback, $25-$35.

Let's Make Love by Andrews. U.S. paperback, $25-$45.

Bus Stop by Inge. U.S. paperback, $35-$50.

Marilyn On Location by Mills. British hardcover, $40-$60.

Alexander WALKER
- *Stardom—The Hollywood Phenomenon*........$10-$15
  Penguin Books, 1974. Paperback. 385 pgs. (£ .55) ISBN-0-14-003750-0 (UK)

WEEGEE
- *Violenti e violentati*........$20-$30
  Mazzotta, 1979. 1st ed. Softcover. (Lit. 18.000) (ITA)

WEEGEE and Mel HARRIS
- *Naked Hollywood*........$20-$30
  Da Capo Press, 1976. 1st ed. Softcover. (£6.95) ISBN-0-306-80047-0 (UK)

Billy WILDER
- *Memories—Et Tout Le Reste Est Folie*........$20-$25
  Publisher unknown, 1993. Softcover. (FRA)

Ken WLASCHIN
- *Les stars du cinema*........$20-$30
  Fernand Nathan, 1981. 1st ed. Hardcover. 232 pgs. ISBN-2-09-293104-0 (FRA)

SEVERAL AUTHORS
- *From Broadway to Picadilly—Encore!* (songbook)........$20-$30
  Wise Publishing, 1988. 1st ed. Softcover. 127 pgs. ISBN-0-7119-1425-7 (UK)
- *Memories of Hollywood* (songbook)........$20-$30
  Wise Publishing, 1991. 1st ed. Softcover. 64 pgs. ISBN-0-7119-2496-1 (UK)
- *Historia del cine—Biblioteca tematica*........$20-$30
  Montaner y Simon, 1979. 1st ed. Hardcover. 190 pgs. ISBN-84-274-0461-1 (SPA)
- *Gran historia ilustrada del cine*........$20-$30
  Sarpe, 1984. Hardcover. 159 pgs. ISBN-84-7291-636-7 (SPA)

Marilyn Movie-Related Novels

Matthew ANDREWS
- *Let's Make Love*........$25-$45
  Bantam Books, 1960. 1st ed. Paperback. 149 pgs. (35¢) (USA)
- *Let's Make Love*........$35-$50
  Corgi Books/Transworld, 1960. Paperback. 188 pgs. (£2.60) (UK)

George AXELROD
- *The Seven Year Itch—A Romantic Comedy*........$35-$50
  Bantam Books, 1955. 1st ed. Paperback. 114 pgs. (25¢) (USA)
- *The Seven Year Itch—A Romantic Comedy*........$35-$50
  Bantam Books, 1955. 2nd re. Paperback. 114 pgs. (25¢) (USA)

W.R. BURNETT
- *La jungla del asfalto*........$20-$30
  Luis de Caralt, 1985. 2nd ed. No. 125. Paperback. 242 pgs. (450 pta.) ISBN-84-217-4239-6 (SPA)
- *La jungla del asfalto*........$20-$30
  Planeta, 1985. 1st ed. No. 11. Paperback. 201 pgs. ISBN-84-320-8620-7 (SPA)
- *La jungla del asfalto* (Greek version)........$20-$30
  Publisher unknown, 1987. 1st ed. Softcover. 300 pgs. (GRE)

William INGE
- *Bus Stop*........$35-$50
  Bantam Books, 1956. 1st ed. Paperback. 113 pgs. (25¢) (USA)
- *Bus Stop*........$50-$75
  Charles Buchan's Publishing, 1956. 1st ed. Softcover. 96 pgs. (£2.60) (UK)

Anita LOOS
- *Les hommes preferent les blondes* ....$50-$75
  Llibrairie Gallimard, 1950s. 1st ed. No. 15. Softcover. 96 pgs. (3.50*f*) (FRA)
- *Les hommes preferent les blondes* ....$50-$75
  Llibrairie Gallimard, 1954. No. 54. Paperback. 180 pgs. (FRA)
- *Les hommes preferent les blondes* ....$50-$75
  Llibrairie Gallimard, 1956. No. 54. Paperback. 180 pgs. (FRA)
- *Les hommes preferent les blondes* ....$50-$75
  Llibrairie Gallimard, 1965. No. 54. Paperback. 180 pgs. (FRA)
- *Les hommes preferent les blondes* ....$40-$60
  J'ai lu, 1973. 1st ed. No. 508. Paperback. 183 pgs. (FRA)
- *Los caballeros las prefieren rubies*..........$50-$75
  Col Popular Literaria, 1955. 1st ed. No. 13. Softcover. 142 pgs. (10 pta.) (SPA)
- *Los caballeros las prefieren rubias*..........$30-$50
  Noguer, 1975. 1st ed. Softcover. 181 pgs. ISBN-84-279-0756-7 (SPA)
- *Los caballeros las prefieren rubias*..........$20-$30
  Tusquets, 1986. 1st ed. No. 129. Paperback. 121 pgs. (800 pta.)
  ISBN-84-7223-629-3 (SPA)

Arthur MILLER
- *The Misfits*..........$50-$70
  The Viking Press, 1961. 1st ed. Hardcover. 132 pgs. (USA)
- *The Misfits*..........$50-$70
  The Viking Press, 1961. 1st ed./book club ed.
  Hardcover. 132 pgs. (USA)
- *The Misfits*..........$30-$40
  Dell, 1961. 1st ed. Paperback. 223 pgs. (50¢) (USA)
- *The Misfits*..........$30-$40
  Penguin Books, 1961. 1st ed. Paperback. 140 pgs. (£2.60) (UK)
- *The Misfits*..........$30-$40
  Rowohlt, 1961. 1st ed. Paperback. 130 pgs. (GER)
- *De ontworteiden*..........$30-$45
  J.M. Meulenhoff, 1961. Paperback. 190 pgs. (HOL)
- *The Misfits*..........$30-$40
  Rowohlt, 1961. 1st ed. Paperback. 130 pgs. (GER)

Arthur MILLER et all
- Film Scripts Three: Charade/The Apartment/The Misfits..........$20-$30
  Irvingthon, 1989. Softcover. 610 pgs. ($19.95) ISBN-0-8290-2277-5 (USA)

Terence RATTIGAN
- The Prince and the Showgirl..........$30-$50
  Signet Books, 1957. 1st ed. Paperback. 127 pgs. (35¢) No. S1409 (USA)
- Plus beau qu'un Reve—Les films pour vous..........$30-$50
  Cine-Periodiques (Franco Bozzesi), 1960. 1st ed. No. 184. Magazine. 66 pgs.
  (0.90*f*) (FRA)
- The Prince and the Showgirl..........$150-$200
  Kenkyusha, year unknown. Paperback. (JPN)

Billy WILDER
- Some Like It Hot..........$30-$50
  Signet Book, 1959. 1st ed. No. S1656. Paperback. 144 pgs. (USA)

Novels With Reference to Marilyn Monroe

Jacques ALMIRA
- *Le passage du desir-Roman*..........$20-$30
  Gallimard, 1978. 1st ed. Softcover. 232 pgs. (FRA)

The Misfits by Miller. U.S. paperback, $30-$40.

The Curious Death of Marilyn Monroe by Slatzer. U.S. paperback, $25-$35.

Forever Marilyn by Cahill. U.S. hardcover, $30-$45.

Warhol: A Postcard Book, 1989 Running Press, $15-$25.

ANONYMOUS
- *Betty & Gay* .... $20-$30
  Zinco, 1990. 1st ed. Softcover. 34 pgs. (325 pta.) (SPA)

Alvah BESSIE
- *The Symbol* .... $25-$35
  Random House, 1966. 1st ed. Hardcover. 305 pgs. ($5.95) (USA)
- *El simbolo* .... $20-$30
  Grijalbo, 1977. 1st ed. No. 97. Paperback. 390 pgs. ISBN-84-253-0774-0 (SPA)

George BERNAU
- *Candle in the Wind* .... $20-$30
  Michael Joseph, 1991. 1st ed. Softcover. 499 pgs. (£8.99)
  ISBN-0-7181-3543-1 (UK)

Leonore CANEVARI, Jeaneette Van WHYE
- *The Murder of Marilyn Monroe* .... $5-$10

Charles CASILLO
- *The Marilyn Diaries* .... $5-$10
  Casillo, year unknown. Paperback. 199 pgs. ISBN-0-9677-6170-0 (USA)

James ELLISON
- *Calendar Girl* .... $5-$10
  Pocket Books, 1993. Paperback. (USA)

Jean-Albert FOEX
- *Satan conduit la belle* .... $30-$40
  EDICA, 1953. 1st ed. Paperback. 159 pgs. (FRA)

William GOLDMAN
- *Oropel*...$20-$30
  Plaza and Janes, 1981. 1st ed. Softcover. 312 pgs. ISBN-84-01-30320-6 (SPA)

Ben HECHT
- *The Sensualists* ....$20-$35
  Messner, 1959. 3rd re. Hardcover. 256 pgs. (USA)

Rafael RAMIREZ HEREDIA
- *Con M de Marilyn*..$10-$15
  Ediciones Alfaguara, 1998. Paperback. 225 pgs. ISBN-9-6819-0330-0 (SAM)

Garson KANIN
- *Hollywood Annees Folles*...$20-$30
  Presses de la Cite, 1975. 1st ed. Hardcover. 249 pgs. (FRA)
- *Moviola—Marilyn, Chaplin, Garbo*...$10-$15
  Bruguera, 1981. 1st ed. No. 1501/52. Paperback. 510 pgs.
  ISBN-84-02-08287-4 (SPA)

Robert S. LEVINSON
- *The Elvis and Marilyn Affair*..$15-$20
  Publisher unknown, 1999. Paperback. 304 pgs. ISBN-0-3128-6968-1 (USA)

Keith LUGER
- *A que hora te mataron Marilyn Monroe?*...$15-$20
  Bruguera, 1971. 1st ed. No. 1102. Paperback. 126 pgs. (10 pta.) (SPA)

MARLIT
- *La Princesa de los Brezos* ....$10-$20
  Orvy, year unknown. 1st ed. No. 14. Paperback. 149 pgs. (SPA)

Arthur MILLER
- *After the Fall*..$20-$35
  The Viking Press, 1964. Limited Ed./500 Deluxe. Hardcover. 129 pgs. (USA)
- *After the Fall*..$15-$20
  Bantam, 1965. 1st ed. Paperback. 164 pgs. (85¢) (USA)
- *Despues de la Caida* ....$20-$30
  Ayma, 1965. 1st ed. No. 8. Paperback. 185 pgs. (SPA)
- *Despues de la Caida* ....$20-$30
  Losada, 1965. 1st ed. Paperback. 128 pgs. (ARG)
- *Despues de la Caida/ Incidente en Vichy*...$20-$30
  Losada, 1967. Paperback. 144 pgs. (ARG)

Terenci MOIX
- *El dia que va morir Marilyn* ....$10-$15
  Edicions 62 Barcelona, 1970. 5th re. No. 60. Paperback. 336 pgs.
  ISBN-84-297-0856-1 (CAT)
- *El dia que murio Marilyn* ....$10-$15
  Lumen, 1970. 1st ed. No. 68. Paperback. 490 pgs. (SPA)
- *El dia que murio Marilyn* ....$10-$15
  Lumen, 1978. No. 541. Paperback. 490 pgs. ISBN-84-264-4001-0 (SPA)
- *El dia en que murio Marilyn* .... $5-$10
  Plaza and Janes, 1990. 1st ed. Vol. 155/2. Paperback. 414 pgs. (795 pta.)
  ISBN-84-01-49502-4 (SPA)
- *Le jour ou est morte Marilyn*..$20-$30
  Le Chemin Vert, 1987. 1st ed. Softcover. 390 pgs. (127*f*)
  ISBN-2-903-533-26-1 (FRA)

Neil NORMAN and Son BARRACLOUGH
- *Insignificance—The Book*...$20-$30
  Sidgwick & Jackson, 1985. 1st ed. Softcover. 128 pgs. (£7.95)
  ISBN-0-283-99218-2 (UK)

Some Like It Hot by Wilder. U.S. paperback, $30-$50.

The Seven Year Itch by Axelrod. U.S. paperback, $35-$50.

The Last Sitting by Stern. U.S. hardcover, $40-$60.

Marilyn Monroe II—The Poster Book by Hillier, $25-$40.

Joyce Carol OATES
- *Blonde*....................$15-$20
Ecco Press, 2000. Hardcover. 737 pgs. ISBN-0-0601-9607-6 (USA)

John RECHY
- *Marilyn's Daughter*....................$20-$30
Carroll and Graf, 1988. 1st ed. Hardcover. 531 pgs. ($18.95) ISBN-0-88184-272-9 (USA)

Sam STAGGS
- *MM II—The Return of Marilyn Monroe*....................$20-$30
Donal I. Fine, 1991. 1st ed. Hardcover. 304 pgs. ($19.95) ISBN-1-55611-179-7 (USA)
- *The Return of Marilyn Monroe*....................$10-$15
SPI Books, 1992. Paperback. 304 pgs. ($5.50) ISBN-1-56171-181-0 (USA)

Victor Di SURERO and Jeanie C. WILLIAMS
- *Marilyn, My Marilyn: An Anthology of Poems*....................$10-$20
Pennywhistle Press, 2001. Paperback. ISBN-0-9386-3119-5 (USA)

Sam TOPEROFF
- *Queen of Desire*....................$10-$15
Harper-Collins, 1992. Hardcover. (USA)

Sergio TOPPI
- *Marilyn Monroe*-No. 23 (Limited edition comic book)....................$20-$30
Bedesup, 1982. 1st ed. Softcover. 47 pgs. (36BEF) (BEL)

Marilyn Postcard Books

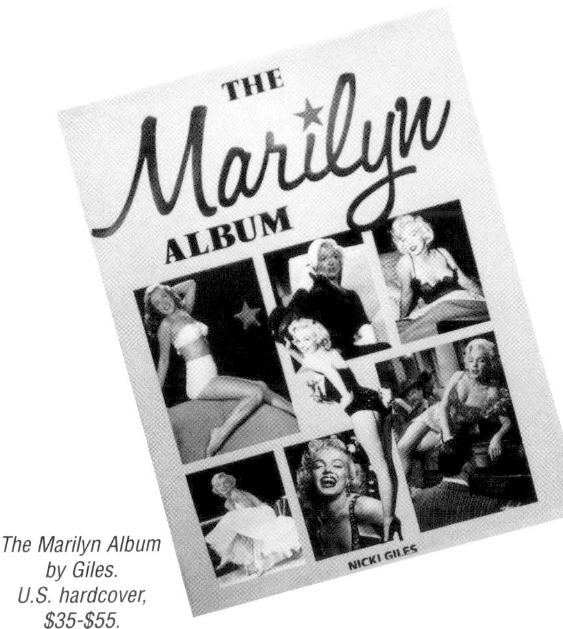

The Marilyn Album by Giles. U.S. hardcover, $35-$55.

- *Marilyn—A Postcard Book*....................$15-$20
Running Press (by John Marriot), year unknown. 30 cards. ($7.95) ISBN-0-89471-898-3 (ORIGIN UNKNOWN)
- *Marilyn Monroe—A Book of Postcards*....................$15-$25
Pomegranate Artbooks, 1990. 30 hand-colored. (USA)
- *Marilyn Monroe—A Book of Thirty Postcards*....................$15-$25
Magna, 1992. Softcover. ISBN-1-85422-319-4 Softcover. 1992 (UK)
- *Marilyn Monroe—A Postcard Book*....................$15-$25
Running Press, 1989. 30 cards. ($6.95) ISBN-0-89471-766-9 (USA)
- *Marilyn Monroe—Classic Postcard Collection*....................$15-$25
Pyramid (by John Marriot), 1990. 30 cards. ISBN-1-85510-059-2 (USA)
- *Marilyn Monroe #11—Nine Detachable Postcards*....................$20-$30
American Postcard Co., year unknown. No. 11. Printed in Italy. (ITA)
- *Marilyn Monroe—Twenty Classic Picture Postcards*....................$10-$20
Godfrey Cave Associates, 1993. (USA)
- *Monroe—A Portfolio of 6 Classic Athena Postcards*....................$15-$25
Athena, 1992. (UK)
- *Schirmer's Twelve*....................$15-$20
Schirmer Art, 1990. No. 2 film stills. (UK)
- *Warhol*....................$15-$25
Running Press, 1989. 30 cards. (USA)

Marilyn Poster Books

Alice HILLIER

- *Marilyn Monroe II*..$25-$40
  Atlanta Press, 1989. 1st ed. Softcover. 20 tear-out posters. ISBN-1-870049-20-9 (UK)

David MALCOLM

- *Sex Symbols—Movie Poster Book*........................$25-$40
  Octopus Books, 1985. 1st ed. Softcover. 47 pgs. ISBN-0-7064-2371-2 (UK)
- *Les Sex Symbols—Un livre a effeuiller*....................$25-$40
  Grum, 1985. 1st ed. Softcover. 46 pgs. ISBN-2-7000-6702-9 (FRA)

Diego A. MANRIQUE

- *Marilyn Monroe Grafic Poster Book*.......................$25-$40
  Gaviota/Productions Compac, 1987. Softcover. (1200 pta.) ISBN-84-7693-039-9 (SPA)

Paul MATHUR

- *Marilyn Monroe Poster Book*................................$25-$40
  Atlanta Press, 1986. 1st ed. Softcover. ISBN-1-8700049-00-4 (UK)

UNKNOWN AUTHOR

- *Marilyn Monroe—The Classic Poster Book: Six Tear-Out Posters*......................................$20-$40
  Mallard Press, 1990. Softcover. (USA)
- *Marilyn Monroe Poster Book*............................$25-$40
  Publisher unknown, 1988. Softcover. 20 tear-out posters. (UK)

The Classic Marilyn Monroe Poster Book, 1990 Mallard Press, $20-$40.

Chapter 4

Calendars & Advertising Collectibles

Marilyn was destined to be a calendar girl. One of her very first modeling assignments was for pinup artist Earl Moran. Moran's work was very well known and was widely distributed in the 1940s and '50s. In 1947, a young Marilyn posed for Moran in various stages of undress. Moran's renditions of Marilyn were not only featured on calendar tops, but also on other items such as advertising blotters, matchbook covers, and notepads.

Moran's series of three paintings entitled *Maid In Baltimore* command the highest prices. These feature Marilyn in a two-piece yellow bikini in different poses. They were also done in a much larger format than the rest of the Moran calendars and were sold between 1947 and 1950. A selection of the original photos Moran took of Marilyn recently appeared in an article *Playboy* did about Marilyn.

A famous Hollywood photographer by the name of Laszlo Willinger also took many early modeling photos of Marilyn in the late-1940s. These photos were later resurrected after Marilyn achieved superstar status in the 1950s. They became the tops for calendars primarily and are printed in beautiful, clear color. All are of the cheesecake variety and were available on different-sized calendars. The photos were taken both in the studio and out on a sunny California beach. In some cases, props were used, such as a giant Mexican sombrero, which Marilyn holds over her nude body.

The most famous of all the Marilyn calendars is, of course, the nude pose on red velvet, taken by photographer Tom Kelley in 1949. Kelley had offered Marilyn "a lift" a few years earlier after he discovered her next to her disabled car on a California street. He presented his business card to her at the time and said that he'd enjoy photographing her sometime. Marilyn did not have a lucrative year in 1949. Out of work and hungry, she needed the $50 Kelley would pay her for posing nude. Marilyn did insist that Kelley's wife be present for the session. A series of shots were taken against a red velvet backdrop, but only two have ever appeared on calendar tops. The most common of these is entitled *Golden Dreams* and the less common is called *A New Wrinkle*. Each pose is slightly different, but the *New Wrinkle* pose is the rarer of the two, and calendars that feature it are worth double those with the *Golden Dreams* poses. John Baumgarth of Chicago, Illinois, purchased the reproduction rights to the *Golden Dreams* pose for a mere $500, and his calendar company went on to gross more than $1 million in sales with it. Remember, Marilyn was paid just $50! These calendars were both released in 1952, coinciding with Marilyn's rapid rise to stardom. When asked what she had on during the photo session, Marilyn coyly replied, "the radio."

The *Golden Dreams* pose was later chosen as *Playboy's* very first centerfold in its premiere issue of December 1953. The *Golden Dreams* pose continued to grace calendar tops through the 1950s, but dropped off dramatically thereafter, with a few reproductions made in the late-1960s and early '70s. These reproductions were usually printed on a heavier stock paper, whereas the originals were printed on a little lighter stock and were still very pliable.

Telltale signs that a calendar is old include: rusty staples where the calendar pad is affixed, yellowed paper on the front and back of the calendar, and the name of the calendar company with the phrase, "Litho—Made in U.S.A." In addition, the originals nearly always featured metal strips along both the top and bottom borders of the calendar, with a loop built into the middle of the top metal strip for hanging purposes. One of the *Golden Dreams* reproduction calendars features simulated wood grain around the outside half-inch border of the calendar, with a dark brown stripe on the very outside border and a light brown stripe just inside of the outer one. One other example has artificially aged shading added to the outer borders of the calendar.

Collectors generally favor calendars with the pad intact, beginning with January, and an advertisement for a store, gas station, etc. on its front somewhere. The old addresses and phone numbers used in these ads are also telltale signs of the age of the calendar.

The last of the beautiful Marilyn advertising calendars were printed around 1960 and, with the exception of a few reproductions of the nude pose years later, have been replaced with our modern calendars.

1947 Earl Moran calendar titled Maid In Baltimore $400-$600.

1948 Earl Moran calendar titled Maid In Baltimore, $400-$600.

Vintage Calendars

Note: These are in order by year (oldest to newest).

1947-1949

- Earl Moran did three different paintings of Marilyn in a two-piece yellow bathing suit entitled *Maid In Baltimore*. These always feature advertising for *American Hammered Piston Rings* by the Kopper's Co. Inc. Buyers beware that there are many other cases of blonde models being used by Moran with the same *Maid In Baltimore* title on the calendar, for the same Kopper's Co. Two examples that are of Marilyn, without any question, are the 1947 and 1948 issued calendars for the Kopper's Co. I have only seen the third example on the back cover of a memorial magazine entirely on Marilyn, released after her death in 1962. Values for each of the three are the same. Dimensions are approximately 16 x 34............$400-$600

1948

- Wallet calendar (the size of a playing card) of the Earl Moran 1948 *Maid in Baltimore* calendar described above in b&w. Calendar months printed on back, along with an ad for a company..$5-$8

Late-1940s-Early 1950s

- Earl Moran Handout Calendars: These small calendars feature various artists' renditions of Marilyn that can be bent back to produce a 3-D effect. These are printed on a heavy cardboard and feature the calendar and advertisement on the bottom. A number of titles for the paintings include: *Little Miss Muffet, What Little Girls Are Made Of, Don't Hope For The Best, Hop For It, Peter, Peter Pumpkin Eater, Rosie's Are Red...*, etc. These generally measure 5 x 10. ....$40-$80

Earl Moran hand-out calendar, $40-$80.

Earl Moran hand-out calendar, $40-$80.

Two sizes of the Dame and Dane calendar tops, $75-$125.

Circa 1952

- A calendar entitled *Dame and Dane*, which features a young Norma Jeane seated next to a Great Dane. Done in both a vertical and a horizontal cut, with the vertical showing more of Marilyn and the dog. It is possible that this calendar was released much later than 1952, but it is still a very desirable calendar. Both valued the same. These generally measure 8 x 10 and 8 x 11, respectively. ....$75-$125

A New Wrinkle 11 x 22½ calendar with Tom Kelley photo of Marilyn, $100-$150.

1952-1960

- Famous nude calendar of Marilyn titled *Golden Dreams*. Features Marilyn lying on red velvet in a 1949 photo by Tom Kelley. A scarcer version with an alternate photo was also done and is titled *A New Wrinkle*. Most of the *New Wrinkle* examples feature advertising. Some of the calendars featuring the *Golden Dreams* pose featured a sheet of acetate with a lace negligee or yellow robe printed on it that could be lifted up to reveal Marilyn in her birthday suit below. These are basically worth the same price as the standard *Golden Dreams* and carry such a title as *Lure of Lace*. A number of the calendars simply came with the lace negligee printed right on the calendar itself. A few of the calendars came with an informational sheet on the back, bound in by the metal strip that ran along the top of the calendar. This informational sheet included a brief biographical sketch on Marilyn. (See tips on how to spot the reproductions earlier.)
  - Wallet (playing card size)—*A New Wrinkle*; 1953; color; entire 12 months printed on front, over MM's image....................$5-$10
  - 9 x 14....................$60-$125
  - 11 x 22½....................$100-$150
  - 16 x 34....................$150-$200
  - Larger sizes....................$175-$250
  - Reproductions (circa 1972 and 1976) measure about 11 x 22. ....each $20-$30

1972 reproduction of the Golden Dreams calendar of 1954, $20-$30.

8½ x 11 Lure of Lace calendar top, $15-$30.

Golden Dreams 11 x 22½ calendar with overlay sheet, $100-$150.

Golden Dreams 11 x 22½ calendar with Tom Kelley photo of Marilyn, $100-$150.

1952

- *Golden Dreams* calendar consisting of four pages. The first page, which shows the first three months of the year, shows MM in the *Golden Dreams* pose. The other three pages feature other models. Marilyn's name is not printed on the front. Measures about 9 x 14....................$50-$125

- RKO Studio handout calendar of Marilyn. Features Marilyn in a one-piece bathing suit to promote her new film *Clash By Night*. Duotone in color. Measures about 4 x 8....................$50-$80

1953

- Earl Moran's *Girls of 1953* calendar. Features Moran paintings of MM on the months of March, May, and June. Spiral bound. Measures 8½ x 14.......$80-$140

Three months of Earl Moran's Girls of 1953 calendar.

1953-1956

- Laszlo Willinger photographed Marilyn in the mid-1940s, and these photos were later resurrected after Marilyn's sudden rise to fame and were used as calendar tops beginning in 1953. All are of the cheesecake variety and are very colorful and clearly printed. All are very scarce. They usually feature a brief bio on Marilyn under the calendar pad (you must lift the pad up), and she is usually identified on the front of the calendar, just below her image. A few of the titles used were *Vivacious Marilyn* (which featured her in a two-piece yellow bathing suit) and *A Friendly Smile* (which featured her in a striped two-piece bathing suit). There are also at least two different calendars featuring MM on the beach with windswept hair and wearing a two-piece striped bathing suit. Yet another features Marilyn holding a huge Mexican sombrero over her nude body, and another features MM seated in a Hawaiian grass skirt outfit.
  - 9 x 14...$75-$125
  - 11 x 22½...$150-$250
  - 16 x 34...$300-$500
  - Larger sizes..$400-$600

9 x 14, $75-$125.

Various examples of calendars featuring photos by Laszlo Willinger.

9 x 14, $75-$125.

11 x 22½, $150-$250.

16 x 34, $300-$500.

16 x 34, $300-$500.

1954 Studio Sketches calendar by T.N. Thompson, $100-$150.

1954

- *Studio Sketches* pinup calendar by T. N. Thompson. Features Marilyn on the first two months. The first page is a painting of Marilyn by Thompson that features Marilyn in the *Golden Dreams* pose, but with black negligee painted over strategic places. The second page features a painting of a young Marilyn in a white "cowgirl" outfit. She is dressed in a white cowboy hat, shorts, and boots, and is topless. The calendar is spiral bound and measures about 8 x 10........$100-$150

1955

- A calendar that came in an envelope that featured a cut-out circle that shows Marilyn's upper torso from the first page of the inside calendar. This is a four-page calendar with three months on each page. The first page shows Marilyn in the famous *Golden Dreams* pose, but with black negligee painted over strategic places. The next three pages feature a young Marilyn in various "cowgirl" poses entitled *Coming Out On Top*, *Caught Short*, and *Southern Exposure*. Marilyn is topless in all of them and has on white cowboy boots, white shorts, and a white cowboy hat. It measures about 8 x 11. ....$100-$175

1956

- A Mexican calendar featuring a photo of MM in a black negligee. Measures about 16 x 34. ....$200-$400

1959

- A calendar, consisting of seven pages, released as a promotional item for Marilyn's 1959 film, *Some Like It Hot*. The calendar features several images of Marilyn in black and white. The outside of the calendar reads, "The New Marilyn Monroe Calendar—Very Hot For March!" It is colored in black, red, and white. Measures approximately 8½ x 11...$75-$125

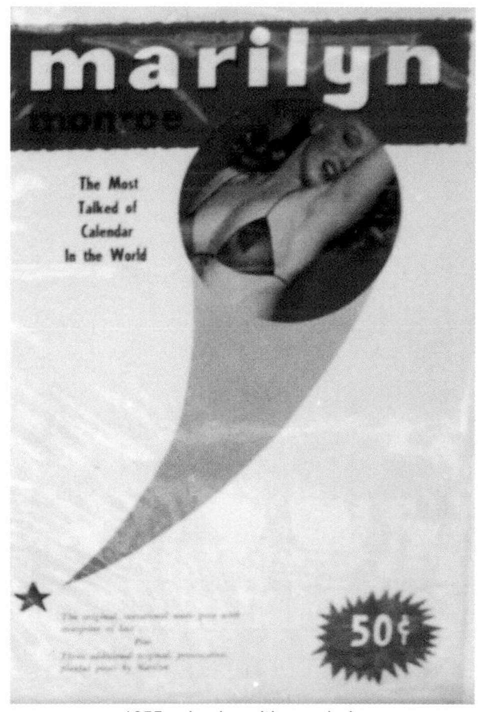

1955 calendar with peephole, $100-$175.

1960

- A Mexican advertising calendar featuring a glamour photo of MM. MM is wrapped in white fur and there is a pinkish-red background. Measures about 16 x 34. ....$200-$400
- Pocket calendar made in Italy. Features Marilyn in full-color on the front and was sold in a glassine envelope. Other stars are featured throughout. Measures about 2 x 3. ....$35-$60

1961

- A calendar featuring the artwork of Ben Hur Baz, depicting Marilyn kneeling in an over-sized yellow shirt, which is quite revealing. Various other examples are known of. Approximately 16 x 34...$100-$150

1974

- Calendar produced in conjunction with Norman Mailer's biography on Marilyn. It is spiral-bound and features eight color and four b&w portraits of the star. Was sold in a colorful envelope featuring a large Bert Stern photo of Marilyn's face. Measures about 8½ x 13...$25-$40

1975

- Poster-calendar of Marilyn in black and gray tones with red lips. Released in conjunction with the movie, *Goodbye Norma Jean*, starring Misty Rowe as Marilyn. Measures about 21 x 35...$25-$35

Note: Quite a few vintage salesmen's sample calendars are on the market that feature the images described above. These date generally from 1952-1960. They are often blank on the top, bottom, or midsection where the advertisements would later go and are either void of a calendar pad or have simply the month of January glued on as a single sheet. They are worth up to one-quarter less than the price of the full calendars unless they are one of the scarcer releases.

Buyers Beware!

There are many fake Marilyn Monroe calendars being sold on various Internet auction sites. Remember, with relative ease, people can now produce excellent color laser copies of the old calendar tops and then affix them to old calendars bought cheaply.

Some sellers use clever terms, such as "new old stock" in an effort to confuse the buyer.

Arrange for a full money-back guarantee with the seller before the auction closes. If they will not grant such, then bid at your own risk.

Calendar featuring the artwork of Ben Hur Baz, $100-$150.

U.S. Calendars (1980-2002)

Beginning around 1983, there have been many calendars printed on Marilyn in the modern square format and measuring about 12 x 12. Most are 12-month calendars, featuring a photo on each page. These have been produced by such companies as Pomegranate, Portal, Landmark, and Hallmark. They feature a wide assortment of Marilyn portraits on each calendar. Some came spiral-bound, and most were shrink-wrapped. An extensive listing of most of them follows.

1980
- MM calendar with fold-out double exposure and scenes from *The Misfits*. .$20-$30

1981
- Unfolds to 22 x 32; has double-exposure nude on one side and the story of the making of *The Misfits* on the other side; color photos. ....$20-$30

1983
- MM calendar with photography by Milton Greene; features beautiful b&w photos. ....$20-$30

1984
- Pomegranate 12 x 14 MM calendar with photos by Milton H. Greene. ....$20-$30
- Harmony Books MM pinup calendar compiled by James Spada, with color and b&w photos. ....$20-$30

1986
- Landmark MM calendar. ....$20-$30

1987
- Landmark MM 25th anniversary calendar; commemorative edition; Ken Galente Collection ....$20-$30

1988
- Portal MM calendar No. 895. ....$20-$30
- Design Look Inc. MM Twentieth Century Fox calendar with fold-out poster, organizer, and planner. ....$20-$30
- Landmark MM calendar. ....$20-$30

1989
- Landmark MM calendar. ....$20-$30
- Portal MM calendar. ....$20-$30
- Portal MM calendar with same cover as 1989 Landmark calendar. ....$20-$30
- Design Look Inc. 16-month MM calendar by Joseph Jasgur with early photos of Norma Jeane. ....$20-$30

1974 calendar featuring photos by Bert Stern, $25-$40.

1992 Portal calendar, $10-$20.

1993 Landmark calendar, $10-$20.

1989 Portal calendar, $20-$30.

1984 Harmony Books calendar, $20-$30.

1994 Landmark calendar, $10-$20.

1990

- Landmark MM calendar. .... $20-$30
- Portal MM calendar. .... $20-$30
- Design Look Inc. MM calendar by Joseph Jasgur with early Norma Jeane photos. .... $20-$30
- Pomegranate MM calendar with b&w photos. .... $20-$30
- Landmark 52-week spiral-bound 7 x 9 MM "engagement calendar" with new b&w portrait each week. .... $20-$30
- Andy Warhol "engagement calendar" with painting of Marilyn on cover. .... $20-$30

1991

- Portal MM calendar. .... $10-$20
- New Seasons Publishing MM calendar. .... $10-$20
- Greystone MM calendar. .... $10-$20
- Landmark general MM calendar. .... $10-$20

1992

- Portal MM calendar. .... $10-$20
- New Seasons Publishing MM calendar. .... $10-$20
- Landmark MM calendar by Bernard of Hollywood.. .... $10-$20
- Pomegranate MM calendar. .... $10-$20
- Day Dream Calendars Inc. "*Playboy's* Marilyn" 16-month calendar. .... $10-$20

1993

- Landmark MM Bernard of Hollywood calendar. .... $10-$20
- Portal 16-month MM calendar. .... $10-$20
- Hallmark MM calendar with different cover than the one below. .... $10-$20
- Hallmark spiral-bound MM calendar. .... $10-$20
- Neues Publishing MM calendar. .... $10-$20

1994

- Portal 16-month MM calendar. .... $10-$20
- Hallmark MM calendar. .... $10-$20
- Bernard of Hollywood MM calendar. .... $10-$20
- Landmark general MM calendar. .... $10-$20
- MM Quote-A-Day calendar. .... $10-$20
- Avalanche Publishing 15 x 15 MM "Collector's Edition Calendar." .... $10-$20

1995

- Landmark MM calendar. .... $10-$20
- Avalanche Publishing 12 x 12 MM calendar with 12 b&w photos by Andre de Dienes. .... $10-$20

1996

- Pomegranate MM pocket calendar with photos by Sam Shaw. .... $10-$20

2002

- Andrews McMeel Publishing MM wall calendar; ISBN-0-7407-1604-2. .... $8-$10

Foreign Calendars (1983-1997)

1983

- Italian MM pocket calendar with color gatefold. ....$30-$45

1980s

- Italian two-year MM calendar – Il Mito. ....$30-$40
- MM calendar by Acorn of London, England ....$25-$35

1987

- MM calendar by Culture Shock of England ....$20-$30
- MM calendar by Danilo Promotions of England ....$20-$30

2000 Avalanche 16-month calendar, $10-$20.

1988 Portal calendar, $20-$30.

1991 Landmark calendar, $10-$20.

1993 Hallmark spiral-bound calendar, $10-$20.

1988 Landmark calendar, $20-$30.

1999 Avalanche calendar, $10-$20.

1992 Landmark calendar, $10-$20.

1994 Portal 16-month calendar, $10-$20.

1992-1993 Gente calendar, $20-$25.

1994 Hallmark spiral-bound calendar, $10-$20.

1993 Portal 16-month calendar, $10-$20.

1989 Landmark calendar, $10-$20.

1994 Cedco calendar, $10-$20.

1956 advertising poster for a Saturday Evening Post article, $200-$350.

1988

- MM 12 x 16½ spiral-bound calendar by Danilo Promotions of England; laminated pages. .... $30-$40
- MM calendar by Atlanta Press of England .... $20-$30

1989

- MM calendar by Danilo Promotions of England .... $20-$30
- MM calendar by Culture Shock of England .... $30-$40
- MM "Big Big Poster Calendar" by Culture Shock of England. .... $30-$40

1990

- "Marilyn Monroe Among Friends" by Sam Shaw and Norm Rosten of Bloomsbury, England .... $20-$35
- MM calendar by Athena. .... $20-$30
- MM 12 x 16½ spiral-bound calendar by Culture Shock of England; laminated pages. .... $25-$35

1991

- MM calendar by Culture Shock of England. .... $20-$30
- MM calendar by Athena. .... $15-$20
- MM spiral-bound calendar by Danilo Promotions of England. .... $25-$30

1992

- MM calendar by Archives Alive. .... $20-$25
- MM calendar by Culture Shock of England. .... $20-$25
- MM calendar by Coles of Canada. .... $20-$25
- MM 8 x 11 calendar by *Gente* magazine of Italy; color photo each month (Aug. 1992-July 1993). .... $20-$25

1993

- MM pocket calendar set with 12 calendars by Rua do salitre, 890 Algarve; each has unique photo .... $8-$12

1995

- MM calendar by Culture Shock of England. .... $20-$30
- MM calendar by Oliver Books of England. .... $15-$20

1996

- MM calendar by Scheurkalender of Holland; has 365 pages, one for each day of the year. .... $30-$35

1997

- MM calendar by Danilo Promotions of England. .... $15-$20

Advertising Posters

1956

- Color poster, 28 x 40; advertising reads, "Pete Martin's candid report on 'The New Marilyn Monroe.' " On bottom, "The Saturday Evening Post." Poster advertises three-part series in the Post on Marilyn. Pete Martin authored the second book published in America on Marilyn entitled, Will Acting Spoil Marilyn Monroe? The photo of Marilyn is a rarely seen one and shows her lying on her side with her head being propped up with her left hand. She's wearing long black gloves and a beautiful red off-the-shoulder dress. A stunning portrait of Marilyn that just oozes glamour. .... $200-$350

Ink Blotters

With and Without Calendar Months

All known examples of these were done by pinup artist Earl Moran. The first were produced in the late-1940s and show a young Marilyn in various poses in full-color and with catchy phrases. These featured advertising for a company on one end and artwork of Marilyn on the other. There were at least two sizes made, and they were 3½ x 6 and 4 x 9. These sometimes featured three calendar months on each blotter. Some of the phrases used were: "Some People Like Boats..."; "What You Don't Owe Won't Hurt You"; "Worry Is The Interest Paid By Those Who Borrow Trouble"; "Things Don't Turn Up Unless You Turn Them Up"; "Little Miss Muffet..."; "Red Riding Hood..."; "Baa, Baa, Black Sheep..."; "Peter, Peter, Pumpkin Eater..."; "Old Mother Hubbard..."; "Little Boy Blue..."; "Rosie's Are Red..."; "Now This Is Just Between You And Me"; "Don't Hope For The Best, Hop For It"; and "What Little Girls Are Made Of."

A selection of handout calendars by Earl Moran.

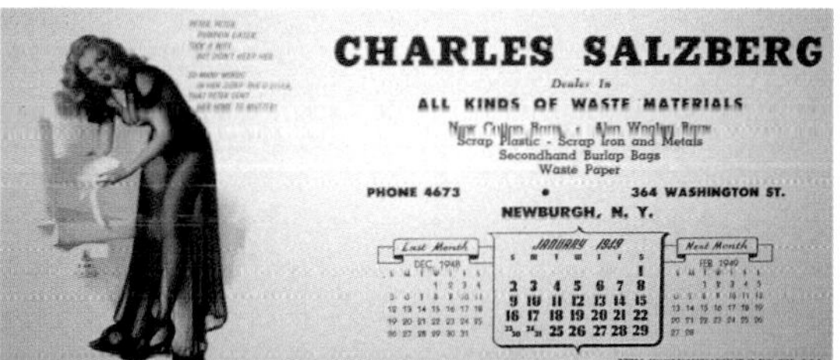

3½ x 6, $25-$35.

3½ x 6, $25-$35.

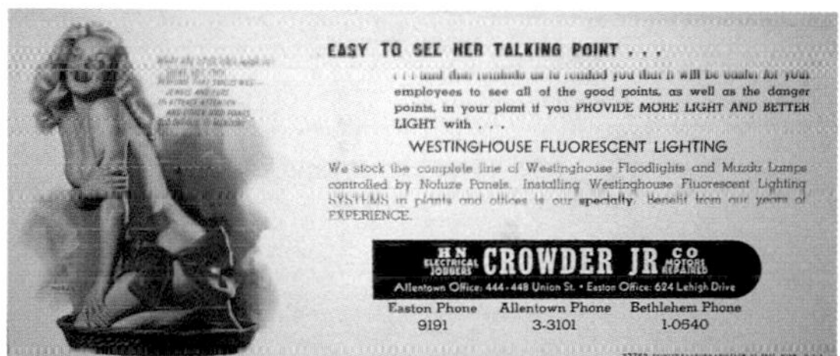

3½ x 6, $25-$35.

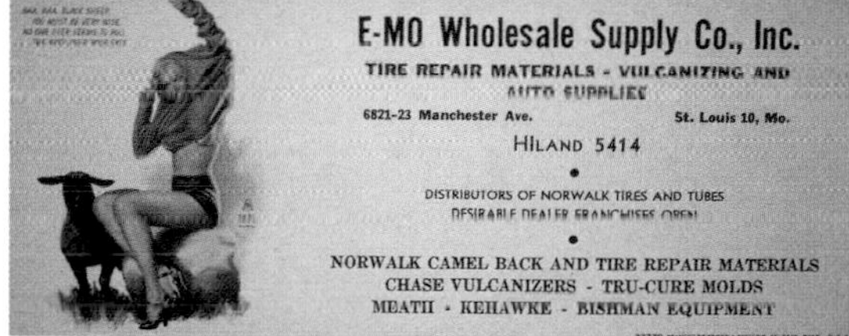

3½ x 6, $25-$35.

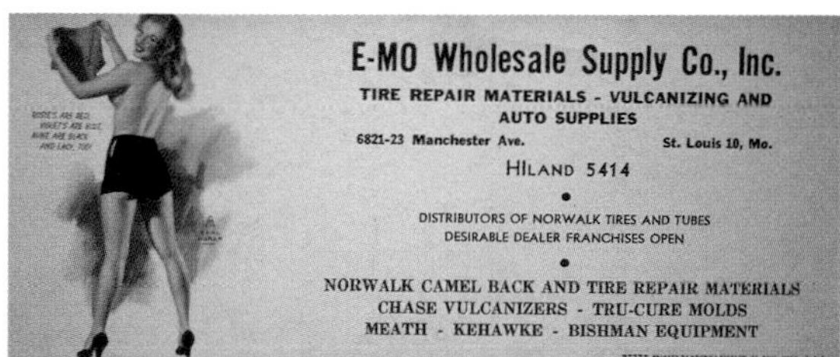

3½ x 6, $25-$35.

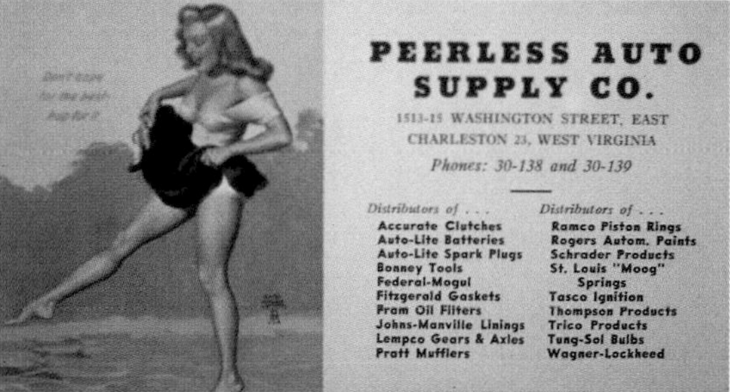

4 x 9, $35-$45.

There were also notepads produced with the previously mentioned phrases on them.

- 3½ x 6 .... $25-$35
- 4 x 9 .... $35-$45
- Notepads, 4 x 8 .... $15-$30

Two 4 x 8 1940s notepads, $15-$30 each.

1946 Album Color Prints ad, $40 $60.

Product Advertisements

Marilyn began modeling for her first product advertisements in 1946 and appeared on the pages of numerous magazines in the U.S. and foreign countries. These advertisements are coveted by today's Marilyn collectors.

By about 1954, Marilyn had ceased to appear in any product ads. This seems ironic, considering that today, her image is used to promote countless products, generating more than $1 million annually for her estate.

Below is a list of ads that she appeared in, along with their approximate values:

- Album Color Prints for Tri-Color Prints of Hollywood, California (color ad—1946). ....$40-$60
- Argoflex Cameras (1940s). ....$30-$50
- Arnold's of Hollywood (modeling the new "Star Suit"—1940s). ....$30-$50
- City Club Shoes for Men (color ad—1951). ....$20-$40
- Close-Up Perfect Make-Up (color ad). ....$20-$30
- Douglas Airlines New DC-6 Airplane (color ad—1946). ....$50-$80
- Hilton Hair Coloring. ....$20-$30
- Hinds Hand Cream. ....$20-$30
- Jantzen Swimwear Catalog (1947). ....$100-$200
- Kyron Way Diet Pills. ....$30-$50
- Louis Creative Hairdressers. ....$20-$40
- Lustre-Creme Shampoo (color ad—1950s). ....$20-$40
- Max Factor Cosmetics (1950s). ....$20-$40
- Maxell Tapes. ....$20-$40
- Nesbitt's California Orange Drink (color ad—1940s). ....$100-$150
- Rayve Creme Shampoo (1951). ....$20-$35
- Roi-Tan Cigars. ....$20-$40
- Tar-Tan Suntan Lotion. ....$20-$30
- Tru-Glo Makeup by Westmore Cosmetics (color ads—1952 and 1954). ....$20-$40

1940s Argoflex Cameras ad, $30-$50.

This page and next: a selection of advertising blotters by Earl Moran.

1951 City Club shoes ad, $20-$40.

Close-Up Perfect make-up ad, $20-$30.

1946 Douglas Airlines ad, $50-$80.

Kyron Way diet pill ad for Cunningham's Drug Stores, $30-$50.

1950s Lustre-Creme Shampoo ad, $20-$40.

1951 Rayve Creme Shampoo ad, $20-$35.

1950s Tru-Glo Make-Up by Westmore Cosmetics ad, $20-$40.

Chapter 5

Dolls

Amazingly, there were only paper dolls produced of Marilyn during her lifetime, and no porcelain or similar dolls such as those made of Shirley Temple, etc. It was not until 1982 that the first Marilyn Monroe dolls were produced—21 years after her death! A testimony, indeed, to the eternal love the world has for a fallen angel named Marilyn Monroe.

The first dolls were made by TRISTAR, and it was quite an extensive series, elaborately packaged in cardboard boxes with see-through cellophane. They did not, however, catch an authentic likeness of Marilyn, though they did duplicate many of the dresses Marilyn wore in her films to some satisfaction.

The next series came the following year, 1983, and was done by World Dolls. This series consisted of five dolls: three in porcelain and two in vinyl. They were a vast improvement over the TRISTAR dolls, but still did not capture the greatest likeness of Marilyn. They were infinitely more expensive than the TRISTAR dolls and even included one that was adorned with real fur and jewels!

The World Dolls set the stage for the next series of Marilyn dolls, which was produced by The Franklin Mint, beginning in 1990 and continuing still today. This series is by far the most exquisite of all, capturing an extremely good likeness of Marilyn and adorning her with elaborate gowns actually worn in her various movies, with the exception of one doll called *Sweater Girl*. For the first time, these dolls were offered in "posed" positions, instead of the traditional "stiff" dolls. They are generally priced in the $200 range, but one $500 doll was produced in 1997 and featured leather shoes and a sequined gown from *There's No Business Like Show Business*. It is twice the size of the rest in the series.

In 1997, a set of three *Barbie* Marilyns were produced by Mattel that were fitted in costumes from Marilyn's films and were very well done, though a bit out of the ordinary.

The only dolls that were produced during Marilyn's lifetime were the four different paper doll books done by Saalfield, beginning in 1952. These four books were in full color and basically replicated each other, just changing color arrangements and composition of the dolls on the front cover. These are now highly prized by Marilyn collectors, with the uncut and intact books preferred.

DSI Dolls

1993

- *Fur Fantasy Marilyn.* 11½" tall; vinyl; gold gown with a black fur; individually numbered; limited edition with Certificate of Authenticity (COA); 50,000 made. Originally $34.99. .... $30-$40
- *Silver Sizzle Marilyn.* 11½" tall; vinyl; silver gown; individually numbered; limited edition with COA; 50,000 made. Originally $34.99. .... $30-$40
- *Sparkle Superstar Marilyn.* 11½" tall; vinyl; red and black gown; individually numbered; limited edition with COA; 50,000 made. Originally $34.99. ..... $30-$40
- *Emerald Evening Marilyn.* 11½" tall; vinyl; green gown; individually numbered; limited edition with COA; 50,000 made. Originally $34.99. .... $30-$40
- *Spectacular Showgirl Marilyn.* 11½" tall; vinyl; blue gown with a blue boa; individually numbered; limited edition with COA; 50,000 made. Originally $34.99 .... $30-$40
- *Spotlight Splendor Marilyn.* 11½" tall; vinyl; black gown with a white fur; individually numbered; limited edition with COA; 50,000 made. Originally $34.99. .... $30-$40
- *Silver Dazzle Marilyn*; 11½" tall; vinyl; silver gown; individually numbered; limited edition with COA; 15,000 made and available at such places as QVC. ...... $50-$75

Silver Dazzle Marilyn, $50-$75.

Sparkle Superstar Marilyn, $30-$40.

Spectacular Showgirl Marilyn, $30-$40.

Silver Sizzle Marilyn, $30-$40.

Spotlight Splendor Marilyn, $30-$40.

Emerald Evening Marilyn, $30-$40.

Fur Fantasy Marilyn, $30-$40.

1990's Gentlemen Prefer Blondes.

Franklin Mint Dolls

1990

- *Gentlemen Prefer Blondes*. 19" tall; porcelain; pink gown; came with COA. Originally $200. ....$150-$200

1991

- *The Seven Year Itch*. 19" tall; porcelain; famous blowing white dress; came with COA. Originally $200. ....$150-$200

1992

- *Gentlemen Prefer Blondes*. 19" tall; porcelain; red sequined gown; came with COA. Originally $200. ....$150-$200

1993

- *Sweater Girl*. 19" tall; porcelain; gray skirt and a pink sweater; came with COA. Originally $200. ....$150-$200

1994

- *Golden Marilyn*. 19" tall; porcelain; gold lamé gown; came with COA. Originally $200. ....$150-$200

1996

- *Some Like It Hot*. 19" tall; porcelain; black dress; came with COA. Originally $200. ....$150-$200
- *River of No Return*. 19" tall; porcelain; red and gold gown; came with COA. Originally $200. ....$150-$200

1991's The Seven Year Itch.

1992's Gentlemen Prefer Blondes.

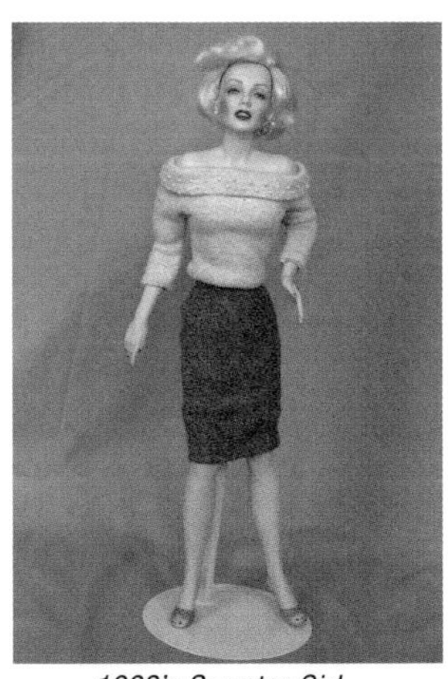
1993's Sweater Girl.

1994's Golden Marilyn.

1996's River of No Return.

1996's Some Like It Hot.

1997's There's No Business Like....

1997's All About Eve.

1998's Bus Stop.

- *The Ultimate Marilyn.* 24" tall; porcelain; beige bejeweled gown from role in *There's No Business Like Show Business*; came with COA; limited edition of 9,500. Originally $500. ....$400-$500

The Ultimate Marilyn doll by The Franklin Mint, $400-$500.

1997

- *All About Eve.* 19" tall; porcelain; white gown with fur coat from movie; came with COA. Originally $200. ....$150-$200
- *There's No Business Like Show Business.* 19" tall; porcelain; blue gown from the movie; came with COA. Originally $200. ....$150-$200

1998/1999

- *Bus Stop.* 19" tall; porcelain; green and gold dance outfit from the movie; came with COA....................$150-$200.
- *Vinyl Portrait Dress-Up Doll.* 15⅛" tall; vinyl; trunk and other ensembles sold separately; individually hand-numbered. Originally $110. ....$70-$110

Ensembles and accessories for the above doll:
- *Gentlemen Prefer Blondes* (pink dress), *The Seven Year Itch*, *Gentlemen Prefer Blondes* (red dress), *Some Like It Hot*, and *Happy Birthday Mr. President*; came with jewelry, shoes, etc.; Originally $69 each. ....$50-$70
- Wardrobe Trunk. Originally $135. ....$100-$135
- Dress Form. Originally $20 ....$15-$20

Vinyl dress-up doll with accessories by The Franklin Mint, $70-$110.

1999

- *Happy Birthday Mr. President!* 18" tall on stand; vinyl portrait dress-up doll; MM sings "Happy Birthday" to President Kennedy in 1962; dress adorned with 1,300 aurora borealis beads and Austrian crystal earrings. .... $150-$200

2000

- *Millennium Marilyn.* 16½" tall; vinyl portrait doll; gold and platinum spangled evening gown; came with genuine diamond earrings; limited edition that closed after Dec. 31, 2000. Originally $195....................$150-$200

2001

- *Love, Marilyn.* 11¼" tall high seated (including bench); porcelain portrait doll; gossamer white-tulle gown, based on actual photograph by Milton H. Greene; individually hand-numbered. Originally $195. ....$150-$200

The Franklin Mint's Happy Birthday Mr. President doll, $150-$200.

Mattel Barbie Dolls

1997

- *The Seven Year Itch.* 11½" tall; vinyl; famous white blowing dress from movie; Hollywood Legends Collection. ....$50-$70
- *Gentlemen Prefer Blondes.* 11½" tall; vinyl; red sequined gown from movie; Hollywood Legends Collection. ....$50-$70
- *Gentlemen Prefer Blondes.* 11½" tall; vinyl; pink gown from the movie; Hollywood Legends Collection. ....$50-$70

At left, the set of Barbie dolls by Mattel, $50-$70 each.

1982 set of 16' TRISTAR dolls, $80-$125 each.

1982 set of 11½' TRISTAR dolls, $50-$100 each.

1983 World Dolls, from left: Seven Year Itch doll ($150-$200); portrait doll in black sequins ($200-$275); portrait doll in white sequins ($200-$275); and portrait doll in red ($150-$200).

TRISTAR/20th Century Fox Film Corp. Dolls

1982

- *There's No Business Like Show Business*; 16" tall; vinyl; gold lamé gown. First Series..........$80-$125
- *How To Marry A Millionaire*. 16" tall; vinyl; red gown. First Series ....$80-$125
- *The Seven Year Itch*. 16" tall; vinyl; famous blowing white dress. First Series. ....$80-$125
- *Gentlemen Prefer Blondes*. 16" tall; vinyl; pink gown from movie. First Series. ....$80-$125
- *How To Marry A Millionaire*. 11½" tall; vinyl; red gown. First Series ....$50-$100
- *There's No Business Like Show Business*. 11½" tall; vinyl; gold gown that was designed for *Gentlemen Prefer Blondes*. First Series. ....$50-$100
- *The Seven Year Itch*. 11½" tall; vinyl; famous white blowing dress from movie. First Series. ....$50-$100
- *Gentlemen Prefer Blondes*; 11½" tall; vinyl; pink gown from movie. First Series. ....$50-$100

1983

- *River of No Return*. 11½" tall; vinyl; red and blue gown (not worn in movie), holding guitar. Second Series..........$50-$100
- *Let's Make It Legal*. 11½" tall; vinyl; green gown not worn in movie. Second Series..........$50-$100
- *Niagara*. 11½" tall; vinyl; red gown with a pink shawl, carrying a record. Second Series. ....$50-$100
- *Gentlemen Prefer Blondes*. 11½" tall; vinyl; beige and black body suit, black stockings, and black top hat. Second Series..........$50-$100

World Dolls

1983

- Original portrait doll. 18½" tall; vinyl; famous blowing white dress from *The Seven Year Itch*; came with COA; one-year edition only. World Doll Celebrity Series. Originally $150..........$150-$200
- Original portrait doll. 18½" tall; vinyl; red formal gown with white feather boa; came with COA; one-year edition only. World Doll Celebrity Series. Originally $75. ....$150-$200
- Original portrait doll. 16½" tall; porcelain; white sequined gown; came with COA; one-year edition only. World Doll Celebrity Series. Originally $300. ....$200-$275
- Original portrait doll. 16½" tall; porcelain; black sequined gown; came with COA; one-year edition only. World Doll Celebrity Series. Originally $400. ....$200-$275
- Original portrait doll. Size unknown; porcelain; gold metallic mesh gown, real white mink fur, glass eyes, and quarter-karat diamond earrings; came with COA; limited and numbered edition. World Doll Celebrity Series. Originally a whopping $3,000. ......$1,200-$1,800

Miscellaneous Dolls

- *Marilyn Monroe Musical Doll.* M.S.R Imports, Inc., 1982. 8" tall; porcelain from waist up; famous white blowing dress and diamond ring on right hand; plays "Diamonds Are A Girl's Best Friend" and rotates on plastic base; made in Taiwan. Item No. 1520. ....$70-$95
- *Kiddle Doll.* Kindiddle Kreations, 2001. Little Biddle Peep as MM, wearing the white billowing dress. ....$550-$650
- *One-of-a-Kind Handmade Doll.* Clark Harford, vintage unknown; 24" tall; in lavendar off-the-shoulder sweater and darker purple satiny skirt. ....$1,000-$1,900
- *Russian Nesting Dolls.* Circa 1990-2001. Several wooden dolls that fit inside each other; handpainted....................$10-$20
- *Spoof Doll-Celebrity Spoofs.* Christhomas Corp., circa 1990s. 8"; packaged with plastic covering; created by Dennis Glassburg....................$5-$15

Rotating musical doll by M.S.R. Imports, $70-$95.

Handmade doll by Clark Harford, $1,000-$1,900.

Paper Dolls

- *American Beauties.* Saalfield No. 1338, circa late-1950s. Stiff cover with two Marilyn dolls on front and a punch-out dressing table on the back. Set issued after the company's contract was up, so it was unable to use MM's name on them, though they are identical to the identified Marilyn paper doll books that follow....................$150-$200
- *Celebrity Fashion Show Statuette Dolls.* Bonnie Books No. 2743. Artist's rendering of MM on book cover, which is designed like a folder, with pockets inside for the dolls. Child Craft Series....................$50-$100
- *Marilyn Monroe Paper Dolls.* Saalfield No. 4323, 1954. Features two standing Marilyn dolls made of heavy cardboard on the cover, which has a blue-and-white striped background; complete wardrobe inside. These dolls are known as "statuette" dolls and are scarce because there were few made.............$200-$300
- *Marilyn Monroe Paper Dolls.* Saalfield No. 4308-25, 1953. Features two hard cardboard "statuette" dolls affixed to the front cover; jacket doors swing open to reveal pages of clothes inside; dressing table featured on back. Original edition of MM paper dolls. ....$200-$300
- *Marilyn Monroe Paper Dolls.* Saalfield No. 158610, 1953. Features two dolls on front cover with "Authorized Edition" printed in lower right corner.......$200-$300
- *Marilyn Monroe Paper Dolls by Tom Tierney.* Dover Publications, 1979. All-color book includes cut-out doll and 32 costumes from 24 of Marilyn's films. ...$5-$10
- *Marilyn Monroe Paper Doll.* 1986. Came with a two-page Cheetos ad; depicts a circa 1952 MM (face), along with *Rambo* and Madonna style clothes; color ....$15-$30
- *Talking Paper Doll.* Adult Toys, circa 1970s. In the famous white blowing dress from *The Seven Year Itch* and says, "I Love You"; image is b&w. ....$15-$25
- *Single dolls* (cut) of MM from the 1950s, with or without clothes. .....each $40-$70

Russian nesting dolls, $10-$20.

Celebrity Spoofs doll, $5-$15.

American Beauties paper doll book, No. 1338, $150-$200.

Celebrity Fashion Show doll book, No. 2743, $50-$100.

Tom Tierney paper doll book, $5-$10.

Chapter 6

Figural Collectibles

Marilyn figural collectibles are among the most sought-after by collectors. The ability to display these collectibles is one of the reasons for their great popularity.

Very few figural pieces were produced during Marilyn's lifetime. In fact, the greatest share of them began to appear in the late-1970s, and continue to be produced in large numbers to this day. The earliest piece produced (to my knowledge) was the Marilyn Monroe head vase by Relpo. It was made in the early to mid-1960s, and was sold through such places as floral shops. Lately, Clay Art and The Franklin Mint have produced some fine Marilyn Monroe figural collectibles.

Marilyn's image has been cast in everything from musical sculptures to whiskey bottles, and from cookie jars to table lamps. What would Marilyn have thought?

No other person, with the possible exception of John Wayne and Elvis Presley, have been immortalized in the way that Marilyn Monroe has, though her life was cut short long before that of Presley's or Wayne's. I think it is safe to say that figural collectibles of Marilyn Monroe will be produced for some time to come, much to the delight of her legions of fans.

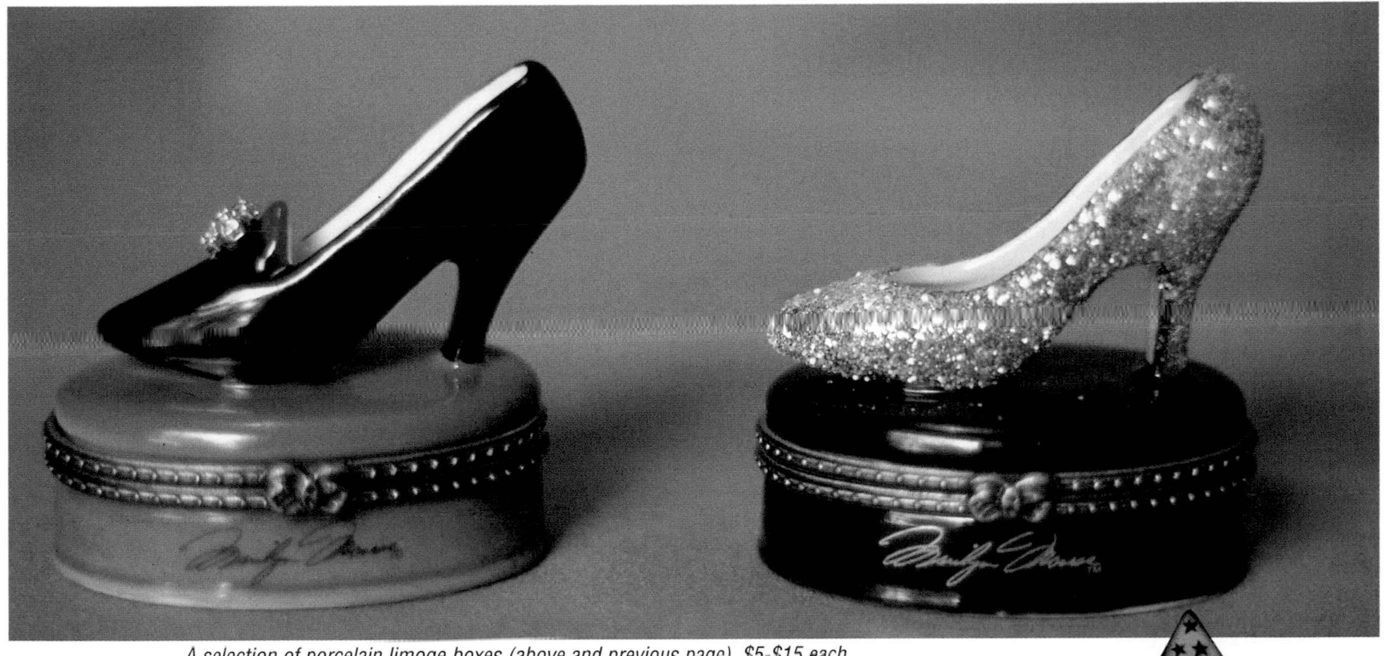

A selection of porcelain limoge boxes (above and previous page), $5-$15 each.

Assorted

- MM Limoge Boxes. PHB Collection, 2000. Three examples depicting MM in a red dress, white sparkle dress, and a swimsuit (with pair of purple sunglasses), and others; limited edition of 3,600 pieces. .....each $5-$15
- Marilyn Monroe Action Toy. Hollywood Memories, 1970s. 7" tall; only known MM toy. ....$80-$90
- Marilyn Monroe Bear. ENESCO, 1990. Ceramic; in famous white blowing dress from *Itch*; part of the "Lucy & Me" collection by Lucy Rigg; made in Sri Lanka..$15-$20
- Marilyn Monroe Bisque Porcelain Night Light. Vandor, 1984; 9" tall; in the famous blowing white dress; made in Japan, and unauthorized ....$125-$175
- Marilyn Monroe Bobbing Head Doll. Sams, 1996. 9" tall; porcelain; in gold lamé dress; packed in a generic box; came with COA and individually numbered; limited edition of 5,000....................$45-$60
- Marilyn Monroe Bust. Foreign-made, late-1990s. Approximately 20" tall; papier-mache or similar "mannequin" material; hollow on inside ....$35-$70
- Marilyn Monroe Bust. Maker unknown, circa 1989. Wearing black strapless dress, with ruffled edges; made in Finland.............................$40-$80
- Marilyn Bust. Fleshpot, vintage unknown. 10" tall; porcelain; made in England. ....$125-$150
- Marilyn Bust, vintage unknown. Foreign-made, possibly New Zealand, maker unknown...........................$50-$75
- Marilyn Caricature Statue. Continental Studios of Burbank, California, 1970s. Plaster; in famous white blowing dress; bumblebee stamped in bottom of piece ....$80-$130

Mask by Clay Art, $40-$70.

Mask by Clay Art, $30-$60.

Two more Limoges boxes, $5-$15 each.

Figure by Ashley Belle, $200-$300.

Night light by Vandor, $200-$250.

Bobbing head doll, $45-$60.

Clay Art salt and pepper set, $30-$40.

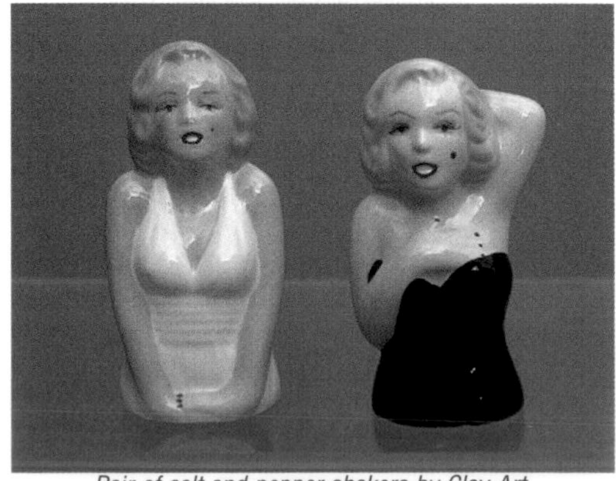
Pair of salt and pepper shakers by Clay Art, $16-$20.

- Marilyn Monroe Caricature Statue. ENESCO, 1980s-90s. 16½" tall; plaster; in a black gown; distributed by Tobacco Stores; head much bigger in proportion to body as is typical with the caricature statues. .... $40-$60
- Marilyn Monroe Ceramic Figure. Maker unknown, early 1980s. 7½" tall; sitting on a piano .... $50-$80
- Marilyn Monroe Ceramic Heart-Shaped Candy Dish. Maker and vintage unknown. Red dish with MM's figure reclining on edge; made in China .... $100-$150
- Marilyn Monroe Coin-Operated Bank. Funtime Savings of China, circa 1982. 12" tall; vinyl MM doll on top of plastic black or white base; in the famous blowing white dress; insert coin and small fan blows dress up............................. $45-$65
- Marilyn Monroe Cookie Jar. ENESCO, 1997. Ceramic; featuring a bust of Marilyn in halter dress and available in pink, white, or teal; limited edition. Originally $300. .... $250-$300
- Marilyn Figurine. Ashley Belle, vintage unknown. In white blowing *Itch* dress. .... $200-$300
- Marilyn Figurine. Royal Dux, circa 1999. 11" tall; depicts MM in *The Seven Year Itch*; designed by V. Daniel; Royal Dux sticker and imprint on figurine; signed,numbered, and hand-painted in the Czech Republic .... $150-$200
- Marilyn Monroe Head Vase. RELPO, 1950s-early 1960s. 6¾" tall; ceramic; in black halter dress with large pearl earrings and a silver bow in the back left bottom corner of her hair, barely visible from front; distributed in floral shops with flower bouquets in them. Very scarce .... $1,000-$1,500
- Marilyn Monroe Head Vase. Malena, 1988; 8½" tall; plaster; not a good likeness; done in pastel hues. .... $30-$40
- Marilyn Monroe Head Vase. Maker unknown, 1980s. 4" tall; ceramic; MM holding a microphone and wearing a white dress; not a great likeness................... $40-$60
- Marilyn Monroe McCormick Decanter. McCormick Distilling Co., 1983. 15" tall; in famous blowing white dress; packed in decorative box; copyright 20th Century Fox Film Corp. .... $350-$450
- Marilyn Monroe McCormick Decanter. McCormick Distilling Co., 1983. 7" tall; in famous blowing white dress, as above; packed in decorative box; copyright 20th Century Fox Film Corp. .... $125-$200
- Marilyn Monroe Metal Figurine. Maker unknown, 1979. 2¼" tall; sculpted in the old toy soldier style; in famous *Itch* dress; limited edition of 200 and made in Blenheim, England, especially for Gerry Alingh of Iowa. .... $25-$45

The set of 9" figurines by Royal Orleans, $175-$275 apiece.

Caricature statue, $40-$60.

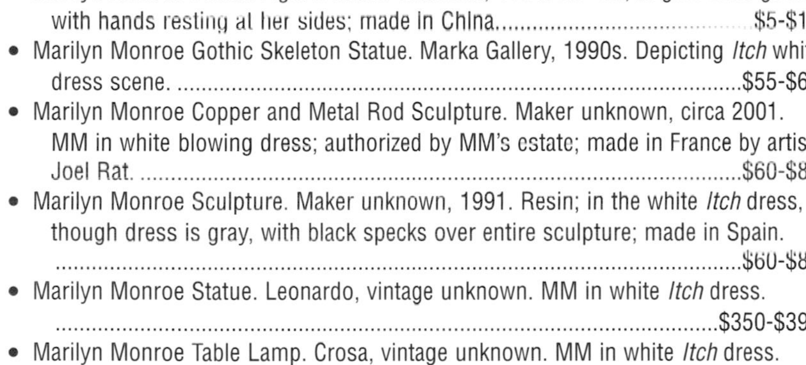

- Marilyn Monroe Plastic Figure. Maker unknown, 1991. 3½" tall; in gold lamé gown with hands resting at her sides; made in China. .... $5-$10
- Marilyn Monroe Gothic Skeleton Statue. Marka Gallery, 1990s. Depicting *Itch* white dress scene. .... $55-$60
- Marilyn Monroe Copper and Metal Rod Sculpture. Maker unknown, circa 2001. MM in white blowing dress; authorized by MM's estate; made in France by artist Joel Rat. .... $60-$80
- Marilyn Monroe Sculpture. Maker unknown, 1991. Resin; in the white *Itch* dress, though dress is gray, with black specks over entire sculpture; made in Spain. .... $60-$80
- Marilyn Monroe Statue. Leonardo, vintage unknown. MM in white *Itch* dress. .... $350-$390
- Marilyn Monroe Table Lamp. Crosa, vintage unknown. MM in white *Itch* dress. .... $150-$225
- Marilyn Monroe Telephone. Telemania, 2000. *Itch* dress; plays "I Wanna be Loved by You." .... $180-$190

Clay Art cookie jar with original box, $50-$70.

Telemania telephone and box, $180-$190.

Plastic figurine, $5-$10.

Pair of coin-operated banks, $45-$65 each.

Royal Dux figurine, $150-$200.

Early 1980s ceramic piano, $50-$80.

Clay Art

- Marilyn Monroe Ceramic Mask. 1988; about 9" wide x 9¾" high..................$30-$60
- Marilyn Monroe Ceramic Mask. 1988; with a star-shaped background........$40-$70
- Marilyn Monroe Ceramic Bust. 1988; in white halter dress; done in pastel hues, glazed; in decorative box..$50-$70
- Marilyn Monroe Ceramic Circular Powder Box. 1988; b&w with color MM on handle; in decorative box...$35-$45
- Marilyn Monroe Ceramic Cookie Jar. 1997. MM in white *Itch* dress. Originally $45. ....$40-$60
- Marilyn Monroe Ceramic Cookie Jar. Circa 2000; MM reclining on a heart-shaped cushion. ....$50-$70
- Marilyn Monroe Millennium Ceramic Cookie Jar. 2000. MM in top hat, wearing sleeveless dress..$50-$70
- Marilyn Monroe Ceramic 3-D Pin. 1988; rhinestones affixed to it; mounted on cardboard..$8-$15
- Marilyn Monroe Covered Heart Box. 1988; MM's face on top; came in decorative packaging ....$25-$35
- Marilyn Monroe Figural Picture Frame. 1988; MM's picture in frame and figure on the rim; in decorative box. ....$40-$65
- Marilyn Monroe Head Mug in 3-D. 1988; came in decorative box. ....$12-$20
- Marilyn Monroe Heart-Shaped Dish. 1988; MM's reclining figure on top; came in decorative box. ....$25-$35
- Marilyn Monroe Light Switch Plate. Circa 1990s; MM faces on front..$15-$20
- Marilyn Monroe Salt and Pepper Shakers. 1988; 3½" tall; in a white and a black dress..$16-$20
- Marilyn Monroe Salt and Pepper Shakers. Vintage unknown; MM seated on a heart-shaped pillow...................................$30-$40
- Marilyn Monroe Welcome Plaque. Circa 1980s; heart shape with "Welcome" on it, affixed to bust...................................$25-$40

Head vase by Relpo, $1,000-$1,500.

1997 ENESCO cookie jar, $250-$300.

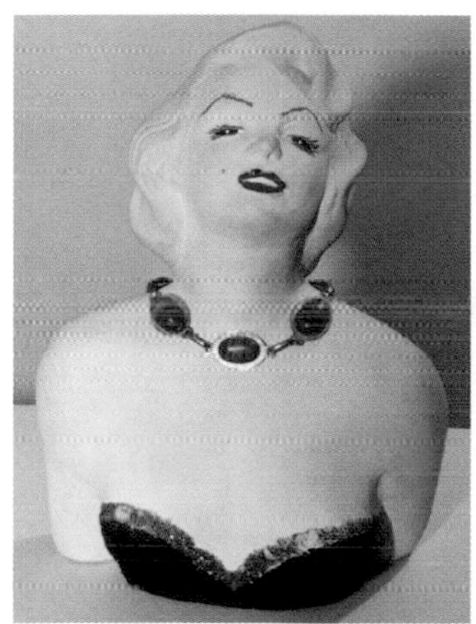

Finnish bust, circa 1989, $40-$80.

1997 Clay Art cookie jar, $40-$60.

Foreign-made bust (possibly New Zealand), $50-$75.

Millennium cookie jar by Clay Art, $40-$70.

Late-1990s foreign-made bust, $35-$70.

Table lamp by Crosa, $150-$225.

Franklin Mint

- Marilyn Monroe Porcelain Sculpture. 1997; 10" tall; in famous blowing white dress; accented with 24-karat gold and platinum; limited to 45 firing days. Originally $200. ....$150-$200
- Marilyn Monroe Porcelain Musical Sculpture. 1995; 5½" tall; in pink dress from *Gentlemen Prefer Blondes*, surrounded by men; plays "Diamond's Are A Girl's Best Friend"; covered with a crystal clear dome; hand-numbered; limited edition, closed after 95 casting days. Originally $55. ....$45-$65
- Marilyn Monroe Porcelain Musical Sculpture. 1998; 5½" tall; in red sequin dress from *Gentlemen Prefer Blondes*; plays "Two Girls From Little Rock"; covered with a crystal clear dome; hand-numbered; limited edition, closed after 95 casting days. ....$45-$65
- Marilyn Monroe Bronze Sculpture. 2001; 10½" tall; in an off-the-shoulder dress; limited edition of 9,500 worldwide. Originally $195. ....$195-$200

Royal Orleans

- Marilyn Monroe Figurine. 1982; 9" tall; in famous white blowing dress from *The Seven Year Itch*; limited numbered edition of 20,000; produced with a matching plate. ....$175-$275
- Marilyn Monroe Figurine. 1982; 9" tall; in pink dress from *Gentlemen Prefer Blondes*; limited numbered edition of 20,000; produced with a matching plate. ....$175-$275
- Marilyn Monroe Figurine. 1982; 9" tall; in red dress from *Niagara*; limited numbered edition of 20,000; produced with a matching plate. ....$175-$275
- Marilyn Monroe Figurine. 1982; 9" tall; in red one-piece bathing suit from *How To Marry A Millionaire*; limited numbered edition of 20,000; produced with a matching plate. ....$175-$275
- Marilyn Monroe Figurine. 1982; 4" tall; in pink dress from *Gentlemen Prefer Blondes*; limited edition; matches its counterpart in the above set. ....$50-$80
- Marilyn Monroe Figurine. 1982; 4" tall; in famous white blowing dress from *Itch*; limited edition; matches its counterpart in the above set. ....$50-$80

Note: The two 4" figurines immediately above also came with a small eyelet affixed to the top of Marilyn's head so that they could be used as ornaments. These are valued the same.

1995 musical sculpture by The Franklin Mint, $45-$65.

Modern sculpture from France, $60-$80

Clay Art mug with box, $12-$20.

Gothic statue, $55-$60.

Resin sculpture from Spain, $60-$80.

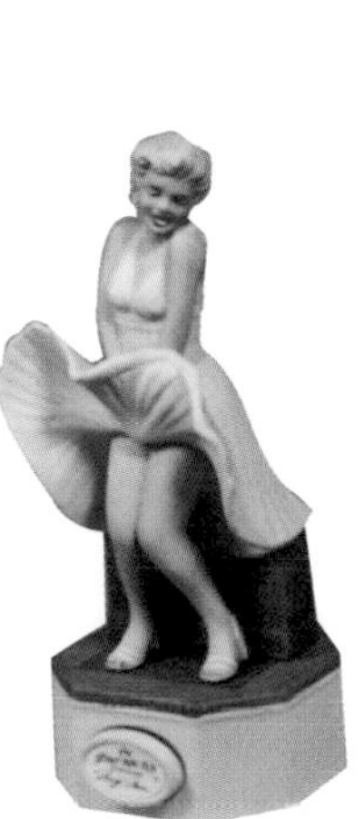

Two sizes of McCormick decanters: far left, $125-$200 and near left, $350-$450.

Chapter 7

Magazines

Marilyn Monroe easily could be called the original cover girl. Her very appearance on a magazine cover ensured a considerable increase in issue sales. Of course, this was true only after she had attained superstar status around 1952. Before then, she had graced the covers of many U.S. and foreign magazines as simply just another pretty face.

Marilyn began her career as a model in 1945 when she was just 19. She learned early on how to best use makeup and would later be a photographer's dream. She took great pride in applying most of her own makeup. Fox studio photographer Frank Powolny once said of her, "She works fast, has her own ideas. She's good for 20 poses an hour."

Marilyn's first cover appearance (although not solo) was on the January 1946 issue of *Douglas Airview*, an in-house publication put out by Douglas Airlines. In late-1945, Norma Jeane posed for photographer Larry Kronquist in one of her first paid modeling jobs, showing off the interior of Douglas's new DC-6 airplane.

Marilyn's first solo cover appearance in the U.S. was on the April 26, 1946 issue of *Family Circle*, which was ironic, considering the reputation she would later attain. Her first solo appearance on a foreign cover was on the April 13, 1946 issue of *Leader* in England.

By this time, Marilyn began to appear on numerous foreign covers as well, often unidentified. Her early U.S. cover appearances tended to be on romance or men's types of publications. Some of the more risqué photographs had to have clothing painted on in strategic areas in order to comply with censorship laws. Marilyn was really ahead of her time and continuously taunted the censors—more than three decades before Madonna was even heard of!

Marilyn's magazine cover appearances are some of the most popular Monroe collectibles, with some fetching prices in the hundreds of dollars. These appearances number more than 1,000 to date, and she continues to grace covers in nearly every country in the world, nearly 40 years after her death.

In general, magazines with collectible Monroe covers come in four sizes: pocket (4 x 6), digest (5½ x 7½), standard (8½ x 11), and large (10½ x 14). In most cases, size makes little difference when determining the value of the magazines. The covers most sought-after by collectors are those in which Marilyn occupies the entire cover.

Douglas Airview, January 1946, $1,200-$1,500.

Laff, June 1946, $250-$350.

Salute, August 1946, $400-$600.

Personal Romances, June 1947, $400-$500.

Sunday World Herald, June 1, 1947, $600-$800.

Sunday News, August 14, 1949, $150-$250.

U.S. Cover Appearances

1946

- *Douglas Airview* Jan. 1946; vol. 8, no. 1; Norma Jeane's first cover. ....$1,200-$1,500
- *Laff*, June 1946; vol. 7, no. 3; her third cover-given credit........$250-$350
- *Laff*, Aug. 1946; vol. 7, no. 5; fourth major cover-given credit as "Jean Norman." ....$250-$350
- *Pageant,* June 1946; vol. 2, no. 5; a shot on this digest issue. ....$100-$200
- *Salute,* Aug. 1946; vol. 1, no. 4; a morale-boosting issue for the soldiers serving in WWII. ....$400-$600

Descriptions of Magazine Grades

The estimated values for each magazine are listed from the very good to near-mint range. Here is a guide to help with determining the proper grade for a particular collectible:

Mint

Never used. Just as it came from the printer, regardless of its age. Appears to be new.

Near-Mint

Looks perfect at a glance. Only minor imperfections evident in the form of tiny tears, corner creases, or spine stresses.

Very Fine

An excellent copy. Minimal surface wear is evident. Staples may show discoloring through paper. Spine may show stress lines.

Fine

An above average issue with minor but noticeable cover wear. Some discoloring at staples. Minor wear at staples and spine, but not serious. Corner creases evident. Multiple creasing will drop it a grade. Cover may be slightly loose.

Very Good

General wear evident. Staples may be rusty. A store stamp or name may be written on cover. Pages may be a bit brittle. A small amount of chipping may be evident or a small piece of a corner may be off. Cover may be stained, spine split, cover creased and slightly soiled. Minor tape repair may be noted.

Good

Below-average copy. Numerous creases; light soiling and staining. Cover may be detached and have both small and large tears. Spine may be split. Pages may be yellowed and a little brittle and may display various areas of chipping.

Fair

Complete issue but with a few pages missing, writing on cover, chunks missing. Cover may be detached and have tape repairs. A good reading copy. Pages brittle and also yellowed with age.

Poor

Much of the cover may be missing, as well as several pages. Heavily soiled with brittle pages. Good reading or research copy. Good copy to clip ads from.

- *Family Circle,* April 26, 1946; vol. 28, no. 17; Norma Jeane as cute farm girl. ....$250-$350
- *U.S. Camera,* May 1946; vol. 9, no. 4; Norma Jeane is on one-quarter of the cover. ....$75-$150

1947

- *Laff,* Jan. 1947; vol. 7, no. 10; given credit as Norma Jeane Daugherty. ....$250-$350
- *Sunday World Herald Magazine,* June 1, 1947; sitting next to babies on floor. ....$600-$800
- *Laff,* Sept. 1947; vol. 8, no. 6; introduced as Marilyn Monroe. ....$250-$350
- *Parade,* Feb. 16, 1947; delivered with the Sunday newspaper. ....$400-$500
- *Personal Romances,* June 1947; vol. 14, no. 2; pictured in a wedding gown. ....$400-$500
- *Personal Romances,* July 1947; vol. 14, no. 3; pictured as a cute sailor girl. ....$400-$500
- *True Experiences,* Sept. 1947; at the steering wheel of a boat. ....$400-$600

1949

- *Film Humor,* Spring 1949; vol. 1, no. 4; as one of four swimsuit models. ....$50-$75
- *Foto-Parade,* Aug. 1949; vol. 1, no. 1; classic cheesecake in a striped bikini. ....$150-$250
- *Hit!,* Sept. 1949; vol. 6, no. 6; in a yellow bikini Marilyn often wore. ....$150-$250
- *Glamourous Models,* Aug. 1949; vol. 4, no. 3; in a white bikini top. ....$150-$250
- *So-Rite Fall Fashions,* Fall 1949; a catalog cover appearance. ....$400-$600
- *Sunday News,* Aug. 14, 1949; stepping out of a pool in a green suit. ....$150-$250
- *Teen-Age Diary Secrets* (comic book), Oct. 1949; vol. 1, no. 6; in a red sweater. ....$400-$500

1950

- *Chicago Tribune,* Aug. 6, 1950; with long red hair and black lace gloves. ....$200-$300
- *Gala,* May-June 1950; vol. 1, no. 1; posing with a polka-dot umbrella. ....$100-$175
- *Glance,* May 1950; vol. 3, no. 1; a vivid cover, sitting on a diving board. ....$250-$350
- *Laff,* Feb. 1950; vol. 10, no. 11; curled up with a powder puff and high heels. ....$150-$225
- *Man to Man,* Feb.-March 1950; vol. 1, no. 2; posed in a lacy top with a telephone. ....$100-$150
- *True Experiences,* May 1950; vol. 48, no. 6; with shorter bobbed hair. ....$200-$375

1951

- *Focus* (pocket), Dec. 1951; vol. 1, no. 5; playing on the rocks in a swimsuit. ....$20-$40
- *People Today* (pocket), Feb. 13, 1951; vol. 2, no. 4; publicity photo from *All About Eve*. ....$20-$40
- *Pittsburgh Press Roto Magazine,* July 1, 1951; full-blown glamour shot with hair up. ....$150-$225
- *Quick* (pocket), Nov. 19, 1951; vol. 5, no. 21; cute cover with a comparison to Harlow. ....$20-$40
- *True Romance,* Sept. 1951; vol. 54, no. 1; in a pink scarf and yellow sweater. ....$150-$250
- *True Story,* Nov. 1951; vol. 65, no. 4; with very short hair in a yellow turtleneck. ....$100-$150
- *Your Money Maker,* Sept. 1951; in a two-piece bathing suit. ....$200-$400

So-Rite Fashions, 1949, $400-$600.

Glance, May 1950, $250-$350.

True Experiences, May 1950, $200-$375.

1952

- *Art Photography,* March 1952; vol. 3, no. 7; a blue-tint cover, playing in the snow. ....$75-$125
- *Chicago Tribune Grafic,* May 25, 1952; in black lace dress. ....$100-$200
- *Chicago Tribune Grafic,* Oct. 12, 1952; with a blue satin halter-top..........$100-$200
- *Down Beat,* Sept. 10, 1952; vol. 19, no. 18; with Ray Anthony in a candid pose. ....$35-$70
- *Eye* (digest), Nov. 1952; vol. 2, no. 8; sitting on a diving board in a gold bikini. ....$50-$100
- *Focus* (pocket), Sept. 1952; vol. 2, no. 8; in a gold bikini top. ....$20-$40
- *Gold Coast News Magazine,* Oct. 15, 1952; vol. 3, no. 43; published only in Florida. ....$80-$120
- *I Confess,* Sept. 1952; a glamour shot in a black strapless dress. ....$100-$175
- *Look,* Sept. 9, 1952; vol. 16, no. 19; as a cheerleader. ....$60-$80
- *LIFE,* April 7, 1952; vol. 32, no. 14; classic image taken by Halsman. ....$60-$100
- *Movie Fan,* Dec. 1952; vol. 7, no. 3; in red dress from *Niagara*. ....$90-$135
- *Movieland,* July 1952; vol. 10, no. 6; in blue satin halter-top. ....$80-$125
- *Movieland,* Oct. 1952; vol. 10, no. 9; curled up in a yellow bikini. ....$70-$125
- *Movie Life,* Nov. 1952; vol. 15, no. 12; in red negligee. ....$60-$100
- *Movie Spotlight,* Oct. 1952; vol. 3, no. 6; glamour shot in a brown fur......$60-$100
- *Movie Pin-Ups,* March 1952; vol. 1, no. 2; sitting, wearing a bikini. ....$60-$90
- *Movie Pix,* Oct. 1952; vol. 3, no. 6; classic Monroe—open mouth, half-mast eyes. ....$75-$125
- *Music Views* (pocket), Oct. 1952; with Ray Anthony. ....$30-$50
- *People Today* (pocket), June 18, 1952; vol. 4, no. 13; in white bikini on a ladder. ....$20-$40
- *People Today* (pocket), Dec. 3, 1952; vol. 5, no. 12; b&w portrait holding a cigarette. ....$20-$40
- *Pic,* Feb. 1952; vol. 23, no. 1; glamour pose, looking up at the camera.....$75-$125
- *Picture Roto Magazine,* July 27, 1952; sultry pose with reflection...........$100-$175
- *Ray Anthony & Co.,* 1952; Marilyn and Ray posing cheek-to-cheek. ....$50-$75
- *Scope,* Nov. 1952; vol. 1, no. 1; a long-haired cheesecake shot. ....$90-$150
- *See,* July 1952; vol. 11, no. 4; with short red hair. ....$75-$125
- *Screen Fan,* Dec. 1952; vol. 1, no. 2; in strapless black gown and earrings. ....$75-$125
- *Screenland,* Aug. 1952; vol. 56, no. 10; an *Asphalt Jungle*-era photograph. ....$60-$100
- *Silver Screen,* Feb. 1952; vol. 22, no. 4; well-known shot with jewels and black lace dress. ....$60-$100
- *Sir!,* Dec. 1952; vol. 8, no. 3; young Norma Jeane on a green barrel. ....$75-$125
- *Sunday News (N.Y.),* Nov. 30, 1952; in red dress before green drapery.....$90-$150
- *Sunday Mirror (N.Y.),* Sept. 7, 1952; a lovely dual image with a mirror. ..$400-$450
- *TV Forecast* (digest), Oct. 4, 1952; vol. 5, no. 23; a pre-*TV Guide* publication. ....$100-$175
- *Vue* (digest), Sept. 1952; vol. 3, no. 2; leaning back in a yellow swimsuit...$50-$80

1953

- *Balco News* (digest), July-Aug. 1953; vol. 13, no. 3; sent to employees of Bausch & Lomb. ....$150-$250
- *Brief* (digest), Dec. 1953; vol. 1, no. 8; in black lacy negligee. ....$40-$80
- *Cheesecake,* 1953; reclining in a yellow halter bikini. ....$75-$125
- *Cue,* June 27, 1953; shared cover with Jane Russell. ....$40-$60
- *Cosmopolitan,* May 1953; vol. 134, no. 5; smiling in a long black lace negligee. ....$75-$125
- *Eye* (digest), Feb. 1953; vol. 3, no. 2; in pink long johns warming by a fire. ....$40-$80
- *Eye* (digest), Aug. 1953; vol. 13, no. 8; a wraparound cover, in a yellow bikini. ....$40-$80

True Romance, September 1951, $150-$250.

Quick, November 19, 1951, $20-$40.

True Story, November 1951, $100-$150.

Focus, *December 1951,* *$20-$40.*

Ray Anthony & Co., *1952,* *$50-$75.*

PIC, *February 1952,* *$75-$125.*

- *Films In Review* (digest), April 1953; vol. 4, no. 4; b&w cover featuring Monroe reading. ....$100-$150
- *Focus* (pocket), March 1953; vol. 3, no. 3; b&w cheesecake shot by Beauchamp. ....$20-$40
- *Focus* (pocket), May 1953; vol. 3, no. 5; wearing a bow necklace. ....$20-$40
- *Hit Parader,* Jan. 1953; practicing typical allure....................$30-$50
- *I Confess,* May 1953; vol. 3, no. 2; young, long-haired early Marilyn. .....$100-$150
- *International Sound Technician,* March 1953; vol. 1, no. 1; with Jane Russell on the set of *Blondes.* ....$100-$150
- *Laff,* Jan. 1953; vol. 14, no. 5; sitting on the beach in a red suit. ....$75-$125
- *Leisure Time,* Dec. 20, 1953; with Jane Russell in *Gentlemen Prefer Blondes.* ....$75-$125
- *LIFE,* May 25, 1953; vol. 34, no. 21; with Jane Russell in *Blondes.*....................$25-$45
- *Look,* June 30, 1953; with Lauren Bacall and Betty Grable. ....$20-$40
- *Look,* Nov. 17, 1953; vol. 17, no. 23; in grey sweater, holding a cigarette. ....$60-$100
- *Marilyn Monroe's Beauty Secrets* (digest), 1953; b&w cover in a lamé halter dress. ....$100-$300
- *Marilyn Monroe Pin-Ups,* 1953; two versions of this issue with different inside photos: one was banned. ....$100-$200
- *Milwaukee Journal Sunday Inset,* Sept. 6, 1953; glamorous image in a white fur. ....$125-$225
- *Modern Man,* Nov. 1953; vol. 3, no. 5-29; a de Dienes image, playing on the beach. ....$40-$80
- *Modern Screen,* Oct. 1953; vol. 47, no. 5; pretty over-the-shoulder pose in a white fur. ....$40-$80
- *Motion Picture and Television Magazine,* Jan. 1953; vol. LXXXIV, no. 6; from *Niagara,* in a white fur-trim robe. ....$40-$80
- *Motion Picture and Television Magazine,* Nov. 1953; vol. LXXXVI, no. 4; in yellow suit, sitting on a wire table. ....$40-$80
- *Motor World,* June 19, 1953; vol. 4, no. 13; b&w image of Marilyn atop a car. ....$90-$125
- *Movieland,* Jan. 1953; vol. 10, no. 12; glamorous in black gloves and upswept hair. ....$75-$125
- *Movieland,* April 1953; vol. 11, no. 3; sitting on the floor in a purple outfit. ....$70-$125
- *Movieland,* Oct. 1953; vol. 11, no. 9; against a stool in a red negligee. .....$70-$100
- *Movie Life,* Dec. 1953; vol. 17, no. 1; in a white dress and diamond jewelry. ....$75-$125
- *3-D Movie Magazine,* Sept. 1953; inside photos printed 3-D, included glasses. ....$75-$125
- *Movie Pix,* April 1953; vol. 4, no. 3; hand on hip, in a red outfit. ....$75-$125
- *Movie Pix,* Dec. 1953; vol. 5, no. 1; with Lauren Bacall and Betty Grable. .$60-$100
- *Movies,* Feb. 1953; vol. 2, no. 6; in the red *Niagara* dress. ....$75-$125
- *Movie Stars Parade,* Oct. 1953; vol. 13, no. 11; a still from *Blondes.* ....$75-$125
- *Movie World,* Sept. 1953; vol. 4, no. 5; a very short-haired MM in a bow necklace. ....$75-$125
- *People Today* (pocket), July 29, 1953; vol. 7, no. 2; in white fringe bikini, cross-legged on floor....................$20-$40
- *People Today* (pocket), Dec. 2, 1953; vol. 7, no. 11; in a red swimsuit, hugging a white pillar.. ....$20-$40
- *Photo* (digest), July 1953; vol. 2, no. 7; in a yellow bikini, sitting on her feet. ....$50-$80
- *Photoplay,* Feb. 1953; vol. 43, no. 2; in a black dress with a white collar.....$50-$90
- *Photoplay,* Dec. 1953; vol. 53, no. 2; in a white fur with a striped background. ....$50-$90
- *Photoplay Pin-Ups,* no. 4; in a black negligee, holding a fur coat. ....$50-$80
- *Pic,* May 1953; vol. 24, no. 3; in a black halter-style one-piece swimsuit. ....$75-$125

- *Picture Scope,* July 1953; vol. 1, no. 5; wearing one of the gowns from *Blondes.* ....$75-$125
- *Playboy,* Dec. 1953; vol. 1, no. 1; the first issue MM is the centerfold in. ....$1,500-$2,000
- *Pocket Pin-Ups* (pocket), 1953; cute b&w image in a short nightie. ....$100-$175
- *Prevue* (pocket), Jan. 1953; vol. 2, no. 1; b&w candid in the *Niagara* dress. ....$20-$40
- *Redbook,* March 1953; vol. 100, no. 5; wearing a sequined cocktail dress. ....$10-$[illegible]
- *Screen Annual,* 1953; in one of the *Blondes* musical number costumes....$75-$125
- *Screen Fan,* June 1953; vol. 1, no. 6; in a dinner jacket from *Blondes*.......$75-$125
- *Screen Life,* Nov. 1953; vol. 6, no. 5; in a red suit with glass shoes and umbrella. ....$75-$125
- *Screen Stars,* Feb. 1953; vol. 11, no. 1; in a low dress and emerald earrings. ....$75-$125
- *Screen World,* Dec. 1953; vol. 1, no. 2; in the red *Blondes* dress. ....$75-$125
- *See,* Nov. 1953; vol. 12, no. 6; lovely in the famous gold lamé gown. ....$60-$95
- *Show* (pocket), March 1953; vol. 1, no. 7; in a black nightie, on a giant pillow. ....$20-$40
- *Silver Screen,* Oct. 1953; vol. 23, no. 12; one of the famous photos in a white fur. ....$50-$80
- *Song Hits,* Nov. 1953; vol. 17, no. 4; an earlier glamour image. ....$30-$50
- *3-D Star Pin-Ups,* Dec. 1953; vol. 1, no. 1; in a red swimsuit hugging a column. ....$90-$125
- *Sunday News (N.Y.),* Feb. 15, 1953; with Jane Russell in a publicity pose. ....$100-$175
- *Sweet Hearts* (comic), Jan. 1953; no.119; with Richard Widmark. ....$100-$200
- *Tab* (digest), Sept. 1953; in a pink one-piece swimsuit. ....$60-$80
- *Tele-views,* Sept. 1953; 1952 glamour shot...$80-$110
- *Tempo* (pocket), Aug. 31, 1953; vol. 1, no. 13; b&w image with an inset of DiMaggio. ....$20-$40
- *That Girl Marilyn!* (pocket), 1953; entire issue devoted to MM. ....$50-$95
- *The American News,* May 1953; vol. 35; typical glamour photo..............$125-$250
- *TV and Movie Screen,* Nov. 1953; vol. 1, no. 1; typical sexy cover..............$60-$90
- *TV Digest,* March 21, 1953; b&w pose on this Pittsburgh TV guide. ....$100-$130
- *TV Guide* (digest), Jan. 23-29,1953; vol. VI, no. 4; portrait from *Niagara* and an article on censors. ....$300-$400
- *TV Starland,* Nov. 1953; vol. 1, no. 2; dancing with Walter Winchell..........$75-$125
- *TV Today,* May 8, 1953; July 17, 1953; Nov. 13, 1953; Detroit's version of *TV Guide.* ....$100-$150
- *Who's Who in Hollywood 1953,* 1953; vol. 1, no. 8; in a clinging lavender gown. ....$60-$90
- *Why* (digest), June 1953; vol. 1, no. 161; b&w image and sex symbol article. ....$40-$60

1954

- *Art Photography,* Oct. 1954; vol. 6, no. 4-64; standing atop a globe............$40-$60
- *Bold* (pocket), Jan. 1954; vol. 1, no. 1; b&w image with DiMaggio. ....$20-$40
- *Film Stars Album Winter,* 1953-1954; vol. 1, no. 1; glamour shot with shorter hair. ....$60-$100
- *Focus* (pocket), June 1954; vol. 4, no. 7; in the *Niagara* dress with gold hoop earrings. ....$20-$40
- *Hollywood Yearbook 1954*, 1954; vol. 1, no. 5; in a red dress and matching earrings. ....$60-$90
- *Marilyn by Sidney Skolsky,* 1954; entire issue devoted to MM..................$80-$125
- *Miami Daily News,* May 7, 1954; delivered with the Sunday newspaper. ....$125-$200
- *Modern Photography,* Aug. 1954; vol. 18, no. 8; sitting on her feet in a yellow bikini. ....$40-$65

Silver Screen, February 1952, $60-$100.

Chicago Sunday Tribune, May 25, 1952, $100-$200.

People Today, June 18, 1952, $20-$40.

See, July 1952, $75-$125.

I Confess, September 1952, $100-$175.

Sunday Mirror, September 7, 1952, $400-$450.

- *Modern Screen,* March 1954; vol. 48, no. 4; in a ruffled blouse with longer hair. ....$40-$60
- *Modern Screen,* Sept. 1954; vol. 48, no. 10; holding up diamonds from *Blondes.* ....$40-$60
- *Movie Fan,* July 1954; vol. 9, no. 4; glamour image wearing pearls....$75-$125
- *Movieland's Annual 1954,* 1954; in a one-strap fuchsia gown. ....$65-$100
- *Movieland,* Feb. 1954; vol. 12, no. 2; in a rhinestone-studded black dress. ....$60-$100
- *Movieland,* Nov. 1954; vol. 12, no. 11; smiling in the one-strap fuchsia dress. ....$60-$100
- *Movie Life,* Aug. 1954; vol. 17, no. 9; lowering one strap of a bathing suit. ....$60-$100
- *Movie Life Yearbook,* 1954; b&w image in a white sweater....$40-$65
- *Movies,* June 1954; vol. 3, no. 2; publicity shot from *How To Marry A Millionaire.* ....$75-$100
- *Movie Spotlight,* Oct. 1954; vol. 5, no. 5; a wide-eyed Monroe with long earrings. ....$65-$95
- *Movie Stars Parade,* March 1954; vol. 14, no. 4; in a gold lamé gown, tinted silver. ....$65-$100
- *Movie Stars Parade,* Sept. 1954; vol. 15, no. 1; wearing a sexy black lace gown. ....$65-$100
- *Movie Time,* Feb. 1954; vol. 2, no. 6; showing off a diamond necklace. ....$65-$100
- *Movie World,* May 1954; vol. 5, no. 3; in a dark one-piece bathing suit. ...$65-$100
- *Night & Day,* Aug. 1954; vol. 6, no. 8; the first star to have a cover alone. ....$65-$100
- *Now* (digest), Jan. 1954; vol. 1, no. 2; candid photo with Joe DiMaggio at a restaurant. ....$40-$60
- *Pic,* June 1954; vol. 25, no. 5; singing to the troops in Korea. ....$60-$90
- *Picture Life* (pocket), April 1954; vol. 1, no. 3; posing in a pair of red long underwear....$20-$40
- *Prevue* (pocket), Jan. 1954; vol. 4, no. 1; a close-up, wearing emerald earrings. ....$20-$40
- *Roto Sunday Magazine,* March 28, 1954; wearing a corset, delivered with the paper....$100-$200
- *Screen Annual 1954,* 1954; holding up a polka-dot scarf....$60-$95
- *Screen Stars,* Nov. 1954; vol. 12, no. 5; a pretty, close-up portrait. ....$60-$95
- *Screen Stories,* Nov. 1954; vol. 52, no. 5; in white costume from *There's No Business Like Show Business.* ....$40-$65
- *See,* Nov. 1954; vol. 13, no. 6; in a corset with fishnet stockings. ....$60-$90
- *Silver Screen,* April 1954; vol. 24, no. 6; sitting in a red lacy negligee....$40-$65
- *Sir!,* April 1954; vol. 11, no. 7; in a red dress with green drapery behind....$40-$65
- *Song Fan,* July 1954; vol. 1, no. 3; with Robert Mitchum in *River of No Return.* ....$40-$60
- *3-D Hollywood Pin-Ups,* Jan. 1954; cheesecake pose in a one-piece suit. ....$90-$130
- *Sunday Mirror (N.Y.),* March 21, 1954; Weekend Sunday section, sexy portrait. ....$125-$200
- *Tempo* (pocket), March 8, 1954; vol. 2, no. 10; in a swimsuit, posed along jagged rocks....$20-$40
- *Tempo* (pocket), Sept. 6, 1954; vol. 3, no. 9; almost full-body photo in red lace. ....$20-$40
- *Tempo* (pocket), Nov. 8, 1954; vol. 3, no. 19; vivid image in the red *Niagara* dress. ....$20-$40
- *The Dynamo,* 1954-55; a Fox Studio publication....$100-$140
- *The Hotel Dixie Host,* Dec. 18, 1954; a digest-size guide to New York. ....$50-$100

1955

- *Behind the Scene* (pocket), July 1953; vol. 1, no. 8; wearing a diamond necklace. ....$20-$40

- *Bold* (pocket), Jan. 1955; vol. 2, no. 1; sitting Indian-style in a white bikini. ....$20-$40
- *Boston Sunday Herald,* Jan. 23, 1955; Weekend Sunday section, sitting in a chair. ....$100-$200
- *Cabaret,* July 1955; vol. 1, no. 3; b&w image, sitting in a bubble bath. ....$40-$75
- *Cartoon Cuties* (digest), Sept. 1955; no. 2; a young glamour shot from *Love Happy*........$100-$150
- *Down Beat,* July 27, 1955; in the blowing white dress from *The Seven Year Itch.* ....$30-$60
- *Focus* (pocket), Jan. 1955, vol. 5, no. 1, sitting on a step in a nightie........$20-$40
- *Focus* (pocket), Nov. 1955; vol. 5, no. 1; the classic gold lamé image.........$20-$40
- *He* (pocket), Feb. 1955; vol. 2, no. 3; cute in a corset from *River*...............$20-$40
- *Inside Hollywood Annual,* 1955; vol. 1, no. 1; coyly looking over her shoulder. ....$60-$90
- *Modern Man,* March 1955; vol. 4, no. 9-45; puckering up for the camera...$40-$65
- *Man to Man,* May 1955; vol. 6, no. 6; with white skirt blowing up..............$40-$65
- *Modern Screen,* June 1955; vol. 49, no. 7; modeling a black fur. ....$40-$65
- *Modern Screen,* Oct. 1955; vol. 49, no. 11; wearing a white terry cloth robe. ....$40-$65
- *Modern Screen Pin-Ups,* 1955; slipping a fur stole behind her back. ....$50-$90
- *Movieland,* June 1955; vol. 13, no. 5; reclining in a red chair. ....$75-$125
- *Movieland,* Dec. 1955; vol. 13, no. 12; three images in a sweater.............$75-$125
- *Movie Life,* April 1955; vol. 18, no. 5; looking over her shoulder. ....$70-$90
- *Movie Play,* Nov. 1955; vol. 9, no. 6; in the red *Niagara* dress. ....$70-$90
- *Movies,* Dec. 1955; sharing a cover with Kim Novak...................................$20-$40
- *Movie Stars Parade,* Sept. 1955; vol. 15, no. 10; in a white dress with her arms up. ....$60-$95
- *Movie World,* June 1955; vol. 6, no. 3; in her "Heatwave" costume from *There's No Business Like Show Business.* ....$75-$125
- *Parts Pups,* May 1955; put out by Napa Parts, riding an elephant. ....$100-$175
- *Pic* (digest), Sept. 1955; vol. 26, no. 4; in her elephant-riding costume ......$40-$65
- *Picture Life* (pocket), Feb. 1955; vol. 2, no. 1; holding a red cover-up to her side. ....$20-$40
- *Picture Scope* (digest), May 1955; vol. 3, no. 4; in a red negligee with a navy blue background.........$40-$65
- *Picture Week* (pocket), Feb. 26, 1955; vol. 1, no. 1; cute b&w image, in a blouse and with a smile. ....$20-$40
- *Picture Week* (pocket), June 4, 1955; vol. 1, no. 14; riding an elephant at Madison Square Garden........$20-$40
- *Picture Week* (pocket), July 16, 1955; vol. 1, no. 17; in the tiger-stripe dress from *Itch.* ....$20-$40
- *Pin-Ups Past and Present,* 1955; vol. 1, no. 1; b&w image for this historical look at sex symbols. ....$40-$80
- *Redbook,* July 1955; V105, no. 3; a close-up in the bathrobe from *Itch.*......$40-$70
- *Screen Annual Pin-Ups,* 1955; sitting on steps in a black nightie. ....$40-$70
- *Screen Hits Annual,* 1955; a full-length cheesecake pose in red lace. ....$30-$60
- *Screen Life,* March 1955; vol. 8, no. 1; sitting on a wire table in a yellow suit. ....$75-$125
- *Screen Stars,* July 1955; vol. 13, no. 4; in tiger dress from *Itch.*..............$75-$125
- *Screen Stories,* July 1955; vol. 54, no. 1; *Itch* is depicted. ....$40-$65
- *See,* July 1955; vol. 14, no. 4; in a black one-piece swimsuit. ....$75-$125
- *Tab* (digest), Aug. 1955; vol. 5, no. 3; in the red *Niagara* dress and earrings. ....$40-$65
- *Tempo and Quick* (pocket), Feb. 14, 1955; vol. 4, no. 7; posing inside a large heart. ....$20-$40
- *Tempo and Quick* (pocket), July 4, 1955; vol. 5, no. 1; posing with a giant firecracker........$20-$40
- *Tempo and Quick* (pocket), Nov. 1, 1955; vol. 5, no. 12; cute in a yellow swimsuit. ....$20-$40

Look, September 9, 1952, $60-$80

Movieland, October 1952, $70-$125.

Movie Pix, October 1952, $75-$125.

Eye, November 1952, $50-$80.

Sunday News, November 30, 1952, $90-$150.

Screen Fan, December 1952, $75-$125.

- *Tempo and Quick* (pocket), Dec. 27, 1955; vol. 5, no. 16; surrounded by wrapped gifts at her feet. ....$20-$40
- *The American Weekly,* Sept. 25, 1955; in black gloves and fur; newspaper section. ....$90-$125
- *The Marilyn Monroe Story* (pocket), no. 3; entire issue devoted to her, Marilyn in red. ....$50-$100
- *The National Police Gazette,* Feb. 1955; vol. 160, no. 9; with skirt blowing up from *The Seven Year Itch.* ....$45-$70
- *True Romance,* Oct. 1955; vol. 61, no. 2; a young Marilyn in a yellow sweater. ....$125-$175
- *TV Today* (digest), Aug. 27, 1955; Detroit-based TV guide. ....$100-$125
- *U.S. Camera,* July 1955; vol. XVIII, no. 7; reclining in a leather chair from *The Seven Year Itch.* ....$40-$60
- *Vue* (digest), Jan. 1955; vol. 6, no. 6; wearing a tight red gown. ....$40-$60
- *Who's Who in Hollywood,* 1955; vol. 1, no. 10; a large laughing portrait from *The Seven Year Itch.* ....$40-$65

1956

- *Films In Review* (digest), Oct. 1956; vol. VII, no. 8; a cover from *Bus Stop.* ....$40-$60
- *Film Life,* June 1956; vol. 1, no. 5; a lovely pose in a white strapped dress. ....$70-$90
- *Guns,* July 1956; vol. 2, no. 7-19; being taught how to shoot a gun. ....$70-$100
- *Look,* May 29, 1956; vol. 20, no. 11; curled up in bed with a sheet. ....$30-$50
- *Modern Man,* June 1956; vol. V, no. 12-60; at a table wearing a red velvet dress. ....$40-$60
- *Modern Screen,* Nov. 1956; wearing a black fur and a serious face. ....$40-$60
- *Movie Life,* April 1956; vol. 19, no. 5; in a black dress decorated with beads. ....$65-$100
- *Movie Stars Parade,* Feb. 1956; vol. 16, no. 3; a close-up, smiling. ....$65-$100
- *Photoplay,* Oct. 1956; vol. 50, no. 4; several images in her *Bus Stop* costume. ....$50-$100
- *Picture Digest* (digest), Feb. 1956; vol. 29, no. 4; warming up by a fireplace, in long underwear. ....$40-$60
- *Picture Week* (pocket), June 5, 1956; vol. 2, no. 8; a red-haired MM in black fur. ....$20-$40
- *Rave,* Aug. 1956; vol. 11, no. 5; glamour image, 28 pages on MM. ....$50-$80
- *Screen Stars,* July 1956; vol. 14, no. 4; wearing a tight red dress. ....$70-$100
- *Sir!,* Oct. 1956; vol. 13, no. 10; the famous image in the gold lamé dress. ....$60-$100
- *Tab* (digest), Dec. 1956; vol. 6, no. 5; sitting in a two-piece yellow suit. ....$50-$80
- *The Male Point of View* (pocket), Feb. 1956; vol. 2, no. 4; reclining in a skimpy yellow bikini. ....$20-$40
- *The National Police Gazette,* March 1956; vol. 161, no. 3; in a button-decorated bikini top. ....$50-$80
- *The Press Photographer,* 1956; an *Itch* cover. ....$80-$125
- *Time,* May 14, 1956; vol. 1XVII, no. 20; an absolutely lovely artwork portrait. ....$75-$125

1957

- *Filmland,* Dec. 1957; vol. 7, no. 6; in the tiger dress from *Itch.* ....$70-$100
- *Hollywood Screen Parade,* March 1957; showing off a diamond necklace. ....$40-$65
- *Man to Man Annual,* Spring 1957; wearing a white terry bathrobe. ....$50-$100
- *Movieland,* April 1957; vol. 15, no. 4; close-up from *Millionaire.* ....$50-$100
- *Movie Screen Yearbook,* 1957; no. 3; with bangs and big earrings. ....$50-$80
- *Screen Stories,* July 1957; vol. 56, no. 7; a pretty, soft-looking image in stripes. ....$40-$60
- *Sunday Mirror (N.Y.),* June 22, 1957; newspaper section, in a black-sequined gown. ....$100-$200

- *The National Police Gazette,* Oct. 1957; vol. CLXII, no. 10; a typical glamorous photograph. ....$30-$50
- *True Romance,* Jan. 1957; vol. 63, no. 5; in a red sweater and scarf.........$75-$125
- *True Strange,* Aug. 1957; several artwork images. ....$30-$55

1958

- *Detective Cases,* July 1958; vol. 3, no. 4; hugging a white pillar. ....$30-$50
- *Inside Story,* April 1958; vol. 4, no. 4; wearing a sexy lacy negligee. ....$30-$50
- *Loco,* Oct, 1958; an artist's internretation [illegible]
- *Movie Mirror,* May 1958; vol. 2, no. 7; glamourous with her eyes half-closed. ....$30-$50
- *Parade,* Dec. 7, 1958; newspaper section, candid from *Some Like It Hot*....$60-$90
- *Sunbathing Review,* Fall 1958; nudist spiral-bound sepia cover, young MM. ....$70-$100

1959

- *Chicago Tribune Magazine,* Nov. 17, 1959; newspaper section, several images in a dress. ....$100-$150
- *Cosmopolitan,* March 1959; vol. 146, no. 3; an illustration by John Whitcomb, all in white. ....$50-$100
- *Family Weekly,* Feb. 22, 1959; newspaper section, posing in front of Niagara Falls. ....$55-$100
- *Inside Story,* May 1959; in her elephant-riding costume. ....$30-$50
- *LIFE,* April 20, 1959; vol. 46, no. 16; playfully biting on diamonds. ....$20-$40
- *LIFE,* Nov. 9, 1959; vol. 47, no. 19; jumping in a black-sequined spangle dress. ....$20-$40
- *National Enquirer,* March 15-21, 1959; vol. 33, no. 28; b&w image on this early scandal issue. ....$75-$100
- *Pictorial and TV View,* March 15, 1959, the subject of an artwork cover......$50-$80
- *The National Police Gazette,* Jan. 1959; vol. 164, no. 1; looking over her shoulder and smiling. ....$40-$60

1960

- *American Weekly,* Dec. 11, 1960; newspaper section, with Clark Gable.......$60-$90
- *Cosmopolitan,* Dec. 1960; vol. 149, no. 6; with Gable in *The Misfits*. ....$40-$60
- *Films In Review* (digest), Oct. 1960; vol. XI, no. 8; in a scene from *Let's Make Love*. ....$20-$40
- *Inside Story,* July 1960; vol. 6, no. 5; a revealing overhead cleavage photo. ....$20-$40
- *LIFE,* Aug. 15, 1960; vol. 49, no. 7; a close-up with Yves Montand. ....$20-$40
- *Modern Screen,* Dec. 1960; vol. 54, no. 12; a tight close-up, wearing dark gloves. ....$25-$45
- *The Californian,* Aug. 19, 1960; a *Love* costume shot. ....$75-$100
- *The National Police Gazette,* Jan. 1960; vol. 165, no. 1; at the *Some Like It Hot* premiere. ....$40-$60
- *This Week,* Aug. 20, 1960; from newspaper, with Yves Montand................$40-$60
- *This Week,* Dec. 11, 1960; from newspaper, wearing a red sweater............$50-$80
- *TV Life,* Oct. 1960; half-cover, in a black dress and gloves. ....$20-$40
- *TV and Movie Screen,* 9, 1960; vol. 7, no. 10; in a white halter dress. ....$35-$50

1961

- *Blast,* Jan. 1961; a publicity photo from *Love*. ....$30-$50
- *Esquire,* March 1961; vol. 1V, no. 3; a painting of her in a *Misfits* costume. ....$20-$40
- *Family Weekly,* Feb. 26, 1961; from newspaper, from *The Misfits*. ....$40-$70
- *Hollywood Tattler,* Nov. 1961; a sad-looking close-up portrait. ....$20-$45
- *Infinity,* May 1961; costume-fitting for riding the elephant. ....$75-$125
- *Look,* Jan. 3, 1961; with Clark Gable. ....$15-$30
- *Modern Screen,* Oct. 1961; vol. 55, no. 10; on the floor with a tiger rug.....$25-$45

Cheesecake, 1953, $75-$125.

Screen Annual, 1953, $75-$125.

That Girl Marilyn!, 1953, $50-$95.

- *Screen Stories,* Feb. 1961; vol. 60, no. 2; wearing a bright orange blouse. ....$20-$40
- *Screen Stories,* May 1961; vol. 60, no. 5; wearing a black hair net in *The Misfits.* ....$20-$40
- *The National Police Gazette,* May 1961; vol. 166, no. 5; a pretty close-up, wearing hoop earrings. ....$25-$45

1962

- *Films In Review* (digest), Oct. 1962; vol. XIII, no. 8; a glamour image on this tribute cover. ....$20-$40
- *LIFE,* June 22, 1962; vol. 52, no. 25; in a blue terry bathrobe from *Something's Got To Give.* ....$20-$35
- *LIFE,* Aug. 17, 1962; vol. 53, no. 7; a farewell in a beige fur hat from *Something's Got To Give.* ....$20-$25
- *Marilyn Monroe—Her Last Untold Secrets,* 1962; entire issue on her life and death. ....$40-$80
- *Marilyn Monroe—Her Tragic Life,* 1962; entire issue on her life and death. ....$40-$80
- *Marilyn's Life Story by Dell,* 1962; entire issue on her life and death............$40-$80
- *Marilyn Monroe—The Complete Story of Her Life, Her Loves and Her Death,* 1962; entire issue on her life and death. ....$40-$80
- *Modern Screen,* Nov. 1962; vol. 56, no. 50; a sad, downcast face from *Something's Got to Give.* ....$30-$40
- *Movieland and TV Time,* Nov. 1962 ; vol. 20, no. 5; in sequins at the 1961 Golden Globes. ....$30-$50
- *Silver Screen,* Dec. 1962; vol. 28, no. 8; a sad-looking memorial shot from *Let's Make Love.* ....$20-$40
- *The National Police Gazette,* Oct. 1962; vol. 167, no. 9; looking happy at the premiere of *Some Like It Hot.* ....$35-$55

Marilyn Monroe Pin-Ups, 1953, $100-$200.

Motion Picture and Television Magazine, January 1953, $40-$80.

Movieland, January 1953, $75-$125.

1963

- *Films In Review* (digest), June-July 1963; vol. XIV, no. 6; a wardrobe shot from *Something's Got To Give.* ....$15-$35
- *Photoplay,* Jan. 1963; vol. 63, no. 6; holding up a striped see-through scarf. ....$25-$45
- *This Week Magazine,* April 12, 1963; newspaper section, half-cover in hat. ....$35-$45

1964

- *LIFE,* Aug. 7, 1964; vol. 57, no. 6; a head-and-shoulders portrait. ....$20-$40

1965

- *Fact,* May-June 1965; a smiling b&w portrait by Bert Stern. ....$10-$20
- *Ladies Home Companion,* Jan. 1965; vol. 3, no. 2; a sad-looking face on this digest. ....$25-$40
- *Screen Legends,* Aug. 1965; vol. 1, no. 2; Marilyn and Paul Newman by an artist. ....$25-$40

1966

- *Coronet* (digest), Jan. 1966; vol. 4, no. 1; in a red costume from *Blondes.* ....$20-$40

1968

- *Avant Garde,* March 1968; no. 2; an artsy Stern shot in sepia tones............$20-$40
- *Modern Photography,* Sept. 1968; biting a strand of pearls. ....$20-$40

1969

- *The Blade Sunday Magazine,* Nov. 2, 1969; newspaper section, half-cover in a fur. ....$20-$35
- *Detroit News Sunday Magazine,* June 22, 1969; newspaper section, *The Misfits* portrait....$20-$30

1970

- *Hollywood Studio Magazine,* Sept. 1970; vol. 5, no. 5; being fitted for a costume by Travilla....$20-$35

1971

- *Pageant* (digest), March 1971; vol. 26, no. 9; a young Norma Jeane in the wind. ....$30-$50
- *Screen Stories,* Sept. 1971; vol. 70, no. 10; the famous image in the white fur. ....$15-$25

1972

- *LIFE,* Sept. 8, 1972; vol. 73, no. 10; reclining on pillows, in a fancy slip. ......$5-$10
- *Ms.,* Aug. 1972; vol. 1, no. 2; a glamorous Monroe face in a circle. ....$5-$10
- *Newsweek,* Oct. 16, 1972; vol. LXXX, no. 16; a joyous MM in black sequins. ....$10-$15

1973

- *Film Comment,* May-June 1973; the cast of *The Misfits* is featured.............$10-$20
- *Hollywood Studio Magazine,* Aug. 1973; vol. 4; holding up an eight ball.....$25-$35
- *Interview,* 1973; no. 19; wearing a white fluffy fur....$10-$20
- *Ladies Home Journal,* July 1973; vol. XC, no. 7; a lovely portrait taken by Stern. ....$10-$15
- *Liberty Fall,* 1973; vol. 1, no. 10; many images of her on an artwork cover. ....$10-$20
- *Parade,* Aug. 5, 1973; newspaper section, a beige fur hat....$10-$20
- *The Atlantic Monthly,* Aug. 1973; vol. 232, no. 2; b&w photo by Milton Greene. ....$10-$25
- *Time,* July 16, 1973; vol. 102, no. 3; a created image of MM and Norman Mailer. ....$15-$30
- *Where It's At,* vol. 2, no. 8; b&w pose from *Hot*....$20-$40

1974

- *Sleazy Scandals* (comic), 1974; an X-rated comic, art of *Golden Dreams*....$20-$40

1975

- *Chicago Sun-Times Magazine—Midwest,* Aug. 17, 1975; newspaper section, white dress blowing....$10-$20
- *Films In Review* (digest), June-July 1975; vol. XXVI, no. 6; publicity photo from *Eve*....$10-$20
- *Motion Picture,* Nov. 1975; vol. 64, no. 777; on the end of a sofa corner. ...$10-$20
- *Photoplay,* Sept. 1975; vol. 88, no. 3; holding up a mink, surrounded by presents. ....$10-$20

1976

- *Chicago Tribune Magazine,* Nov. 14, 1976; newspaper section, in the gold lamé dress....$20-$30
- *Hollywood Studio Magazine,* Feb. 1976; nude in the *New Wrinkle* pose. ......$20-$40
- *In the Know,* March 1976; vol. 2, no. 3; a beautiful portrait from *Give*.........$10-$20
- *The Velvet Light Trap,* Fall 1976; no. 16; b&w profile in a glamorous lamé gown. ....$10-$20

Laff, January 1953, $75-$125

Screen Stars, February 1953, $75-$125.

Photoplay, February 1953, $50-$90.

Sunday News,
February 15, 1953,
$100-$175.

Redbook,
March 1953,
$40-$65.

PIC,
June 1954,
$60-$90.

1977

- *American Classic Screen,* Nov.-Dec. 1977; vol. 2, no. 2; an unflattering artist's rendition. .... $10-$20
- *Film Collectors World,* Sept. 1, 1977; no. 22; tinted cover in a one-piece swimsuit. .... $10-$20

1979

- *Films In Review,* March 1979; vol. XXX, no. 3; a soft, pretty portrait from *Something's Got To Give.* .... $10-$20
- *Marilyn Monroe by Bonomo,* 1979; no. 78; a tiny grocery store check-out issue. .... $10-$20
- *National Enquirer,* May 1979; as the main subject on cover. .... $5-$10
- *San Francisco Datebook,* Feb. 11, 1979; newspaper section, white skirt from *The Seven Year Itch.* .... $10-$20

1980

- *Celebrity Skin,* 1980; artwork cover, cross-eyed in gold lamé. .... $10-$20
- *San Francisco Datebook,* Nov. 9-15, 1980; newspaper section, *Niagara* portrait. .... $10-$20
- *Screen Greats: Monroe,* 1980; vol. 2; entire issue on her, in a corset from *River Of No Return.* .... $10-$20

1981

- *After Dark,* Sept. 1981; vol. 14, no. 3-4; a romantic windswept image in sequins. .... $20-$30
- *San Francisco Datebook,* Nov. 1, 1981; newspaper section, MM on half the cover. .... $10-$20
- *Hollywood Studio Magazine,* Dec. 1981; vol. 15, no. 4; with Jane Russell in *Gentlemen Prefer Blondes.* .... $10-$20
- *LIFE,* Oct. 1981; vol. 4, no. 10; leaning back in a turquoise swimsuit. .... $10-$20
- *Sunday Life,* March 15, 1981; in a tinted glamour pose. .... $10-$20

1982

- *Collectibles Illustrated,* Nov.-Dec. 1982; vol. 1, no. 4; leaning back in a turquoise swimsuit. .... $10-$20
- *Film Comment,* Sept.-Oct. 1982; vol. 18, no. 5; sultry in a black lacy dress .... $10-$20
- *LIFE,* Aug. 1982; vol. 5, no. 8; a lovely 1962 portrait by Stern. .... $10-$20
- *Sunday News Magazine* (N.Y.), Aug. 1, 1982; newspaper section, holding a mirror. .... $10-$20
- *The Globe,* Nov. 23, 1982; main star on this far-fetched issue. .... $5-$10
- *The Newsday Magazine,* Aug. 1, 1982; newspaper section, artwork portrait. .... $5-$10

1983

- *Butterick Sewing World,* Winter 1983; vol. 15, no. 4; in a pretty ruffled, off-the-shoulder top. .... $10-$20
- *Entertainment N.Y.,* Feb. 1983; typical glamour pose. .... $10-$20
- *Human Digest* (digest), 1983; wearing the one-strap *Millionaire* dress. .... $30-$40
- *Films In Review* (digest), Aug.-Sept. 1983; vol. XXXV, no. 7; a scene from *The Misfits* is featured. .... $10-$20

1984

- *American Photographer,* July 1984; vol. XIII, no. 1; on a bicycle, portraying Lillian Russell. .... $10-$20
- *San Francisco Datebook,* Feb. 12, 1984; newspaper section, famous white dress blowing up. .... $10-$20

1985

- *Crossfire* (comic); June 1985; no. 12; fantasy artwork image of MM in bed. ....$10-$20
- *Hollywood Studio Magazine,* Aug. 1985; vol. 18, no. 8; pretty portrait from *Millionaire.*....................$5-$10
- *Hollywood Then & Now,* Dec. 1985; vol. 18, no. 12; the common image in the white fur. ....$5-$10
- *Horoscope,* March 1985; a candid image in a white fur and a smile. ....$10-$20
- *Picture Week,* Oct. 14, 1985; a 1962 portrait taken by Stern.............. $5-$10

1986

- *Esquire,* March 1986; vol. 105, no. 3; in pearl-drop earrings and a white fur. ....$5-$10
- *Films In Review* (digest), May 1986; vol. XXXVII, no. 5; a scene from *Don't Bother To Knock*....................$5-$10
- *Filthy Funnies* (comic); Aug. 1986; appropriate artwork, considering the title. ....$5-$10
- *National Examiner,* March 25, 1986; a tabloid cover appearance. ....$5-$10
- *Nevada,* Dec. 1986; a portrait of *The Misfits* cast, 1961 ....$10-$20
- *Picture Week,* Sept. 1, 1986; a young portrait of Norma Jeane......................$5-$10
- *The Sharper Image Catalog,* July 1986; a beautiful airbrush work of Norma Jeane. ....$5-$10

1987

- *Celebrity Focus,* Aug. 1987; vol. 1, no. 8; in a sad-looking portrait from 1962. ....$5-$10
- *Gallery,* Sept. 1987; wearing the very well-known gold lamé. ....$5-$10
- *Hollywood Then & Now,* Aug. 1987; vol. 20, no. 8; a *Niagara* shot is on this tribute issue. ....$5-$10
- *Michael's Thing Weekly,* Aug. 24, 1987; vol. 17, no. 34; in a black spaghetti-strap dress....................$15-$20
- *Newsweek-The Fifties,* 1987; a typical glamour image of the star. ....$5-$10
- *Palm Springs Life,* Aug. 1987; vol. XXIX, no. 12; wearing a sexy black lace dress. ....$5-$10
- *Parlcé,* July 1987; vol. 13, no. 2, sitting on rocks in a light blue suit..........$20-$40
- *People Extra Weekly,* Spring 1987; this issue had to be purchased through the mail....................$5-$10
- *Screen Greats Presents Marilyn,* 1987; extra-thick issue entirely on MM. .....$5-$10

1988

- *American Movie Classics,* Aug. 1988; no. 3; a close-up portrait, wearing the gold lamé....................$5-$10
- *Fibrearts,* vol. 15, no. 2; a psychedelic colorized image. ....$5-$10
- *Hollywood Studio Magazine,* Oct. 1988; vol. 21, no. 10; sharing the cover in a glamour pose. ....$5-$10
- *L.A. Style,* Feb. 1988; vol. 111, no. 9; extra-large b&w cover in New York City, 1955. ....$20-$40
- *The Sun Sign Astrologer,* Aug. 1988; cute photo holding jewelry..................$5-$10

1989

- *American Heritage,* Feb. 1989; vol. 40, no. 1; a wistful look in a white sweater. ....$10-$20
- *Art & Auction,* Sept. 1989; vol. XII, no. 2; a colorful artwork cover. ....$5-$10
- *Condé Nast Traveler,* Aug. 1989; on the beach filming *Hot*...........................$5-$10
- *Facets,* March 1988; vol. 10, no. 15; a public TV guide in Alabama, art cover. ....$5-$10
- *National Examiner,* Nov. 7, 1989; another cover to help boost sales. ....$5-$10

Movie World, May 1954, $65-$100.

Man To Man, May 1955, $40-$65.

Screen Stars, July 1955, $75-$125.

Cartoon Cuties, September 1955, $100-$150.

Film Life, June 1956, $70-$90.

Sir!, October 1956, $60-$100.

1990

- *American Movie Classics,* Dec. 1990; vol. 3, no. 12; looking out the window in *The Seven Year Itch.* ....$5-$10
- *Fortunoff Jewelry Catalog,* 1990; a publicity shot from *Asphalt Jungle.* ....$5-$10
- *Screen Greats Hollywood Nostalgia,* no. 1; a typical Marilyn in a black fur. ...$5-$10
- *Sports Collectors Digest,* April 20, 1990; vol. 17, no. 16; a colorized photo, holding a baseball bat. ....$10-$15
- *Sun,* Sept. 11, 1990; vol. 8, no. 37; a glamour picture included on the cover. ....$5-$10
- *Weekly World News,* Dec. 18, 1990; yet another exciting tabloid appearance. ....$5-$10

1991

- *Hollywood Then & Now,* Oct. 1991; vol. 24, no. 10; in a green velvet dress from *River.* ....$5-$10
- *In Vermont,* Aug. 1991; a sexy and glamorous photograph. ....$5-$10
- *Personality Classics-Marilyn Monroe,* 1991; by Revolutionary Comics. ....$5-$10
- *The Sharper Image Catalog,* vol. 2, no. 3; looking like a ballerina for Greene. ....$10-$15
- *Woman's World,* Dec. 17, 1991; vol. XII, no. 51; smiling and joyful in a white fur. ....$5-$10

1992

- *Hollywood Then & Now,* June-July 1992; vol. 25, no. 5; on half the cover, in a director's chair. ....$5-$10
- *Hollywood Then & Now,* Aug. 1992; vol. 25, no. 6; a glamorous photograph. ....$5-$10
- *Hot Air,* Oct.-Nov. 1992; b&w glamour pose on this airline issue. ....$15-$25
- *Hot Spots,* July-Aug. 1992 (summer issue); looking sultry in gold lamé. ....$10-$15
- *McCall's,* July 1992; vol. CXIX, no. 10; a cute portrait in a black turtleneck. ..$5-$10
- *National Examiner,* Oct. 6, 1992; another appearance on a scandal issue. ....$5-$10
- *People Weekly,* Aug. 10, 1992; vol. 38, no. 6; a 1962 sad portrait taken by Stern. ....$5-$10
- *The Sharper Image Catalog,* June 1992; a stunning young Norma Jeane by a net. ....$20-$30
- *Weekly World News,* Sept. 29, 1992; continuing to appear on tabloids. ....$5-$10

1993

- *Autograph Collector,* April 1993; vol. 2, no. 4; a full-body profile in the gold lamé gown. ....$5-$10
- *Movie Collectors World,* April 23, 1993; no. 419; with Jane Russell in *Gentlemen Prefer Blondes.* ....$5-$10
- *Marilyn by Revolutionary Comics,* 1993; devoted to her life and death theories. ....$10-$15
- *Tailwinds Catalog,* 1993; in Korea, standing on top of a plane. ....$25-$40
- *Visions Magazine,* Spring 1993; no. 9; a Sam Shaw photo, holding her hair. ....$5-$10

1994

- *Camera & Darkroom,* July 1994; vol. 16, no. 7; an Eve Arnold photo from *The Misfits.* ....$5-$10
- *Collect!,* June 1994; in a ruffle blouse, with longer hair. ....$5-$10
- *Premiere Telecard Magazine,* Feb. 1994; vol. 2, no. 2; a young Norma Jeane on the beach in pink. ....$5-$10
- *Remember,* Aug.-Sept. 1994; a blue-tinted image of MM and DiMaggio. ....$5-$10
- *Marilyn by Starlog Group,* 1994; entire issue on her, optical 3-D cover image. ....$5-$15
- *Who,* May 2, 1994; no. 114; a sexy glamour photograph. ....$5-$10

1995

- *American Movie Classics,* Feb. 1995; vol. 8, no. 2; a smiling Marilyn in the black lace dress. ....$5-$10
- *American Photo,* March-April 1995; an Eve Arnold portrait, in a car from *The Misfits.* ....$5-$10
- *Collecting,* April 1995; vol. 1, no. 1; throwing her head back laughing. ....$5-$10
- *Digital Hollywood Awards Catalog,* Feb. 22, 1995; in a white lamé gown. .....$5-$10
- *Image Laserdisc Preview,* Jan. 1995; no. 12; a color publicity still from *River Of No Return.* ....$5-$10
- *The Sciences,* Nov.-Dec. 1995; vol. 35, no. 6; a pop-art-oriented artwork cover. ....$5-$10
- *Stamps,* May-June 1995; a well-done artwork cover. ....$5-$10

1996

- *Dance & The Arts,* July-Aug. 1996; vol. 14, no. 1; a rare candid, in a black mink and a gown. ....$10-$15
- *Entertainment Weekly,* Fall 1996; a 1962 profile, holding beads by Stern. .....$5-$10

1997

- *American Photo,* June-July 1997; vol. 111, no. 3; a portrait from 1962 by Stern. ....$5-$10
- *Cable TV,* Dec. 1997; vol. 1, no. 1; a smiling b&w glamour photo. ....$5-$10
- *Collect,* Dec. 1997; a common publicity glamour photo. ....$5-$10
- *Doll Collector,* Jan. 1997; Franklin Mint's $500 MM doll. ....$5-$15
- *Drive-In Cinema,* Feb. 1997; no. 2; a glamorous, sultry Monroe. ....$10-$15
- *Ocean Drive,* Oct. 1997; a less common white fur frontal shot. ....$10-$15
- *Playboy,* Jan. 1997; vol. 44, no. 1; wrapped up in a black sweater. ....$10-$20
- *The Red Diaries* (comic), no. 1; art of Marilyn and the Kennedys. ....$10-$15
- *Worth,* Oct. 1997; vol. 6, no. 10; a full-body profile, in a blue swimsuit. ....$5-$10

1998-2002

U.S. Marilyn covers are generally worth the cover price only.

Partial U.S. Cover Appearances

Below is a list of issues in which Marilyn appears on part of the cover. Those listed are only a sampling of her partial cover appearances, and their values are much less than a full-cover appearance. Each collector has to decide for himself how much he is willing to pay for these shared partial covers. These titles serve only as a sampling of what has been published. They are generally worth $15-$30.

- *Movie Teen,* Sept. 1951
- *Sensation,* Jan. 1954
- *Private Lives,* May 1955
- *Inside Story,* Oct. 1956
- *Hush-Hush,* Sept. 1960 and Aug. 1956
- *Look,* Oct. 23, 1951 and June 3, 1952
- *Stateside,* Feb. 1954
- *True Police Cases,* Jan. 1955
- *Movie World,* Feb. 1956
- *Inside Hollywood,* May 1960
- *Suppressed,* Sept. 1954
- *TV,* Sept. 1955
- *Sir!,* May 1956 and Aug. 1955
- *Cavalier,* Aug. 1961 and March 1960
- *Colliers,* Aug. 1953, July 1954, and Aug. 1956
- *Confidential,* Aug. 1953, Sept. 1955, May 1957, May 1956, Nov. 1956, and May 1954
- *Bunk,* Feb. 1956
- *On The QT,* July 1961 and Jan. 1963
- *The Lowdown,* April 1955 and Jan. 1963
- *Tip-Off,* Aug. 1957
- *Uncensored,* Feb. 1962
- *Whisper,* April 1957
- *Playboy,* Sept. 1955
- *Top Secret,* April 1959
- *Pic,* Feb. 1954
- *Police Dragnet,* Sept. 1955

True Romance, January 1957, $75-$125.

Family Weekly, February 1961, $40-$70.

Cine Universal, September 1962 (Mexico), $90-$130.

Foreign Cover Appearances

Country Codes

ARG-Argentina	INT-International
ATA-Austria	ITA-Italy
AUS-Australia	JPN-Japan
BEL-Belgium	KUW-Kuwait
BRA-Brazil	MEX-Mexico
CAN-Canada	NZ-New Zealand
CHI-Chile	POL-Poland
CNA-China	PR-Puerto Rico
CUB-Cuba	RUS-Russia
DEN-Denmark	SAF-South Africa
ENG-England	SAM-South America
FIN-Finland	SPA-Spain
FRA-France	SWE-Sweden
GER-Germany	SWI-Switzerland
GRE-Greece	TUR-Turkey
HOL-Holland	URU-Uruguay
IND-India	VEN-Venezuela

V,
February 8, 1948
(France),
$100-$175.

Votre Sante,
February 15, 1949
(France),
$175-$250.

1946

- *Leader,* April 13, 1946; first solo cover in the world. (ENG) ....$500-$700
- *Votre Amie,* Sept. 1946; colorized, playing in leaves. (FRA) ....$400-$600

1947

- *Intimitá,* Aug. 1, 1947; no. 75; standing in a floral bikini. (ITA) ....$200-$400
- *Picture Post,* Dec. 13, 1947; vol. 37, no. 11; wearing a sweater, arm up. (ENG) ....$175-$275
- *Puerto Rico Illustrado,* March 22, 1947; wearing checkered pants. (PR) ....$200-$350

1948

- *Hela Varlden,* July 1948; no. 27; at a ship's wheel in a striped shirt. (SWE) ....$400-$600
- *Intimitá,* Aug. 6, 1948; no. 128; Norma Jeane sitting in a floral bikini. (ITA) ....$200-$400
- *New Screen News,* May 28, 1948; cheesecake pose in a striped bikini. (AUS) ....$250-$400
- *Prins Reporter,* Aug. 14-28, 1948; no. 17; young Norma Jeane on the beach. (HOL) ....$200-$350
- *V,* Feb. 8, 1948; no. 175; in dress from *Ladies of the Chorus.* (FRA) ....$100-$175
- *Wereld Kroniek,* Sept. 25, 1948; sitting in road. (HOL) ....$200-$300
- *Wereld Kroniek,* Oct. 30, 1948; waving in a sweater. (HOL) ....$200-$300

1949

- *Kroniek Van De Week,* March 12, 1949; no. 24; dressed as a farmgirl holding a goat. (HOL) ....$150-$250
- *Opden Uitijk,* June 1949; no. 9; a rare de Dienes photo by a barn door. (HOL) ....$300-$500
- *Picture Post,* March 26, 1949; vol. 42, no. 13; b&w Norma Jeane in the wind and sun. (ENG) ....$175-$275
- *Picture Post,* Aug. 13, 1949; vol. 44, no. 7; squatting in a bikini on the beach. (ENG) ....$175-$275
- *V,* Oct. 31, 1949; no. 265; colorized Norma Jeane as a sailor. (FRA) ....$175-$275
- *Votre Santé,* Feb. 15, 1949; no. 35; in a tailored suit. (FRA) ....$175-$250
- *Wereld Kroniek,* Jan. 9, 1949; no. 2; Norma Jeane sitting in the snow. (HOL) ....$200-$300

1950

- *Das Magazin,* 1950; no. 13; in a red one-piece swimsuit on beach. (GER) ....$200-$300
- *Paris Hollywood,* 1950; a colorized cheesecake photograph. (FRA) ....$100-$200
- *Paris Tout Bas,* 1950; no. 1; an early Norma Jeane portrait. (FRA) ....$100-$200
- *Piccolo,* Oct. 29, 1950; no. 26; a pretty *Eve* portrait. (HOL) ....$125-$175
- *Revue,* May 27, 1950; no. 21; wearing a print blouse by de Dienes. (GER) ....$200-$300
- *Roman Magasinet,* circa 1950; n. 1; an *Eve* publicity still. (DEN) ....$50-$100

1951

- *Billed Bladet,* June 26, 1951; no. 26; in the grass with a dandelion. (DEN) ....$100-$175
- *Cinemonde,* 1951; no. 870; in a bathing suit on half the cover. (FRA) ....$50-$100
- *Confidenze,* June 17, 1951; vol. VI; wearing a turtleneck and reclining in a lawnchair. (ITA) ....$200-$300
- *Cuentame,* Dec. 5, 1951; vol. 5, no. 214; in a yellow sweater with her hair blowing. (ARG) ....$150-$200

- *Hela Varlden,* 1951; no. 25; holding a bouquet of roses for *Eve.* (SWE) ....$100-$175
- *Le Soir Illustré,* Sept. 20, 1951; no. 10004; smiling with her hair blowing in the wind. (FRA) ....$100-$150
- *Novell Magisinet* (digest), 1951; no. 15; an *Eve* publicity still. (SWE) ....$50-$100
- *Pix,* Aug. 11, 1951; vol. 26, no. 25; glamourous in a red velvet dress. (AUS) ....$100-$175
- *Resimli Romans,* 13 Aralik 1951; with bobbed hair in a yellow turtleneck. (TUR) ....$100-$150
- *Wereld Kroniek,* June 2, 1951, no. 22, a de Dienes, playing on the beach. (HOL) ....$200-$300
- *Zondagsvriend,* Sept. 27, 1951; playing on the ground in a leaf pile. (HOL) ....$200-$300

1952

- *Billed Bladet,* Nov. 4, 1952; reclining in a lamé dress with arms up. (SWE) ....$90-$130
- *Bolero Film,* July 27, 1952; no. 271; smiling with a bouquet of red roses. (ITA) ....$100-$150
- *Chic,* 1952; a de Dienes photo of Norma Jeane. (CUB) ....$150-$200
- *Cine Mundo,* Sept. 27, 1952; vol. 1, no. 28; smiling in b&w glamour image. (SPA) ....$100-$175
- *Cine Revue,* Oct. 3, 1952; vol. 32, no. 40; showing Cary Grant her leg. (FRA) ....$50-$100
- *Dien Gluck,* 1952; no. 7; an early studio publicity photo. (SWI) ....$100-$150
- *Die Truhe Marjetta* (digest), circa 1952; an early glamorous artwork image. (SWI) ....$40-$60
- *Ecran,* Nov. 5, 1952; no. 1098; holding up a white cat. (CHI) ....$55-$85
- *8 Otto,* March 2, 1952; no. 9; posing within a big heart. (ITA) ....$100-$140
- *8 Otto,* April 6, 1952; n. 14; testing the water in a pool with her toe. (ITA) ....$100-$140
- *Estampa,* April 14, 1952; vol. XIV, no. 708; *Asphalt Jungle* colorized photo, MM in suit. (ARG) ....$125-$175
- *Film Journalen,* May 25, 1952; no. 21; having her photo taken by a ladder. (SWE) ....$65-$95
- *Film Magazin,* 1 Jng., 1952; no. 20; hugging a white cat. (SWI) ....$100-$150
- *Fotographia Artistica,* March 1952; vol. 3, no. 7; sitting in the snow in a hat. (SPA) ....$100-$150
- *Fotogramas,* Nov. 28, 1952; a glamorous photo with a hand to her chin. (SPA) ....$100-$125
- *Fotogramas,* Dec. 12, 1952; embracing with Keith Andes. (SPA) ....$100-$125
- *Funk Illustrierte,* April 13, 1952; a glamorous publicity photo. (GER) ......$100-$150
- *Il Lavoro Illustrato,* Sept. 7, 1952; no. 36; smiling, holding a white cat. (ITA) ....$100-$125
- *La Settimana Incom Illustrada,* Aug. 9, 1952; vol. V, no. 32; holding envelope, looking surprised. (ITA) ....$100-$125
- *Novellmagisinet* (digest) 1952 no. 11; a photo from *The Asphalt Jungle.* (SWE) ....$40-$60
- *Mein Film,* 1952; no. 49; embracing Richard Widmark. (ATA) ....$60-$100
- *Movie Pictorial,* June 1952; vol. 17, no. 6; wearing a striped shirt from *Clash By Night.* (JPN) ....$100-$140
- *Mundo Uruguayo,* June 5, 1952; vol. XXXIV, no. 1728; with Keith Andes in a romantic pose. (URU) ....$90-$120
- *Noir Et Blanc,* July 16, 1952; no. 386; dancing on the beach in a swimsuit. (FRA) ....$85-$125
- *Paris Frou Frou,* 1952; an early glamorous publicity still. (FRA) ....$85-$125
- *Photoplay,* Nov. 1952; vol. 3, no. 2; a lovely shot of Marilyn reclining in a brown mink. (ENG) ....$90-$125
- *Picturegoer,* Aug. 9, 1952; vol. 24, no. 901; sitting in a director's chair at the studio. (ENG) ....$50-$80

Das Magazin, 1950 (Germany), $200-$300

Roman Magasinet, circa 1950 (Denmark), $50-$100.

Confindenze, June 1951 (Italy), $200-$300.

The Photoplayer, 1952 (Australia), $100-$150.

Estampa, April 14, 1952 (Argentina), $125-$175.

Movie Pictorial, June 1952 (Japan), $100-$140.

- *Se,* Nov. 20-26, 1952; vol. 15, no. 47; in a sultry pose, reclining and wearing a lamé dress. (SWE)....................$60-$90
- *Tele Cine,* 1952; no. 29; a classic glamorous Marilyn. (FRA)....................$60-$90
- *The Photoplayer,* Oct. 4, 1952; vol. XXX, no. 23; in a swimsuit holding on to a palm tree. (AUS)....................$100-$150
- *True Story,* May 1952; with bobbed hair, in a yellow turtleneck. (JPN)....$125-$200
- *Voir,* Nov. 23, 1952; no. 425; looking over her shoulder, in a skirt. (FRA) ....$125-$175
- *Weekend Picture Magazine,* Aug. 9, 1952; vol. 2, no. 32; newspaper section, candid pose in dress. (CAN)....................$150-$250
- *Zondagsvriend,* March 20, 1952; no. 12; as a farm girl holding a baby lamb. (HOL) ....$100-$175

1953

- *Acena Muda,* Oct. 21, 1953; no. 43; a glamour shot for *Niagara.* (BRA)....$80-$125
- *A.M. Australian Magazine,* April 24, 1953; posing with Betty Grable and Lauren Bacall. (AUS)....................$50-$90
- *Amour Film,* Sept. 1, 1953; no. 9; getting cozy with Richard Widmark. (FRA) ....$40-$60
- *Antena,* Feb. 17, 1953; a glamorous MM with diamond jewelry. (ARG).......$50-$90
- *Antena,* Oct. 1953; the common shot with the white fur. (ARG)....................$50-$70
- *Beauty Book,* Sept. 1953; Norma Jeane in a white robe on the beach. (JPN) ....$200-$300
- *Billed Bladet,* Nov. 24, 1953; no. 47; in a black dress decorated with jewels. (DEN) ....$60-$90
- *Cahiers Du Cinema,* June 1953; no. 24; with her co-stars from *Millionaire.* (FRA) ....$40-$55
- *Capriccio* (digest), 1953; no. 9; an early glamour publicity pose. (GER)......$50-$90
- *Cinelandia,* June 1953; vol. 11, no. 15; wearing the racey black negligee. (BRA) ....$50-$90
- *Cinelandia,* Nov. 1953; vol. 2, no. 25; all three women in *Millionaire.* (BRA) ....$50-$80
- *Cinema,* Sept. 30, 1953; no. 118; with Jane Russell on a ladder. (ITA)........$40-$65
- *Cinemin,* Dec. 1953; no. 27; wearing a gold bow necklace. (ARG)............$75-$125
- *Cine-Miroir,* Feb. 1953; no. 952; at the Ray Anthony party in red dress. (FRA) ....$100-$135
- *Cine Radio Actualdad,* Dec. 1953; by a Christmas tree. (BRA)....................$40-$65
- *Cine Revue,* Feb. 27, 1953; vol. 33, no. 9; with Jane Russell in wedding dresses. (FRA)....................$40-$65
- *Cine Revue,* Nov. 13, 1953; vol. 33, no. 46; with Bacall and Grable in *Millionaire.* (FRA)....................$40-$65
- *Confessioni,* Nov. 19, 1953; vol. V, no. 269; wearing a gold lamé gown. (ITA) ....$50-$80
- *De Post,* May 1953; in *Don't Bother To Knock.* (BEL)....................$75-$100
- *Der Spiegel,* Sept. 30, 1953; vol. VII, no. 40; an unretouched glamour photo. (GER) ....$60-$90
- *Deutsche Illustrierte,* Sept. 19, 1953; no. 38; Marilyn holding a Greek column. (GER)....................$60-$85
- *Ecran,* June 16, 1953; no. 1169; a *Niagara* glamour pose. (CHI)....................$40-$70
- *Ecran,* Sept. 29, 1953; no. 1184; a glamorous publicity still. (CHI)..............$40-$70
- *Ecran,* Dec. 22, 1953; no. 1196; looking sexy on the Christmas issue. (CHI) ....$40-$70
- *Eiga No Tomo,* Oct. 1953; no. 249; the well-known white fur pose. (JPN)...$60-$90
- *Epoca,* June 14, 1953; no. 141; a close-up in the black lace dress. (ITA)....$40-$70
- *Fick Journalen* (digest), April 16, 1953; no. 16; Norma Jeane climbing some steep rocks. (SWE)....................$100-$140
- *Film Complet,* 1953; no. 402; kissing Richard Allen in *Niagara.* (FRA).........$40-$65
- *Film en Toneel,* Oct. 1953; no. 4; in a blue satin halter top. (HOL)...............$40-$65
- *Film Journalen,* Oct. 4, 1953; no. 40-41; on a wire table in a yellow suit. (SWE) ....$40-$65

- *Film Magazin,* 2 Jhg., 1953; no. 19; black-gloved hands touching her face. (SWI) ....$50-$75
- *Film Strip* (digest), Nov. 24, 1953; full figure from *The Asphalt Jungle.* (RUS) ....$70-$120
- *Follie!,* March 1953; vol. VI, no. 3; a young Norma Jeane under an umbrella. (ITA) ....$150-$225
- *Follie!,* Sept.-Oct. 1953; no. 9; with Jane Russell in top hats. (ITA)...........$75-$125
- *Garbo,* Oct. 3, 1953; vol. 1, no. 29; color-tinted with short bobbed hair. (SPA) ....$40-$70
- *Glamor,* Nov. 24, 1953; early publicity shot with bobbed hair. (ENG).........$75-$100
- *Gondel,* 1953; no. 54; a typical sexy shot. (GER) ....$60-$90
- *Grand Hotel,* Feb. 28, 1953; no. 349; an artwork cover in a red dress. (ITA) ....$50-$100
- *Ibz/Berliner Illustrierte,* April 10, 1953; no. 44; the common white fur publicity pose. (GER) ....$50-$90
- *Illustrated,* Jan. 31, 1953; vol. XIV, no. 49; in a lacy dress, with red hair. (ENG) ....$70-$100
- *Illustrated,* Aug. 8, 1953; vol. XV, no. 24; the three women in *Millionaire.* (ENG) ....$50-$90
- *Illustrierte Post,* Nov. 4, 1953; no. 15; a glamorous studio publicity pose. (GER) ....$50-$90
- *Imagenes,* April 1953; no. 20; reclining in a lamé gown. (SPA) ....$100-$200
- *Intimitá,* Oct. 15, 1953; no. 399; in the red *Niagara* dress with arm up. (ITA) ....$75-$100
- *La Domenica Della Donna,* June 7, 1953; no. 23; with Richard Widmark. (ITA) ....$75-$125
- *La Domenica Della Donna,* Dec. 18, 1953; no. 50; holding 500-year-old diamond. (ITA) ....$75-$125
- *Le Film Complet,* 3rd trimester 53; no. 402; a glamorous studio photo. (FRA) ....$40-$65
- *Le Ore,* Aug. 1, 1953; vol. 1, no. 12; colorized, holding an umbrella. (ITA)..$50-$70
- *Le Ore,* Aug. 29, 1953; vol. 1, no. 16; looking over her shoulder in jeans. (ITA) ....$60-$90
- *Le Ore,* Nov. 21, 1953; vol. 1, no. 28; Halsman photo, in white dress. (ITA) ....$50-$70
- *Mein Film,* Jan. 23, 1953; no. 52; in the black dress with white collar. (ATA) ....$50-$80
- *Me Naiset,* 1953; no. 5; a young Norma Jeane in a pink sweater. (FIN) ....$225-$375
- *Mignon,* Jan. 1, 1953; no. 1; a pretty glamour pose. (ITA)..........................$40-$60
- *Mujer,* May 1953; no. 191; sultry in the *Niagara* dress with arm up. (SPA) ....$100-$125
- *Munchner Illustrierte,* Jan. 17, 1953; no. 3; with Jane Russell in top hats. (GER) ....$50-$80
- *Munchner Illustrierte,* Sept. 12, 1953; no. 37; Halsman photo, in white dress. (GER) ....$50-$80
- *Mundo Uruguayo,* Nov. 5, 1953; vol. XXXV, no. 1802; in black dress with jewels on straps. (URU) ....$50-$80
- *Motion Picture Times,* July 1953; no. 67; with her hair up for *Eve.* (JPN) ....$100-$150
- *Neue Illustrierte,* July 25, 1953; vol. 8, no. 30; with her arm up from *How To Marry A Millionaire.* (GER) ....$90-$125
- *New Liberty,* March 1953; vol. 30, no. 1; a double-image mirror reflexion. (CAN) ....$50-$80
- *New Screen News,* Jan. 16, 1953; a tinted studio portrait. (AUS) ....$50-$80
- *Noir Et Blanc,* Feb. 25, 1953; no. 418; a long-haired Marilyn coming out of a pool. (FRA) ....$45-$75
- *Noir Et Blanc,* July 20, 1953; vol. 9, no. 438; two side-by-side full-length photos. (FRA) ....$50-$75
- *Novella,* Jan. 4, 1953; no. 1; a studio publicity photograph. (ITA)................$40-$80

Screen, June 1953 (Japan), $70-$100.

Weekend Picture Magazine, August 9, 1952 (Canada), $150-$250.

Cine Revue, October 3, 1952 (France), $50-$100.

Photoplay, November 1952 (England), $90-$125.

Cine Revue, February 27, 1953 (France), $40-$65.

Follie, March 1953 (Italy), $150-$225.

- *Novella,* Nov. 1, 1953; vol. XXXIV, no. 44; a picture from *Niagara.* (ITA) .....$40-$80
- *Novelle Film,* Jan. 17, 1953; no. 265; embracing Richard Widmark. (ITA) ...$40-$80
- *Novelle Film,* July 25, 1953; no. 292; with Richard Allen in *Niagara.* (ITA) ....$40-$80
- *Otto Volante,* March 16-31, 1953; vol. 11, no. 6; intently reading a script on a set. (ITA) ....$50-$80
- *Paris Frou Frou,* circa 1953; no. 1; a coy look in the black lace negligee. (FRA) ....$100-$140
- *Paris Frou Frou,* circa 1953; no. 11; posing with Charles Laughton and Jane Russell. (FRA) ....$65-$95
- *Paris Hollywood,* Dec. 1953-Jan. 1954; vol. 2, no. 22; standing by a snowman. (SWE) ....$80-$120
- *Parisia,* March 1954; no. 4; a typical glamour image. (FRA) ....$70-$90
- *Paris Match,* July 25, 1953; no. 226; hugging a white pillar. (FRA)..........$70-$95
- *Photoplay,* Aug. 1953; Marilyn wearing a top hat. (ENG) ....$40-$75
- *Photoplay,* May 1953; in a black dress with jewel-studded straps. (AUS)..$60-$100
- *Photoplay,* Oct. 1953; wearing a gold halter dress. (AUS)..........$60-$100
- *Piccolo,* Jan. 18, 1953; vol. 29, no. 2; standing in front of Niagara Falls. (HOL) ....$55-$100
- *Piccolo,* Dec. 27, 1953; posing with big sticks of dynamite. (HOL)..........$55-$100
- *Picturegoer,* May 9, 1953; vol. 25, no. 940; in lacy black negligee. (ENG) ...$40-$60
- *Picture Post,* Aug. 15, 1953; vol. 60, no. 7; with Charles Laughton and Jane Russell. (ENG)..........$50-$80
- *Pin-Up,* Sept. 2, 1953; digest-size colorized shot by a pier. (SWE) ....$50-$80
- *Pix,* May 9, 1953; vol. 29, no. 10; a cute pose in a jewel-decorated dress. (AUS) ....$50-$90
- *Radio Revue,* Sept. 27-Oct. 3, 1953; no. 39; posing in a glamorous fashion. (GER) ....$50-$90
- *Radio Revue,* Oct. 3-9, 1953; no. 40; with Jane Russell in *Gentlemen Prefer Blondes.* (GER)..........$50-$80
- *Regal* (digest), May 1953; no. 44; a cheesecake image in a yellow bikini. (FRA) ....$80-$100
- *Regal* (digest), June 1953; no. 45; a cheesecake image in a striped bikini. (FRA) ....$80-$100
- *Regards,* June 1953; no. 45; a close-up in dangling earrings. (FRA) ....$100-$145
- *Screen,* June 1953; leaning back over green satin. (JPN) ....$70-$100
- *Screen Parade,* Sept. 1953; the three women in *Millionaire.* (AUS) ....$50-$80
- *Tempo,* April 18, 1953; vol. XV, no. 16; holding roses in her arms from *All About Eve.* (ITA) ....$50-$80
- *Tempo,* Nov. 26, 1953; vol. XV, no. 48; close-up with a cigarette by Greene. (ITA) ....$45-$70
- *Tempo,* Dec. 17, 1953; vol. XV, no. 51; the three women in *How To Marry A Millionaire.* (ITA)..........$35-$50
- *Triunfo,* Feb. 25, 1953; no. 367; a sexy glamour pose. (SPA) ....$50-$80
- *Triunfo,* Sept. 30, 1953; no. 398; a sexy glamour pose in a dress. (SPA) ....$50-$80
- *20th Century Fox,* April-May 1953; no. 7; with Jane Russell, both are wearing top hats. (ITA) ....$100-$130
- *20th Century Fox,* Dec. 31, 1953; no. 24; posing with a snowman. (ITA) ....$100-$130
- *Uge Revyen,* June 30, 1953; vol. II, no. 26; a tinted digest, wearing the red *Niagara* dress. (DEN)..........$25-$35
- *Uge Revyen,* Sept. 29, 1953; vol. II, no. 39; a tinted digest with the *Millionaire* women. (DEN) ....$25-$45
- *Une Semaine De Paris,* Sept. 15, 1953; no. 356; a sultry publicity pose. (FRA) ....$25-$45
- *Vea,* Sept. 19, 1953; no. 462; in swimsuit, holding white pillar. (MEX)....$100-$150
- *Vea,* Oct. 10, 1953; no. 465; sitting in a one-piece swimsuit. (MEX) ....$100-$150
- *Vision,* July 24, 1953; vol. 5, no. 6; at the *Niagara* party in the red dress. (CHI) ....$75-$125

- *Weiner Bilderwoche,* Nov. 14, 1953; no. 46; black dress with jewel straps. (ATA) ....$60-$90
- *What's On In London?,* May 8, 1953; a publicity pose in a tight dress. (ENG) ....$60-$90

1954

- *Amor Film,* Sept. 15, 1954; no. 34; with Jane Russell in *Blondes.* (FRA).....$40-$60
- *Antologia Otto Volante,* Aug. 1954; no. 4; holding polka-dot scarf. (ITA).....$60-$90
- *Australasian Post,* March 25, 1954; in a green velvet dress from *River Of No Return.* (AUS) ....$80-$120
- *Australasian Post,* May 27, 1954; on steps, undoing swimsuit strap. (AUS) ....$80-$120
- *Blighty,* Jan. 30, 1954; cutting a cake. (ENG) ....$40-$80
- *Capriccio Journal,* 1954; no. 7; digest with a diamond necklace. (GER) ......$40-$70
- *Chi é Marilyn Monroe Collana Biogaphica,* June 1, 1954; entire issue on her; going up a ladder. (ITA) ....$150-$275
- *Cinelandia,* Feb. 1954; vol. 3, no. 30; glamour pose in white fur. (BRA) ......$50-$80
- *Cinelandia,* Sept. 1954; vol. IV, no. 45; a sultry portrait. (BRA) ....$50-$80
- *Cinemondé,* April 16, 1954; in the gold lamé gown. (FRA)........$40-$60
- *Cinema Nuovo,* Dec. 10, 1954; vol. 3, no. 48; a typical studio photograph. (ITA) ....$40-$65
- *Cinemin,* June 1954; no. 33; full-length, holding white pillar. (ARG)........$100-$130
- *Cine Radio Actualdad,* Sept. 24, 1954; vol. XIX, no. 950; with Gina Lollobrigida. (URU) ....$40-$60
- *Cineromanzo,* Oct. 28, 1954; no. 11; a sexy glamour picture. (ITA).........$100-$130
- *Clubman,* Summer 1954; no. 43; in a costume from *River.* (ENG) ....$75-$125
- *Cronache Della Politica E Del Costume,* Dec. 10, 1954; no. 22; a studio portrait. (ITA) ....$70-$100
- *Der Stern,* Jan. 31, 1954; wearing the famous gold lamé gown. (GER) ....$60-$95
- *Ecran,* June 29, 1954; no. 1221; a pretty glamour portrait. (CHI) ....$30-$50
- *Ecran,* Aug. 3, 1954; no. 1226; the three women from *Millionaire.* (CHI) ....$30-$50
- *Ecran,* Dec. 28, 1954; no. 1249; showing off a diamond necklace. (CHI) ....$30-$50
- *Eiga No Tomo,* March 1954; no. 254; in a fur with a striped background. (JPN) ....$60-$90
- *Epoca,* Jan. 17, 1954; vol. V, no. 172; hanging out a car window in Canada. (ITA) ....$40-$65
- *Epoca,* March 21, 1954; vol. V, no. 161; the classic image in the white fur. (ITA) ....$30-$40
- *Epoca,* Aug. 15, 1954; no. 202; leaning forward and laughing. (ITA) ....$40-$60
- *Estudio,* May 5, 1954; no. 27; a studio publicity pose. (SPA) ....$100-$140
- *Festival,* Feb. 24, 1954; no. 243; on the back cover as well. (FRA) ....$60-$90
- *Frau Im Spiegel,* Oct. 16, 1954; vol. 9, no. 42; tinted photo from *River Of No Return.* (GER) ....$50-$80
- *Intimitá,* March 18, 1954; no. 421; smiling in the white fur. (ITA)........$40-$65
- *Joulu Iso Kalle,* Dec. 5-20, 1954; no. 23; wearing a black negligee. (FIN) ....$100-$140
- *La Cinematographie Francaise,* Dec. 4, 1954; no. 1595; a cute publicity photograph. (FRA)........$50-$90
- *Le Film Complet,* Nov. 25, 1954; no. 488; a 20th Century Fox publicity shot. (FRA) ....$40-$65
- *Le Ore,* Jan. 2, 1954; no. 34; hugging a white Greek column. (ITA)............$40-$65
- *Le Ore,* April 3, 1954; vol. II, no. 47; putting her hands in cement at Chinese Mann's Theatre. (ITA)........$50-$80
- *Le Ore,* July Oct. 1954; vol. II, no. 61; leaning back against green satin. (ITA) ....$45-$65
- *Le Ore,* Oct. 9, 1954; vol. II, no. 74; full-length pose hugging the white pole. (ITA) ....$45-$65
- *Marilyn—by Skolsky,* 1954; South American version of the American issue. (ARG) ....$90-$120

Tempo, April 1953 (Italy), $50-$80.

Imagenes, April 1953 (Spain), $100-$200.

La Domenica Della Donna, June 1953 (Italy), $75-$125.

Cinelandia, June 1953 (Brazil), $50-$90.

Motion Picture Times, July 1953 (Japan), $100-$150.

Picture Post, August 15, 1953 (England), $50-$80.

- *Mexico Dia,* Aug. 10, 1954; a studio publicity image. (MEX)....................$100-$150
- *Min Melodi,* May 7, 1954; no. 19; three paintings of Marilyn poses. (SWE) ....$50-$80
- *Min Melodi,* June 4, 1954; no. 23; on a rock in *River.* (SWE) ....$70-$90
- *Movie Life,* March 1, 1954; vol. VIII, no. 9; wearing a yellow dress and hugging a white cat. (AUS) ....$100-$140
- *Movie Life,* Oct. 1954; three different images on cover. (AUS)....................$100-$130
- *Movie Stars Parade,* Sept. 1954; a glamorous and sexy pose. (AUS) ......$100-$130
- *Munchener Illustrierte,* Feb. 27, 1954; no. 9; with Jane Russell, both wearing costumes. (GER) ....$60-$90
- *New Screen News,* Feb. 12, 1954; wearing a red one-piece swimsuit. (AUS) ....$40-$65
- *New Screen News,* March 12, 1954; holding the white Greek column. (AUS) ....$40-$65
- *Notte E Giorno,* Nov. 8, 1954; no. 7; in front of Niagara Falls. (ITA)............$60-$90
- *Novella,* Sept. 26, 1954; no. 39; typical smiling, glamorous MM. (ITA) ....$40-$80
- *Oggi,* Jan. 28, 1954; vol. X, no. 4; DiMaggio on their wedding day. (ITA)....$30-$50
- *Oggi,* March 18, 1954; vol. X, no. 11; posing with the troops in Korea in 1954. (ITA) ....$30-$50
- *Oggi,* Oct. 21, 1954; vol. X, no. 42; with Billy Wilder on the *The Seven Year Itch* set. (ITA)....................$30-$50
- *Paris Frou Frou,* 1954; no. 40; a common glamorous photo. (FRA) ....$50-$90
- *Paris Hollywood,* Sept. 1954; vol. 3, no. 17; publicity still for *River Of No Return.* (SWE) ....$80-$110
- *Photoplay,* March 1954; vol. 5, no. 12; on a wire table in a yellow bathing suit. (ENG)....................$40-$80
- *Photoplay,* Dec. 1954; vol. 5, no. 12; in a green velvet dress from *River Of No Return.* (ENG) ....$40-$80
- *Photoplay,* April 1954; a profile shot in the gold lamé gown. (AUS) ....$50-$100
- *Photoplay,* July 1954; in a white fur with a striped background. (AUS) .....$50-$100
- *Picturegoer,* Jan. 16, 1954; vol. 27, no. 976; tinted cover, holding a diamond necklace. (ENG) ....$35-$45
- *Picturegoer,* Oct. 23, 1954; vol. 28, no. 1016; tinted with her white dress blowing up. (ENG)....................$35-$45
- *Picture Post,* April 24, 1954; hands behind her, in gold lamé. (ENG)...........$40-$60
- *Picture Show,* Sept. 25, 1954; vol. 63, no. 1643; with Robert Mitchum in *River Of No Return.* (ENG) ....$30-$40
- *Piff* (digest), Sept. 1954; no. 10; in a colorful corset and headdress from *River Of No Return.* (ENG) ....$35-$50
- *Quic,* circa 1954; vol. 1, no. 1; a pose from *How To Marry A Millionaire*; also on back cover. (ITA)....................$60-$90
- *Reves,* Aug. 12, 1954; no. 424; a studio publicity pose. (FRA) ....$50-$70
- *Revue,* May 29, 1954; no. 22; showing off a 500-year-old diamond. (GER) ....$60-$90
- *Rosso E Nero,* Jan. 31-Feb. 28, 1954; vol. 2, no. 1; a color shot from *The Asphalt Jungle.* (ITA) ....$100-$150
- *Rosso E Nero,* Nov. 1954; no. 8; in yellow swimsuit on rocks. (ITA) ....$80-$125
- *Screen Stars,* April-May 1954; vol. 1, no. 2; posing in a swimsuit with an umbrella. (AUS)....................$80-$125
- *Se,* Jan. 29-Feb. 4, 1954; vol. 17, no. 5; with Joe DiMaggio, on three-quarters of the cover. (SWE)....................$30-$45
- *Se,* Oct. 1-7, 1954; in the white dress from *Itch.* (SWE) ....$30-$50
- *Seduction,* Feb. 1954; vol. 1, no. 2; a profile in the red *Niagara* dress. (ITA) ....$100-$175
- *Semaine Du Monde,* Jan. 29, 1954; no. 64; wearing white fur and a smile. (FRA) ....$40-$65
- *Semaine Du Nord Magazine,* Oct. 28, 1954; no. 31; an early glamour photo, smiling in gloves. (FRA) ....$100-$140
- *Serena,* Jan. 28, 1954; no. 50; in a red suit holding the white pillar. (ITA) ....$70-$100

- *Settimo Giorno,* Dec. 23, 1954; vol. VII, no. 51; looking over her shoulder in a dress. (ITA) .... $80-$125
- *Sight and Sound,* Jan.-March 1954; vol. 23, no. 3; with Bacall and Grable in *How To Marry A Millionaire.* (ENG) .... $20-$35
- *Star,* May 1954; wearing a fur and a serious face. (JPN) .... $75-$120
- *Tabarin,* March 1954; no. 3; a double-image cheesecake shot in a suit. (ITA) .... $50-$80
- *The Eiga Story,* Sept. 1954; a younger Marilyn, with wide eyes. (JPN) .... $80-$120
- *True Confessions,* Feb. 1954; in the red *Niagara* dress and gold hoops. (ENG) .... $125-$175
- *TV Sorrisi E Canzoni,* July 11, 1954; no. 28; tinted cover, with Robert Mitchum. (ITA) .... $60-$90
- *20th Century Fox,* Feb. 28, 1954; vol. IX, no. 3-4; sitting in a lacy red negligee and heels. (ITA) .... $80-$120
- *20th Century Fox,* Dec. 17, 1954; no. 23; cutting a cake in the white *Itch* dress. (ITA) .... $80-$120
- *Une Semaine De Paris,* April 28, 1954; no. 388; a classic, glamorous Monroe. (FRA) .... $40-$65
- *Une Semaine De Paris,* Sept. 27, 1954; no. 406; a studio-released publicity still. (FRA) .... $40-$65
- *Visto,* July 10, 1954; no. 28; dreamy image, sitting with a guitar. (ITA) .... $80-$125
- *Visto,* Sept. 25, 1954; vol. III, no. 39, the common, white fur image. (ITA) .... $50-$80
- *Voila Europe Magazine,* Feb. 21, 1954; no. 472; Marilyn glamour at its best. (FRA) .... $80-$100
- *Wiener Film Revue,* 1954; no. 6; a publicity photograph. (ATA) .... $50-$80

1955

- *A.M. Australian Magazine,* April 5, 1955; in white satin dress by a bookcase. (AUS) .... $125-$175
- *A.M. Australian Magazine,* July 5, 1955; full-length profile in a red negligee. (AUS) .... $125-$175
- *Amor Film,* March 16, 1955; no. 56; a studio publicity pose. (FRA) .... $40-$60
- *Amor Film Hebdo,* May 25, 1955; no. 66; posing with Donald O'Connor. (FRA) .... $40-$60
- *Amor Film,* Dec. 28, 1955; no. 97; full-length in the tiger-stripe dress. (FRA) .... $40-$60
- *Bild Journalen,* April 1955; n. 13; tinted image with her makeup man, Whitey Snyder. (SWE) .... $100-$140
- *Cahiers Du Cinema,* Noel 1955; no. 54; in blowing white *Seven Year Itch* dress. (FRA) .... $40-$65
- *Cine Aventuras,* Feb.-March 1955; in a red-and-white striped blouse. (ARG) .... $40-$60
- *Cinelandia,* Dec. 1955; vol. IV, no. 74; two pictures in a white terry robe. (BRA) .... $50-$80
- *Cinema,* Nov. 25, 1955; vol. XIV, no. 155; *Itch* publicity pose. (ITA) .... $50-$70
- *Cine-Revelation,* May 12, 1955; no. 58; sitting, in a photo by Halsman. (FRA) .... $100-$150
- *Cine Revue,* July 15, 1955; vol. 35, no. 28; with Tom Ewell in *Itch.* (FRA) .... $40-$65
- *Cine Revue,* Nov. 18, 1955; vol. 35; wrapped in deep red with a choker. (FRA) .... $50-$80
- *Der Stern,* Oct. 4, 1955; no. 15; sitting near mirrors and reflections. (GER) .... $90-$125
- *Ecran,* June 21, 1955; no. 1274; with DiMaggio at the *The Seven Year Itch* premiere. (CHI) .... $30-$45
- *Eiga No Tomo,* Sept. 1955; no. 272; sitting in a director's chair, wearing a jeweled gown. (JPN) .... $60-$90
- *Epoca,* July 24, 1955; vol. VI, no. 251; coyly looking over her shoulder. (ITA) .... $60-$90

Cine Mundo, September 27, 1952 (Spain), $100-$175.

A Cena Muda, October 21, 1953 (Brazil), $80-$125.

Cinelandia, November 1953 (Brazil), $50-$80.

Clubman, 1954 (England), $75-$125.

Rosso E Nero, January-February 1954 (Italy), $100-$150.

Se, January-February 1954 (Sweden), $30-$45.

- *Filmlandia,* Sept. 1955; no. 10; sitting in a director's chair, wearing a jeweled gown. (ARG) .... $60-$90
- *Film Magazin,* Jan. 4, 1955; no. 52; tinted, in director's chair. (SWI) .... $40-$60
- *Flix,* circa 1955; no. 4; wearing high heels and a potato sack. (ENG) .... $60-$100
- *Flix,* circa 1955; no. 5; from *Itch* by a staircase. (ENG) .... $60-$100
- *Flix,* circa 1955; vol. 1, no. 8; international edition; with Tom Ewell. (ENG) .... $60-$95
- *Fotogramas*, 1955; vol. X, no. 319; a tinted glamour cover from *Niagara.* (SPA) .... $60-$90
- *Garbo,* Sept. 17, 1955; vol. III, no. 131; Joe DiMaggio escorting MM to *The Seven Year Itch* premiere. (SPA) .... $40-$60
- *Grand Hotel,* July 2, 1955; no. 471; an artwork cover of Marilyn. (ITA) .... $50-$90
- *Hemmets Veckotidning,* July 2, 1955; vol. 27, no. 27; young Norma Jeane on the beach in pants. (SWE) .... $125-$200
- *Illustrierte Alm Buhne*, 1955; no. 2755; in a white costume from *There's No Business Like Show Business.* (GER) .... $50-$80
- *Junior Women's Weekly,* Aug. 22, 1955; a digest insert with Tom Ewell. (AUS) .... $50-$70
- *Jours De France*, March 24-31, 1955; no. 20; with a surprised look and a flower choker. (FRA) .... $90-$130
- *L'Europeo,* Dec. 4, 1955; no. 49; a standard movie-star glamour face. (ITA) .... $40-$80
- *Le Grande Firmi Orchidea*, Sept. 1, 1955; no. 293; a glamour portrait. (ITA) .... $100-$150
- *Le Ore,* June 4, 1955; vol. III, no. 108; a close-up in a striped turtleneck. (ITA) .... $50-$80
- *Le Ore,* Nov. 19, 1955; vol. III, no. 132; standing in the striped turtleneck. (ITA) .... $50-$80
- *Liberty*, July 1955; vol. 32, no. 5; wearing the one-strap *Millionaire* dress. (CAN) .... $40-$70
- *Marilyn,* circa 1955; vol. 1, no. 1; a comic about MM, with an art cover. (ARG) .... $80-$120
- *Marilyn,* circa 1955; vol. 1, no. 2; a comic about MM, with an art cover. (ARG) .... $80-$120
- *Marilyn Monroe* (pocket), 1955; entire issue is dedicated to her. (SPA) .... $75-$100
- *Mein Film,* Jan. 1955; with Rory Calhoun in *River.* (ATA) .... $40-$65
- *Mimosa* (digest), Jan. 1955; no. 23; the three women from *How To Marry A Millionaire.* (ITA) .... $40-$65
- *Movie Life,* Nov. 1955; holding the 500-year-old diamond. (AUS) .... $100-$140
- *New Screen News,* Nov. 1, 1955; with Tom Ewell in *Itch.* (AUS) .... $40-$60
- *Photoplay,* July 1955; vol. 6, no. 7; in a black swimsuit on steps. (ENG) .... $40-$65
- *Photoplayer,* Feb. 19, 1955; on the couch from *Itch.* (AUS) .... $40-$80
- *Piccolo,* April 3, 1955; vol. 31, no. 12; with Donald O'Connor. (HOL) .... $40-$80
- *Radio Revue,* May 22-28, 1955; no. 2; typical glamour image. (GER) .... $50-$90
- *Radio Revue,* Sept. 18, 1955; no. 38; a studio publicity pose. (GER) .... $50-$90
- *Revue,* Aug. 6, 1955; no. 32; wearing the gold lamé gown, on three-quarters of the cover. (GER) .... $40-$65
- *Rhythme,* April 15, 1955; a studio publicity pose. (HOL) .... $50-$80
- *Ricu Ritas,* circa 1955; vol. 11, no. 49; sitting on Tom Ewell's lap. (ARG) .... $100-$130
- *Rosso E Nero,* Jan. 1955; no. 11; blowing a kiss to the camera. (ITA) .... $80-$120
- *Seura,* Nov. 9, 1955; no. 45; dancing barefoot in a red skirt. (FIN) .... $100-$150
- *Show* (digest), circa 1955; no. 4; sitting in a swimsuit and lace-up sandals. (ENG) .... $60-$100
- *Sixty-Six (66)* (pocket), circa 1955; no. 2; entire issue is on her; in the tiger-stripe dress. (ENG) .... $100-$150
- *Stars & Sterne,* 1955; no. 8; in a suit with a polka-dot scarf. (GER) .... $60-$90
- *Tempo,* Nov. 14, 1955; no. 47; a semi-profile in the gold lamé gown. (ITA) .... $40-$60

- *The Showgirl* (pocket), circa 1955; no. 21; wearing a blue satin halter dress. (ENG) ....$80-$100
- *Visioni,* May 14, 1955; no. 18; the white *Itch* dress blowing up. (ITA).......$90-$120
- *Visto,* Aug. 27, 1955; vol. IV, no. 35; a large portrait from *Itch.* (ITA)..........$50-$90
- *Weiner Film Revue,* 1955; n. 12; in the red dress, posed with Lassie. (ATA) ....$100-$140

1956

- *ABC,* July 7, 1956; seated at the *Bus Stop* press conference. (BEL) ....$60-$90
- *Bella,* Sept. 24-Oct.7, 1956; a glamour shot with the white fur. (GER).........$60-$95
- *Billed Bladet,* July 10, 1956; next to Arthur Miller. (SWE) ....$40-$60
- *Blighty,* Oct. 6, 1956; no. 884; in a purple off-the-shoulder dress. (ENG) ....$100-$150
- *Bolero Film,* July 15, 1956; no. 479; in the red *Niagara* dress. (ITA)..........$80-$100
- *Bravo,* Aug. 26, 1956; no. 1; a studio glamour pose. (GER) ....$60-$80
- *Cahiers Du Cinema,* Nov. 1956; no. 64; on stage during *Bus Stop.* (FRA) ...$60-$95
- *Cine Revelation,* Jan. 5, 1956; no. 92; in a blue bejeweled dress. (FRA)....$75-$100
- *Cine Revelation,* July 19, 1956; no. 120; with arm up, from *Niagara.* (FRA) ....$75-$100
- *Cine Revue,* July 20, 1956; vol. 36, no. 29; standing in front of a house. (FRA) ....$50-$80
- *Cine Universal,* circa 1956; holding her arm, wearing black lace dress. (MEX) ....$80-$120
- *Das Schweizer Magazin* (digest), no. 156; in a blouse, sitting on rocks. (SWI) ....$40-$80
- *Eiga No Tomo,* Dec. 1956; no. 287; in a black spaghetti-strap dress. (JPN) ....$80-$100
- *Elle,* July 16, 1956; no. 551; in a sleeveless white blouse, looking up. (FRA) ....$125-$175
- *Entre Nous,* 1956-57; lying on the ground. (FRA) ....$125-$170
- *Festival,* May 9, 1956; no. 358; sitting on silver foil steps. (FRA) ....$50-$90
- *Fotogramas,* July 27, 1956; no. 400; with Laurence Olivier at a press conference. (SPA)..$50-$90
- *Funk Und Film,* April 7, 1956; tinted shot with Tom Ewell. (GER) ....$40-$80
- *Gondel* (digest), 1956; no. 89; seated on steps. (GER) ....$40-$70
- *Grand Hotel,* Oct. 6, 1956; no. 537; Marilyn, portrayed on this artwork cover. (ITA) ....$60-$90
- *Hayat,* May 4, 1956; no. 5; sitting on large rocks in a pantsuit. (TUR).........$50-$80
- *Hjemmet,* Nov. 6, 1956; vol. 59, no. 45; in the red dress in front of Niagara Falls. (DEN)..$75-$90
- *Hola!,* July 22, 1956; on half the cover. (SPA)..$30-$40
- *Hollywood Festival,* Sept. 1, 1956; vol. XII, no. 164; a double-mirror-reflected image. (ITA)..$65-$125
- *Illustrated,* July 14, 1956; vol. XVIII, no. 21; lying back against green satin. (ENG) ....$55-$85
- *Il Travaso,* July 1, 1956; no. 27; art cover. (ITA) ....$30-$40
- *La Cinematographie Francaise,* Feb. 1, 1956; no. 1698; a typical studio glamour image. (FRA) ....$30-$50
- *La Cinematographie Francaise,* Oct. 3, 1956; no. 1885; a studio glamour portrait. (FRA)..$30-$50
- *La Vida Escandolosa De M. Monroe,* Aug. 1956; no. 1; entire issue on her; a candid photo cover. (ARG) ....$150-$200
- *Le Film Complet,* May 4, 1956; no. 566; a studio publicity pose. (FRA).......$40-$60
- *Le Ore,* March 3, 1956; vol. IV, no. 147; in a lacy black negligee with clouds behind. (ITA)..$40-$65
- *Le Ore,* May 5, 1956; vol. IV, no. 156; holding a guitar in a corset. (ITA) ....$40-$65
- *Le Ore,* Sept. 22, 1956; vol. IV, no. 176; profile in the red *Niagara* dress. (ITA) ....$50-$75
- *L'Europeo,* July 8, 1956; no. 28; wearing the black lace negligee. (ITA) ......$40-$65

Munchner Illustricrte, February 27, 1954 (Germany), $60-$90.

Movie Life, March 1954 (Australia), $100-$130.

Australasian Post, March 25, 1954 (Australia), $80-$120.

Oggi, March 18, 1954 (Italy), $30-$50.

Le Ore, April 3, 1954 (Italy), $50-$80.

Star, May 1954 (Japan), $75-$120.

- *Mandens Blad,* Oct. 1956; on half the cover. (DEN) ....$30-$40
- *Mascotte,* March 28, 1956; vol. 3, no. 44; *Golden Dreams* nude with a blue bikini. (ITA) ....$80-$110
- *Men Only,* Aug. 1956; an artist's cartoon like rendering of MM. (ENG)........$40-$60
- *Munchner Illustrierte,* March 17, 1956; no. 11; wearing a black-and-white striped turtleneck. (GER)....................................$40-$70
- *Novella,* July 1, 1956; no. 27; Marilyn's glamour at its height. (ITA)............$50-$75
- *Novella,* Aug. 5, 1956; no. 32; a studio glamour shot. (ITA) ....$50-$75
- *Oggi,* Nov. 8, 1956; no. 45; meeting Queen Elizabeth. (ITA)........................$40-$60
- *Parade,* Oct. 1956; no. 2; in the detailed gold lamé gown. (ITA) ....$45-$75
- *Paris Frou Frou,* no. 40; in a skirt, sitting on a suitcase. (FRA) ....$50-$85
- *Paris Hollywood* (digest), 1956; vol. 5, no. 24; an image from *Bus Stop.* (DEN) ....$40-$65
- *Paris Match,* July 7, 1956; no. 378; with husband Arthur Miller. (FRA) ....$40-$60
- *People,* July 25, 1956; vol. 7, no. 11; wrapped in white sheets. (AUS)....$100-$150
- *Photoplay,* Aug. 1956; vol. 7, no. 8; standing in a tight detailed dress. (ENG) ....$40-$70
- *Picturegoer,* Nov. 17, 1956; in red velvet dress at a dinner table. (ENG)......$30-$40
- *Picture Show,* Oct. 13, 1956; vol. 67, no. 1750; with Don Murray in *Bus Stop.* (ENG)....................................$30-$40
- *Picture Post,* July 14, 1956; vol. 71, no. 15; in a khaki shirt, sitting in front of a rock. (ENG)....................................$50-$75
- *Picture Post,* Oct. 22, 1956; vol. 73, no. 3; a tight portrait from *Bus Stop.* (ENG) ....$50-$75
- *Point De Vue Images Du Monde,* July 7, 1956; no. 421; close-up in the striped turtleneck. (FRA) ....$90-$125
- *Radio Cinema Television,* Nov. 18, 1956; no. 357; in a white costume from *There's No Business Like Show Business.* (FRA) ....$50-$80
- *RCA Victor Cancionero,* 1956; Monroe is featured on this digest. (SAM) ....$40-$65
- *Realta Illustrata,* Dec. 5, 1956; no. 47-48; in the gold lamé gown. (ITA)......$50-$75
- *Revelation,* 1956; c.no. 3; a close-up in a long-sleeved, lace dress. (FRA) ....$100-$150
- *Revue,* Oct. 27, 1956; no. 43; common image in the white fur. (GER).........$40-$60
- *Settimo Giorno,* July 7, 1956; vol. IX, no. 28; in white fur, sitting in a chair. (ITA) ....$100-$150
- *Tempo,* Sept. 13, 1956; vol. XVII, no. 37; in a long-sleeved lace dress. (ITA) ....$45-$65
- *The Australian Woman's Weekly,* July 25, 1956; vol. 24, no. 8; a bluebird is perched on her finger. (AUS)....................................$175-$250
- *Vea,* 1956; no. 899; in the white *Itch* dress on half the cover. (CHI) ....$25-$35
- *Vie Nuove,* July 21, 1956; vol. XI, no. 30; arm in arm with Arthur Miller. (ITA) ....$40-$70

1957

- *ABC,* Jan. 5, 1957; no. 1; a large, tinted portrait. (BEL) ....$40-$65
- *ABC,* June 22, 1957; in a dress on a soccer field. (BEL) ....$50-$85
- *ABC Film Review,* Oct. 1957; vol. 7, no. 10; in a white dress from *The Prince and the Showgirl.* (ENG)....................................$90-$120
- *Amour Film,* Sept. 1, 1957; no. 149; pretty, studio-released photo. (FRA)...$40-$60
- *Billed Bladet,* Feb. 12, 1957; vol. 20, no. 7; eyes closed, holding a little bird. (DEN) ....$60-$100
- *Billed Bladet,* Oct. 11, 1957; vol. 20, no. 42; hanging out the window, from *The Seven Year Itch.* (DEN) ....$50-$90
- *Bild Journalen,* Nov. 16-23, 1957; no. 46; a tinted, dreamy image depicting MM with blowing hair. (SWE)....................................$60-$85
- *Cinemonde,* Oct. 10, 1957; vol. 25, no. 1209; an extra-large full-face photo from *The Seven Year Itch.* (FRA) ....$50-$80
- *Cine Revelation,* Sept. 5, 1957; no. 179; wearing a flame-colored dress with spangles. (FRA) ....$55-$85

- *Cine Revue,* April 12, 1957; vol. 35, no. 15; with the white fur. (FRA) ....$30-$40
- *Deutsche Illustrierte,* Sept. 14, 1957; no. 37; romantic image by Jack Cardiff. (GER) ....$50-$85
- *Din Tidning,* Nov. 25, 1957; no. 22; in black sequins and a fur, taken by Richard Avedon. (SWE) ....$50-$85
- *Ecran,* July 23, 1957; no. 1383; standard, studio-released photo. (CHI) ......$30-$40
- *Film D'Oggi,* Oct. 19, 1957; no. 42; hanging out a window from *Showgirl.* (ITA) ....$40-$70
- *Films and Filming,* July 1957; with Laurence Olivier in *Showgirl.* (ENG) ......$30-$40
- *Garbo,* Sept. 28, 1957; vol. V, no. 237; cheek to cheek with Laurence Olivier. (SPA) ....$30-$40
- *Hjemmet,* Jan. 29, 1957; vol. 60, no. 5; with Don Murray in *Bus Stop.* (DEN) ....$50-$80
- *Il Travaso,* May 26, 1957; no. 21; an artwork cover. (ITA) ....$30-$40
- *Kavalkad,* Nov. 7, 1957; a cover from *Bus Stop.* (DEN) ....$60-$90
- *Le Film Complet,* April 18, 1957; no. 613; in a skirt, sitting on a suitcase in *Bus Stop.* (FRA) ....$40-$60
- *LIFE* (International), July 8, 1957; vol. 23, no. 1; seated with Laurence Olivier in *The Prince and The Showgirl.* (INT) ....$200-$275
- *Mon Film,* Dec. 4, 1957; no. 589; in ruffled dress from *Showgirl.* (FRA) .....$30-$50
- *Neue Illustrierte,* Nov. 16, 1957; vol. 12, no. 46; in a dress, in a photo by Jack Cardiff. (GER) ....$80-$120
- *Paseo,* May 4, 1957; wearing a long green satin gown. (MEX) ....$75-$125
- *Picture Show,* July 4, 1957; with Laurence Olivier in *Showgirl.* (ENG) ....$30-$50
- *Rotosei,* Oct. 25, 1957; vol. 1, no. 32; by Avedon, dreamy in a black-sequined dress. (ITA) ....$50-$85
- *Screen,* Nov. 1957; wrapped in a fur, wearing black sequins. (JPN) ....$60-$90
- *Se,* Oct. 11-18, 1957; vol. 20, no. 41; lying on the floor in a flowing dress. (SWE) ....$60-$85
- *Settimo Giorno,* May 25, 1957; vol. X, no. 21; a profile-like shot in the gold lamé dress. (ITA) ....$60-$85
- *Sight and Sound,* Summer 1957; vol. 27, no. 1; a scene in a dress from *The Prince and The Showgirl.* (ENG) ....$30-$50
- Stage and *Cinema,* Nov. 15, 1957; vol. 44, no. 10; glamorous in a gold halter-style dress. (SAF) ....$90-$120
- *Svensk Damtidning,* Sept. 12, 1957; with Laurence Olivier. (SWE) ....$60-$90
- *Tele Magazine,* Oct. 1957; no. 6; a pretty, glamorous Monroe. (FRA) ....$60-$90
- *The New Fiesta,* July 1957; vol. 2, no. 6; digest with a romantic ruffle-clad Marilyn. (ENG) ....$60-$90
- *Towa,* 1957; in a flowing dress on the floor by Greene. (JPN) ....$50-$90
- *Vecko Revyn,* Sept. 27, 1957; no. 39; wearing the long black-sequined gown. (SWE) ....$50-$80
- *Visto,* Oct. 19, 1957; vol. VI, no. 42; in a blue blouse, a Milton Greene photo. (ITA) ....$60-$90
- *Weekend,* Oct. 5, 1957; vol. 4, no. 7; in a black dress with a white collar. (AUS) ....$60-$100

1958

- *Antena,* May 13, 1958; vol. XXVII, no. 1409; in a *Bus Stop* costume. (ARG) ....$60-$90
- *Grand Hotel,* Feb. 13, 1958; no. 608; an artwork rendering. (ITA) ....$50-$85
- *Idolos* (digest), July 17, 1958; vol. 1, no. 5; all on her; wearing a white coat and gloves. (SPA) ....$50-$75
- *Lectures d'Aujord'hui,* May 3, 1958; no. 296; a candid, smiling Marilyn in a white terry robe. (BEL) ....$60-$90
- *Le Ore,* June 21, 1958; vol. V, no. 267; a close-up, hugging the white pole. (ITA) ....$40-$65
- *L'Europeo,* April 13, 1958; no. 15; wearing the famous gold lamé gown. (ITA) ....$40-$65

Revue, May 29, 1954 (Germany), $60-$90.

The Eiga Story, September 1954 (Japan), $80-$120.

Piff, September 1954 (Sweden), $35-$50.

Cineromanzo, October 1954 (Italy), $100-$130.

Voir, November 23, 1954 (France), $125-$175.

Joulu Iso Kalle, December 1954 (Finland), $100-$140.

- *New Screen News,* Jan. 10, 1958; embracing Laurence Olivier. (AUS) ....$40-$60
- *Novella,* Nov. 23, 1958; vol. XXXIX, no. 47; candid, with her eyes closed, smiling. (ITA) ....$60-$90
- *Oggi,* Sept. 25, 1958; vol. XIV, no. 39; with her hair blowing around her face. (ITA) ....$40-$65
- *Settimo Giorno,* Jan. 4, 1958; vol. XI, no. 1; a close-up with her eyes shut by Avedon. (ITA) ....$100-$140
- *Settimo Giorno,* May 22, 1958; vol. XI, no. 21; a hazy profile in an oversized hat. (ITA) ....$100-$140
- *Settimo Giorno,* Oct. 9, 1958; no. 41; in a black dress and white gloves. (ITA) ....$90-$130
- *Star Weekly,* Nov. 22, 1958; newspaper section; in a red dress. (CAN)........$40-$80
- *Tempo,* Nov. 4, 1958; vol. XX, no. 45; in the fuschia one-strap dress with a hand to her face. (ITA) ....$40-$65

1959

- *Bild Journalen,* June 10, 1959; no. 24; tinted in a robe by a bathtub. (SWE) ....$85-$125
- *Cocktail,* April 25, 1959; in a black jewel-decorated dress, laughing. (ENG) ....$75-$125
- *De Post,* Feb. 15, 1959; vol. 11, no. 7; at the *Bus Stop* press conference in a suit. (BEL) ....$60-$90
- *Deutsche Illustrierte,* Feb. 14, 1959; no. 7; with Jane Russell in *Blondes.* (GER) ....$40-$55
- *Epoca,* March 8, 1959; vol. X, no. 440; a half-cover, by Avedon. (ITA) ....$30-$40
- *Epoca,* June 7, 1959; no. 453; a partial cover. (ITA) ....$30-$40
- *Fan's Star Library—Monroe,* 1959; no. 18; entire issue is on her; a glamour cover. (ENG) ....$125-$175
- *Films and Filming,* June 1959; vol. 5, no. 9; with Tony Curtis and Jack Lemmon. (ENG) ....$30-$50
- *Gran Via,* 1959; no. 109; wearing a black jeweled-strap dress. (SPA) ....$50-$80
- *Hollywood Festival,* Aug. 22, 1959; no. 167; in a bandana skirt with her arm up. (ITA) ....$100-$130
- *Il Musichiere,* April 30, 1959; vol. 1, no. 17; portrayed by an artist. (ITA) ....$60-$100
- *Jours De France,* June 13, 1959; no. 239; biting a strand of pearls. (FRA ....$50-$100
- *La Settimo Incom Illustrata,* Nov. 7, 1959; vol. XII, no. 45; a picture from *Niagara.* (ITA) ....$50-$90
- *L'Europeo,* July 19, 1959; no. 29; playing on the beach in a swimsuit. (ITA) ....$50-$80
- *Liberty,* March 1959; wearing the white fur on three-quarters of the cover. (CAN) ....$30-$40
- *Lunes,* July 6, 1959; in a black negligee from *Hot.* (URU) ....$50-$80
- *Marie Claire,* Sept. 1959; no. 59; a very tight close-up from *Hot.* (FRA) ....$60-$80
- *Mundo Argentino,* May 13, 1959; no. 2515; a tinted cover with her hand to her cheek. (ARG) ....$50-$80
- *Neue Illustrierte,* Dec. 12, 1959; vol. 14, no. 50; jumping in a dress. (GER) ....$60-$90
- *Noi Donne,* May 3, 1959; vol. XIV, no. 18; in the red *Niagara* dress and hoops. (ITA) ....$60-$90
- *Oggi,* April 19, 1959; vol. XV, no. 16; sitting in a chair, wearing triple pearls. (ITA) ....$40-$60
- *Oggi,* Oct. 8, 1959; vol. XV, no. 41; in a black dress, biting a strand of pearls. (ITA) ....$40-$60
- *Paris Match,* Feb. 28, 1959; no. 516; a close-up from *Bus Stop.* (FRA) ....$40-$60
- *Picture Show,* Dec. 26, 1959; a portrait decorated by Christmas ornaments. (ENG) ....$35-$45
- *Pix,* April 11, 1959; in a cocktail dress, wearing a lot of jewelry. (AUS) ....$60-$100

- *Platea,* Dec. 4, 1959; vol. 1, no. 5; in a beaded gown, holding an earring. (ARG) .... $80-$120
- *Regards,* Nov. 1959; a close-up from *River.* (FRA) .... $80-$110
- *Revue,* Feb. 21, 1959; no. 8; in a white dress with gold drapes behind her. (GER) .... $125-$175
- *Se,* Dec. 17, 1959; vol. 22, no. 51; two images of Marilyn jumping, by Halsman. (SWE) .... $40-$65
- *Se Og Hor,* Feb. 13, 1959; vol. 20, no. 7; sitting with Karen Blixen. (DEN) .... $75-$100
- *Sissi,* 1959; vol. 2, no. 76; holding the 500 year old diamond. (SPA) .... $40-$50
- *Sissi,* 1959; vol. 2, no. 77; with shorter hair and black gloves. (SPA) .... $40-$50
- *Sissi,* Aug. 24, 1959; vol. 2, no. 78; with Arthur Miller. (SPA) .... $40-$50
- *Sissi,* 1959; vol. 2, no. 79; a younger glamour portrait with hand up. (SPA) .... $40-$50
- *Star Revue,* Nov. 1959; no. 24; a standard studio-released photo. (GER) .... $60-$90
- *Star Weekly,* Oct. 3, 1959; Marilyn on top in sequins; Arthur Miller on bottom. (CAN) .... $30-$50
- *The Australian Women's Weekly,* April 8, 1959; in the black-sequined dress, a profile by Avedon. (AUS) .... $70-$110
- *The Queen,* March 17, 1959; a photo that shows Marilyn at her best. (ENG) .... $75-$125
- *TV Cine Actualite,* June 14, 1959; no. 272; a glamorous publicity photo. (FRA) .... $60-$90
- *Vie Nuove,* Oct. 3, 1959; no. 39; in a black negligee in *Hot.* (ITA) .... $60-$90
- *Weekend,* Oct. 21-25, 1959; no. 2852; biting playfully on a strand of pearls. (ENG) .... $85-$111
- *Zondagsvriend,* Dec. 31, 1959; no. 53; jumping up with Halsman. (HOL) .... $50-$80

1960

- *Bild Journalen,* May 11, 1960; in the famous gold lamé halter dress. (SWE) .... $40-$60
- *Bonnes Soirees,* April 10, 1960; no. 1991; displaying "the Marilyn look." (FRA) .... $35-$50
- *Bravo,* July 17-23, 1960; no. 29; in a glamorous gown. (GER) .... $40-$60
- *Capri,* May 1960; no. 18; a studio publicity pose. (FRA) .... $45-$60
- *Cinemondo,* May 10, 1960; vol. 28, no. 1344; a less common white fur pose. (FRA) .... $40-$60
- *De Post,* Oct. 9, 1960; vol. 12, no. 41; in a black dress and a sad face. (BEL) .... $50-$80
- *Ecran,* Dec. 16, 1960; no. 1638; a serious face in a white fur. (CHI) .... $30-$40
- *Elite,* Oct. 29, 1960; in the plunging gold lamé gown. (VEN) .... $60-$90
- *Elokuva Aitta,* no. 12; a tinted glamour photo. (FIN) .... $50-$70
- *Epoca,* Feb. 14, 1960; vol. XI, no. 489; in a beige dress, holding a champagne glass. (ITA) .... $40-$60
- *Frau Im Spiegel,* Feb. 20, 1960; vol. 15; a glamorous portrait. (SWI) .... $50-$70
- *Funk Und Film,* Sept. 24, 1960; no. 39; a standard studio photograph. (GER) .... $50-$70
- *Gaceta Illustrada,* May 21, 1960; no. 189; sitting on the floor throwing money in the air. (SPA) .... $100-$150
- *Gente,* Jan. 29, 1960; no. 5; a typical glamour studio shot. (ITA) .... $60-$90
- *Jours De France,* Aug. 6, 1960; no. 299; being embraced by Yves Montand. (FRA) .... $60-$80
- *Jours De France,* Nov. 26, 1960; no. 315; a close-up from *The Misfits,* with bangs. (FRA) .... $60-$80
- *La Cinematographie Francaise,* Oct. 1, 1960; no. 1885; a studio glamour photograph. (FRA) .... $50-$70
- *La Settimana Incom Illustrata,* Nov. 24, 1960; no. 47; in a silver lamé gown. (ITA) .... $60-$90
- *L'Ecran Lorrain,* Nov. 1960; no. 161; a studio publicity photo. (FRA) .... $40-$60

Settimo Giorno, December 23, 1954 (Italy), $80-$125.

Ricu ritas, circa 1955 (Argentina), $100-$130.

Flix, circa 1955 (England), $60-$100.

Jours de France, March 1955 (France), $90-$130.

A.M. Australian Magazine, April 5, 1955 (Australia), $125-$175.

Bild Journalen, April 1955 (Sweden), $100-$140.

- *Lecturas,* Sept. 1, 1960; a studio glamour image. (SPA)............................$45-$65
- *Le Films Pour Vous,* June 20, 1960; no. 184; Marilyn at her best. (FRA) ....$50-$70
- *Le Films Pour Vous,* Sept. 12, 1960; no. 196; Marilyn in a glamorous-style dress. (FRA) ....$50-$70
- *Le Ore,* April 6, 1960; no. 363; jumping up in a black-sequined dress. (ITA) ....$40-$60
- *Le Ore,* Sept. 6, 1960; vol. VIII, no. 382; dancing in a purple sweater, from *Let's Make Love.* (ITA) ....$40-$60
- *Le Ore,* Dec. 13, 1960; vol. VIII, no. 396; looking at money on the floor. (ITA) ....$60-$90
- *L'Europeo,* April 10, 1960; no. 15; a glamour shot in a chair from *Let's Make Love.* (ITA) ....$40-$65
- *L'Europeo,* Sept. 18, 1960; vol. XVI, no. 38; doing the Charleston in a black dress. (ITA) ....$40-$65
- *L'Europeo,* Nov. 20, 1960; vol. XVI, no. 47; sitting on a table, looking at diamonds. (ITA) ....$40-$65
- *Liberty,* Oct. 1960; vol. 37, no. 7; three-quarters of cover with a reflection from a mirror. (CAN) ....$30-$40
- *L'Officiel Des Spectacles,* Oct. 12, 1960; no. 726; a glamour photograph. (FRA) ....$30-$40
- *Manana,* July 9, 1960; no. 880; in a red spaghetti-strap dress. (MEX) ....$125-$175
- *Me Naiset,* Dec. 6, 1960; no. 18; with Yves Montand in director's chair. (FIN) ....$50-$80
- *Meridiano,* Jan. 10, 1960; no. 2; a large b&w candid portrait. (ITA) ....$50-$80
- *Munchner Illustrierte,* Sept. 30, 1960; no. 36; a publicity shot with Montand. (GER) ....$50-$80
- *Neue Illustrierte,* Oct. 22, 1960; vol. 15, no. 43; a portrait by Avedon. (GER) ....$60-$80
- *Noir Et Blanc,* Jan. 29, 1960; no. 778; with Yves Montand. (FRA) ....$40-$65
- *Noir Et Blanc,* Nov. 16, 1960; no. 820; a candid with husband Arthur Miller. (FRA) ....$40-$65
- *Paris Match,* Feb. 13, 1960; no. 566; embracing Yves Montand. (FRA).......$34-$45
- *Photo Roman,* June 15, 1960; no. 10; a tinted cover, being held by Keith Andes. (FRA) ....$100-$135
- *Piccolo,* Nov. 1960; a glamorous face shot. (HOL)....................................$50-$75
- *Picture Show,* Oct. 15, 1960; in a leotard from *Love.* (ENG).......................$30-$40
- *Popular Hi-Fi,* Oct. 1960; in a negligee by a bookcase. (ENG)................$100-$130
- *Revue,* March 26, 1960; no. 13; dancing in a black sheath dress. (GER)...$80-$100
- *Revue,* Dec. 17, 1960; no. 51; an unretouched portrait from *The Misfits.* (GER) ....$50-$86
- *Roman Bladet,* Sept. 1, 1960; no. 314; in a gold halter dress. (DEN) ....$60-$90
- *Romanschatz,* 1960; no. 204; a pose with Tony Curtis. (GER)....................$40-$65
- *Settimo Giorno,* Nov. 27, 1960; vol. XIII, no. 49; with Yves Montand. (ITA) ....$60-$90
- *Sight and Sound,* Autumn 1960; vol. 29, no. 4; a shot from *Love.* (ENG)....$30-$40
- *Stage And Cinema,* April 1, 960; vol. 55, no. 2; a glamorous Marilyn. (SAF) ....$100-$120
- *Star Revue,* May 1960; no. 10; a close-up by Avedon. (GER) ....$60-$90
- *Star Weekly,* Sept. 24, 1960; newspaper section; holding pole from *Let's Make Love.* (CAN) ....$45-$60
- *Stern,* June 18, 1960; vol. 13, no. 25; surrounded by men in a number from *Let's Make Love.* (GER) ....$60-$90
- *Stern,* Sept. 17, 1960; vol. 13, no. 38; with Yves Montand. (GER) ....$50-$80
- *Stern,* Dec. 17, 1960; vol. 13, no. 51; a cute photo, looking at diamonds. (GER) ....$60-$90
- *Tempo,* Aug. 27, 1960; vol. XXII, no. 35; hair blowing, wearing the black-sequined dress. (ITA)....................$50-$80
- *The Australian Woman's Weekly,* Dec. 7, 1960; a less common shot in white gloves. (AUS) ....$90-$110
- *Today,* Oct. 1, 1960; with Yves Montand. (ENG)..$60-$90

- *Vecko Revyen,* Sept. 1960; no. 37; on stage with men from *Love.* (SWE)...$60-$80
- *Visto,* Oct. 6, 1960; no. 41; a candid shot in a suit with a bouquet of roses. (ITA) ....$60-$80
- *Weekend,* April Sept. 1960; vol. 6, no. 34; a candid with Arthur Miller. (AUS) ....$60-$90
- *Weekend,* March 30-April 3, 1960; no. 2875; with Frankie Vaughn. (ENG) ..$60-$90
- *Weekend,* Sept. 7-11, 1960; on stage with men from *Love.* (ENG) ....$60-$90

1961

- *ABC Met TV Gids,* April 15, 1961; with her idol, Clark Gable. (BEL)............$60-$80
- *Bild Journalen,* May 24, 1961; in a chair, photo by Arnold. (SWE)..............$60-$80
- *Cinelandia,* April 1961; vol. X, no. 203; in a bright orange blouse. (BRA)....$50-$80
- *Cinelandia,* June 1961; vol. X, no. 207; in a black hair net from *The Misfits.* (BRA) ....$50-$70
- *Cinemonde,* Feb. 21, 1961; vol. 28, no. 1385; in a black dress with white gloves. (FRA) ....$50-$70
- *Cine Universal,* July 1, 1961; no. 119; embracing Clark Gable. (MEX).......$80-$110
- *Epoca,* Feb. 5, 1961; vol. XII, no. 540; on the floor in a white terry robe. (ITA) ....$40-$60
- *Filmski Svet,* Oct. 10, 1961; no. 345; a typical glamour shot. (POL)...........$40-$60
- *Funk Und Film,* April 8, 1961; a studio-released publicity still. (GER) ....$60-$80
- *Hayat,* May 18, 1961; no. 21; three different tinted portraits. (TUR)...........$50-$80
- *Hayat,* Aug. 24, 1961; no. 35; in a bikini, sitting in a director's chair on *The Misfits* set. (TUR) ....$70-$100
- *Hebdo Roman,* Jan. 25, 1961; no. 4; a glamorous photograph. (FRA) ......$70-$100
- *Jours De France,* Feb. 18, 1961; no. 327; a close-up by Arnold. (FRA)........$60-$90
- *Kristall,* 1 VJ; b&w image by Greene, in a top. (GER)...............................$75-$100
- *Le Monde Et La Vie,* Sept. 1961; no. 100; smiling in the black-sequined dress. (FRA) ....$60-$90
- *Lecturas,* 1961; no. 511; a portrait from *Love.* (SPA)..................................$50-$80
- *L'Espresso Mese,* March 1961; no. 3; a photo by Arnold in a car. (ITA).......$50-$80
- *L'Europeo,* March 12, 1961; vol. XVII, no. 11; from *Misfits,* in a black polka-dot hair net. (ITA) ....$40-$60
- *L'Europeo,* June 25, 1961; vol. XVII, no. 26; in a black fur and black leather gloves. (ITA) ....$40-$60
- *L'Europeo,* Dec. 17, 1961; vol. XVII, no. 51; in a black strapless dress decorated with beadwork. (ITA) ....$40-$60
- *Manana,* July 1, 1961; no. 931; reflection from *Misfits* in a car mirror. (MEX) ....$100-$150
- *Mi Vida,* Aug. 24, 1961; no. 176; a tinted glamour photo in a dress. (CHI) ....$75-$110
- *Radio,* Nov. 1, 1961; no. 130; a typical glamour photograph. (SPA)...........$60-$80
- *Star Weekly,* Sept. 16, 1961; a candid from the set of *Hot.* (CAN) ....$75-$110
- *Tempo,* April 11, 1961; no. 15; tinted shot with Clark Gable and Montgomery Clift. (DEN) ....$60-$90
- *The Eiga Geijutsu,* 1961; a shot from *Love* on a chair. (JPN) ....$60-$90
- *Today,* Feb. 4, 1961; vol. 3, no. 50; standing with husband Arthur Miller. (ENG) ....$60-$90
- *Visto,* Feb. 16, 1961; no. 7; a sexy studio photograph. (ITA) ....$60-$90
- *Weekend,* March 1-5, 1961; no. 2923. (ENG)...$60-$90

1962

- *ABC,* Aug. 12, 1962; no. 33; a b&w Greene photo. (ITA).............................$50-$80
- *Antena TV,* Sept. 4, 1962; in a costume from *Love.* (ARG)..........................$40-$65
- *Avondlectur,* March 23, 1962; in the cherry-print dress from *The Misfits.* (HOL) ....$40-$60
- *Billed Bladet,* Aug. 10, 1962; vol. 25, no. 32; a shot with a surprised look from *Some Like It Hot.* (DEN) ....$60-$85

Der Stern, April 10, 1955 (Germany), $90-$125.

Piccolo, April 3, 1955 (Holland), $40-$80.

Liberty, July 1955 (Canada), $40-$70.

A.M. Australian Magazine, July 5, 1955 (Australia), $125-$175.

Epoca, July 24, 1955 (Italy), $60-$90.

Cine Revue, November 1955 (France), $50-$80.

- *Bunte Illustrierte,* Aug. 22, 1962; no. 34; in the black-sequined dress by Avedon. (GER)....$60-$85
- *Celuloid,* Sept. 22, 1962; a glamour image on this death issue. (SPA) ....$50-$65
- *Cine Avance,* Aug. 1962; no. 1; a close-up in gold hoop earrings and a smile. (MEX)....$125-$175
- *Cine Monde,* Aug. 14, 1962; no. 1462; in dark pink halter dress. (FRA) ......$50-$75
- *Cine Tele-Revue,* Aug. 8, 1962; no. 33; entire issue devoted to her; two images on cover. (FRA)....$75-$100
- *Cine Universal,* Sept. 1, 1962; a candid photo from her last trip to Mexico. (MEX) ....$90-$130
- *Contre Champ,* Oct. 1962; no. 4; a glamour photograph on another memorial. (FRA)....$50-$80
- *Ecran,* June 15, 1962; no. 1560; a photo from *Love.* (CHI)....$30-$40
- *Ecran,* Aug. 10, 1962; no. 1646; another image from *Love.* (CHI) ....$30-$40
- *El Aventuras,* Aug. 8, 1962; entire issue is on her; a profile in the gold lamé. (MEX) ....$125-$200
- *Epoca,* Aug. 12, 1962; vol. XIII, no. 620; at her last Golden Globes Awards. (ITA) ....$40-$50
- *Everybody's,* Sept. 19, 1962, in a blue terry robe from *Give.* (AUS).............$60-$90
- *Everybody's,* Sept. 26, 1962; wearing the cherry dress from *The Misfits.* (AUS) ....$70-$100
- *Fatos & Fotos,* Aug. 18, 1962; typical Marilyn on this memorial-oriented cover. (SPA)....$80-$110
- *Festival Film Special,* 1962; entire issue devoted to her; in the white fur. (FRA) ....$100-$150
- *Fotogramas,* March 16, 1962; vol. XVII, no. 694; a studio publicity still. (SPA) ....$60-$90
- *Fotogramas,* June 8, 1962; vol. XVII, no. 706; tinted, in the flower dress from *Something's Got To Give.* (SPA)....$60-$90
- *Frau Im Spiegel,* Aug. 25, 1962; vol. 17, no. 34; face shot at an awards show in Hollywood. (SWI)....$60-$90
- *Gaceta Illustrada,* Aug. 11, 1962; vol. VII, no. 305; a still from *Let's Make Love.* (SPA)....$60-$90
- *Gente,* Aug. 17, 1962; no. 33; with Yves Montand. (ITA) ....$60-$90
- *Hemmets Journal,* Dec. 27, 1962; vol. 42, no. 52; in a beige fur hat from *Something's Got To Give.* (SWE)....$60-$90
- *Idilio,* Oct. 16, 1962; in a white dress from *Love.* (ARG)....$60-$80
- *Intervalo De Cine Presenta-MM,* 1962; entire issue is dedicated to her life and death. (ARG)....$150-$200
- *Kavalkad* (digest), April 1962; vol. 14, no. 9; a young Norma Jeane holding ski poles. (SWE) ....$90-$120
- *La Grande Tragedia—MM,* 1962; entire issue on her, looking over her shoulder. (ARG) ....$150-$200
- *Le Soir Illustre,* Aug. 9, 1962; no. 1572; in white-collared dress. (FRA) ......$60-$90
- *L'Europeo,* March 25, 1962; no. 12; three pictures from the Golden Globe Awards. (ITA) ....$40-$60
- *L'Europeo,* June 18, 1962; no. 24; in a swimming pool from *Give.* (ITA).....$40-$60
- *L'Europeo,* Aug. 12, 1962; no. 32; in a black fur and black gloves on this tribute issue. (ITA) ....$40-$70
- *Luxembourg Selection,* Nov. 1962; no. 8 ; in the black negligee from publicity stills. (FRA)....$40-$70
- *Manchet,* Aug. 1962; another publication says good-bye to Monroe. (MEX) ....$70-$100
- *Maschere,* Aug. 1962; a glamorous Marilyn in a publicity still. (ITA) ....$40-$80
- *Mi Vida,* Aug. 30, 1962; no. 229; in a red dress standing next to a green chair. (CHI)....$100-$130
- *Mujer,* Feb. 1962; a Greene photo, lying on the floor. (SPA)....$90-$125
- *Neue Illustrierte,* Aug. 12, 1962; vol. 17, no. 32; in a beige fur hat, biting her tongue. (GER)....$80-$110

- *Noir Et Blanc,* Aug. 10, 1962; no. 910; a glamour shot in a necklace and earrings. (IRA) .... $60-$90
- *Oggi,* Aug. 12, 1962; vol. XVIII, no. 33; a moment with her hair up from *Love.* (ITA) .... $50-$80
- *Oggi,* Sept. 20, 1962; vol. XVIII, no. 38; with her eyes closed in a pink shirt. (ITA) .... $50-$80
- *Paris Match,* June 23, 1962; no. 689; lying her head on her arm. (FRA) ..... $50-$80
- *Paris Match,* Aug. 18, 1962; no. 697; a close-up portrait from1962. (FRA) .... $50-$80
- *Piccolo,* Sept. 2, 1962; no. 704; wearing a jean jacket on the *The Misfits* set. (HOL) .... $50-$80
- *Point De Vue Images Du Monde,* Aug. 10, 1962; vol. 18, no. 739; in a blue gown with jewels. (FRA) .... $60-$90
- *Positif,* Oct. 1962; no. 48; a b&w image with her hair up. (FRA) .... $40-$80
- *Radio Film,* Sept. 30, 1962; a publicity still from *Love.* (ARG) .... $50-$90
- *Sabado Grafico,* Aug. 11, 1962; no. 306; at a press conference. (SPA) .... $50-$80
- *Se,* June 28, 1962; vol. 25, no. 26; almost naked, seated by the pool in *Give.* (SWE) .... $40-$65
- *Se,* Aug. 9, 1962; vol. 25, no. 32; with her eyes shut in the black sequined dress. (SWE) .... $40-$60
- *Se Apago La Estrella –MM,* 1962; entire issue is on her life and death. (ARG) .... $150-$200
- *Se Og Hor,* June 29, 1962; vol. 23, no. 27; in the swimming pool during the filming of *Give.* (DEN) .... $50-$80
- *Stop,* Aug. 1962; no. 16; in the common gold lamé gown. (FRA) .... $40-$60
- *Svensk Damtidning,* Aug. 22, 1962; no. 34; a portrait from *Love.* (SWE).... $50-$80
- *Tempo,* Aug. 18, 1962; vol. XXIV, no. 33; seated on a sofa in the black sequined dress. (ITA) .... $50-$85
- *Todo,* Aug. 16, 1962; no. 1349; a glamorous Marilyn in a dress. (MEX).. $125-$175
- *Town,* Nov. 1962; a portrait by George Barris during her last summer. (ENG) .... $80-$120
- *TV France,* Aug. 18-24, 1962; no. 20, smiling in a white terry robe from *Itch.* (FRA) .... $60-$90
- *Vie Nuove,* Aug. 9, 1962; vol. XVII, no. 32; a close-up portrait on this tribute issue. (ITA) .... $50-$80
- *Wereld Kroniek,* Aug. 1962; a three-quarters cover with a large face shot. (HOL) .... $40-$60
- *Woman's Day,* March 19, 1962; no. 274; a pretty portrait from *Love.* (AUS) .... $50-$80
- *Cine Monde,* July 30, 1962; vol. 31, no. 1512; in the beige fur hat, biting her tongue. (FRA) .... $50-$80

1963

- *Cine Hoy,* Nov.-Dec. 1963; a close-up. (ARG) .... $40-$60
- *Crapouillot,* Jan. 1963; no. 59; by the swimming pool in *Give.* (FRA) .... $30-$50
- *Epoca,* Aug. 11, 1963; vol. XIV, no. 672; a semi-profile in the gold lamé gown. (ITA) .... $40-$60
- *Frissons Films,* June 1963; no. 3; a studio publicity still. (FRA) .... $30-$50
- *Movie TV & Show Times,* 1963; holding a pole from *Love.* (JPN) .... $60-$90
- *Se,* May 9, 1963; no. 19; a tinted Stem shot with a scarf. (SWE) .... $40-$65
- *Successo,* May 1963; no. 5; an artwork cover of Marilyn dancing. (ITA) ..... $30-$50
- *Towa,* 1963; sitting by the swimming pool in *Give.* (JPN) .... $60-$90

1964

- *Idun Vecko Journalen,* Nov. 6, 1964; no. 45; a portrait in the blue terry robe from *Something's Got To Give.* (SWE) .... $40-$60
- *Le Ore,* March 2, 1964; no. 13; curled up in a bed with a red carnation on it. (ITA) .... $30-$45

Cinema, November 25, 1955 (Italy), $50-$70.

Entre Nous, 1956 (France), $125-$170.

Hayat, May 4, 1956 (Turkey), $50-$80.

The Australian Women's Weekly, July 1956 (Australia), $175-$250.

Settimo Giorno, July 7, 1956 (Italy), $100-$150.

Point De Vue Images Du Monde, July 7, 1956 (France), $90-$125.

- *L'Europeo,* Feb. 9, 1964; vol. XX, no. 6; a portrait in the blue terry robe from *Something's Got To Give.* (ITA) ....$30-$45
- *Listener,* Aug. 28, 1964; vol. 51, no. 1300; posing for a picture. (NZ) ....$60-$100
- *Panorama,* Oct. 1964; vol. 2, no. 25; wearing the gold lamé gown. (ITA) ....$30-$45
- *Tidens Kvinder,* Oct. 6, 1964; a pretty portrait in the beige fur trimmed hat. (SWE) ....$40-$60
- *Vecko Revyen,* Nov. 4, 1964; wrapped in a fur wearing the black-sequined dress. (SWE) ....$35-$55

1965

- *Film Ideal,* Aug. 1, 1965; with a stand-in during a scene from *Gentlemen Prefer Blondes.* (SPA) ....$30-$45
- *Marie Claire,* Jan. 18, 1965; no. 128; a joyful face in the black-sequined dress. (FRA) ....$40-$60
- *7 Dias,* Oct. 1965; a sad face, holding up a tinted scarf over her torso. (CHI) ....$30-$55
- *Tele Demiere,* Oct. 20, 1965; no. 186; a portrait from her last summer. (FRA) ....$30-$40

1966

- *Cine Tele Revue,* April 28, 1966; in the flame-colored dress from *Gentlemen Prefer Blondes.* (FRA) ....$30-$40
- *Gente,* Aug. 31, 1966; vol. X, no. 35; in a black spaghetti-strap dress. (ITA) ....$30-$50
- *Interview,* Aug. 1966; no. 6; a classic glamour photograph. (FRA) ....$30-$50
- *Kristall,* Sept. 23, 1966; in a sweater in the mid-1950s. (GER) ....$60-$90
- *La Storia Del Cinema,* March 30, 1966; no. 1; jumping in a Halsman picture. (ITA) ....$40-$50
- *Mi Vida,* Nov. 1966; vol. VIII, no. 442; sitting in the flame-colored gown from *Gentlemen Prefer Blondes.* (CHI) ....$60-$80
- *Mujeres Celebras,* 1966; a glamour still by the studio. (SPA) ....$40-$65
- *Secretos,* Jan. 8, 1966; an Arnold portrait on *The Misfits* set. (ARG) ....$40-$60
- *Stern,* Aug. 7, 1966; no. 32; in the blue terry robe by the pool from *Something's Got To Give.* (GER) ....$40-$65

1967

- *La Storia Del Cinema,* Feb. 1, 1967; no. 44; with Laurence Olivier on the set of *The Prince and The Showgirl.* (ITA) ....$40-$60
- *Noir Et Blanc,* Dec. 6, 1967; vol. 22, no. 1187; a candid shot, posing with her hand on her chin. (FRA) ....$40-$70

1968

- *Cine Avance,* Aug. 10, 1968; close-up portrait in gold lamé. (MEX) ....$50-$90
- *Historia Hors Serie,* 1968; no. 10; typical glamour image. (FRA) ....$30-$50
- *Observer,* July 14, 1968; a sad portrait taken by Steen. (ENG) ....$30-$40

1969

- *Buenhogar,* 1969; the overused photo in the white fur. (SWE) ....$30-$40
- *Gente,* Jan. 22, 1969; no. 4; a half-cover close-up from *Love.* (ITA) ....$30-$40
- *Se,* Dec. 23, 1969; sitting in a director's chair for *Love.* (SWE) ....$30-$40

1971

- *Fotogramas,* Feb. 12, 1971; vol. XXVI, no. 1165; romantic glamour photo. (SPA) ....$20-$35
- *Headlines,* Dec. 1971; various newspaper clippings. (ENG) ....$20-$35
- *Stop,* July 17, 1971; no. 1189; with John Kennedy. (ITA) ....$20-$35
- *Tele 7 Jours,* Aug. 7, 1971; no. 589; a classic Marilyn at her best. (FRA) ....$20-$30

1972

- *Cine Revue,* Dec. 21, 1972; vol. 52, no. 51; a Barris photo by the ocean. (FRA) ....$20-$30
- *Grand Hotel,* Oct. 12, 1972; vol. XXVII, no. 1371; an artwork cover depicting Monroe. (ITA) ....$20-$30
- *Hitweek,* Sept. 22, 1972; a reproduction of the 1952 *LIFE* cover. (HOL) ......$20-$30
- *Oggi,* Oct. 3, 1972; no. 40; on most of cover, in an orange shirt. (ITA)........$20-$30
- *Skema,* Nov. 1972; no. 11; dancing with a large ostrich plume. (ITA)..........$20-$30
- *Vogue,* Dec. 1971-Jan. 1972; no. 522; a glamour portrait. (FRA) ....[illegible]

1973

- *Film Index,* 1973; no. 15; with Richard Widmark. (AUS).............................$10-$20
- *Film Index,* 1973; no. 16; with Cary Grant and Charles Coburn. (AUS)........$10-$20
- *HP,* Aug. 11, 1973; vol. 60, no. 32; in blue terry robe from *Give.* (HOL) ......$20-$30
- *Q-Quick,* Sept. 6, 1973; lying on the floor by Greene. (GER)........................$20-$30
- *The Sunday Times Magazine,* Sept. 16, 1973; a young Norma Jeane holding a ball. (ENG) ....$20-$30
- *Thursday,* Nov. 22, 1973; a Barris photo from her final summer. (AUS) ......$20-$30
- *Vecko Journalen,* Aug. 8, 1973; no. 32; a classic glamour image. (SWE)....$20-$30
- *Women's Weekly,* Oct. 17, 1973; holding a champagne glass. (AUS) ....$20-$30

1974

- *Domenica Del Corriere,* July 7, 1974; no. 27; an Avedon photo in a glamorous dress. (ITA)...$20-$30
- *Historia,* March 1974; no. 328; partially featured on the cover. (FRA)..........$10-$20
- *La Fiera Letteraria,* Jan. 20, 1974; no. 3; a glamour photograph. (ITA)........$20-$30
- *Le Grand Journal Illustre,* July 20, 1974; Monroe at her best. (FRA)...........$20-$30
- *L'Express,* Oct. 21, 1974; no. 1215; a studio-released publicity photo. (FRA) ....$15-$20
- *L'Express,* Oct. 28, 1974; no. 1216; another publicity still. (FRA) ....$15-$20
- *Miroir De L'Historie,* 1974; no. B 280; looking seductive in a black negligee. (FRA) ....$15-$20
- *Movie,* 1974; part 1; a classic glamour image. (ENG) ....$15-$20
- *Movie,* 1974; part 2; another glamour photo. (ENG) ....$15-$20
- *Photo,* 1974; no. 86; dressed as a ballerina in white. (FRA).........................$15-$20
- *Samedi Teleguide,* July 27, 1974; no. 2196; an image from her final summer. (BEL) ....$15-$20
- *Telerama,* Oct. 30, 1974; no. 1294; the majority of the cover is an image by Stern. (FRA) ....$15-$20

1975

- *Le Nouvel Observateur,* July 21, 1975; no. 558; holding a mirror in an Arnold shot. (FRA) ....$15-$20
- *Positif,* Jan. 1975; no. 165; a sexy and glamorous Marilyn. (FRA)...............$15-$20
- *Tele Magazine,* July 19, 1975; no. 1028; a standard studio photograph. (FRA) ....$15-$20
- *Tele 7 Jours,* Jan. 25, 1975; no. 767; another studio publicity still. (FRA) ....$15-$20

1976

- *Guida TV,* Oct. 1, 1976; no. 29; wearing a tight dress and a smile. (ITA).....$10-$20
- *Le Vedettes (Internationales),* June 26, 1976; looking glamorous in a studio photo. (FRA) ....$10-$20
- *Panorama,* Nov. 26, 1976; a studio-produced photograph. (ITA) ....$10-$20
- *Top Tele,* Dec. 22, 1976; no. 15; in a low-cut sexy gown. (FRA) ....$10-$20

Vie Nuove, July 21, 1956 (Italy), $40-$70.

Photoplay, August 1956 (England), $40-$70.

Radio Cinema Television, November 18, 1956 (France), $50-$80.

Eiga No Tomo, December 1956 (Japan), $80-$100.

Settimo Giorno, May 1957 (Italy), $60-$85.

The New Fiesta, July 1957 (England), $60-$90.

1977

- *Comment,* Aug. 1977; no. 5; an overused publicity still. (FRA) ....$10-$20
- *Revue,* May-June 1977; no. 79; another 20th Century Fox still. (FRA).........$10-$20
- *Settimana TV,* Aug. 21, 1977; no. 35; a smiling MM at her finest. (ITA) ......$10-$20

1978

- *Encyclopedia Alpha Du Cinema,* Sept. 20, 1978; vol. 1, no. 1; pretty portrait from her final summer. (FRA) ....$10-$20
- *Figure,* May 1978; vol. 1, no. 2; artwork by artist Tempest. (ITA)................$10-$20
- *Film Portraits,* March-April 1978; no. 2; a portrait by Arnold. (FRA) ....$10-$20
- *Le Soir Illustre,* Aug. 24, 1978; wearing beige fur hat from *Give.* (FRA) ......$10-$20
- *Metal Hurlant,* Dec. 1978; no. 36; artwork of MM and a lion head. (FRA)....$10-$20
- *Panorama,* July 14, 1978; a typical glamour image. (ITA) ....$10-$20

1979

- *Bravo,* April 5, 1979; a standard glamour portrait. (GER).............................$10-$20
- *Bravo,* Nov. 15, 1979; another glamour photograph. (GER) ....$10-$20
- *Confidences,* May 1979; no. 1638; smiling in a sexy dress. (FRA) ....$10-$20
- *Epoca,* July 7, 1979; no. 1500; a smiling glamorous Monroe. (ITA) ....$10-$20
- *Golboy,* Jan. 1979; no. 81; a studio still. (FRA) ....$10-$20
- *Golboy,* Oct. 1979; no. 89; another studio portrait. (FRA) ....$10-$20
- *Grafiti,* July 1979; a smiling portrait. (FRA) ....$10-$20
- *Titbits,* Aug. 25, 1979; a sexy Monroe pose. (ENG).....................................$10-$20

1980

- *Bravo,* May 29, 1980; in a low-cut dress. (GER) ....$10-$20
- *Cahiers Du Cinema,* April 1980; no. 310; a studio publicity pose. (FRA)......$10-$20
- *Confidences,* June 1980; no. 1696; classic glamorous Marilyn. (SPA) ....$10-$20
- *Encyclopedie Alpha Du Cinema,* July 2, 1980; no. 93; sexy shot. (FRA) ......$10-$20
- *Encyclopedie Alpha Du Cinema,* Aug. 30, 1980; no. 132; an overused publicity still. (FRA) ....$10-$20
- *Dizionario Del Film,* 1980; no. 10; Monroe glamour. (ITA) ....$10-$20
- *Guida TV,* Sept. 21, 1980; no. 38; a studio-released photo. (ITA)................$10-$20
- *I Grandi Fatti,* 1980; a pretty, soft-looking portrait. (ITA)..............................$10-$20
- *Mikro Gids,* July 12-18, 1980; a studio photograph. (ITA) ....$10-$20
- *Movies Chap,* 1980; a glamour image in a dress. (ENG).............................$10-$20
- *Oggi,* Sept. Oct. 1980; no. 37; a flattering portrait. (ITA).............................$10-$20
- *Paris Liosirs,* Sept. 1980; no. 9; a typical Marilyn pose. (FRA) ....$10-$20
- *Ragazza,* Aug. 20, 1980; no. 35; wearing a bright orange blouse. (ITA).......$10-$20
- *Se,* May 1980; no. 20; wearing an expensive silk slip. (SWE) ....$10-$20
- *Tele Cine Video,* Dec. 1980; no. 2; a studio-released publicity still. (FRA)....$10-$20
- *Tele Guide,* Nov. Dec. 1980; no. 189; a smiling, vibrant Marilyn. (FRA) ....$10-$20
- *Telerama,* July 2, 1980; no. 1590; a glamorous photo. (FRA) ....$10-$20
- *Tele Sette,* May 1, 1980; no. 18; posing with the white fur. (ITA) ....$10-$20
- *Tele Star,* Aug. 5, 1980; no. 201; in velvet green dress from *River Of No Return.* (FRA) ....$10-$20
- *Vara Gids,* July 12, 1980; vol. 51, no. 28; in a white bikini top with a sky background. (HOL)..$10-$20

1981

- *Bunte,* Feb. 7, 1981; a close-up portrait. (GER)..$10-$20
- *Cult Movie,* Dec. 1981-Jan. 1982; entire issue; in *Itch* dress. (ITA) ....$10-$20
- *Encyclopedie Alpha Du Cinema,* April 15, 1981; vol. X, no. 132; in the pool from *Something's Got To Give.* (IRA)...$10-$20
- *Fotogramas,* March 4, 1981; vol. 32, no. 647; wrapped in a towel on the beach. (SPA) ....$10-$20
- *Grand Hotel,* July 20, 1981; no. 30; in the train from *Hot.* (ITA) ....$10-$20
- *La Recherche,* Dec. 1981; no. 128; a studio publicity still. (IRA) ....$10-$20

- *Metal Hurlant,* July 1981; no. 64; in a sexy pose. (FRA) ....$10-$20
- *Photo,* March 1981; no. 162; wrapped in white sheets, by Douglas Kirkland. (FRA) ....$10-$20
- *Pilote,* March 1981; no. 82; a studio publicity pose. (FRA) ....$10-$20
- *Pilote,* May 1981; no. 84; a studio publicity pose. (FRA)..............................$10-$20
- *Popular Video,* Oct. 1981; a studio publicity photo. (ENG)..............................$10-$20
- *Presse,* Dec. 26, 1981; no. 4; a studio glamour shot. (FRA) ....$10-$20
- *Q-Quick,* Jan. 1981; a studio publicity photo. (GER) ....$10-$20
- *Q-Quick,* Oct. 1981; a smiling glamour image. (GER) ....$10-$20
- *Star Club,* 1981; entire issue on her; in black lace. (GER)..............................$10-$20
- *Telerama,* May 23, 1981; no. 1636; a studio glamour photograph. (FRA)....$10-$20
- *Video News,* March-April 1981; no. 2; a classic Monroe image. (FRA) ....$10-$20

1982

- *Amica,* June 22, 1982; no. 25; majority of issue is on her; in the gold lamé. (ITA) ....$10-$20
- *Bravo,* Aug. 3, 1982; no. 66; a peekaboo nude by Stern. (CHI)..............................$10-$20
- *Cinema & Cinema,* Nov.-Dec. 1982; no. 33; in the sheets, by Kirkland. (ITA) ....$10-$20
- *Cosmos,* March 1982; a pretty portrait. (VEN) ....$10-$20
- *El Cine Enciclopedia Salvat,* 1982; a close up from her final summer. (SPA) ....$10-$20
- *Emma,* June 1982; in the white dress, by Halsman. (GER) ....$10-$20
- *France Soir Magazine,* May 2, 1982; no. 11746; a typical glamour image by Stern. (FRA) ....$10-$20
- *Il Cinema,* 1982; no. 59; a studio-released photograph. (ITA)..............................$10-$20
- *Intimidades,* 1982; in the gold lamé gown. (SPA) ....$10-$20
- *Le Cinema,* 1982; no. 1-2; a classic glamour photo. (FRA)..............................$10-$20
- *Lecturas,* Aug. 1982; a smiling glamour-clad Monroe. (SPA)..............................$10-$20
- *Le Nouveau F,* July-Aug. 1982; no. 6/6; tight close-up from *River.* (FRA)....$10-$20
- *Metal Extra,* April 1982; no. 1; an artwork cover of Marilyn. (ITA) ....$10-$20
- *Piejk,* Aug. 1982; a pretty, flattering portrait. (JPN)..............................$10-$20
- *Q-Quick,* Aug. 1982; no. 32, a glamour pose by Greene. (GER)..............................$10-$20
- *Ragazza In,* April 1982; no. 16; a studio glamour publicity still. (ITA)..........$10-$20
- *Salut,* Sept. 1, 1982; no. 181; a glamour photograph. (FRA) ....$10-$20
- *Star Retro,* June 1982; no. 2; a classic and famous Monroe shot. (FRA) ....$10-$20
- *Star System,* Sept. 1982; no. 10; entire issue on her; in a dress from *Gentlemen Prefer Blondes.* (FRA)..............................$10-$20
- *Stern,* Aug. 5, 1982; no. 32; a close-up portrait by Stern. (GER) ....$10-$20
- *Sunday,* 1982; no. 31; a young Marilyn demonstrates many exercises. (ENG) ....$10-$20
- *Super Tele,* Nov. 13, 1982; no. 184; classic glamour photo. (FRA) ....$10-$20
- *Tele Guide,* Feb. 2, 1982; no. 253; another glamour shot. (FRA)..............................$10-$20
- *Tele Guide Jeux,* Jan. 1982; no. 9; a smiling, vibrant Monroe. (FRA)...........$10-$20
- *Tele Poche,* March 27, 1982; no. 116; a sexy, smiling Marilyn. (FRA) ....$10-$20
- *Telerama,* July 28, 1982; no. 1698; a studio-released pose. (FRA) ....$10-$20
- *Tele 7 Jours,* July 31, 1982; no. 1157; a pretty studio portrait. (FRA)..........$10-$20
- *Titbits,* Sept. 25, 1982; no. 5020; drinking a glass of champagne, by Stern. (ENG) ....$10-$20
- *TV Radio Corriere,* Aug. 1, 982; no. 31; a flattering photograph by the studio. (ITA) ....$10-$20
- *TV Sorrisi E Canzoni,* Aug. 8, 1982; no. 32; a typical sexy Monroe. (ITA)....$10-$20
- *Video,* July-Aug. 1982; no. 12; a classic well-known photograph. (FRA) .....$10-$20
- *Video TV Jaquettes,* May 1, 1982; no. 1; wearing a sexy dress and big smile. (FRA) ....$10-$20

Weekend, October 5, 1957 (Australia), $60-$100.

Cinemonde, October 1957 (France), $50-$80.

Screen, November 1957 (Japan), $60-$90.

Bild Journalen, November 1957 (Sweden), $60-$85.

Neue Illustrierte, November 16, 1957 (Germany), $80-$120.

Settimo Giorno, January 4, 1958 (Italy), $100-$140.

1983

- *Christiane,* Jan. 1983; no. 390; a glamour photo, often used. (FRA)............$10-$20
- *Grandi Temi Della Fotografia,* 1983; no. 6; a studio glamour still. (ITA).......$10-$20
- *Histoire De L'Art,* Feb. 1983; no. 154; a common photograph. (FRA)..........$10-$20
- *Le Cinema,* 1983; no. 59; wearing a tight, sexy dress. (FRA).......................$10-$20
- *Positif,* July-Aug. 1983; no. 269, 1970; a smiling, glamorous Monroe. (FRA) ....$10-$20
- *Psychologies,* Sept. 1983; no. 3; an often-seen studio still. (FRA)..............$10-$20
- *Q-Quick,* July 7, 1983; vol. 7, no. 28; four photos of MM. (GER) ....$10-$20
- *Q-Quick,* Oct. 1983; in the well-known white *Itch* dress. (GER) ....$10-$20
- *Retro Revue,* Jan. 1983; no. 2; on this nostalgia-oriented issue. (FRA).......$10-$20
- *Salut,* Dec. 21, 1983; no. 215; a studio-released publicity still. (FRA)..........$10-$20
- *Screen,* Feb. 25, 1983; holding up a striped scarf over her torso. (JPN) .....$10-$20
- *Skoop,* Nov. 1983; another common publicity pose. (HOL) ....$10-$20
- *Tele Cine Video,* Feb. 1983; no. 26; a studio-released publicity still. (FRA)..$10-$20
- *Tele De Aaz,* July 9, 1983; no. 43; wearing a sexy tight dress. (FRA)...........$10-$20
- *Tele K-7,* Sept. 17, 1983; no. 1; a well-known photograph. (FRA)................$10-$20
- *Telerama,* Aug. 17, 1983; no. 1753; smiling and looking vibrant. (FRA) ......$10-$20
- *Telerama,* Dec. 10, 1983; no. 1759; a shot of the ultimate star. (FRA) ....$10-$20
- *Tele Star,* March 1, 1983; no. 335; in a glamorous gown. (FRA) ....$10-$20
- *TV Couleur,* July 9, 1983; no. 8; another common studio shot. (FRA) ....$10-$20
- *Video Actualite,* Feb. 1983; no. 26; a common publicity pose. (FRA)...........$10-$20

1984

- *Cine Revue,* June 28, 1984; vol. 64, no. 26; a studio publicity phtograph. (FRA) ....$10-$20
- *L'Ebdo Des Savanes,* Nov. 2, 1984; no. 3; in a glamorous gown. (FRA) ......$10-$20
- *Le Cinema,* vol. 1, no. 2; in the black sequined gown and fur. (FRA) ....$10-$20
- *Novella 2000,* Nov. 6, 1984; no. 45; a common familiar photo. (FRA) ....$10-$20
- *Observer,* May 6, 1984; a young Norma Jeane in shorts. (ENG) ....$10-$20
- *Rev'Ameriques Ete,* 1984; a familiar, often-used photo. (FRA).....................$10-$20
- *Revista Veronica,* March 10, 1984; no. 34; looking glamorous for the camera. (CHI)..........$10-$20
- *Tele Cine Video,* July-Aug. 1984; no. 42; an over-used still. (FRA)..............$10-$20
- *Tele Star,* Jan. 31, 1984; no. 383; in the white fur. (FRA) ....$10-$20
- *Telegraph Sunday Magazine,* July 22, 1984; no. 404; Norma Jeane posing for artist Earl Moran. (ENG) ....$10-$20
- *Tele Magazine,* April 7, 1984; no. 1483; a common publicity still. (FRA) .....$10-$20
- *The Movie,* 1984; vol. 1, no. 1; in the black sequined dress and a long fur. (ENG) ....$10-$20
- *Unsolved,* 1984; vol. 1, no. 3; glamour shot, in a pearl necklace. (ENG) .....$10-$20
- *Veronica,* March 10, 1984; holding a striped scarf over her torso. (CHI)....$10-$20

1985

- *Bolero,* July 17, 1985; no. 28; a well-known glamour photo. (ITA) ....$10-$20
- *Cine Revue,* April 25, 1985; no. 17; in a costume from *River.* (FRA) ....$10-$20
- *Conoscerti,* 1985; no. 3; a studio publicity still. (ITA).................................$10-$20
- *Cos,* Nov. 14, 1985; posing for Stern in 1962. (CHI)......................................$10-$20
- *Epoca,* Nov. 22, 1985; n. 1833; a common glamour photograph. (ITA) ....$10-$20
- *Grandeur Nature,* 1985; no. 4; another publicity shot. (FRA) ....$10-$20
- *Just Seventeen,* Oct. 2, 1985; no. 68; in the well-known gold lamé gown. (ENG) ....$10-$20
- *La Lettre Du Livre,* Dec. 1985; no. 3; a typical Marilyn glamour image. (FRA) ....$10-$20
- *Orient Express,* Feb. 1985; no. 29; an artwork cover. (ITA) ....$10-$20
- *Prima Stripblad,* Sept. 1985; 4 comic book cover. (HOL) ....$10-$20
- *Rev'Ameriques,* 1985-86; continues to fascinate France. (FRA)...................$10-$20
- *Silence On Tourne,* May 1985; no. 5; a well-used publicity photo. (FRA).....$10-$20

- *Speciale Demiere,* Sept. 21, 1985; no. 1201; wearing a smile and a dress. (FRA) ....$10-$20
- *Super Tele,* April 27, 1985; no. 312; a common publicity shot. (FRA)..........$10-$20
- *Telerama,* July 3, 1985; no. 1851; looking as glamorous as possible. (FRA) ....$10-$20
- *Tele Star,* April 2, 1985; no. 447; a common studio-released still. (FRA) .....$10-$20
- *TV Couleur,* April 27, 1985; no. 102; a common studio portrait. (FRA)........$10-$20
- *Vous Et Votre Avenir,* June 1985; no. 25; a close-up portrait from *River of No Return.* (FRA) ....$10-$20

1986

- *Bunte,* March 20, 1986; with her eyes closed, from *Bus Stop.* (GER)..........$10-$20
- Cimoc, 1986; no. 6; nude artwork by Gonzalez. (SPA) ....$10-$20
- *Clic Photos,* April 1986; no. 61; a common studio portrait. (FRA) ....$10-$20
- *Gente Mese,* Aug. 1986; no. 8; looking sexy for the camera. (ITA) ....$10-$20
- *Le Grand Alpha De La Peinture,* 1986; no. 89; looking like the biggest movie star. (FRA) ....$10-$20
- *Le Nouvel Absolu,* Nov. 1986; no. 10; a classic Monroe pose. (FRA)...........$10-$20
- *Perfection,* Dec. 1986; no. 2; in white-collared dress and earrings. (FRA)...$10-$20
- *Playboy,* 1986; art cover, in a fur. (JPN) ....$10-$20
- *Primer Plano,* Sept. 1986; in the detailed gold lamé gown. (FRA) ....$10-$20
- *Rev'Amoriques,* 1986-87; a common publicity photograph. (IRA) ....$10-$20
- *Selection Du Readers Digest,* Jan. 1986; common studio portrait. (FRA)....$10-$20
- *Super Flash,* June 1986; vol. XVIII, no. 216; a pretty pose in a gown, by Avedon. (ITA) ....$10-$20
- *You,* March 23, 1986; Norma Jeane kneeling down with a lamb. (ENG) ......$10-$20

1987

- *Cahiers Du Cinema,* Aug. 1987; no. 398; lying down, reading a book. (FRA) ....$10-$20
- *Cine Tele Revue,* July 23, 1987; no. 30, in the one-piece yellow swimsuit. (FRA) ....$10-$20
- *Circus-Hors Serie 106,* Feb.-March 1987; a classic photo. (FRA) ....$10-$20
- *Confidences Magazine,* June 1987; entire issue on her; in the white fur. (FRA) ....$10-$20
- *Eclipse Comics,* June 1987; Marilyn appears on this comic book. (FRA).....$10-$20
- *Esquire,* Autumn 1987; vol. 1, no. 3; jumping in the red dress, by Halsman. (JPN) ....$10-$20
- *Rev'Ameriques Ete,* 1987-88; a classic glamour pose. (FRA)......................$10-$20
- *Fantastik,* Oct. 1987; no. 31; a studio publicity still. (FRA)..........................$10-$20
- *Funk Uhr,* Aug. 31, 1987; a young Norma Jeane wearing a sailor hat. (GER) ....$10-$20
- *Gente Mese,* Jan. 1987; no. 13; wrapped in the white fur boa. (ITA) ....$10-$20
- *Gente Mese,* July 1987; vol. 2, no. 19; in the gold lamé gown. (ITA)...........$10-$20
- *Gente,* Aug. 7, 1987; no. 31; a common glamour publicity still. (ITA)..........$10-$20
- *Icones,* Oct.-Nov. 1987; no. 9; a sexy, glamour-oriented image. (FRA) ....$10-$20
- *Jours De France,* Oct. 1, 987; no. 1976; a studio publicity photograph. (FRA) ....$10-$20
- *La Epoca,* March 22, 1987; no. 1; a young Norma Jeane by a fence in jeans. (CHI) ....$10-$20
- *La Tribuna Illustrata,* May 1987; no. 5; a glamorous studio-released image. (ITA) ....$10-$20
- *Librum-Pistas Sensitivas Por Marilyn,* Nov. 1987; art cover. (SPA) ....$10-$20
- *Observer,* Aug. 2, 1987; Norma Jeane holding a camera, in a red sweater. (ENG) ....$10-$20
- *Okapi,* May 10, 1987; no. 371; a still taken by the studio. (FRA) ....$10-$20
- *Onda TV,* Aug. 8, 1987; no. 32; a common glamour photograph. (ITA) ....$10-$20
- *Playboy,* 1987; young Norma Jeane posing for Moran. (GRE) ....$10-$20
- *Promenades Americaines,* 1987; TWA; a well-used glamour shot. (FRA) ....$10-$20

Settimo Giorno, May 1958 (Italy), $100-$140.

Novella, November 1958 (Italy), $60-$90.

Tempo, November 4, 1958 (Italy), $40-$65.

- *Psychologies,* Oct. 1987; no. 47; over-used publicity photo. (FRA) ....$10-$20
- *Seven,* Nov. 14, 1987; in white bikini with a sky background. (ITA)............$10-$20
- *7 Corriere Della Sera,* Nov. 14, 1987; a common publicity photo. (ITA).......$10-$20
- *Subway,* July-Aug. 1987; wearing a sexy, tight dress. (ITA).........................$10-$20
- *Spotlight,* 1987-88; no. 5; looking coyly at the camera. (FRA)....................$10-$20
- *Tele Star,* Aug. 1, 1987; no. 565; posing in a smile and a dress. (FRA)........$10-$20
- *Titanic,* 1987; no. 31; an artwork image. (HOL)..$10-$20
- *You,* July 26, 1987; a sad portrait from her last summer. (ENG)..................$10-$20
- *Vrig,* Aug. 1, 1987; wrapped in white bed sheets, by Kirkland. (HOL).........$10-$20

Se Og Hor, February 13, 1959 (Denmark), $75-$100.

de Post, February 15, 1959 (Belguim), $60-$90.

Oggi, April 19, 1959 (Italy), $40-$60.

1988

- *BD Magazine,* June 2, 1988; an overused publicity photo. (FRA)................$10-$20
- *Bologna In Anterrima,* Jan. 9, 1988; no. 2; a cool-looking glamour photo. (ITA) ....$10-$20
- *Canal + Magazine,* Dec. 1988; no. 15; another common still. (FRA) ....$10-$20
- *Cine Tele Revue,* Aug. 18, 1988; no. 33; airbrushed artwork. (BEL)............$10-$20
- *Cine Tele Revue,* Aug. 18, 1988; no. 33; wearing white robe at a window. (FRA) ....$10-$20
- *Elle,* April 11, 1988; no. 2205; looking like a ballerina in a chair. (FRA) ....$10-$20
- *Emois,* July-Aug. 1988; no. 13; an often-used common still. (FRA)............$10-$20
- *Foto Music,* Aug. 1988; no. 29; smiling sweetly for the camera. (FRA) ....$10-$20
- *Il Venerdi Di Republica,* Feb. 19, 1988; no. 17; in a car from *The Misfits* set. (ITA) ....$10-$20
- *La Recherche,* Feb. 1988; no. 196; wearing a tight dress and a smile. (FRA) ....$10-$20
- *Network Pictorial,* Oct. 1988; curled up in bedsheets, by Kirkland. (IND) ....$10-$20
- *Paris Match,* Sept. 2, 1988; no. 2049; wearing a long black sweater for Greene. (FRA) ....$10-$20
- *Rev' Ameriques Ete,* 1988; posing in a tight dress for the camera. (FRA)....$10-$20
- *Tele Cine Fiches,* Dec. 17, 1988; no. 4; a common glamour photo. (FRA) ...$10-$20
- *Tele K-7,* April 4, 1988; no. 239; a studio-released publicity still. (FRA) ......$10-$20
- *TV France Soir Magazine,* April 11, 1988; no. 13581; one of the more common shots. (FRA) ....$10-$20
- *TV Hebdo La Voix Du Norde,* April 1, 1988; no. 13602; wearing one of the common gowns. (FRA) ....$10-$20
- *Video 7,* July-Aug. 1988; no. 80; the typical movie-star pose. (FRA) ....$10-$20
- *Woman,* Aug. 6, 1988; in the white dress, by Halsman. (AUS) ....$10-$20

1989

- *Art Dossier,* June 1989; no. 36; an artwork cover. (ITA)................................$5-$10
- *Beux Arts,* Feb. 1989; no. 65; a common publicity pose. (FRA) ....$5-$10
- *Breve Storia Del Cinema,* Nov. 24, 1989; wearing a tight, sexy dress. (ITA) ..$5-$10
- *Business Art,* Dec. 1989-Jan. 1990; no. 1; a nice artwork cover. (ITA) ....$5-$10
- *Ca M'Interesse,* Sept. 1989; no. 103; a typical Marilyn pose. (FRA)...............$5-$10
- *Contact Fnac,* April 1989; no. 267; a studio publicity still. (FRA) ....$5-$10
- *Errol's,* Dec. 1989; vol. 1, no. 1; an artsy image from *Niagara.* (CHI).............$5-$10
- *Idoles Magazine,* Oct. 1989; no. 1; the common shot in the white fur. (FRA) ....$5-$10
- *La Gazette De L'Hotel Drout,* March 24, 1989; no. 12; hamming it up for the camera. (FRA) ....$5-$10
- *New Idea,* June 10, 1989; two shots MM and Norma Jeane. (AUS)...............$5-$10
- *Riza Psicosomatica,* June 1989; no. 100; an artwork cover. (ITA)..................$5-$10
- *Spotlight,* 3rd Trimester 1989; no. 27; an overused publicity still. (FRA) ....$5-$10
- *The Sunday Telegraph,* Nov. 19-25, 1989; Norma Jeane sitting on the beach in pants. (ENG)..$5-$10
- *Tele Coulisses,* Jan. 7, 1989; no. 29; wearing a smile and glamorous dress. (FRA) ....$5-$10

- *Tele Loisirs,* July 31-Aug. 6, 1989; no. 179; in the white fur and long earrings. (FRA) .... $5-$10
- *Tele 7 Video,* July 1, 1989; no. 16; a common publicity still. (FRA) .... $5-$10
- *Tele Video,* Jan. 7, 1989; no. 5; posing as only Marilyn can. (FRA) .... $5-$10
- *TV Magazine Figaro,* July 29, 1989; no. 13972; a studio-released portrait. (FRA) .... $5-$10
- *Vocable,* Oct. 1989; no. 112, a commonly used studio portrait. (FRA) .... $5-$10
- *Voici,* May 13, 1989; no. 79; wearing the gold lamé gown. (FRA) .... $5-$10
- *Zoom,* March 1989; no. 88; in a blue swimsuit holding a rope. (ITA) .... $5-$10

1990

- *Arri Yadah Wa'Shabab,* May 15-22, 1990; no. 474; in a bright orange blouse. (KUW) .... $5-$10
- *Blitz,* Feb. 2, 1990; no. 3; a studio publicity still. (ITA) .... $5-$10
- *Chip Chats,* April 3, 1990; vol. 37, no. 2; a Monroe statue by artist Chris Rees. (CAN) .... $5-$10
- *Flash Art,* Dec. 1989-Jan. 1990; no. 153; another piece of Monroe artwork. (ITA) .... $5-$10
- *Il Venerdi Di Republica,* March 16, 1990; no. 110; a portrait in a car, by Arnold. (ITA) .... $5-$10
- *L'Amateur De L'Art,* June 1990; no. 768; a common studio shot. (FRA) .... $5-$10
- *L'Arte Moderna,* 1990; no. 10; an artwork cover. (ITA) .... $5-$10
- *Memorie & Ricordi,* March 1990, no. 3; smiling sweetly for the camera. (ITA) .... $5-$10
- *Minuti Menardni,* April 1990; vol. XIV, no. 244; artwork by Andy Warhol. (ITA) .... $5-$10
- *Non Solo Poster,* Nov. 1990; no. 4; a studio publicity still. (ITA) .... $5-$10
- *Paris Match Hors Serie,* 1990; a classic Marilyn pose. (FRA) .... $5-$10
- *Raro!,* Jan.-Feb. 1990; no. 7; holding a guitar from *River.* (ITA) .... $5-$10
- *Saturday Night,* March 1990; vol. 105, no. 3; in the bedsheets, posing for Kirkland. (CAN) .... $5-$10
- *Sound & Vision,* Nov.-Dec. 1990; no. 17/18; an artwork cover. (ITA) .... $5-$10
- *Speak-Up,* Aug. 1990; no. 65; a common publicity pose. (ITA) .... $5-$10
- *Speak-Up,* Nov. 1990; vol. VI, no. 63; in a red bathing suit. (SPA) .... $5-$10
- *Speciale Demiere,* July 28, 1990; no. 2356; wearing a sexy, tight dress. (FRA) .... $5-$10
- *Studio Magazine,* Sept. 1990; no. 41; classic glamour image. (FRA) .... $5-$10
- *Tele Video Scope,* May 12, 1990; no. 7; posing coyly. (FRA) .... $5-$10
- *The Paris Free Voice,* July 1990; no. 6; classic glamour photo. (FRA) .... $5-$10
- *The Sun Pictorial Daily,* Aug. 30, 1990; a candid at a press conference. (JPN) .... $5-$10
- *TV Cable Hebdo,* Oct. 13, 1990; no. 23; an appearance on a television guide. (FRA) .... $5-$10
- *TV Cable Hebdo,* Dec. 1, 1990; no. 30; a common glamour photo. (FRA) .... $5-$10
- *TYNAIKA,* 1990; Norma Jeane posing on the beach. (GRE) .... $5-$10
- *Zoom,* Dec. 1990; wearing a bulky coat in the mid-1950s. (HOL) .... $5-$10

1991

- *Al Mawed,* Aug. 24, 1991; no. 1470; close-up face shot in color. (KUW) .... $5-$10
- *Chat,* June 1, 1991; in a jewel-studded-strap dress. (ENG) .... $5-$10
- *Cine Fiches,* April 15, 1991; wearing the gold lamé gown. (FRA) .... $5-$10
- *Cineteca TV,* June 14, 1991; no. 14; glamourous studio photo. (ITA) .... $5-$10
- *Diagonal,* March 1991; vol. V, no. 20; artwork by Warhol. (SPA) .... $5-$10
- *El Pais Seminal,* 1991; an often-seen studio shot. (FRA) .... $5-$10
- *Emma,* Aug. 1991; no. 8; Marilyn blowing her fans a kiss. (GER) .... $5-$10
- *Flix,* May 1991; vol. 12; a glamour picture with hoop earrings. (JPN) .... $5-$10
- *Focus,* Oct. 1991; holding fabric flowers over her breasts (HOL) .... $5-$10

Bild Journalen, June 1959 (Sweden), $85-$125.

Lunes, July 6, 1959 (Uruguay), $50-$80.

Cinemonde, February 21, 1961 (France), $50-$70.

Stage and Cinema, April 1960 (South Africa), $100-$120.

Le Ore, December 1960 (Italy), $60-$90.

Weekend, March 1961 (England), $60-$90.

- *Globe,* July-Aug. 1991; no. 59; a studio glamour pose. (FRA) ....$5-$10
- *Grazia,* Dec. 15, 1991; no. 2650; a common studio photograph. (ITA) ....$5-$10
- *L'Autre Journal,* June 1991; no. 13; sleeping in a chair. (FRA) ....$5-$10
- *L'Evenement Du Jeudi,* May 30, 1991; no. 343; a glamourous studio photograph. (FRA) ....$5-$10
- *Le Nouvel Observateur,* Oct. 1991; no. 7; Marilyn continues to fascinate. (FRA) ....$5-$10
- *Max,* Dec. 1991; an airbrushed artwork. (GER) ....$5-$10
- *Observer,* 1991; a common studio photograph. (ENG) ....$5-$10
- *Psy Autrement,* 1991; no. 2; wearing a tight dress and a smile. (FRA) ....$5-$10
- *7A Paris,* June 19-25, 1991; embracing Tom Ewell. (FRA) ....$5-$10
- *Raccolta Skorpio,* Sept. 3, 1991; no. 188; an artwork cover. (ITA) ....$5-$10
- *Speak-Up,* Feb. 1991; no. 46; a common studio photo. (FRA) ....$5-$10
- *Studio Magazine,* July-Aug. 1991; no. 52; a sad portrait by Greene. (FRA) ...$5-$10
- *Sunday,* May 5, 1991; a young Marilyn in a white robe. (ENG) ....$5-$10
- *Sunday Sun,* May 26, 1991; vol. 18, no. 35; posing in Canada during *Niagara.* (CAN) ....$5-$10
- *Super TV,* Nov. 2-8, 1991; no. 44; in the gold lamé dress. (GER) ....$5-$10
- *Tele K-7,* Aug. 19, 1991; no. 415; looking glamorous as always. (FRA) ....$5-$10
- *Touch It,* May-June 1991; no. 1; living on in more artwork. (ITA) ....$5-$10
- *TV Movie,* 1991; no. 26; in a black dress with jewel-studded straps. (GER) ..$5-$10
- *Tele Poche,* Aug. 19, 1991; no. 1332; a common publicity still. (FRA)...........$5-$10
- *Zoom,* March 1991; no. 108; a studio publicity still. (ITA) ....$5-$10

1992

- *Anteprima,* Aug. 28, 1992; with Jane Russell in *Blondes.* (ITA) ....$5-$10
- *Auf Einen Blick,* July 30, 1992; no. 32; with fellow legend, James Dean. (GER) ....$5-$10
- *Blanco Negro,* 1992; an artsy photo of Marilyn posing. (SPA) ....$5-$10
- *Bolero,* Aug. 1992; no. 8; a common publicity still for *Niagara.* (SWI)...........$5-$10
- *Ciak,* Aug. 8, 1992; vol. 8, no. 8; a glamorous-looking Marilyn. (ITA) ....$5-$10
- *Cinemazero,* April 1992; no. 4; many pictures of her on the floor. (ITA) ....$5-$10
- *Cine Revue Hors-Serie,* circa 1992; entire issue is on her; in gold lamé. (BEL) ....$5-$10
- *Cine Tele Revue,* July 30, 1992; no. 31; a side profile taken by Stern. (FRA) .$5-$10
- *Corriere Cultura,* April 19, 1992; an often-used photograph. (ITA) ....$5-$10
- *Enigmistika,* Oct. 1992; no. 3; a sexy Monroe pose. (ITA) ....$5-$10
- *Flix,* Sept. 1992; vol. 27; in the white-collared dress. (JPN) ....$5-$10
- *Foto Pratica,* Dec. 1991-Jan. 1992; no. 276-7; in pink longjohns, by the fire. (ITA) ....$5-$10
- *Foto Pro,* Aug. 1992; no. 53; portrayed by an artist. (ITA) ....$5-$10
- *Friday,* 1992; no. 29; a photo by Stern that MM crossed out. (JPN) ....$5-$10
- *Funk Uhr,* July 24, 1992; Monroe is on the majority of the cover. (GER) ....$5-$10
- *Gente,* Feb. 24, 1992; vol. XXXVI, no. 9; on only half the cover, in a fur. (ITA) ....$5-$10
- *Gente Mese,* Aug. 1992; vol. VII, no. 8; in a costume from *Blondes.* (ITA) ....$5-$10
- *Good Weekend,* Sept. 1, 1992; wearing a blue robe by a pool. (AUS) ....$5-$10
- *Hp De Tijd,* July 3, 1992; a common publicity still. (HOL)..............................$5-$10
- *Il Venerdi Di Republica,* July 31, 1992; no. 233; a nice artwork cover. (ITA) ....$5-$10
- *Intimita "Vita Vera Di M.Monroe,"* Aug. 20, 1992; no. 2424; a special tribute; in the gold lamé. (ITA) ....$5-$10
- *I Maestri Del Colore,* 1992; no. 50; an attractive artwork cover. (ITA) ....$5-$10
- *Impacto,* Aug. 20, 1992; no. 2216; sitting on steps, holding a purse by Greene. (SPA) ....$5-$10
- *Kai,* May 1992; no. 32; young Norma Jeane combing her hair. (GRE) ....$5-$10
- *Le CoQ Gourmand,* 1992; no. 14; a common publicity pose often seen. (FRA) ....$5-$10

- *L'Express,* 1992; no. 1; full-length profile in the black-sequined-dress. (FRA) .... $5-$10
- *Life Stories,* 1992; no. 3; entire issue is devoted to her; in the white fur. (FIN) .... $5-$10
- *Madame Jours De France,* Aug. 3, 1992; another issue exploring 30 years since her death. (FRA) .... $5-$10
- *Marilyn—Super Star,* 1992; all on her; art cover in white sheets. (SPA) .... $5-$10
- *Marilyn—The Complete Story,* 1992; all on her; in the white collared dress. (SPA) .... $5-$10
- *Paralleli,* Aug. 1992; no. 8; a common often seen photo. (ITA) .... $5-$10
- *Pin's Collection,* June 15, 1992; no. 20; a well-known publicity photo. (FRA) .... $5-$10
- *Popcorn,* April 1992; no. 4; a photo on the rocks, by Greene. (ITA) .... $5-$10
- *Premiere "Movie Extra,"* Sept. 1992; no. 9; sitting in a director's chair in a blue dress. (JPN) .... $5-$10
- *Premiere,* Sept. 1992; no. 9; looking out a window, by Sam Shaw. (JPN) .... $5-$10
- *Prisma,* Aug. 1992; no. 32; in a black dress with jewel-decorated straps. (SWI) .... $5-$10
- *Ragazza,* 1992; with hands clasped at her breast. (ITA) .... $5-$10
- *SAT-TV International,* Aug. 1992; in a black lacy negligee. (GER) .... $5-$10
- *Serai,* May 21, 1992; in a bubblebath from *Itch.* (JPN) .... $5-$10
- *7 Corriere Della Sera,* July 11, 1992; no. 27; several 1952 photos by Halsman. (ITA) .... $5-$10
- *Sorrisi E Canzoni TV,* Aug. 2-8, 1992; no. 31; a Stern photo with a bead necklace. (ITA) .... $5-$10
- *Stern,* Aug. 6, 1992; no. 33; lying face down and naked on a bed by Stern. (GER) .... $5-$10
- *Stop,* Aug. 8, 1992; no. 2289; entire issue on her; in the gold lamé gown. (ITA) .... $5-$10
- *Sunday Express Magazine,* July 19, 1992; a gorgeous, smiling portrait from (ENG) .... $5-$10
- *Super!,* July 16, 1992; in the gold lamé gown and a shot from her autopsy. (GER) .... $5-$10
- *Super TV,* Aug. 8-14, 1992; no. 32; in the white-collared black low-cut dress. (GER) .... $5-$10
- *Tele Cable,* Aug. 1, 1992; no. 109; a common publicity photo. (FRA) .... $5-$10
- *Tele Cable,* Oct. 14, 1992; no. 121; another photo used too often. (FRA) .... $5-$10
- *Tele K-7,* July 27, 1992; no. 464; in a white bikini on orange cushions. (FRA) .... $5-$10
- *Tele Loisirs,* July 27-Aug. 2, 1992; no. 335; wearing the white fur. (FRA) .... $5-$10
- *Tele Moustique,* July 30, 1992; no. 3470; publicity still from *River.* (BEL) .... $5-$10
- *Tele Poche* (digest), July 27, 1992; no. 1381; a portrait in the jewel-studded-strap dress. (FRA) .... $5-$10
- *Television Programmes,* 1992; no. 32; in a white ruffled dress looking beautiful. (FRA) .... $5-$10
- *Tele 7 Jours,* Aug. 29, 1992; no. 1683; a common publicity still. (FRA) .... $5-$10
- *The Records Thursday Entertainment Guide,* July 30, 1992; newspaper section; glamour face. (CAN) .... $5-$10
- *Timbroloisirs,* Feb. 15, 1992; no. 35; a studio publicity still. (FRA) .... $5-$10
- *Time Out,* July 8-15, 1992; no. 1145; in a sleeveless shirt, reading a book. (ENG) .... $5-$10
- *Tip Berlin Magazine,* Aug. 13-26, 1992; vol. 21, no. 17; a shot from *Let's Make Love.* (GER) .... $5-$10
- *TV Cable Hebdo,* July 6, 1992; no. 114; common publicity photo. (FRA) .... $5-$10
- *TV France Soir Magazine,* Aug. 1, 1992; no. 14923; one of the more common studio shots. (FRA) .... $5-$10
- *TV Magazine Centre France,* Aug. 2, 1992; no. 1157; the typical Monroe allure. (FRA) .... $5-$10
- *TV Magazine Corse Matin,* Aug. 1992; no. 10227; studio publicity shot. (FRA) .... $5-$10

Cinelandia, April 1961 (Brazil), $50-$80

Billed Bladet, August 10, 1962 (Denmark), $60-$85.

Tempo, August 18, 1962 (Italy), $50-$85.

L'Europeo, December 17, 1961 (Italy), $40-$60.

Kavalkad, April 1962 (Sweden), $90-$120.

Cine Avance, August 1962 (Mexico), $125-$175.

- *TV Magazine Le Figaro,* Aug. 1, 1992; no. 14912; glam and sexy. (FRA).......$5-$10
- *TV France Soir Magazine,* Aug. 1, 1992; no. 14923; one of the often-used pictures. (FRA) ....$5-$10
- *TV Movie,* July 25-Aug. 7, 1992; a lovely, soft portrait. (GER) ....$5-$10
- *TV Sorrisi E.Canzoni,* Aug. 2, 1992; no. 31; a portrait by Stern from 1962. (ITA) ....$5-$10
- *TV Studio,* July 10, 1992; no. 27; in the dress with the white collar. (HOL)...$5-$10
- *Veronica,* July 10, 1992; in the dress with the white collar. (HOL).......$5-$10
- *Video Magazine,* Aug. 1992; on majority of the cover, in a dress. (GER) ....$5-$10
- *Vita Vera,* Aug. 13, 1992; no. 2424; entire issue; in gold lamé. (ITA).......$5-$10
- *Weekend,* Aug. 1, 1992; news supplement with a tinted glamour shot. (ENG) ....$5-$10
- *World Report,* Dec. 1992; no. 09424520; a portrait from 1962 by Stern. (GER) ....$5-$10

1993

- *Flight Jacket Museum Catalog,* 1993; in Korea with a U.S. pilot during the war. (JPN) ....$5-$10
- *Globe Hebdo,* Aug. 14, 1993; no. 28; in bed holding a flower to her chest. (IRA) ....$5-$10
- *Cirandes Ciclos TV,* 1993; a glamour photograph, seldom used. (SPA) ....$5-$10
- *Le Cable Video,* Aug. 23, 1993; no. 83; a studio still for publicity. (FRA).......$5-$10
- *Le Nouvel Observateur,* July 15, 1993; no. 1497; a lovely portrait of Monroe's beauty. (FRA).......$5-$10
- *Les Beux Films D'Hollywood,* Jan. 1993; a classic publicity photo of the queen. (FRA) ....$5-$10
- *Pins Collection,* Feb. 15, 1993; no. 26; an often-used portrait. (FRA) ....$5-$10
- *Positif,* July 1993; a photo of the band from *Hot.* (FRA) ....$5-$10
- *Stern,* April 1, 1993; no. 1; a tinted glamour pose with half-closed eyes. (GER) ....$5-$10
- *TV Cable Hebdo,* Aug. 23, 1993; no. 173; studio promotion shot. (FRA).......$5-$10
- *Vogue Hommes,* Nov. 1993; no. 164; a sad b&w portrait taken by Avedon. (FRA) ....$5-$10

1994

- *El Caso Extra,* 1994; all on her; sitting on steps with a purse. (SPA) ....$5-$10
- *Foto Revista,* Nov. 1994; vol. XII, no. 43; three photos by Avedon, in the black dress. (SPA) ....$5-$10
- *Gong,* July 23-29, 1994; no. 29; tinted cover in the jewel-studded-strap dress. (GER).......$5-$10
- *Playboy,* Dec. 1994; in the black dress with the white collar. (GER).......$5-$10
- *TV Times,* March 12-18, 1994; a digest with a portrait by Greene. (AUS)......$5-$10
- *Weekend,* June 4, 1994; a young Norma Jeane and her sister on the beach. (ENG) ....$5-$10

1995

- *Airbrush,* Nov.-Dec. 1995; an airbrushed art image. (HOL) ....$5-$10
- *Brief Marken Spiegel,* June 1995; vol. 35, no. 6; the United States Monroe postal stamp art. (GER) ....$5-$10
- *Cinema,* Feb. 1995; no. 201; curled up in bedsheets with hand on head. (GER) ....$5-$10
- *Filmihullu,* May 1995; a tinted glamour pose, in a dress. (FIN) ....$5-$10
- *Sette Corriere Della Sera,* Feb. 23, 1995; no. 8; on the beach with an umbrella. (ITA) ....$5-$10
- *The Australian Magazine,* May 27-8, 1995; jumping in the black spangle dress. (AUS).......$5-$10

- *Trova Roma,* Nov. 1995; the *Golden Dreams* nude pose. (ITA) ....$5-$10
- *TV Krant,* Jan. 7-13, 1995; an artist's portrait. (HOL) ....$5-$10
- *Un Ospite A Roma* (digest), Dec. 16-31, 1995; no. 23; in white-collared dress. (ITA) ....$5-$10
- *Weekend,* March 9, 1995; a newspaper section; with a glamour photo. (ENG) ....$5-$10

1996

- *OK! Weekly,* June 2, 1996; with the ever-present white fur. (ENG) ....$5-$10
- *Horzu,* May 25-31, 1996; beautiful portrait all in white, by Greene. (GER).....$5-$10
- *Premiere,* Jan. 1996; vol. 3, no. 12; in the black-lace negligee looking sexy. (ENG) ....$5-$10
- *Satellite (Veronica),* May 21-31, 1996; a common publicity pose. (HOL).......$5-$10
- *Saturday Night,* Sept. 1996; vol. III, no. 7; smoking a cigarette on the *Niagara* set. (CAN)..$5-$10
- *Specchio Della Stampa,* April 27, 1996; no. 14; wearing a long black knit sweater. (ITA) ....$5-$10
- *Today's Seniors,* Aug. 1996; a lovely photo from *Give* in 1962. (CAN)...........$5-$10

1997

- *Cine Action Performance,* 1997; no. 44; a frontal glamour shot in a white fur. (CAN)..$5-$10
- *De Puzzelaar,* 1997; no. 3; a classic, well-known studio photo. (HOL)...........$5-$10
- *Eye,* May 1997; the *New Wrinkle* nude pose. (ENG) ....$5-$10
- *Hp De Tijd,* Nov. 21, 1997; a studio publicity pose. (HOL) ....$5-$10
- *Intemet Magazine,* June 1997; no. 31; smiling, holding a pile of jewels in her hands. (ENG) ....$5-$10
- *Playboy,* Jan. 1997; holding a scarf in front of her nude torso. (CNA).........$40-$50
- *Playboy,* Feb. 1997; in a long black sweater open on one side. (FRA) ....$20-$30
- *Playboy,* Oct. 1997; a lovely, smiling portrait from *Niagara* set. (JPN).........$30-$40
- *Viva!,* Sept. 2, 1997; no. 13; in the white collared dress (POL)...................$10-$15

1998-2002

- Nearly all issues. ....$5-$10.

Mi Vida, August 30, 1962 (Chile), $100-$130.

Cine Universal, September 1962 (Mexico), $90-$130.

Panorama, October 1964 (Italy), $30-$45.

Chapter 8

Miscellaneous Collectibles

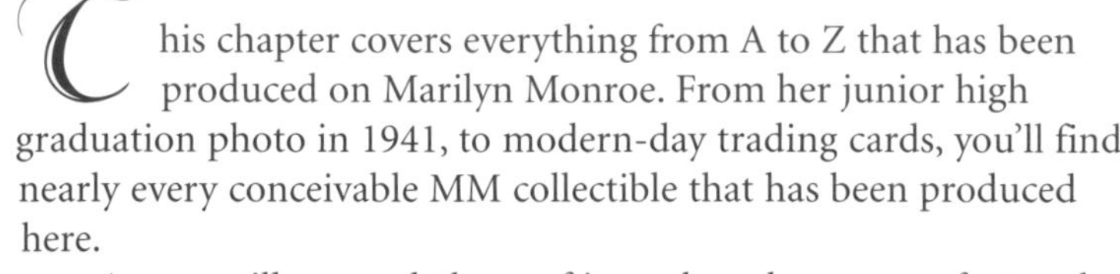

This chapter covers everything from A to Z that has been produced on Marilyn Monroe. From her junior high graduation photo in 1941, to modern-day trading cards, you'll find nearly every conceivable MM collectible that has been produced here.

As you will see, a plethora of items have been manufactured over the years that feature MM's likeness—many of which are not very expensive. That's part of the fun in collecting items on Marilyn, though, because no matter your age or income level, there's something available for everyone to own in rememberance of this fascinating blonde.

And the licensing of products bearing Marilyn's image is a very lucrative business. Beginning in the 1980s, the Roger Richman Agency was the official licensing representative of Marilyn's estate.

Anna Strassburg, the second wife of Marilyn's famed acting coach, Lee Strassburg, had inherited all the rights to Marilyn's image when Lee passed away.

More recently, Marilyn's estate has been represented by CMG Worldwide, which is based in Indiana.

The irony of it all is that nearly 40 years after her death, Marilyn's estate is generating huge amounts of money in comparison to what she had made when she was alive. She has truly become an everlasting icon.

A selection of contemporary bookmarks, $2-$4 each.

- Action Figure, circa 1970s. MM in red one-piece swimsuit; labeled "Hollywood Memories." ....$20-$10
- Act Now Products, 1995. Various products featuring Andre de Dienes' photos on them; titled "The Lost Photos of Marilyn"; consisting of the following items (see cigarette lighters described elsewhere):
  - Key Chain....$2-$3
  - Mirror....$2-$3
  - Magnet....$2-$3
  - Button (2½")....$2-$3
  - Button Covers (set of four)....$2-$3
- Address Book, vintage unknown. Andy Warhol photos on front and back; Nues Publishing; item no. 8083; ISBN-3-82-38-8083-7....$3-$5
- Airbrushing, 1995. Color airbrushing by Daytona. Originally $125. ....$125-$140
- Apron, vintage unknown. Featuring MM images on it. ....$15-$25
- Ashtray, vintage unknown. Clear crystal *Seven Year Itch* ashtray/candy dish; made in China. ....$45-$50
- Ballpoint Pen, 1970s. 4"; plastic; shaped like a match; head removes to reveal pen; MM's face etched on it and reads, "Marilyn Monroe Likes It Hot." ....$5-$10
- Balsa Wood Boxes, circa 1990s-2001. Three oval boxes with artists' renderings of Marilyn on the tops; all glamour shots. ....each $15-$20
- Beach Towels, circa 1980s-'90s. With MM in gold lamé gown, famous *Itch* dress, and a black gown. ....each $10-$25
- Belt Buckle, 1995. By U.S. Postal Service. ....$30-$40
- Body and Bath Massager, 1992. Made by Salton of China. ....$20-$30
- Bookmark, circa 1980-'90s. Color painting of MM in a caricature fashion, in white blowing *Itch* dress; glossy surface to paper; various others. ....each $2-$4
- Book Token, vintage unknown. With MM gift card (valued at £1). ....$3-$8
- Bottle Opener, vintage unknown. Heavy-duty. ....$15-$20
- Box, circa 1990s-2001. Decoupage box with various MM photos on it; maker unknown. ....$10-$20

Bridge and canasta set, $75-$150.

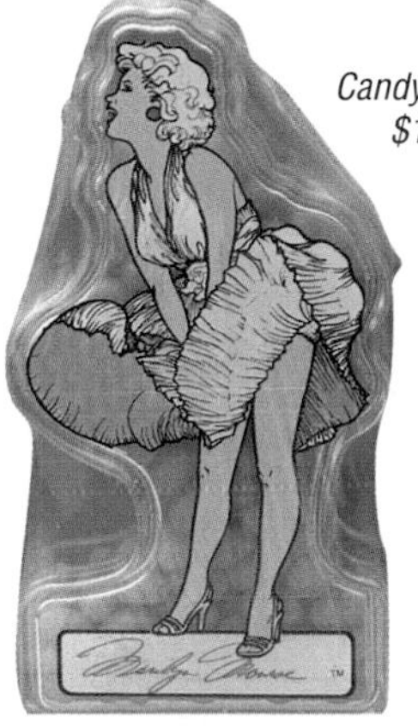

Candy container, $10-$20.

Checks and checkbook cover, $5-$8.

Cell phone cover, $12-$20.

Reproduction California driver's license, $3-$5.

- Bridge and Canasta Set, 1950s. Boxed set of two decks of playing cards; one of the *Golden Dreams* pose and one of the *New Wrinkle* pose; includes four metal coasters showing two each of the poses; came in either cardboard or black velvet-covered box.
  - Cardboard Set..$75-$150
  - Velvet Set..$100-$200
- Brush-Up Brush, vintage unknown. Made by Banning. ....$15-$25
- Candy Container, 1989. 3½ x 7; MM in famous white *Itch* dress on top; came filled with bubble gum..$10-$20
- Car Deodorizer, 1955. 3 x 4; hanging color deodorizer sealed in cellophane showing MM in *Golden Dreams* pose with black lace overlay; reads "Hang Glamourette Pamela Wherever A Fragrance Is Desired"; made by Presto Products Co., Detroit, Michigan. ....$20-$40
- Car Deodorizer Display, 1954. 12 x 13; cardboard display featuring four different scent cards called Monroe scent; by Monroe Manufacturing Co., New Castle, Pennsylvania..$75-$135
- Cedar Box, vintage unknown. 8 x 10; with nude *Golden Dreams* pose laminated to top, with lock and key. ....$50-$75
- Cell Phone Cover, circa 1990s-2001. Features a painting of MM in black negligee. ....$12-$20
- Ceramic Tiles, 1990s; two 7⅞ x 7⅞; one b&w of *Itch* dress scene; one color of MM in black negligee. ....each $15-$25
- Checkbook Cover, vintage unknown. MM in famous white billowing dress pose from *Itch*. ....$5-$8

Zippo cigarette lighter, $30-$40.

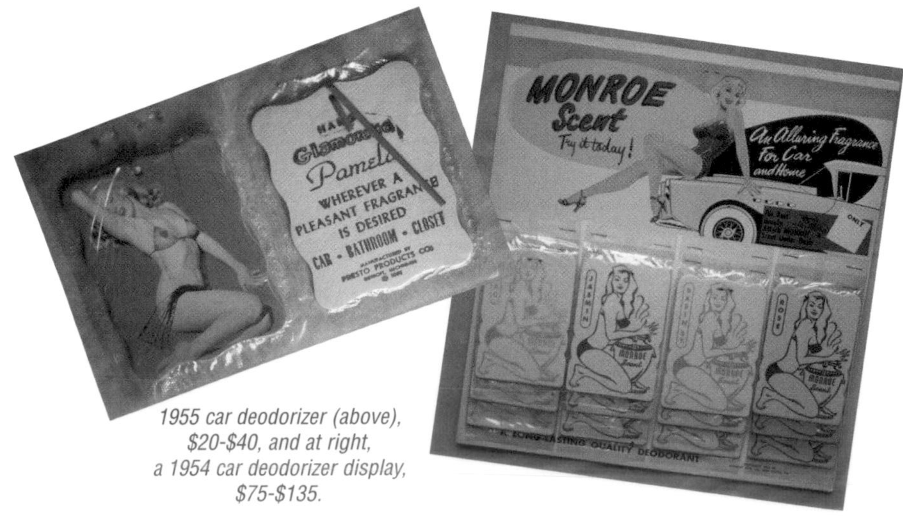

1955 car deodorizer (above), $20-$40, and at right, a 1954 car deodorizer display, $75-$135.

Just one of many variations of gift bags made in the 1980s-1990s, $3-$10 each.

A selection of contemporary clocks; they range in price from $15-$35.

- Cigar Box, vintage unknown. Adorned with Andy Warhol images of MM. ...$30-$40
- Cigar Box, 1960s-'70s. Features nude *Golden Dreams* pose on top. ....$35-$50
- Cigarette Holder, vintage unknown. Elegant, with built-in cigarette lighter. ....$125-$150
- Cigarette Lighters, circa 1990s-2001. *Golden Dreams* pose on front, with white fur Milton Greene photo. ....each $10-$20
- Cigarette Lighters, 1992. Set of several lighters, each with b&w Andre de Dienes' photos; entitled, "The Lost Photos of Marilyn"; produced by Weston Editions Ltd. and labeled "Djeep" disposable lighters. ....each $5-$10
- Cigarette Lighter, 1990s. Chrome Zippo lighter with the famous pose of MM in black halter dress with white collar; photo is beneath the classic glass dome; packaging reads, "Zippo-U.S.A.-Lighter-Lifetime Guarantee"; various other images on same lighters. ....$30-$40
- Cigarette Lighter, 1990s. Zippo lighter in film canister labeled "Stars of Hollywood" with Marilyn's face on front of lighter. ....$30-$40
- Cigarette Lighter, 1992. Zippo lighter with belt and coin; numbered limited edition; made in Japan. ....$160-$190
- Clock, 1991. Plastic red or black wall clock with MM's legs as the pendulum; made by Kirch of New York. ....$20-$30
- Clock, 1991. "Marilyn by Moonlight" alarm clock by Centric; made in China. ....$25-$35
- Clock, 1999. Assorted alarm clocks by Bernard of Hollywood. ....each $20-$30
- Clock, 1995. Alarm clock with Michael Dias painting used on the 1995 U.S. postage stamp. ....$20-$35
- Clock, 1995. Commemorative wall clock released by U.S. Postal Service; features Michael Dias painting. ....$15-$30
- Clock, 1980s. 2½' x 3'; Affixed to wood with MM photo on it; covered with polyurethane; various examples. ....$15-$30
- Clocks, 1985-2001. Assorted contemporary wall clocks, with MM photos on faces. ....each $8-$20
- Coasters, 1991. Set of four with color glamour shots on each; made by Clay Art; style 1621. ....$10-$15
- Coasters, circa 1970s-'80s. Set of six with same color artwork of MM's face on each; made in Italy. ....$20-$30

Set of coasters by Clay Art, $10-$15.

Italian coasters from a set of six, $20-$30 set.

1974 datebook,
$15-$30.

1998 Collecticritters Bear (above), $20-$40, and the 1999 Collecticritters Bear, $18-$30.

1972 drawing aid,
$15-$20.

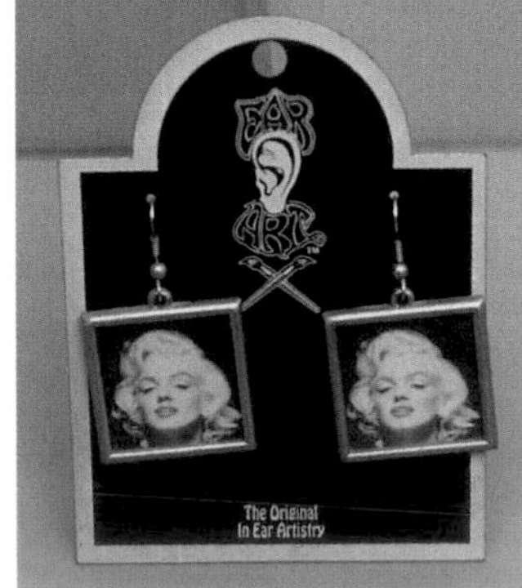

Pair of contemporary earrings,
$15-$30.

- Coasters, originally 1950s. 4"; metal coasters of MM in *Golden Dreams* and *New Wrinkle* poses. ....each $20-$30
- Coat Hanger, circa 1980s. Full-color face shot of Marilyn mounted on a coat hanger........$5-$10
- Coin, vintage unknown. Aluminum collector coin with *Golden Dreams* pose and "1926-1962" on front and MM with DiMaggio on back. ....$5-$8
- Coin Bank, 1997. Features MM's face on a TV; made by Vandor. ....$125-$150
- Collecticritters Marilyn Bear, 1998. Red with embroidered diamond on chest. ....$20-$40
- Collecticritters Marilyn Bear, 1999. Pink with rhinestone necklace and brooch, and embroidered MM signature on foot; 10,000 made; holographic numbered tag. ....$18-$30
- Collector Card, 1992. Harold Lloyd Presents Marilyn, HL TRUSTA; 1992; the word "PROTOTYPE" printed on reverse (no image). ....$9-$15
- Cologne Spray, 1983. 3.3 oz. Bottle; Marilyn concentrated cologne spray; came in decorative box showing color photo of Marilyn; made in U.S........$15-$20
- Color-Tinted Portrait, 1950s. 5 x 7; circa 1949 photo of MM that was sold in five-and-dime stores in a picture frame; bottom has Marilyn's name and "Printed in U. S. A." (not in frame). ....$10-$20
- Cosmetic Kit, vintage unknown. With small purse and 5 oz. of perfume. ....$20-$30
- Cribbage Board, 1950s. With *Golden Dreams* nude photo in center of board. ....$175-$200
- Dart Flights, vintage unknown. MM dart flights from England. ....$20-$35
- Datebook, 1974. Many color and b&w MM photos with commentary by Norman Mailer; printed on slick heavy paper and spiral-bound. ....$15-$30
- Datebook, 1993. "Marilyn Datebook" by Cedco Publishing Co. ....$10-$20
- Diary, circa 1990s-2001. Locking diary; made by Vandor. ....$20-$25
- Dice, vintage unknown. Set of four with "Chevrolet" and MM's image on them. ....$4-$8
- Drawing Aid, circa 1972, though dated 1956. 8" long; female-shaped plastic drawing form; MM's photo on envelope with the phrase, "Whether the angle's acute, or the slope is so great, that you need a directional change, you will find what you want on the back or the front of Marilyn's beautiful frame."......$15-$20
- Driver's License, 1990s. Reproduction California driver's license with MM's color photo on it........$3-$5
- Ear Muffs, vintage unknown. Pair of ear muffs with MM's face inset on them by R.G. Barry Co. ....$90-$110

Flag, circa 1999, $10-$20

Holograms, 1992, $10-$20.

A selection of contemporary key chains, $4-$8.

1951 license plate for Marilyn's Lincoln, $1,000-$2,000.

1990s goose egg from France, $100-$150.

- Earrings, vintage unknown. Pair of earrings by Vitreous Co. showing a head shot of Marilyn .... $15-$30
- Ed Weston Fine Art of Northridge, California, 1992. Various items produced for a *Some Like It Hot* New Year's Eve bash at the Riviera Hotel and Casino in Las Vegas, Nevada, on Dec. 31, 1992:
  - Pin. 2½"; features b&w photo of MM; numbered; limited edition of 5,000. .... $5-$10
  - Brochure. 4½ x 11 folded, eight pages; 54 photos of MM by George Barris, Bert Stern, Laszlo Willinger, and others inside; photos issued in limited edition of 99 at $250 for a 5 x 7 and $3,000 for an 8 x 10. .... $10-$20
  - Single photo. 7 x 10; limited edition of 2,500. .... $20-$30
- Emerson Junior High Graduating Class Photo, June 1941. Approximately 8 x 25; showing entire class in front of school in panoramic view; glossy finish. .... $1,000-$2,000
- Eraser, vintage unknown. MM eraser; maker unknown .... $3-$8
- Exhibition Catalog, 1967. Homage to Marilyn Monroe at Sydney Janis Gallery in New York, Dec. 6-30, 1967; MM photo on cover; features works by Bert Stern, Richard Avedon, Warhol, Rosenquist, Segal, Rotella, Dali, de Kooning, Marisol, and others on the inside.. .... $30-$45
- Exhibition Catalog, 1960s. 10½ x 10½; "Marilyn, The Legend and the Truth"; photographic retrospective with silver softcover, small b&w photo of MM, and 16 pages of b&w and color photos from the exhibit and list of photographers. .... $50-$80
- Flag, circa 1999. About 2½' x 5'; American flag, with a screen printing of MM's face and signature .... $10-$20
- Frame Up!, 1990s. 7 x 8 and 7 x 9; cardboard picture frame in two styles with MM's photo in one and two photos in the other; easels on the back. .... each $5-$10
- Gift Bags, 1980s-'90s. Numerous gift bags; various sizes from tiny to large. .... each $3-$10
- Gift Cards, vintage unknown. Pack of three cards that read, "Especially for you" next to Marilyn's image. .... $3-$5
- Glassware, vintage unknown. Warhol MM art on beverage, wine, and champagne glasses; set of four. .... set $40-$50
- Glassware, 1990s. Set of four shot glasses by Hollywood Legends featuring MM in the white *Itch* dress, a black one-piece bathing suit, a white dress, and a black dress with white polka-dots .... set $20-$35
- Goose Egg, circa 1990s. Handpainted goose egg from France .... $100-$150
- Halloween Mask, 1950s. Latex mask of Marilyn Monroe; few remain .... $50-$100

Lunch box by Vandor, $25-$35.

Limited-edition ENESCO Jack-in-the-box, 1990, $100-$150.

- Holograms, 1992. Four in set with decorative box by Hollywood Legends, Harold Lloyd Collection. .... $10-$20
- Invitations, 1984. Set of eight made by Hallmark and read, "Wanna Party?" .... $5-$10
- Jack-In-The-Box, 1990. Beautifully done in decorative porcelain box featuring MM pictures on sides; entitled, "Stars of the Silver Screen"; limited edition of 10,000 by ENESCO. .... $100-$150
- Jeans, circa 1996. Marilyn Monroe Signature Jeans; have tag attached with a color photo of MM in jeans, along with a phone card featuring her photo on it .... $40-$50
- Jewelry, 1997-98. Marilyn jewelry called "The Hollywood Collection; replicas of actual jewelry worn by MM in her films; rings, pendants, etc. ....each $40-$60
- Jewelry Box, 1994. MM's image on box; made by Vandor. .... $35-$40

Contemporary Marilyn Monroe jewelry, $40-$60 each.

1950s matchbook with artwork by T.N. Thompson, $15-$30.

- Kaleidoscope, 1988. 8½" long; Says "Kiss," shows many colored Marilyns; made in Taiwan by Applause Inc. ....$5-$10
- Key, 1970s. 2" diameter; solid brass with 20th Century Fox logo on one side and "Marilyn Monroe-Dressing Room No. 5" on the other; attached to a small ring on a nylon wristband ....$20-$40
- Key Chain, 1950s. 1½ x 2; clear Lucite plastic with b&w photos of Marilyn in *Golden Dreams* pose on one side and *New Wrinkle* pose on other; has a bead link chain that opens and closes. ....$30-$40
- Key Chain, circa 1970s. Large and plastic in shape of the white dress blowing scene, has "Some Like It Hot" on it, and face is empty to insert whatever photo you like. ....$5-$10
- Key Chain, circa 1980s. Plastic case with color photo of MM lying on her side in a two-piece yellow bathing suit like the one featured on the earlier Lusterchrome postcard. ....$4-$8
- Key Chain, circa 1996. Plastic case with two photos of Marilyn on each side. $4-$8
- Key Chain, 1990. Warhol MM artwork; made by Reed Productions of San Fransisco, California. ....$4-$8
- Key Chain, 1989. Gold trimmed with face shot of MM by Gift Creations; made in Taiwan. ....$4-$8
- Korea Photos, 1954. Original photos taken by GIs while MM performed for troops in Korea in February 1954; various sizes, with no negative available......$40-$100
- Lapel Pin, 1953. Small metal pin of Marilyn in one-piece red bathing suit; dated on back. ....$30-$50
- Lapel Pins, vintage unknown. Ceramic hand-painted pins of MM; came with rhinestone earrings or necklace. ....each $10-$15
- Letter/Envelope, circa 1954. Typed letter, sent by the studio, and featuring MM's facsimile signature; postmarked "Beverly Hills, CA, P.O. Box 900"; came with 2¾ x 3¼ glossy photo; gives prices on larger photos, explaining that they have too many requests to send the larger photos..$30-$60
- Letter/Envelope, 1961. Typed letter on MM's stationery, though signed by a secretary; thanking writer for get well wishes to Marilyn. ....$50-$90
- License Plate, circa 1984. Pink license plate depicting the 1984 Olympics held in Los Angeles; MM's face and name on the front. ....$15-$20

Light switch covers, $12-$15 each.

Memory cube, $5-$10.

Shot glasses by Hollywood Legends, $20-$35 set.

Vintage photos taken in Korea, $40-$100 each.

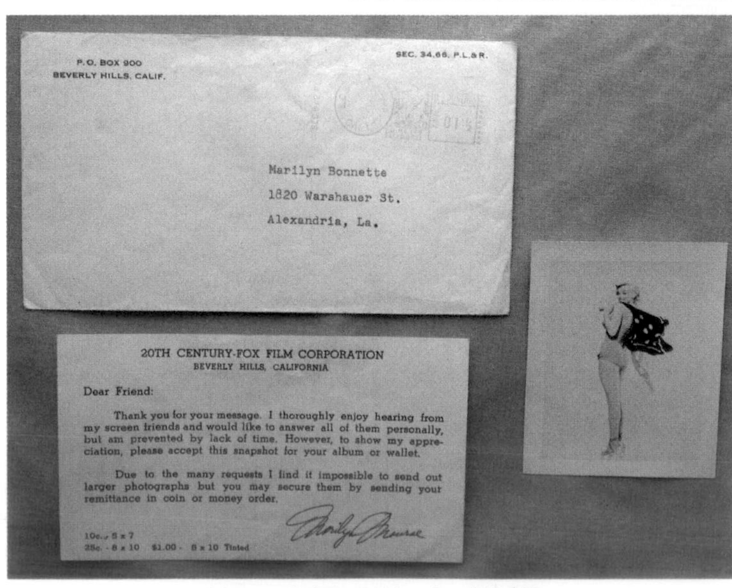

P.O. BOX 900
BEVERLY HILLS, CALIF.

SEC. 34.66, P.L.&R.

Marilyn Bonnette
1820 Warshauer St.
Alexandria, La.

20TH CENTURY-FOX FILM CORPORATION
BEVERLY HILLS, CALIFORNIA

Dear Friend:

Thank you for your message. I thoroughly enjoy hearing from my screen friends and would like to answer all of them personally, but am prevented by lack of time. However, to show my appreciation, please accept this snapshot for your album or wallet.

Due to the many requests I find it impossible to send out larger photographs but you may secure them by sending your remittance in coin or money order.

Marilyn Monroe

10c. - 5 x 7
25c. - 8 x 10 $1.00 - 8 x 10 Tinted

A letter and photo sent to a fan, $30-$60.

- License Plate, 1951. California-issued front plate to MM's Lincoln; license number 3P 88 603. . . . . $1,000-$2,000
- Light Switch Covers, vintage unknown. Single and double; by Hollywood Legends.. each $12-$15
- Limoge, 1992. MM's face handpainted; each one-of-a-kind; only 50 made. . . . . $400-$450
- Lithograph, 1990s. Earl MacPherson litho of a nude Marilyn standing and bending her left leg up. . . . . $40-$60
- Lithograph, circa 1990. 22 x 28; entitled "Gentlemen Prefer Blondes" and "Niagara"; came in museum-quality framing; were mates to the plates done same year in conjunction with 20th Century Fox; made by Royal Orleans; signed and numbered by artist; limited edition of 500. . each $100-$150
- Lithograph, 1985. Printed on litho in Fantazya-Provincetown, Massachusetts, by JUREK; came with COA; limited edition of 500.. . . . . $100-$200
- Lottery Tickets, circa 1998. Set of four Illinois tickets with different photos (scratched or unscratched). . . . each $1-$3
- Lunch Box, vintage unknown. Large box featuring MM image by Andy Warhol; made by Vandor. . . . . $30-$35

- Lunch Box, vintage unknown. Features MM's face on TV screen; made by Vandor. .... $25-$35
- Magnet, 1997. Giant magnet by Ata-Boy Inc., Los Angeles, California; made in China .... $5-$10
- Magnet, vintage unknown. Titled "Legends of the Fridge"; features MM photo by Bernard of Hollywood. .... $5-$10
- Magnet Dolls, vintage unknown. 9" tall; MM dress-up magnets by Caryco. .... [illegible]
- Makeup Bag, vintage unknown. By Andre de Dienes Collection. .... $35-$40
- Mannequin, 1990s. By Dector Mannequin Co. of Los Angeles (now American Mannequin Co.). .... $1,000-$1,200
- Marble, vintage unknown. Larger "shooter" marble featuring MM on it. .... $3-$5
- Mask, circa 1990s. Halloween mask; maker unknown. .... $15-$30
- Mask, 1983. Postcard-size with color painting of MM's face, with hole for your nose; artwork by Betty Levine. .... $3-$8
- Matchbook Covers, 1950s. Depict MM art on front with captions such as, "Look Here Pardner" (showing MM in a white cowgirl outfit) by T.N. Thompson, or "Maid in Baltimore" (showing MM in a two-piece yellow bathing suit) by Earl Moran. .... each $15-$30
- Max Factor Store Display, 1999. 2' x 3'; cardboard; in red sweater pulled over knees (Milton Greene photo) .... $20-$40
- Memory Cube, vintage unknown. Featuring color photos of MM on each side .... $5-$10
- Metal Sign, circa early 1990s. 12½ x 16½; reproduces Marilyn's Lustre Cream Ad in color. .... $10-$20
- Metal Sign, 1994. 12½ x 16½; reproduces Marilyn's Tru-Glo Makeup Ad in color. .... $10-$20
- Metal Tray, circa 1980s-90s; 12 x 16½; shows b&w ballerina photo of MM titled "Marilyn Forever"; made by Tropico of Paris, France. .... $10-$15
- Mirror, circa 1952-1954. 8½ x 11; advertising mirror with MM in the famous nude *Golden Dreams* pose, with a black lace negligee painted on. .... $50-$100
- Mirror, 1950s. 8 x 10; advertising mirror with the nude *Golden Dreams* pose in color on it. .... $60-$100
- Mirror, circa 1990. 16 x 20; screen printing of MM's face and signature in sepia tone. .... $20-$30
- Mirror, 1992. Glamour Starlight makeup mirror by Salton .... $30-$40
- Model Car, 1993. White Cadillac convertible (1955) with red interior and shows MM's facsimile signature and image on the car; by Solido; limited edition "Signature Series." .... $80-$110
    - Above car by Solido also done in a pink Buick convertible; smaller size than above car. .... $50-$85
- Money Clip, circa 1970s. MM in famous nude *Golden Dreams* pose. .... $10-$20
- Mouse Pad, circa 1998-2001. Various examples of MM mouse pads. .... each $10-$20
- Movie Script Reprints, circa 1990-2000. From some of MM's bigger films, such as *Some Like It Hot*. .... each $20-$30
- Mug, 1990. 12 oz. ceramic; depicts colorized Warhol images of MM; made by Clay Art; style No. 1620. .... $5-$12
- Mug, late-1970s-early 1980s. Art portrait with "Some Like It Hot" written on reverse; made by Famous Mugs of Nostalgia Lane. .... $5-$12
- Mug, circa 1980s. Entitled "Marilyn The Cat," showing white Persian cat with blue dress like white *Itch* dress. .... $5-$12
- Mug, circa 1999. Travel mug; "Collectible Marilyn" by Allison Lefcort/Estate of Marilyn Monroe. .... $5-$10
- Mug, circa 1990s. Shows MM in a gold lamé dress. .... $5-$10
- Mug, circa 1990s. "Very Merry Kissmas" printed on it. .... $5-$10
- Mug, circa 1990s. Shows a photo of MM on the beach by Sam Shaw. .... $5-$10
- Mug, 1992. Vandor pearls mug .... $25-$35

Music box, 1990s, $20-$40

Advertising mirror, circa 1952-1954, $50-$100.

A selection of Polonaise ornaments, $35-$40 each.

Notepaper and envelopes by Erica Products, $5-$12.

- Mug, 1992. "Want to be wonderful" printed on it; by Vandor. .... $15-$20
- Music Box, 1990s. MM in the gold lamé dress. .... $20-$40
- Neon Poster, circa 1955. 24 x 36; titled "Neon Lights Marilyn"; depicts MM putting on Channel No. 5 and neon lights come out of the bottle; very heavy-weight. .... $100-$150
- Night Light, 1984. MM in white *Itch* dress on the famous Hollywood sign; made by Vandor. .... $200-$250
- Notebook and Folder, vintage unknown. Featuring b&w drawings of Marilyn; made by Lisa Frank. .... $10-$15
- Notecards, early 1990s. 5 x 7; boxed set of 10 cards from France with two cards each of five different Eve Arnold photos in color; cards are blank and came with envelopes. .... $10-$15
- Notepad Cube, 1990. 3 x 2¾ cube of paper. .... $2-$5
- Notepaper and Envelopes, 1999. Featuring the Andy Warhol artwork of MM; by Erica Products. .... $5-$12
- Numismatic Marilyn Items:
  - 1 troy oz. silver medallion; vintage unknown. .999 FS; MM in white blowing dress on one side and the reverse says, "Marilyn Monroe 1926-1962"; limited edition. $20-$30
  - 1 troy oz. silver coin; vintage unknown. .999 FS; nude *Golden Dreams* pose on one side and ."1" on other side. .... $20-$30
  - 1 troy oz. silver coin; vintage unknown. .999 FS; nude *Golden Dreams* pose on one side and John F. Kennedy on the other. .... $20-$30
  - 1 troy oz. silver wafer; vintage unknown. .999 FS; nude *Golden Dreams* pose on one side and blank on other except for a decorative border. .... $20-$30
  - silver coin set, 1971; by The Franklin Mint; Marilyn is one of 10 coins in set; each bears a legendary stars' likeness; stars' image on one side and his/her facsimile signature on other; limited to 500 sets. .... $200-$300
  - 2 oz. bronze wafer, vintage unknown. *Golden Dreams* pose with initials T.P. to right of MM's image on one side and completely blank on other. .... $15-$25
  - aluminum coin, 1985. MM's face on one side and the words, "Krewe of Jefferson" on the other; came in blue, gold, red, and silver; says, "Famous Americans—A Tribute to Marilyn Monroe 1926-1962." .... $5-$10

A mug by Vandor, $25-$35.

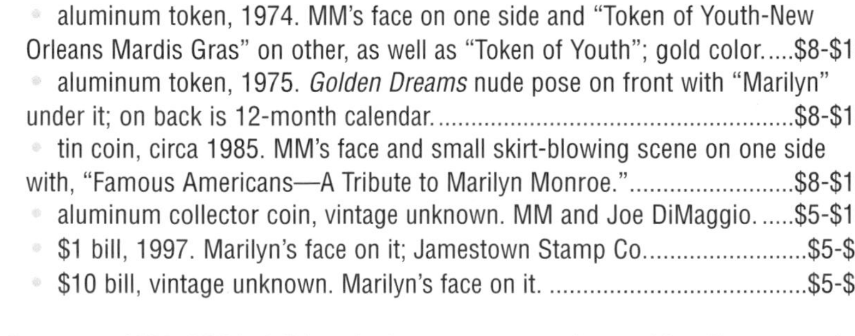

  - aluminum token, 1974. MM's face on one side and "Token of Youth-New Orleans Mardis Gras" on other, as well as "Token of Youth"; gold color. .... $8-$12
  - aluminum token, 1975. *Golden Dreams* nude pose on front with "Marilyn" under it; on back is 12-month calendar. .... $8-$10
  - tin coin, circa 1985. MM's face and small skirt-blowing scene on one side with, "Famous Americans—A Tribute to Marilyn Monroe." .... $8-$10
  - aluminum collector coin, vintage unknown. MM and Joe DiMaggio. ...... $5-$10
  - $1 bill, 1997. Marilyn's face on it; Jamestown Stamp Co. .... $5-$8
  - $10 bill, vintage unknown. Marilyn's face on it. .... $5-$8

Party mask, $3-$8.

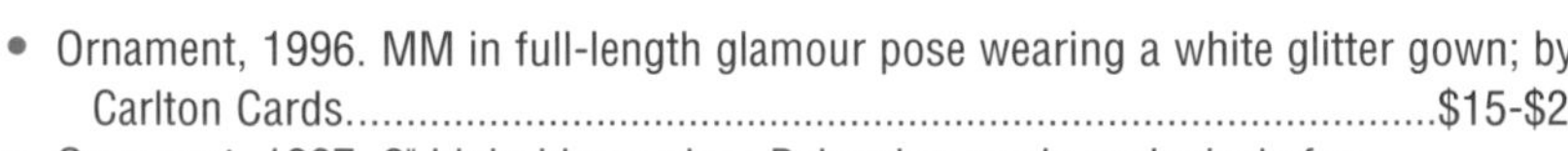

- Ornament, 1996. MM in full-length glamour pose wearing a white glitter gown; by Carlton Cards. .... $15-$20
- Ornament, 1997. 6" high; blown glass Polonaise; made exclusively for Kurt S. Adler Inc. .... $35-$40
- Ornament, 1998. Another edition of the above Polonaise ornament. .... $35-$40
- Ornament, circa 1995. Featuring 1995 U.S. postage stamp of MM; made for Kurt S. Adler Inc. .... $7-$15
- Ornament, 1997. *Gentlemen Prefer Blondes* by Hallmark. .... $15-$20

- Ornament, 1998. *The Seven Year Itch* by Hallmark. ....$15-$20
- Ornament, 1999. *How to Marry a Millionaire* by Hallmark..$15-$20
- Ornaments, 2001. Porcelain set of four by The Bradford Editions; depict MM in dresses she wore in *The Seven Year Itch, Gentlemen Prefer Blondes, How To Marry A Millionaire,* and *There's No Business Like Show Business*; artwork by Chris Notorile. Originally $9.99 each. ....$9-$12
- Ornament, vintage unknown. MM in a red bathing suit and towel; Patricia Andrews keepsake...........$45-$50
- Ornament, 1990s. MM in a gold lamé gown with outstretched arms; by ENESCO......................$15-$30
- Painting, circa 1995. 18½ x 13¼; oil on canvas by Michael Deas; same pose as on '95 U.S. postage stamp...$125-$175
- Painting, 1956. 28 x 36; oil on canvas by Abe Kazuni; famous *Golden Dreams* nude pose.........$1,300-$1,600
- Party Set, circa 1993. By Hallmark; included table cloth, cups, etc...$15-$20
- Peep Show TV Set, 1970s-'80s. 2" tall, color case shows eight different views of Marilyn inside. ....$5-$10
- Peep Viewer, 1970s-'80s. Marilyn in the nude *Golden Dreams* pose inside; green case. ....$5-$10
- Pen, 1999. "Marilyn by Moonlight" pen. ....$5-$10
- Pencil Holder, circa 1980s. Approved by the Roger Richman Agency; made in Italy. ....$15-$20
- Pencil Sharpener, 1979. Made by Trevu Italiana – MI Italy.............................. $3-$8
- Pens, vintage unknown. Ink pens by Writek. ....each $20-$25
- Perfume, 1985. 1.7 oz., Marilyn Golden Musk; in decorative box; made in U.S. ....$10-$20
- Perfume, 1980s. Deluxe Golden Musk perfume in black box; Marilyn Monroe Beauty Corp...$80-$85

Dollar bill, $5-$8.

A selection of silver medallions, $20-$30 each.

Dress-up magnets by Caryco, $60-$70 set.

Model collectible cars by Solido, $80-$110 (Cadillac, above) and $50-$85 (Buick, at right).

Bearilyn Monroe bear, 1984, $50-$70.

A selection of contemporary playing card decks, $10-$25 each.

- Perfume Bottle, circa 2001. Cobalt blue and various other hues and shapes, with MM's image on top from *Itch* in gold; made in China.......................each $55-$60
- Perfume Kit, vintage unknown. 1 oz. of perfume. ....$50-$65
- Phone Cards, 1995. Set of two by Gem International with George Barris photos on them; $3 face value each..$30-$40
- Phone Cards, 1995. Two sets of three phone cards by Worldlink with various glamour shots along with MM's facsimile signature; all have $10 face value. ....$40-$50
- Phone Card, 1995. Single phone card by Worldlink with Richard Avedon photo; special issue for Cardex '95 convention held in the Netherlands; face value of $5. ....$5-$10
- Phone Cards, circa 1990s. Set of three cards by Global Com 2000 with Bernard of Hollywood photos on each; face value of $3 on two and $10 on one.......$40-$50
- Phone Cards, circa 1990s. Set of four cards by Laser Radio, each with different photo of MM; came in three-ring binder with printing on it; also came with COA for each; face values of $10, $12, $15, and $20. ....$50-$80
- Phone Card, circa 1990s. By France Telecom Cable shows a scene from *The Seven Year Itch* with Tom Ewell and MM; card has a microchip on its front. ....$20-$30
- Phone Card, 1994. Official Telcom card by Pacific Coin Co. of New Zealand; limited to 5,500; $20 face value. ....$30-$40
- Phone Cards, 1994. Set of seven by George Barris with Barris photos of MM on each; five have face values of $10, one of $20, and one of $1,000 (which is signed by Barris)...$20-$40 and $1,000-$1,200
- Phone Cards, circa 1996. Set of two by American National Phone Card Co.; one is jumbo (5 x 7) and worth 20 units, other is super jumbo (8 x 10) worth 50 units; both feature artwork on them.
  - Jumbo ....$30-$40
  - Super Jumbo ....$45-$55
- Phone Cards, 1995. Set of two Gem International WORLD '95 cards produced for international phone cards show in Singapore on Dec. 15-19, 1995; each feature George Barris photos; one is worth 8 units, other is worth 88 units.
  - 8 Unit...$15-$20
  - 88 Unit...$35-$40
- Phone Card, circa 1996. Sold at Kmart stores and affixed to Marilyn Monroe brand clothes..$10-$20
- Photo Album, vintage unknown. With MM's images; made by Vandor. ....$30-$35
- Photos, 1955. Set of six 8 x 10 b&w photos of MM in the white *Itch* dress sold through magazines by Star Pix of New York City. Originally $3 for set. ....$200-$275
- Picture Frame, vintage unknown. Paper frame by Vandor...........................$15-$20
- Picture Frame, vintage unknown. "At the Movies-take clacker" picture frame. ....$40-$45

Stained glass sun catcher, $15-$20.

- Pill Box, vintage unknown. Original Italian pill box; promotional item for *The Seven Year Itch*....................$20-$25
- Pillow, 1996. 19"; white toss pillow with MM's face on it; sold at Target stores. ....$10-$20
- Pillow, vintage unknown. Toss pillow featuring photo of MM in the gold lamé dress....................$5-$10
- Pin, vintage unknown. Featuring McDonald's, Disney characters, and MM. ....$15-$20
- Pinback Buttons, various years. Numerous examples produced—some by fan clubs, others by individuals, and several by companies; sizes vary....each $2-$12
- Planter, vintage unknown. Features MM's face on TV screen; made by Vandor. ....$30-$40
- Playing Cards, circa 1976. Two decks: one with *Golden Dreams* pose and another with *New Wrinkle* pose; reproductions of the two decks done in the 1950s; came in clear plastic case....................each $10-$25

One cup from a party set by Hallmark, $15-$20 set.

1980s perfume, $80-$85.

A selection of Hallmark ornaments, $15-$20 each.

A selection of pinback buttons, $2-$12 each.

A pair of contemporary toss pillows,
$5-$10 for the black and $10-$20 for the white.

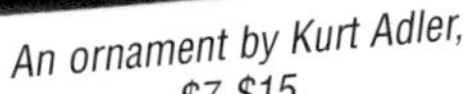

An ornament by Kurt Adler,
$7-$15.

- Pocketknife, circa 1972. Features nude *Golden Dreams* pose encased in hard plastic on handle. ....$5-$10
- Pocketknife, 1982. Pearl two-bladed pocket knife; came in velvet box; Collector Series. ....$65-$80
- Pocket Mirrors, 1970s. Several 2 x 3 mirrors with photos of Marilyn or of her film posters; some dated on the edge and some not; some dated earlier than '70s, but were not made earlier. ....each $8-$15
- Pool Cue, 1993. Marilyn Legend Cue by McDermott Cue Mfg. Co., Menomonee Falls, Wisconsin, features color art and came with a choice of nylon, Irish linen, or leather wrap; came in a soft black case with MM's facsimile signature on it in blue. Originally $295; case was $34. ....cue and case $300-$350
- Print, 1994. 19 x 24; Earl Moran color print entitled "Spanish Girl"; print 1; printed on 80 lb. archival acid-free paper; numbered limited edition of 7,500. ...$80-$120
- Print, circa 1992. "Boulevard of Broken Dreams" by Helnwein; color painting of MM and other Hollywood greats at a bar. ....$40-$50
- Print, circa 1980s. 20 x 25; Earl MacPherson pencil drawing with a little color added "Marilyn II" and "Barely Yours, Marilyn" printed on it; limited edition of 250. ....$50-$100
- Print, 1981. 10 x 13; photographic print of MM by Philippe Halsman; same photo that appeared on the 1952 cover of *LIFE* magazine; stamped on reverse; limited edition of 250. ....$400-$600
- Print, circa 1980s. 16 x 20; color laser print of MM in common gold lamé dress; well done on heavy paper. ....$20-$30

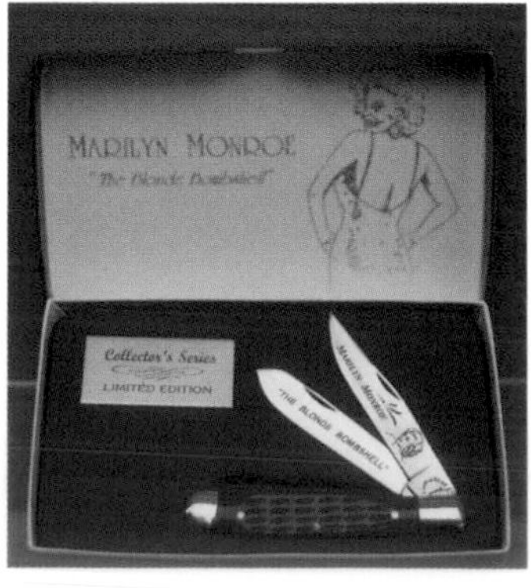

Collector's Series
pocketknife,
$65-$80.

- Print, 1973. Silkscreen print with white paint on gold foil by Bert Stern featuring close-up of MM from Stern's *The Last Sitting*; signed and numbered; limited to 100. ....$2,500-$2,900
- Print, circa 1980s. 19 x 19; silkscreen by Bert Stern of nude from *The Last Sitting*; limited edition of 250. ....$1,200-$1,600
- Print, 1967. Silkscreen print by Bert Stern; green and orange color, in the Warhol style; signed, dated; numbered "3/15." ....$1,200-$1,500
- Print, 1968. Silkscreen print by Bert Stern called "Blue Chiffon" of nude Marilyn concealing her breasts; signed and dated. ....$1,200-$1,500
- Print Portfolios, 1990. 13 x 15; set of eight hand-colored prints of selected MM glamour shots. ....$20-$40
- Print Portfolio, vintage unknown. 11 x 14; set of six color images of MM by photographer friend Sam Shaw. ....$20-$30
- Print Portfolio, 1990s. 10 x 12; Bernard of Hollywood set of three color prints by MM's photographer friend Bruno Bernard. ....$40-$80
- Bernard; came hand-stamped with COA; offered by International Collectors Society, among others. ....$100-$200
- Print Portfolio, 1991. 16 x 20; set of four prints by Earl Moran; actual photos from the 1940s; came in cream-colored slipcase. ....$80-$100
- Print Portfolio, 1990s. 11 x 14; set of five prints by George Barris; photos taken between June 1 and July 18, 1962; numbered. ....$125-$150
- Puzzle, circa 1980s-'90s. 8" tall; multicolored foam puzzle which assembles into standing figure in the blowing white skirt scene; from Gift Creations. ....$10-$15
- Puzzle, 1973. *Playboy* puzzle of MM in the famous nude pose. ....$50-$90
- Puzzle, 1972. *Playboy* puzzle of MM in the famous blowing white skirt pose. ....$50-$90
- Puzzle, 1973. Features a Bert Stern photo. ....$40-$60
- Puzzle, circa 1997. 20 x 27; "Memories of Marilyn" 1,000-piece puzzle featuring collage of photos; by Bernard of Hollywood. ....$15-$20
- Puzzle, 1967. Round 300-piece "Marilyn Star Puzzle" by Alpsco; came in metal film-type canister; catalog no. 82; by Adult Leisure Products Corp., Locust Valley, New York. ....$30-$50
- Puzzle, 1986. 24 x 30; 1,000-piece "Forever Ours—Marilyn Monroe" jigsaw puzzle by Springbok shows many pastel-painted images of MM; artwork by Steve Carter; no. PZL6115. ....$25-$35
- Puzzle, 1980s-'90s. 250-piece jigsaw puzzle by Jigstars showing Milton Greene's photo of MM in ballerina outfit and facsimile signature on bottom right; came put-together with collapsed box compressed inside and shrink-wrapped; made in England. ....$20-$30
- Puzzle, 1972. 8 x 10; jigsaw puzzle of nude *Golden Dreams* pose and encased in plastic; came put together with gold and red emblem on front that said, "1962-1972—10th Anniversary—Never Before, Never Again." ....$10-$25
- Puzzle, 1988. Airbrushed image of MM; a clock was produced with the same image. ....$20-$30
- Puzzle, 1964. MM "eternal" puzzle. ....$20-$30
- Puzzle, 1990. Made of various tiles with different MM image on each. ....$30-$35
- Puzzle, 1970s-80s. Hand-size puzzle postcard with several beads under cellophane cover featuring painting of MM's face; Patent No. 8410391; by Hall and Keane Design Ltd.; British. ....$5-$10
- Radio, 1983. Large tabletop size MM jukebox radio by Cicena, with pink and white neon lights; China. ....$350-$400
- Reading Glasses, vintage unknown. MM's trademarked signature on one lens; came in case; made by Renaissance; rare. ....$45-$50
- Ring, vintage unknown. MM coin face 14-karat gold ring. ....$125-$150
- Ring, 1990s. Gold-colored adjustable band, with the nude *Golden Dreams* pose on top. ....$3-$5
- *Ripley's Believe It or Not* Press Kit, early 1990s. Issued in conjunction with the Marilyn Exhibit at the Ripley's Museum chain; came with a color slide ....$10-$15

Print by Philippe Halsman, circa 1981, $400-$600.

Laser print, circa 1980s, $20-$30.

Print by Bert Stern, 1973, $2,500-$2,900.

A selection of contemporary puzzles, prices vary.

• Rubber Stamps, 1993. Three different stamps by Rubber Stampede entitled "Marilyn Monroe" on first two and "Glamour Girl" on third; numbered A313-C, A313-D and A313-E. ....each $5-$15

• Rug, vintage unknown. Featuring color image of MM by Andy Warhol. ....$10-$20

• Ruler, vintage unknown. MM's image covers entire length. ....$8-$18

• Salt and Pepper Shakers, vintage unknown. MM's face on a TV; made by Vandor. ....$15-$20

• Salt and Pepper Shakers, vintage unknown. Diamond design; made by Vandor...$15-$20

• Salt and Pepper Shakers, vintage unknown. Featuring a pair of high heel shoes; made by Vandor. ....$15-$20

• Scarf, vintage unknown. Silk scarf with the Andy Warhol art of MM on it. ....$30-$50

• Screen Saver, 1994. Depicts several rare Sam Shaw photos of MM and entitled "Sam Shaw's Stars Photo Screen Saver"; manufactured by Desktop Software Inc. ....$25-$30

• Sculpture, circa 1990s. Life-sized animated Marilyn, anatomically correct, of famous *Itch* skirt scene above grate; very few made by a Dutch sculptor. ....$15,000-$20,000

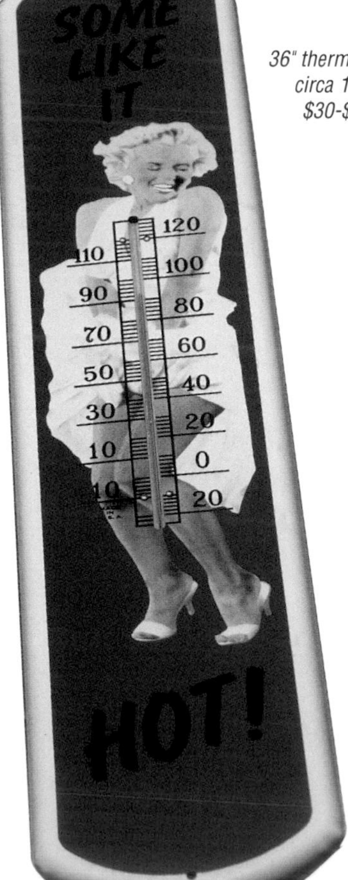

36" thermometer, circa 1972, $30-$50.

• Sculpture, 1991. Life-sized fiberglass and resin sculpture of MM in gold lamé gown; made by Canadian sculptor Chris Rees; limited edition of 10. ....$4,000-$5,000

• Sculpture, 1991. Cast stone bust of MM in same gold lamé gown as above; made by Canadian sculptor Chris Rees; limited edition of 100. ....$500-$600

• Serving Trays, circa 1950s-60s. 13 x 18, 18 x 24, or 20 x 24; each have a laminated color photo of either the nude *Golden Dreams* pose or the nude *New Wrinkle* pose; framed in "blonde" wood. ....each $80-$135

• Serving Tray, 1950s-60s. Same style and vintage as above described trays, only all metal..........$50-$80

• Serving Tray, vintage unknown. *Some Like It Hot* tray; all metal..........$50-$100

• Shoes, 1999. Kelly's Collectible high heel MM shoes; limited edition. ....$40-$60

• Shoes, 1950s. Black platform shoes worn by MM; made by Jeweltone; COA from Guido Ortenzio and signed letter of provenance from Elenore "Bebe" Goddard; from Goddard's collection..........(auction estimate) $9,000-$12,000

• Shot Glass, vintage unknown. Depicts MM in a red bikini, sitting on edge; rare. ....$100-$140

• Shower Head, vintage unknown. Made by Banning..........$30-$35

• Snow Globe, circa 1990s. Famous nude *Golden Dreams* pose; by Hollywood Hot. ....$15-$25

• Snow Globe, circa 1990s. MM in a director's chair from *There's No Business Like Show Business.* ....$55-$65

• Socks, 1993. Pair of green cotton nylon elastane valentine's adult socks by Fan Club Fitwear; No. C31991; made in Korea..........$10-$15

• Socks, 1992. Pair of white or pink ankle socks by Hot Socks Inc..........$8-$10

Contemporary reading glasses, $45-$50.

- Souvenir, circa 1956. "Guide to the Homes of Television and Movie Stars"; shows MM's 1956 home (with car parked outside), as well as homes of many other stars; could be mailed back to relatives. ....$20-$40
- Spoon, vintage unknown. Metallic spoon featuring MM in a black v-neck dress with white collar. ....$5-$10
- Spoon, vintage unknown. Collector spoon of MM, featuring famous nude *Golden Dreams* pose. ....$5-$10
- Standees, late-1980s to present. Numerous life-sized cardboard standees featuring blown-up photos of MM, some color and some b&w (not vintage standees produced by the studios for promoting MM's films, which are listed in chapter 9, page 156)................each $20-$30
- Standees, 1990-94. 9"-12" tall; Miniature versions of those listed above; by Triangle Enterprises. ....$5-$10
- Statue, circa 2000. Life-size cast statue in famous *Itch* dress; displayed in front of cigar and novelty stores. ....$300-$400
- Steering Wheel Knob, circa 1950s. Used on steering wheels to aid in steering vehicles and has color *Golden Dreams* pose on it; newer version features a head and shoulders photo of Marilyn, as well as the nude pose; these were also known as suicide, spinner, or necker knobs; originals have single band (to attach to steering wheel); made by "Hollywood" company................$50-$75
- Steering Wheel Knob, circa 1990s. Reproduction of original knob described above; reproductions have double band (to attach to steering wheel). ....$10-$20
- Steins, 1991. 3 11/16" wide and 5 3/16" high; released by Ernst Inc. in conjunction with its series of Marilyn ceramic plaques by Susie Morton; serially numbered:
  - Marilyn (first issue in the collection). . . . . $40-$50
  - Lights, Camera, Action! . . . . $40-$50
  - New York, New York. $40-$50
- Steins, 1997. Set of MM steins by Longton Crown; featuring the artwork of Chris Notorile, who did many of the Bradford Exchange plates of MM......each $15-$25
- Stickers, circa 1980s. Set of eight color stickers of MM. ....$5-$10
- Sun Catcher, vintage unknown. Gallery stained glass sun catcher of MM in the white *Itch* dress. ....$15-$20
- Sunglasses, 1989. Titled "Marilyn Monroe—The Legend Lives"; came with white case and were on 11 x 16 display board; made by Eyewear by Renaissance. ....$30-$40
- Tapestry, 1983. MM in either gold lamé gown or in famous white skirt-blowing scene. ....each $20-$30
- Tapestry, 1975. 34 x 54; MM holding an umbrella, with small photos around outer border. ....$30-$40
- Tapestry, 1999. 35 x 54 (not including tassels); 100% cotton; velvet; made in Turkey. ....$20-$30

An ornament by ENESCO, $15-$30.

A selection of contemporary rubber stamps, $5-$15 each.

Platform shoes worn by Marilyn Monroe, $9,000-$12,000, and below are contemporary shoes, $40-$60.

1999 Travel Mug set, $5-$10.

- Teddy Bear, 1984. 21" tall; "Bearilyn Monroe" designed by Barbara Isenberg of pink fabric with dress and headband covered with large black polka dots; made by The North American Bear Co. Inc. of Chicago; U.S. material sewn in Haiti. ....$50-$70
- Telephone, 1990. High-heel phone in red; made by Columbia Telephones; first MM phone made..$80-$90
- Thermometer, circa 1970s. 3 x 7; reads, "Some Like It Hot—Marilyn Monroe"; boxed..$10-$15
- Thermometer, circa 1970s. As above, only 8 x 24. ....$20-$25
- Thermometer, circa 1970s. 6 x 36; reading, "Some Like It Hot" with MM in white *Itch* dress. ....$30-$50
- Thermometer, 1984. 2½' high; indoor/outdoor thermometer reading, "Some Like It Hot" and showing white *Itch* dress, as above but smaller; with two suction cups to adhere to a window, etc. ....$20-$30
- Thimble, 1992. Fine bone china and titled "The Seven Year Itch"; made in England by Finsbury...$10-$20

Souvenir guide to stars' homes, circa 1956, $20-$40.

- Thimble, 1992. Pink plastic construction with MM's image on it ....$3-$5
- Ties:
  - 1993; "Flying Skirt" by Bernard of Hollywood; color. ....$20-$30
  - 1993; MM in one-piece bathing suit; by Bernard of Hollywood; color. ....$20-$30
  - 1990s; MM in a black dress with studded straps; by Bernard of Hollywood. ....$20-$30
  - 1990s; MM in three color glamour poses; by Bernard of Hollywood. ..$20-$30
  - 1990s; MM in sectional glamour pose; Bernard of Hollywood. ....$20-$30
  - 1990s; Two 100% polyester color ties; made in U.S. by Ralph Marlin. ....each $20-$30
- Tie Bar and Cuff Link Set, 1972. Nude *Golden Dreams* pose on them; released on the 10th anniversary of MM's death; came in a black or red felt-covered hinged box. ....$40-$60
- Tie Bar and Cuff Link Set, older than above set. Done with very poor MM graphics. ....$30-$40
- Tin, vintage unknown. Small tin with MM in the gold lamé dress on cover. ....$3-$5
- Tin Signs, 1990s. 11 x 16; various tin signs featuring color photos of MM on them; some by Bernard of Hollywood's estate. ....each $10-$20
- Tin Tray, vintage unknown. 12" round, with simulated wood edges; has California map and MM in *Itch* dress. ....$15-$30
- Tip Tray, 1950s. Original tip tray from Italy; promotion for *The Seven Year Itch*. ....$35-$40

Serving tray, vintage unknown, $30-$50.

A selection of steins by R.J. Ernst, $40-$50 each.

Tie bar and cuff link set, 1972, $40-$60.

A stein by Longton Crown, $15-$25.

At right, a selection of contemporary life-size standees, $20-$30 each.

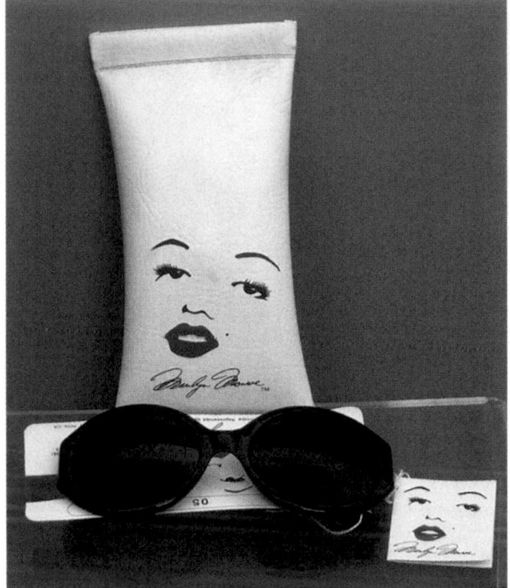

Sunglasses, 1989, $30-$40.

A selection of contemporary ties, $20-$30 each.

- Trade Cards:
  - 1963, but likely from the early 1970s; set of 20 cards labeled, "Marilyn and Her Music"; copyright NMMM; numbered 1-20. ....$15-$25
  - 1993-94; set of 100 cards by Sports Time; all different and beautifully done in high-gloss featuring many nice photos. ....$30-$40
  - 1993-94; 26 x 36 uncut sheet of 100 of the above Sports Time cards. ....$15-$20
  - 1995; set of 100 cards by Sports Time, as above; Second Series; numbered 101-201..$30-$40
  - 1993-94; Diamond card from the Sports Time series above..............$75-$100
  - 1993-94; Ruby card from the Sports Time series above....................$75-$100
  - 1993; "Cover Girl" hologram card set by Sports Time; featuring MM magazine covers...set $20-$30
  - 1993; set of 75 collector cards by The Private Collection; feature photos by Joseph Jasgur; boxed. ....$20-$30
  - 1993; set of trade cards by the Andre de Dienes estate and distributed by The Private Collection; two series of 100 were done. ....each $20-$30
  - 1991; set by Silver Screen Production Ltd.; numbered 1-21; printed in England..$15-$30

- Transparencies, 1940s-'60s. 8 x 10; color transparencies put out by studios for promotion; rare. ....each $100-$300
- T-Shirt, 1999. T-shirt with MM's image on front and "Marilyn Monroe Signature Jeans" label; came with phone card and sample bottle of perfume attached. ....$20-$35
- Tumblers, 1999. "Collectible Marilyn"; estate of Marilyn Monroe/Allison Lefcort; licensed by MMI NYC; distributed by Gifts Inc. ....$10-$15
- Umbrella, vintage unknown. Features dozens of MM faces done in the "Warhol" style; by Museum Masters. ....$30-$40
- Urn, 1970. 24"; one-of-a-kind; titled "A Shattered Life"; by Liebowitz. ....$190-$200
- USO Identification Card, 1980s. Laminated card showing a color close-up photo of MM's face; often thought to be vintage but reproduction....................$2-$5
- View-Master, circa 1990s. Heart-shaped red View Master; boxed, with COA. ....$20-$30
- Wastebasket, vintage unknown. Several MM photos on it. ....$20-$40

- Watches:
  - Circa 1980s; color art of MM on the face, white band; by Bradley. ......$30-$40
  - 1950s; small tin children's watch with elastic band, various colors; MM's image on the face. ....$15-$20
  - Vintage unknown; silver wind-up pocket watch; glamour shot of MM in white fur pose on the face. ....$20-$30
  - Circa 1970s; ladies wristwatch with flexible gold band, metal case, anstainless steel back; bust shot of MM on the dial. ....$25-$35

Miniature standees (above), $5-$10 each, and Series II trading cards by Sports Time (below), $30-$40.

A selection of contemporary tin signs, $10-$20 each.

A small tin, $3-$5.

1986 Chardonnay, $30-$50.

1994 Merlot, $50-$75.

1995 Merlot, $100-$150.

- Watches (continued):
  - 1987; wristwatch with black suede band, fact card, and artwork box; glamour shot on face; part of "The Movie Star Watch Collection"; numbered ASU-876005. .... $20-$40
  - 1980s; rectangular watch with gold finish by Fossil; postage stamp design in full color; packed in wooden box with same graphic. .... $60-$80
  - Vintage unknown; watch by Fossil; features MM photo from *East of Eden* premiere; came in wooden box with MM's handprints carved in top. .... $60-$80
  - Vintage unknown; as above, Fossil watch, except this one came with photo of MM from East of Eden, with her facsimile signature. .... $80-$100
  - 1996; watch by Club Marilyn. .... $20-$40
  - Circa 1999; him-and-her watches with deluxe leather bands; featuring pose used on the U.S. postage stamp; boxed. .... each $40-$60
  - Vintage unknown; dress-up watch featuring MM in Itch dress; plays "I Wanna Be Loved By You." .... $40-$60
  - Vintage unknown; diamond bracelet watch by Seiko; limited edition; in black box. .... $90-$95

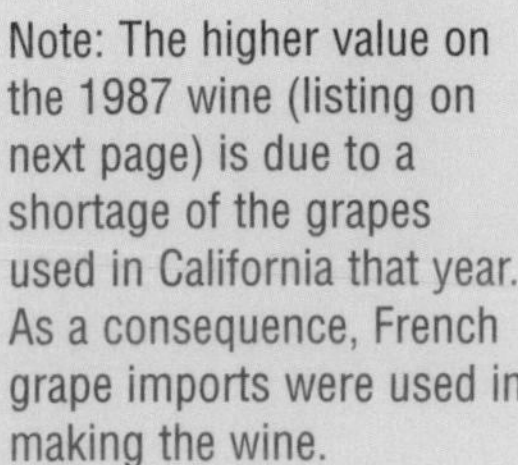

Note: The higher value on the 1987 wine (listing on next page) is due to a shortage of the grapes used in California that year. As a consequence, French grape imports were used in making the wine.

1998 Norma Jeane "A Young Merlot," $30-$40.

1980s Fossil watch, $60-$80.

- Wig, 1991. One-size flame retardant Marilyn wig by Franco American; style No. 24-0025-11; made in Korea; sold out of Glendale, New York. ....$30-$40
- Window Waver, 1982. Shrink-wrapped in color of MM's face; by Starpool of Santa Monica, California. ....$20-$30
- Wine, first appeared in 1988 with sale of vintage 1985 Merlot. Each June 1 (Marilyn's Birthday), there are 3,000 cases produced by Nova Partners of St. Helena, California, bearing Marilyn's image in color on the label; 1986 vintage the only one to also feature a Chardonnay. Remember: There is a three-year difference between the vintage year and the release year; prices below are for the year printed on the bottle:
  - 1985 Merlot; color white fur pose. ....$1,000-$1,500
  - 1986 Merlot; color gold lamé dress pose. ....$800-$1,200
  - 1986 Chardonnay; same color white fur pose as the 1985 Merlot. ......$30-$50
  - 1987 Merlot; color black sequin gown and fur stole pose by Richard Avedon (French Import). ....$400-$600
  - 1988 Merlot; color gold lamé dress with her chin resting on her hand. ....$400-$500
  - 1989 Merlot; in an off-the-shoulder dress. ....$250-$350
  - 1990 Merlot; in a blue bathing suit, holding an umbrella. ....$175-$250
  - 1990 Sparkling Wine; bottled by Marilyn Cuvees of Grafton, California, for Nova Wines Inc.; Cuvee One, Cabneros; MM's image inside large star, surrounded by smaller ones. ....$20-$40
  - 1991 Merlot; putting on Channel No. 5. ....$125-$175
  - 1992 Merlot; Sam Shaw photo of MM on the beach. ....$125-$175

Window waver, 1982, $20-$30.

Contemporary spoon, $5-$10.

University High Yearbook (classmate's copy), 1942, $1,000-$3,000.

- Wine (continued):
  - 1992 Sparkling Wine; Cuvee Two; no description of bottle available. ..$20-$40
  - 1993 Cabernet Sauvignon; no description available. ....$400-$500
  - 1993 Merlot; Sam Shaw photo of MM in white bathing suit ....$50-$75
  - 1994 Cabernet Sauvignon; no description available. ....$50-$100
  - 1994 Merlot; Milton Greene photo of MM in ballerina outfit. ....$50-$75
  - 1995 Merlot; Milton Greene photo of MM in white fur. ....$100-$150
  - 1995 Cabernet Sauvignon; no description available. ....$30-$40
  - 1996 Merlot; Milton Greene photo of MM in black hat and nightie. ...$50-$100
  - 1996 Cabernet Sauvignon; Milton Greene photo of MM in black fur. ...$30-$40
  - 1997 Merlot; Milton Greene photo of MM holding scarf over her face. ....$40-$60
  - 1998 Merlot; MM "Graduation" photo by Milton Greene. ....$30-$40
  - 1998 Norma Jeane; color photo by David Conover. ....$30-$40
  - 1999 Norma Jeane; description not available. ....$20-$30
  - 1999 Merlot; Milton Greene photo of MM in full-length black sweater. ....$20-$30
  - 2000 Norma Jeane; on beach in bikini. ....$10-$15
  - Vertical Set of Marilyn Merlot (1985-1996) ....$5,000-$6,000

- Wrapping Paper, 1988. MM images and trademark signature all over it; three large sheets; by Rock Wraps. ....$3-$8
- Yearbook, 1942. Classmate's copy of yearbook from University High School in California (Marilyn pictured in the 10th grade) ....$1,000-$3,000

At left, oil painting by Michael Deas, circa 1995, $125-$175.

Oil painting by Abe Kazuni, 1950s, $1,300-$1,600.

Chapter 9

Movie-Related Collectibles

From the art departments of the major Hollywood studios came a myriad of beautiful advertising posters, lobby cards, pressbooks, publicity stills, and other materials. All were used to publicize the more than two dozen films Marilyn Monroe played a role in.

Today, these items are exceedingly collectible. Some posters featuring big-name stars and movies are bringing tens of thousands of dollars. After all, we cannot forget some of the legendary actors Marilyn worked with: Betty Grable, Cary Grant, Clark Gable, Jack Lemmon, Tony Curtis and Jane Russell, to name a few.

Fortunately for the collector though, Marilyn posters and related items are bringing much less. You won't have to break your bank to add a couple of these fine pieces of memorabilia to your collection.

America has had a longstanding fascination for the movies, and the collectibles listed within this chapter appeal not only to Marilyn Monroe collectors, but to collectors of more general Hollywood memorabilia as well.

Pressbooks (Campaign Books)

Nearly every movie has had a pressbook produced for publicity purposes. There is no set size, but they generally are 14 x 18. They consist of a variety of ads, articles, and photos that may be clipped and run in the local newspaper by the theater owners. Of great help to the Marilyn collector is the fact that they show each of the various movie posters, lobby cards (in many cases), banners, slides, and publicity stills produced for the movie.

Pressbooks are usually valued at from 5 to 20 percent of the price of a one sheet movie poster for the film involved. Pressbooks vary slightly in size and content from one film to another.

In some cases supplements were produced in addition to the main pressbook. Note that these must not be mistaken for the original release; these will almost always be identified as supplements on their front covers.

- *A Ticket to Tomahawk*, 1950. Fox. .... $40-$80
- *All About Eve*, 1950. Fox. .... $75-$125
- *As Young As You Feel*, 1951. Fox. .... $40-$80
- *Bus Stop*, 1956. Fox. .... $75-$125
- *Clash By Night*, 1952. RKO. .... $40-$80
- *Dangerous Years*, 1947. Fox. .... $50-$100
- *Don't Bother To Knock*, 1952. Fox. .... $75-$125
- *Gentlemen Prefer Blondes*, 1953. Fox. .... $75-$125
- *Home Town Story*, 1951. MGM. .... $40-$80
- *How To Marry A Millionaire*, 1954. Fox. .... $75-$125
- *Ladies of the Chorus*, 1948. Columbia. .... $75-$125
- *Let's Make Love*, 1960. Fox. .... $40-$80
- *Love Happy*, 1950. United Artists. .... $50-$100
- *Love Nest*, 1951. Fox. .... $40-$80
- *Monkey Business*, 1952. Fox. .... $40-$80
- *Niagara*, 1953. Fox. .... $75-$125
- *O. Henry's Full House*, 1952. Fox. .... $40-$80
- *Right Cross*, 1950. MGM. .... $30-$60
- *River of No Return*, 1954. Fox. .... $50-$100
- *Scudda Hoo! Scudda Hay!*, 1948. Fox. .... $30-$50
- *Some Like It Hot*, 1959. United Artists. .... $100-$150
- *The Asphalt Jungle*, 1950. MGM. .... $75-$125
- *The Fireball*, 1950. Fox. .... $40-$80
- *The Misfits*, 1961. United Artists. .... $40-$70
- *The Prince and the Showgirl*, 1957. Warner Brothers. .... $75-$125
- *The Seven Year Itch*, 1955. Fox. .... $100-$150
- *There's No Business Like Show Business*, 1954. Fox. .... $75-$125
- *We're Not Married*, 1952. Fox. .... $40-$80

A selection of pressbooks from several of Marilyn's better-known movies. Values vary, depending on the movie. See listings at left.

Note: Marilyn was to appear in the 1962 film *Something's Got To Give*, but she died before filming was completed. It is possible that there are a few posters, pressbooks, and other materials that were produced for this film. Their rarity would make them quite sought-after and valuable.

A color film still for The Prince and the Showgirl, $40-$60.

Publicity Stills

These photos were usually taken by a studio photographer and measure 8 x 10 or 11 x 14. They were produced in both glossy and matte form and came in color as well as black and white. Other sizes produced are generally smaller than those listed above.

Most were made in conjunction with Marilyn's current film and included the photographer's name, studio name, information on the film, and were numbered either on the front or back. Quite often, this information was typed on a sheet of paper and affixed to the bottom border or the back of the photo.

All of these photos are highly sought-after, as they are first generation and are of high quality/sharpness.

- 5 x 7 .... $20-$40
- 8 x 10 .... $40-$80
- 11 x 14 .... $100-$200

Door panel posters for The Seven Year Itch, $300-$500.

Film Stills

For each of the films produced by the studios, a series of between eight and twelve 8 x 10 stills were produced to be displayed in theater lobbies. These featured scenes from the films and were done in black and white, color, or both. They were produced on glossy stock paper and featured an information strip along the bottom half-inch or so of the photo. This information strip included a listing of the actors/actresses, producer, director, studio, copyright date, title of the movie, and other information. They also featured a number, usually in the bottom right corner, and are especially known for their sharpness.

The earlier color versions were simply hand-tinted, and in the late-1950s they became more like color photographs as we know them today.

- 8 x 10 (black and white) .... $25-$40
- 8 x 10 (color) .... $40-$60

Note: The prices for the stills listed above are pretty general and would pertain to all of those produced during Marilyn's lifetime.

Two souvenir programs, $80-$125 each.

Heralds

These promotional "mini newspapers" consisted of four pages printed on newsprint paper and opened to reveal a centerfold featuring artwork similar to the film's poster. More information and graphics were printed on the front and back. They were made in various sizes over the years and ranged between 10½ to 17" wide and 15 to 22½" long when folded.

- Films where MM has top billing. .... $50-$100
- Early MM films (with MM appearing in graphics). .... $40-$80
- MM films with no graphics featuring her. .... $20-$40

Door-Panel Posters

Produced for selected films, these featured similar graphics to the film's posters. Many were done in a three-color process and measured 20 x 60. Few have survived, and they are extremely collectible.

- Films where MM has top billing. ....$300-$500
- Films with MM in bit parts with small photo of Marilyn on poster. ....$100-$200
- MM films with no graphic of MM. ....$50-$100

Cardboard Promo Poster

- 1956 Promo Poster for the movie tie-in book *Bus Stop*; 11 x 14; large duo-tone picture of MM and stating "Read the Book! See the Movie!"................$100-$150

A giant lobby or entrance photo, $1,500-$2,000.

Souvenir Programs

These were handed out at select theaters to moviegoers and consisted of several pages of black and white and color photos of the stars and/or scenes from the film. They are very attractive and quite collectible. Those that feature color throughout are the most valuable, but all are highly prized.

- Films where MM has top billing. ....$80-$125
- Films with MM in bit parts, with small photos of Marilyn on program. ....$40-$80
- MM films with no graphic of Marilyn. ....$20-$40

Note: Foreign programs for Marilyn's films tend to be much less elaborate and consist of either black and white graphics, or of duo-tone or tinted graphics. They are done on much lighter-weight paper and are valued one-quarter the value of those prices listed above.

Drive-In Theater Program

These were given out at drive-in theaters throughout the 1950s and '60s. They generally measure 3½ x 5 and reproduce graphics from the movies playing for the week.

- Program with MM on cover. ....$5-$10

Giant Lobby or Entrance Display Photo

- Measures about 4' x 5'; depicts MM reclining on a satin pillow; framed in pine; hand-tinted color photo; hung in theater in Janesville, Wisconsin; extremely rare, possibly one-of-a-kind..$1,500-$2,000

TV Tel-Ops/Slides

These were distributed by the studios through their promotional pressbooks and are extremely rare. They were generally done in sets of three or four and would show scenes from the film. A script would accompany them to be read by the TV announcer as each particular slide appeared on the screen. These were available on cardboard or in glass slide form.

They are so scarce that it is difficult to affix a value.

- For those showing MM (per set). ....$100-$200
- For those not showing MM (per set). ....$40-$80

A selection of TV tel-ops/slides, $100-$200 each.

Playbills/Handbills

These were single-page handouts that reproduced the film's poster, or similar artwork to that of the poster, on their fronts. They also stated (usually at the top) when the movie was to be shown at a particular theater. They were printed on various shades of paper.

- Films where MM has top billing. ....$25-$50
- Those not featuring image of MM. ....$10-$20

Several standees featuring Marilyn, $800-$1,500.

Standees

These were produced for most films and may feature a small image of Marilyn in those films in which she did not have top billing. Some of these cardboard standees reproduced the film's poster, but the ones that featured a large blow-up of Marilyn are the most valuable and highly prized by Monroe collectors.

For some of Marilyn's bigger films, two or three different standees were often made that featured her prominently. They were generally about 5 feet tall and could be ordered with or without an easel. They were printed in at least three colors and cost between $12 and $15 to the theater owners. Few examples remain.

- Those featuring only Marilyn..........$800-$1,500
- Those with a small image of Marilyn. ....$300-$700
- Those with no image, but from an MM film. $100 $200

Buyers Beware!

Usually along the bottom right- or left-hand corner of all posters is a copyright statement that will give a name of the studio and the year of release, along with a number, such as 32-41. If the number is preceded by an R, such as R32-41, it signifies that the poster was a reissue at a later date—sometimes many years later. A reissue is in essence a reproduction, and they do not have the value of the original releases. However, some of the reissues are now quite old themselves and are bringing decent prices.

Beginning in the 1960s and continuing through today, there were many reproductions made of Marilyn's classic films by such companies as Portal Publications. Many are dated and identified as such, but if they're not, look for an address that includes a ZIP code along the bottom edge of the poster, as there were no ZIP codes in use during Marilyn's day.

Miscellaneous Movie Posters and Lobby Cards

Three-Sheet (41 x 41)

These came in two sections generally and are three times the size of a one-sheet movie poster. As well, they are valued at approximately three times the value of a one-sheet.

Six-Sheet (81 x 81)

These came in three or four sections and are very scarce. They are valued at six times the value of a one-sheet for any particular film.

24-Sheet (9' x 20')

Made primarily for billboards on light stock paper. These are almost nonexistent today.

40 x 60

These posters were done on a heavy stock paper using a rare silk-screening process. They were meant to hang outside at bus stops, etc., and therefore, most were destroyed by the weather. They are highly sought-after and are valued at one-and-a-half to two times the value of a one-sheet for the particular film.

Banners

These were done on light stock and are very rare.

Foreign Posters

These are valued at a much lower prices than U.S. posters and were issued in different sizes than the U.S. posters.

One-Sheet (27 x 41)

These were the posters most often seen by the public, which still holds true today. They are the most sought-after size of poster. Because these posters were printed on a lighter-stock paper, many collectors choose to have them linen- or paper-backed to help stabilize them. They also appeal to collectors because they are of a size easy to display, and most of our movie poster memories are associated with the standard one-sheet that hung either in or out of the theater's lobby.

Half-Sheet (22 x 28)

These were done on a heavier-stock paper than the one-sheets. In general, they sell for about 30 to 35 percent of the value of a one-sheet and can feature graphics equal to or at times better than the one-sheets. In these instances the value increases considerably.

Window Card (14 x 17 and up to 22")

Printed on very heavy-stock paper, these posters were made for window displays, as their name implies. They came with a blank area on their tops where the local theaters could print show dates and times. This information was sometimes just handwritten, and in other instances, is printed professionally. Often, the border that displayed this information has been trimmed away, which reduces the value of the card.

Inserts (14 x 36)

These are a tall, narrow poster usually printed on heavy stock. They sometimes feature more attractive graphics than the one-sheets. In these cases, they are worth more. Inserts are valued at about the same price as the half-sheets or about 30 to 35 percent of the one-sheet value.

Lobby Cards (11 x 14)

These generally feature scenes from the film and can be quite colorful. They are printed on heavy stock paper and come in sets of eight as a rule, but sets of 10 were also created. Those featuring Marilyn are of course worth more than those that do not. For some of Marilyn's earlier movies, she may only be featured in one or two.

The cards are nearly all numbered along the bottom margin and include the studio's name and year of release. Card No. 1 is always called the "Title Card" and is different from the rest in that it features photos of the star players and bold letters featuring the film's title. These are valued at higher levels that the remainder of the cards as a rule.

The theaters were required to return all posters and lobby cards to the studios. Fortunately, not all theaters complied and many examples of these wonderful items exist today.

A selection of lobby cards from Bus Stop, $75-$125 each.

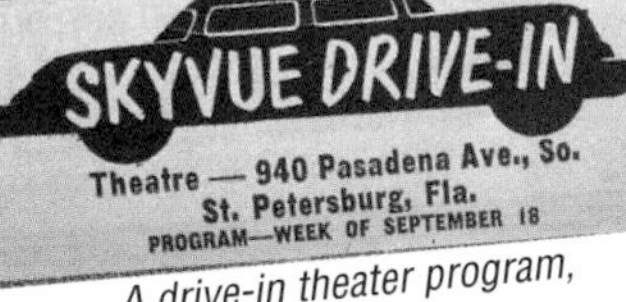

A drive-in theater program, $5-$10.

Title card for Clash By Night, $100-$150.

A selection of lobby cards for Don't Bother To Knock, $75-$125 each.

Lobby cards from Gentlemen Prefer Blondes, $75-$125 each.

Note: Certain posters and lobby cards for *The Asphalt Jungle* were re-released in 1953 with larger Marilyn graphics. These are valued at about half the value of the originals, so look for the capital "R" before the year printed on the items.

All About Eve (1950, Fox)
- One-Sheet....................$300-$500
- Lobby Title Card....................$300-$500
- Lobby Card (MM only on card No. 3)....................$250-$400
- Insert....................$250-$400

The Asphalt Jungle (1950, MGM)
- Lobby Title Card....................$250-$450
- Lobby Card (MM on card No. 8 only)....................$200-$300

As Young As You Feel (1951, Fox)
- One-Sheet....................$100-$200
- Half-Sheet....................$50-$100
- Window Card....................$50-$100
- Lobby Title Card....................$75-$125
- Lobby Card.................... $50-$75
- Insert....................$100-$200

Bus Stop (1956, Fox)
- One-Sheet....................$300-$500
- Half-Sheet....................$200-$375
- Three-Sheet....................$1,200-$1500
- 24-Sheet....................$8,000-$9,000
- Window Card....................$200-$300
- Lobby Title Card (MM and Don Murray in embrace, plus four scenes from film along bottom of card.)....................$150-$225
- Lobby Cards....................each $75-$125
- Card No. 2 (Marilyn dancing at a club.)
- Card No. 3 (MM and Don Murray standing near a jukebox.)
- Card No. 4 (Marilyn at a bus stop in her dancing outfit.)
- Card No. 5 (MM and Don Murray in a bedroom.)
- Card No. 6 (Don Murray carrying Marilyn on his shoulder.)

- Card No. 7 (Marilyn outside near a bus.)
- Card No. 8 (Marilyn throwing away a map.)
- Insert ....$200-$375

Clash By Night (1952, RKO)
- One-Sheet ....$150-$250
- Half-Sheet ....$200-$375
- Window Card ....$100-$200
- Lobby Title Card (MM being choked at a table by Paul Douglas.) ....$100-$150
- Lobby Card (MM only on No. 3) ....$100-$175
- Insert ....$150-$275

Dangerous Years (1947, Fox)
- Lobby Title Card ....$300-$400
- Lobby Card (MM only on No. 8.) ....$300-$400

Don't Bother To Knock (1952, Fox)
- One-Sheet ....$475-$750
- Half-Sheet ....$175-$375
- Three-Sheet ....$2,000-$2,500
- Window Card ....$125-$250
- Lobby Title Card (MM on left side in red one-piece swimsuit; also five scenes from film along the bottom.) ....$100-$175
- Lobby Cards (Marilyn on all.) ....each $75-$125
- Card No. 3 (MM and Richard Widmark in embrace, with young girl looking on.)
- Card No. 4 (MM being held by the shoulders and shaken by a man.)
- Card No. 5 (MM and Richard Widmark talking by a door.)
- Card No. 7 (Richard Widmark and MM seated, with Widmark holding her hand; MM has scratch on her cheek.)
- Card No. 8 (MM seated on bed in nightgown, with Richard Widmark standing above her.)
- Insert ....$375-$750

The Fireball (1950, Fox)
- Lobby Card (MM on No. 5 only.) ....$175-$225

Gentlemen Prefer Blondes (1953, Fox)
- One-Sheet ....$450-$800
- Half-Sheet ....$200-$400
- Three-Sheet ....$1,500-$1,800
- Window Card ....$150-$250
- Lobby Title Card (Artwork of MM and Jane Russell.) ....$100-$175
- Lobby Cards ....each $75-$125

Lobby card for Ladies of the Chorus, $200-$300.

One-sheet poster for Let's Make Love, $150-$275.

Window card for Let's Make Love, $70-$125.

Let's Make Love lobby card, $40-$70.

Title card for Love Nest, $150-$200.

An array of lobby cards from How To Marry A Millionaire, $65-$100 each.

- Card No. 2 (Jane Russell impersonating Marilyn in a court room scene.) ...$15-$30
- Card No. 3 (MM and Jane Russell pulling off Elliot Reed's pants.)
- Card No. 4 (MM and Russell in their dance outfits.)
- Card No. 5 (Marilyn singing, "Diamonds are a Girl's Best Friend.")
- Card No. 6 (MM and Russell seated at a table in a dining room.
- Card No. 7 (Marilyn and Charles Coburn.)
- Card No. 8 (MM and Russell in a French dance number that was cut from the movie.)
- Insert ....$125-$200

Home Town Story (1951, MGM)
- One-Sheet ....$125-$225
- Half-Sheet ....$75-$125
- Window Card ....$50-$100
- Lobby Title Card ....$65-$125
- Lobby Card (MM on No. 2.) ....$125-$175
- Insert ....$50-$100

How To Marry A Millionaire (1954, Fox)
- One-Sheet ....$400-$800
- Half-Sheet ....$175-$375
- Three-Sheet ....$1,100-$1,300
- British Quad (30 x 40—artwork of MM, Grable, and Bacall with fingers raised, as to say, "Come here.") ....$700-$900
- Window Card ....$150-$225
- Lobby Title Card (MM, Betty Grable, and Lauren Bacall seated.) ....$60-$125
- Lobby Cards ....each $65-$100
- Card No. 2 (MM and Bacall meeting William Powell.)
- Card No. 3 (MM, Bacall, and Grable with groceries.)
- Card No. 4 (MM and Bacall at a diner.)
- Card No. 5 (MM, Bacall, and David Wayne at the wedding.)
- Card No. 6 (MM and Alex D'Arcy.)
- Card No. 7 (Marilyn and the wedding party.)
- Card No. 8 (MM and Bacall with packages.)
- Insert ....$175-$375

Ladies of the Chorus (1948, Columbia)
- Lobby Title Card (MM in center of chorus line, holding a baby.) ....$300-$400
- Lobby Cards (Marilyn on cards No. 4, 7, and 8.) ....each $200-$300

Let's Make It Legal (1951, Fox)
- One-Sheet ....$175-$300
- Half-Sheet ....$100-$200
- Window Card ....$75-$125
- Lobby Title Card ....$100-$150
- Lobby Card ....$50-$100
- Insert ....$200-$300

Let's Make Love (1960, Fox)
- One-Sheet ....$150-$275
- Half-Sheet ....$75-$150
- 24-Sheet ....$4,000-$5,000
- Window Card ....$70-$125
- Lobby Title Card ....$60-$100
- Lobby Cards ....each $40-$70
- Card No. 1 (Depicts artwork of Marilyn.)
- Card No. 2 (MM in red tights, with Frankie Vaughn.)
- Card No. 3 (Marilyn in a rehearsal with other cast members.)
- Card No. 4 (MM reading a book, with Yves Montand.)

- Card No. 5 (Marilyn sipping coffee.)
- Card No. 6 (Montand dancing; MM not shown.)
- Card No. 7 (MM in a red coat, with Frankie Vaughn.)
- Card No. 8 (Marilyn surrounded by dancers.)
- Insert....................$70-$125

Love Happy (1950, United Artists)
- Lobby Card (MM on No. 8 only.)....................$400-$600

Love Nest (1951, Fox)
- One-Sheet....................$150-$275
- Half-Sheet....................$75-$125
- Window Card....................$75-$125
- Lobby Title Card (MM seated with hands on knees on the right side of the card.) ....$150-$200
- Lobby Card....................$100-$150
- Insert....................$175-$225

The Misfits (1961, United Artists)
- One-Sheet....................$150-$300
- Half-Sheet....................$70-$125
- Window Card....................$70-$125
- Lobby Title Card....................$60-$100
- Lobby Cards....................each $50-$70
- Card No. 1 (MM, Clark Gable, and Montgomery Clift in a close-up.)
- Card No. 2 (MM, Gable, and Clift, with Gable in the center.)
- Card No. 3 (MM and Gable planting flowers.)
- Card No. 4 (MM, Gable, and Eli Wallach drinking.)
- Card No. 5 (Marilyn with a cowboy hat full of cash.)
- Card No. 6 (Marilyn playing paddleball at a bar.)
- Card No. 7 (Marilyn in a truck.)
- Card No. 8 (Clark Gable; MM not shown.)....................$15-$30
- Insert....................$100-$200

Monkey Business (1952, Fox)
- One-Sheet....................$175-$375
- Half-Sheet....................$100-$200
- Window Card....................$100-$200
- Lobby Title Card (used as No. 1.)....................$75-$125
- Lobby Cards (MM on cards 2, 5, and 8.).................... each $60-$100
- Card No. 2 (Charles Coburn handing MM a piece of paper, with Cary Grant looking on.)
- Insert....................$100-$200

Niagara (1953, Fox)
- One-Sheet....................$500-$700
- Half-Sheet....................$200-$350
- Window Card....................$175-$300
- Lobby Title Card....................$100-$150
- Lobby Cards....................each $60-$125
- Card No. 4 (MM wants a specific record to be played.)
- Card No. 5 (MM lies lifeless on the concrete while Joseph Cotten kneels over her.)
- Card No. 7 (MM talks to Cotten while another couple stands by.)
- Card No. 8 (MM pauses before walking out the door from the stairwell as Cotten tries to catch up to her.)
- Insert....................$250-$400

Several lobby cards for The Misfits, $50-$70 each.

Lobby card for Monkey Business, $60-$100.

Window card for Niagara, $175-$300.

A selection of lobby cards for Niagara, $60-$125 each.

Lobby card for O. Henry's Full House, $50-$100.

O. Henry's Full House (1952, Fox)

- One-Sheet....................$150-$250
- Half-Sheet....................$60-$125
- Window Card....................$50-$100
- Lobby Title Card....................$100-$200
- Lobby Card (MM on No. 4 only; depicting her talking to a man outside a store.) ....$50-$100
- Insert....................$60-$100

The Prince and the Showgirl (1957, Fox)

- One-Sheet....................$500-$1,000
- Half-Sheet....................$250-$450
- Three-Sheet (MM and Laurence Olivier in embrace.)....................$1,500-$1,700
- Window Card....................$200-$400
- Lobby Title Card....................$125-$175
- Lobby Cards (MM on all.)....................each $75-$125
- Card No. 1 (Marilyn lying down in the white dress.)
- Card No. 2 (MM kneeling next to Olivier, who is seated in a chair.)
- Card No. 3 (Marilyn adjusting her dress.)
- Card No. 4 (MM being embraced by Olivier; solid blue background.)
- Card No. 5 (Marilyn reaching for a glass.)
- Card No. 6 (Marilyn lying down with a feather boa.)
- Card No. 7 (Marilyn holding her stomach in the white dress.)
- Card No. 8 (Marilyn in a special seated pose, wearing a red leotard.)
- Insert....................$200-$400

River of No Return (1954, Fox)

- One-Sheet....................$400-$800
- Half-Sheet....................$200-$350
- French 63 x 47 poster (Artwork of MM superimposed over river with a raft.) ....$1,200-$1,600
- Window Card....................$150-$250
- Lobby Title Card (Artwork of MM and Robert Mitchum.)....................$75-$125
- Lobby Cards....................each $60-$100
- Card No. 2 (MM, Robert Mitchum, and a young boy, all seated on the ground outside a log cabin.)
- Card No. 3 (Marilyn singing.)
- Card No. 4 (Marilyn with an old hunter.)
- Card No. 5 (Marilyn lying on a piano.)
- Card No. 6 (MM wrapped in a towel next to Mitchum.)
- Card No. 7 (MM and Mitchum on a raft in the river.)
- Card No. 8 (MM kissing Mitchum, with a young boy in the background.)
- Insert....................$125-$200

The Seven Year Itch (1955, Fox)

- One-Sheet....................$800-$1,400
- Half-Sheet....................$500-$1,000
- 30 x 40 (Tom Ewell gazing at MM in the white blowing dress.)....................$2,000-$3,000
- Three-Sheet....................$2,000-$2,500
- Window Card....................$200-$500
- Lobby Title Card (Artwork of MM and Ewell.)....................$200-$300
- Lobby Cards....................each $75-$140
- Card No. 2 (MM and Ewell drinking.)
- Card No. 3 (MM pulling a bottle that is stuck on Ewell's finger.)

Lobby cards for The Prince and the Showgirl, $75-$125 each.

- Card No. 4 (MM kissing Ewell; she is wearing the "tiger" dress.)
- Card No. 5 (Marilyn serving coffee on a tray.)
- Card No. 6 (Marilyn in a bathtub.)
- Card No. 7 (Marilyn in a yellow dress with other cast members.)
- Card No. 8 (MM and Ewell playing the piano.)
- Insert .... $200-$400

Some Like It Hot! (1959, United Artists)
- One-Sheet $400 $800
- Half-Sheet .... $200-$400
- Three-Sheet .... $1,500-$2000
- Window Card .... $200-$400
- Lobby Title Card (Artwork of MM, Tony Curtis, and Jack Lemmon) .... $100-$200
- Lobby Cards .... each $75-$135
- Card No. 2 (Curtis and Lemmon running; MM not shown.) .... $15-$30
- Card No. 3 (Curtis and Lemmon in drag; MM not shown.) .... $15-$30
- Card No. 4 (Curtis and Lemmon on a train; MM not shown.) .... $15-$30
- Card No. 5 (MM kissing Curtis.)
- Card No. 6 (MM and Lemmon lying down in a hotel room.)
- Card No. 7 (MM, Lemmon, and Curtis winking; same photo as the one used on the one-sheet.)
- Card No. 8 (Marilyn singing, "Runnin' Wild.")
- Insert .... $250-$450

Lobby card for River of No Return, $60-$100.

Lobby cards for The Seven Year Itch, $75-$140 each.

Lobby card for *There's No Business Like Show Business*, $60-$100.

There's No Business Like Show Business (1954, Fox)
- One-Sheet....................$100-$225
- Half-Sheet....................$60-$100
- Window Card....................$60-$100
- Lobby Title Card (Artwork of the cast.)....................$50-$80
- Lobby Cards....................each $60-$100
- Card No. 2 (Cast, other than Marilyn.)....................$15-$30
- Card No. 3 (MM in a leotard, with Donald O'Connor.)
- Card No. 4 (Marilyn lying on a couch while singing.)
- Card No. 5 (Marilyn and the cast during show finale.)
- Card No. 6 (Marilyn singing in a white dress.)
- Card No. 7 (Ethel Merman with cast; MM not shown.)....................$15-$30
- Card No. 8 (Marilyn during "Heat Wave" number.)
- Insert....................$100-$200

A Ticket to Tomahawk (1950, Fox)
- Lobby Title Card....................$125-$175
- Lobby Card (MM on No. 4 only.)....................$200-$250

We're Not Married (1952, Fox)
- One-Sheet....................$100-$225
- Half-Sheet....................$60-$100
- Window Card....................$60-$100
- Lobby Title Card (Depicts a small 2" high image of MM, dressed in a red one-piece bathing suit.)....................$50-$80
- Lobby Cards (MM on cards No. 4 and 6.)....................$75-$125
- Card No. 4 (Marilyn in red one-piece bathing suit as "Miss Mississippi.")
- Card No. 6 (Marilyn in a wedding scene.)
- Insert....................$60-$100

Some Like It Hot lobby cards, $75-$135.

Marilyn—Narrated by Rock Hudson (1963, Fox)
- One-Sheet....................$100-$200
- Half-Sheet....................$75-$150
- Three-Sheet....................$200-$300
- Window Card....................$60-$125
- Lobby Title Card....................$40-$80
- Lobby Cards (MM on all.).................... each $40-$65
- Card No. 1 (MM and Wally Cox seated in chairs while talking from *Something's Got To Give.*)
- Card No. 2 (Marilyn in the blowing dress from *The Seven Year Itch.*)
- Card No. 3 (Marilyn singing "Diamonds Are A Girl's Best Friend" from *Gentlemen Prefer Blondes.*)
- Card No. 4 (MM, Clark Gable, and Eli Wallach drinking from *The Misfits.*)
- Card No. 5 (Marilyn in a sweater from *Monkey Business.*)
- Card No. 6 (Marilyn next to a jukebox in *Bus Stop.*)
- Card No. 7 (Marilyn during "Heat Wave" number on *There's No Business Like Show Business.*)
- Card No. 8 (Marilyn being reflected in a mirror from *How To Marry A Millionaire.*)
- Insert....................$50-$90

Vintage Marilyn Personality Poster

It is widely believed that only one poster featuring Marilyn was made available to the general public during her lifetime. Most of these are printed very clearly, but some are not. The original issue price was $2; the photo is done in Kodachrome, and the posters were made by a Boston company.

An ad featuring this poster for sale can be found in the January 1954 issue of Ebony magazine, and a photo of Marilyn exists signing one of the posters for a GI during her trip to Korea in 1954 to entertain the troops.

- Measures 21½ x 62 and is in color, showing a photo of Marilyn in a two-piece red-and-white striped bikini against a white background. Marilyn's hands are drawn to her left side as if she's tucking in some fabric; her legs are spread apart, and she's wearing an ankle bracelet and a pair of pumps. .... $150-$300

Lobby cards for We're Not Married, $75-$125 each.

Contemporary Marilyn Posters

A great many posters of Marilyn were printed after her death in 1962, the bulk of which were done in the 1980s and '90s. The list is endless, but a good cross-section of the more valuable editions is listed below. Any poster created after 1975 and not in a limited edition is generally worth $10-$20.

- 1967—30 x 42; b&w poster featuring photo of MM as Roslyn from *The Misfits*; produced by Famous Faces. .... $50-$75
- 1979—23½ x 30; "Marilyn 62—Bert Stern Photographs" poster shows nude MM holding see-through scarf over her body; by Boris Gallery of Photography, Boston. .... $75-$100
- 1980s—23 x 27; "The Last Sitting" promotional poster for Bert Stern's book of same title; 10 images. .... $50-$75
- 1980s—As above, only showing color photo of MM nude holding a see-through scarf in front of her. .... $50-$75
- 1980s—As above, only showing MM on her stomach in b&w photo. .... $50-$75
- 1980s—23 x 31; from Germany and showing MM lying nude on her side. .... $75-$125
- 1984—20 x 28; 1st ed.; four color posters by Richard Avedon, featuring MM from 1958 photo session in which she dressed up as various other stars, including Theda Bara, Jean Harlow, Lillian Russell, and Clara Bow; distributed by Andrew Grenshaw Ltd. of New York; some sold pre-framed. Originally $25 each unsigned and $50 signed; also sold in set of four at $90 unsigned and $180 signed.
- Signed .... $100-$150
- Unsigned .... $20-$40
- 1989—18 x 24; Phil Stern b&w photo of Marilyn; printed on heavy paper. .... $100-$200
- 1992—Released to advertise set of MM movies by Fox on VHS; shows MM in pink dress from *Gentlemen Prefer Blondes*, with her arms outstretched above her head; movie titles listed to the left of MM's image. .... $15-$25
- Date Unknown—"Art America Proudly Presents Two Legends" by Earl MacPherson; John Wayne on one side, and MM on the other, with four lovely drawings by MacPherson. .... $100-$150

Lobby card for 1963 film, Marilyn, $40-$65.

Chapter 10

Newspapers

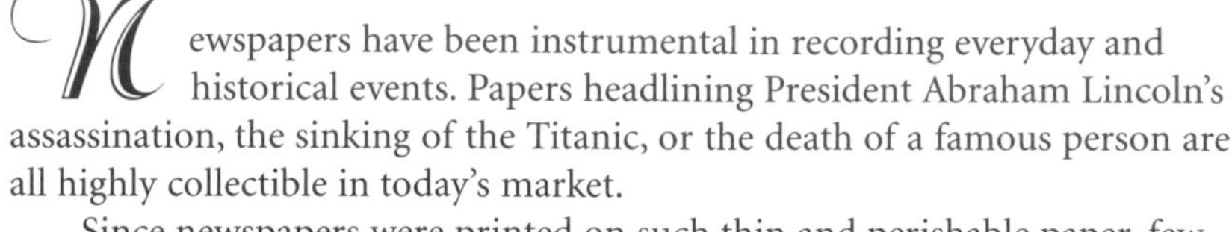

Newspapers have been instrumental in recording everyday and historical events. Papers headlining President Abraham Lincoln's assassination, the sinking of the Titanic, or the death of a famous person are all highly collectible in today's market.

Since newspapers were printed on such thin and perishable paper, few have held up against the test of time. Furthermore, most were thrown out shortly after they were read. A few people, though, had the foresight to save what they deemed important issues, and safely stashed them away to be enjoyed by future generations.

Marilyn Monroe made the papers often, beginning very early on in her career. Most of the earliest references and photos appeared in the Hollywood-related papers—and those in the immediate area of Hollywood—chronicling Marilyn's various roles and/or promotional campaigns for the studios.

The earliest that I have been able to buy is a Chicago paper featuring a prominent photo of Marilyn on its front cover. Marilyn is holding on to several baseball bats and was part of a Hollywood baseball team on a promotional tour to promote her film, *Love Happy*.

Whenever Marilyn is featured on the paper's front-page headlines, the value is increased considerably. The most collectible of these are the issues that carried a full report of Marilyn's death in August 1962.

The following is a selection of collectible Marilyn newspapers from across the country. They are listed by title, date, description, and value. Price range covers very good to near-mint condition.

Today! Film Stars 'World Series'
Ask Congress Probe Hiss Trial
5 CENTS
Herald American
CITY
TURF
Rush Baby Hanging Indictment

Chicago Herald-American, July 9, 1949, $175-$275.

- *Chicago Herald American*, July 9, 1949. "Today! Film Stars 'World Series' "; "Film Stars Stage World Series Here"; "It'll Be a Lovely Game With Marilyn Monroe As Bat Girl"; large photo of Marilyn holding six baseball bats is shown along with the aforementioned headlines....$175-$275
- *Chicago Sun-Times*, Aug. 6, 1962. "Marilyn Monroe Dies of Drug Overdose." ....$80-$120
- *Evening Sentinel* (Keene, New Hampshire), Aug. 6-9, 1962. Four consecutive days of the paper, with articles throughout. ....(set of four) $60-$70
- *The Honolulu Advertiser*, Aug. 6, 1962. "Movie Star Marilyn Monroe Dies from Overdose of Pills" (top story); "Studios Halt Stars' Rule"; "Movie Colony's Reaction: 'Can't Believe She's Dead'"; "Highlights of a Career That Ended in Tragedy." ....$125-$175
- *Los Angeles Times*, Aug. 6, 1962. Monday Preview Extra; "Marilyn Monroe Dies—Blame Pills" (top story); "First Details of Actress' Death In Brentwood"; "Nude Body Found In Bed, Empty Capsule Bottle At Her Side"; "Help She Sought Eluded Marilyn"; large photo of MM on front, with articles and photos inside. ....$125-$175
- *New York Journal American*, Oct. 6, 1954. "Louella O. Parsons Reveals: Joe Fanned On Jealousy" (top story); photos of Marilyn and drama coach on front; articles inside on filed divorce papers. ....$60-$80
- *New York Journal American*, Oct. 12, 1956. "Bombshell In London—Tightly Clad Marilyn Steals London Show"; photos of MM and Arthur Miller. ....$60-$80
- *New York Journal American*, June 23, 1959. "Marilyn Under Knife" (top story); "Doctor Calls Condition Excellent"; pictures of Marilyn on front. ....$60-$80
- *New York Journal American*, Nov. 13, 1960. "Dorothy Kilgallen Exclusive: Inside Story of the Marilyn-Yves Romance"; "MM: Secrets of Her Life By Zolotow (Part One)"; "Marilyn Won't Talk About Divorce"; all are lengthy articles. ....$40-$60
- *New York Journal American*, March 29, 1961. "Don't Grab Joe"; pictures of MM and Joe DiMaggio on front and one more inside. ....$20-$40
- *New York Journal American*, Aug. 6, 1962. "Why did Marilyn End Life?" (top story); "Star's Last Hours Being Checked"; "A Girl Who Found Stardom, But Not Happiness"; "Star's Death Stunning Blow To Film World"; "Three Ex-husbands React—As MM Foretold"; "MM Was Many Things To Many People"; "A Stairway To Stardom: Bit By Bit A Star Is Born and Glows and Dies"; one large photo and six small ones on front. ....$125-$175
- *New York Mirror*, Oct. 5, 1954. "DiMag's Split!" (top story); "Boredom, Sexy Photos Split Dimag's"; "Some Of The Reasons Why"; features large photos of Marilyn on front. ....$60-$80

EXTRA

COMPLETE RACING BASEBALL

Los Angeles Times

MONDAY PREVIEW

MONDAY MORNING, AUGUST 6, 1962

MARILYN MONROE DIES; BLAME PILLS

First Details of Actress' Death in Brentwood

FOUND LITTLE HAPPINESS

Help She Sought Eluded Marilyn

Nude Body Found in Bed, Empty Capsule Bottle at Her Side

Los Angeles Times, August 6, 1962, $125-$175.

- *New York Mirror*, Oct. 6, 1954. "Marilyn Sobs, Joe Gets Walking Papers" (top story); "Nights Were Dull At Joe And Marilyn's"; "Marilyn Starts Suit, Wept All Night Over It"; photos of MM on front. ....$60-$80
- *New York Mirror*, Oct. 7, 1954. "Joe Goes: 'I'll Never Be Back' Any Other Man? Marilyn Weeps"; big photo of Marilyn and Joe on front. ....$70-$90
- *New York Mirror*, Nov. 12, 1960. "Marilyn Miller All Washed Up" (top story); "MM Admits It's Over"; "See No Break-Up For Montand's"; photos of MM and Arthur Miller and Yves Montand on front. ....$50-$75
- *New York Mirror*, Aug. 6, 1962. "Marilyn Monroe Kills Self. Found Nude In Bed...Hand On Phone...Took 40 Pills" (top story); "Marilyn's Tragic Life: World's Golden Girl"; "MM Witty Philosopher"; "Friends Here and Abroad Stunned by News"; "MM's Toughest Role—Life"; no cover photo, but centerfold of photos included. ....$100-$130
- *New York Mirror*, Aug. 6, 1962. Same issue as above, only MM is featured on the cover....................$125-$175
- *New York Mirror*, Aug. 7, 1962. "Marilyn's Last Day Of Life" (top story); "Story Of MM's Last Days"; "Marilyn's Tragic Life... Her World Of Pretending"; "Pill Victims Pattern: Nearly All Want Back"; two photos of MM on front....................$100-$140
- *New York Mirror*, Aug. 9, 1962. "Joe's Goodbye: A Kiss, A Tear" (top story); several inside articles and two-page centerfold of photos. ....$100-$140
- *New York Mirror*, Aug. 15, 1962. "Marilyn's Last Happy Day" (top story); "Gaiety That Death Stilled"; large MM photos on front, photos of MM at her 36th birthday party inside, and centerfold of photos. ....$100-$140
- *New York Mirror*, Aug. 18, 1962. "Find Marilyn 'Wanted To Die'" (top story); "Left Over 500G"; "MM Often Wished To Die...She Left 500G, 142G To Coach."....................$30-$40
- *New York News*, Jan. 15, 1952. "DiMaggio and Marilyn Wed" (top story); more on page 3. ....$50-$90
- *New York News*, May 31, 1956. "Marilyn's Next Near Divorce" (top story); "Marilyn And Miller Tune Wedding Bells"; no photos of MM on front. ....$30-$40
- *New York News*, Nov. 12, 1960. "Miller Walks Out On MM" (top story); "Arthur Packs His Pulitzer Prize, Walks Out on MM"; photos of MM on front and inside. ....$40-$60
- *New York News*, Aug. 6, 1962. "Did He Make a Mystery Call?" (top story); "Seek Mexican in MM's Mystery Call"; more articles inside....................$50-$70
- *New York News*, Aug. 9, 1962. "Joe Whispers 'I Love You'" (top story); "Joe to Marilyn At Rites: ' I Love You'"; "Lawford: 'I Phoned MM on Death Night'; photos of DiMaggio and son on front. ....$75-$100
- *New York News*, Aug. 9, 1962. As above, only different edition; "Last Goodbye" (top story); "Joe To Marilyn At Rites"; "MM's Mexican Pal Is in Beverly Hills"; "Stars Barred At Rites—Lawford's 'shocked'"; Joe DiMaggio photo on front and a two-page centerfold of photos. ....$80-$100
- *New York News*, Aug. 14, 1962. "Marilyn Speaks...Star's Own Words to Biographer in Last Weeks Before Death....MM's Last Picture" (top story); "Twilight Of A Star: Here's MM, Barefoot And Bubbly"; large photo of MM on front, many pictures inside, and centerfold of photos....................$100-$140
- *New York News*, Aug. 15, 1962. "MM Relives Tragic Childhood" (top story); "The Tragic Childhood Days"; large photo of MM on front and more photos inside. ....$80-$100
- *New York News*, Aug. 18, 1962. "MM's Estate May Hit Million. Death Held 'Probable Suicide'" (top story); "Marilyn Returns the Fire in Last Tiff With Gossips"; "MM Left the Million $ She Looked Like"; "Final Verdict on Finale: Probable Suicide"; "Bolanos says Last Good-bye With Flowers"; photos of Jose Bolanos at crypt and beneficiary of will on front; many photos inside......$60-$80

FINAL

DAILY NEWS

NEW YORK'S PICTURE NEWSPAPER®

5¢

Vol. 44. No. 36 — New York 17, N.Y., Monday, August 6, 1962 — WEATHER: Fair.

MARILYN DEAD

Marilyn Monroe: "I was never used to being happy."

THE MONROE SAGA: 7 PAGES OF STORIES AND PICTURES

New York News, August 6, 1962, $50-$70.

- *New York Post*, Aug. 6, 1962. "Marilyn's Last Days." .... $100-$150
- *New York Post*, Aug. 10, 1962. "Marilyn—Tragedy's Child." .... $80-$100
- *New York Post*, June 21, 1965. "Taxes Take Marilyn's Millions"; more inside. .... $40-$60
- *Philadelphia Bulletin*, Aug. 6, 1962. "Marilyn Monroe's Death Starts Hunt for Motive"; "Officials Wonder If She Intended to Kill Herself!"; photos of MM, DiMaggio, Arthur Miller, and Yves Montand. .... $125-$175
- *Philadelphia Daily News*, Feb. 2, 1952. "No Diva, Film Lassie Marilyn Monroe Attains Glamour in Other Lines. Like Them?"; large photo of MM on front sitting on a diving board with more information inside .... $60-$80
- *Philadelphia Evening Bulletin*, Aug. 8, 1962. "MM Found It Impossible to Live Up to Her Screen Reputation." .... $20-$30

Note: There are countless miscellaneous newspapers with small photos and articles about Marilyn. These can be broken down as follows:

1946-1962 .... $20-$40
1963-Present .... $5-$20

Chapter 11

Plates and Plaques

The modern-day phenomenon of collector plates has taken full advantage of the enormous potential for sales of plates featuring Marilyn Monroe's image on them.

The first plates to be produced were the Royal Orleans set in 1982. This set also came with a set of matching figurines. The R.J. Ernst plates were the next made and featured the artwork of Susie Morton.

In 1990, the famous Bradford Exchange got on the bandwagon and produced a set of no less than 12 MM plates, featuring the artwork of Chris Notarile. These plates were a vast improvement over the earlier plates. Technology allowed for much clearer images, and the likeness of Marilyn was so aptly captured by Notarile. Recently, a set of plates was produced by Bradford that feature actual photographs of Marilyn by photographer Milton H. Greene. These represent near perfection in collector plates.

R.J. Ernst also produced a set of Marilyn Monroe plaques in 1991. Companies are getting more and more creative all the time, with Bradford Exchange producing Marilyn connecting and sculptural plates. One wonders what they might come up with next? The end result is a plethora of plates, in all shapes and sizes, and Marilyn collectors scrambling to find enough shelving and wall space to display them all.

Bradford Exchange Plates

Series I

- *The Seven Year Itch*, 1990. 8½"; plate 1 in the Marilyn Monroe Collection; limited numbered edition; limited to 150 firing days; a Delphi plate painted by Chris Notarile; Bradex No. 84-D19 5.1. Originally $27.94. ....$30-$40
- *Gentlemen Prefer Blondes*, 1990. 8½"; plate 2 in the Marilyn Monroe Collection; limited numbered edition; limited to 150 firing days; a Delphi plate painted by Chris Notarile; Bradex No. 84-D19-5.2. Originally $27.94. ....$20-$35
- *How To Marry A Millionaire*, 1991. 8½"; plate 3 in the Marilyn Monroe Collection; limited numbered edition; limited to 150 firing days; a Delphi plate painted by Chris Notarile; Bradex No. 84-D19-5.3. Originally $27.94. ....$20-$35
- *Niagara*, 1992. 8½"; plate 4 in the Marilyn Monroe Collection; limited numbered edition; limited to 150 firing days; a Delphi plate painted by Chris Notarile; Bradex No. 84-D19-5.4. Originally $27.94. ....$20-$35
- *There's No Business Like Show Business*, 1992. 8½"; plate 5 in the Marilyn Monroe Collection; limited numbered edition; limited to 150 firing days; a Delphi plate painted by Chris Notarile; Bradex No. 84-D19-5.5. ....$20-$35
- *How To Marry A Millionaire*, 1992. 8½"; plate 6 in the Marilyn Monroe Collection; limited numbered edition; limited to 150 firing days; a Delphi plate painted by Chris Notarile; Bradex No. 84-D19-5.6....................$20-$35
- *My Heart Belongs To Daddy*, 1992. 8½"; plate 7 in the Marilyn Monroe Collection; limited numbered edition; limited to 150 firing days; a Delphi plate painted by Chris Notarile; Bradex No. 84-D19-5.7....................$20-$35
- *Bus Stop*, 1992. 8½"; plate 8 in the Marilyn Monroe Collection; limited numbered edition; limited to 150 firing days; a Delphi plate painted by Chris Notarile, Bradex No. 84-D19-5.8. ....$20-$35

All twelve plates from Bradford Series I: The Marilyn Collection. Each is worth $20-$35, except plate 1 (The Seven Year Itch shown above left), which is $30-$40

All eight plates from the Bradford Series II: The Magic of Marilyn, $30-$40 each.

- *All About Eve*, 1992. 8½"; plate 9 in the Marilyn Monroe Collection; limited numbered edition; limited to 150 firing days; a Delphi plate painted by Chris Notarile; Bradex No. 84-D19-5.9. ....$20-$35
- *Monkey Business*, 1992. 8½"; plate 10 in the Marilyn Monroe Collection; limited numbered edition; limited to 150 firing days; Delphi plate painted by Chris Notarile; Bradex No. 84-D19-5.10. ....$20-$35
- *Don't Bother To Knock*, 1992. 8½"; plate 11 in the Marilyn Monroe Collection; limited numbered edition; limited to 150 firing days; Delphi plate painted by Chris Notarile; Bradex No. 84-D19-5.11. ....$20-$35
- *We're Not Married*, 1992. 8½"; plate 12 and the final plate in the Marilyn Monroe Collection; limited numbered edition; limited to 150 firing days; a Delphi plate painted by Chris Notarile; Bradex No. 84-D19-5.12....................$20-$35

Series II

- *For Our Boys In Korea-1954*, 1992; 8¼"; plate 1 in the Magic of Marilyn Collection; limited numbered edition; limited to 95 firing days; a Delphi plate painted by Chris Notarile; Bradex No. 84-D19-12.1. ....$30-$40

The eight plates that make up Bradford Series III: Reflections of Marilyn, each $30-$40.

- *Opening Night*, 1992; 8¼"; plate 2 in the Magic of Marilyn Collection; limited numbered edition; limited to 95 firing days; a Delphi plate painted by Chris Notarile; Bradex No. 84-D19-12.2. ....$30-$40
- *Rising Star*, 1993; 8¼"; plate 3 in the Magic of Marilyn Collection; limited numbered edition; limited to 95 firing days; a Delphi plate painted by Chris Notarile; Bradex No.84-D19-12.3. ......$30-$40
- *Stopping Traffic*, 1993. 8¼"; plate 4 in the Magic of Marilyn Collection; limited numbered edition; limited to 95 firing days; a Delphi plate painted by Chris Notarile; Bradex No. 84-D19-12.4. ....$30-$40
- *Strassburg's Student*, 1993. 8¼"; plate 5 in the Magic of Marilyn Collection; limited numbered edition; limited to 95 firing days; a Delphi plate painted by Chris Notarile; Bradex No. 84-D19-12.5. ....$30-$40
- *Photo Opportunity*, 1993. 8¼"; plate 6 in the Magic of Marilyn Collection; limited numbered edition; limited to 95 firing days; a Delphi plate painted by Chris Notarile; Bradex No. 84-D19-12.6. ....$30-$40
- *Shining Star*, 1993. 8¼"; plate 7 in the Magic of Marilyn Collection; limited numbered edition; limited to 95 firing days; a Delphi plate painted by Chris Notarile; Bradex No. 84-D19-12.7. .....$30-$40
- *Curtain Call*, 1994. 8¼"; plate 8 and final plate in the Magic of Marilyn Collection; limited numbered edition; limited to 95 firing days; a Delphi plate painted by Chris Notarile; Bradex No. 84-D19-12.8. ....$30-$40

Series III

- *All That Glitters*, 1994. 8⅛"; plate 1 in the Reflections of Marilyn Collection; limited numbered edition; limited to 95 firing days; artwork by Chris Notarile; Bradex No. 84-B10-169.1. Originally $29.90. ....$30-$40
- *Shimmering Heat*, 1994. 8⅛"; plate 2 in the Reflections of Marilyn Collection; limited numbered edition; limited to 95 firing days; artwork by Chris Notarile; Bradex No.84-B10-169.2. ....$30-$40
- *Million Dollar Star*, 1994. 8⅛"; plate 3 in the Reflections of Marilyn Collection; limited numbered edition; limited to 95 firing days; artwork by Chris Notarile; Bradex No. 84-B10-169.3. ...$30-$40
- *A Twinkle In Her Eye*, 1995. 8⅛"; plate 4 in the Reflections of Marilyn Collection; limited numbered edition; limited to 95 firing days; artwork by Chris Notarile; Bradex No. 84-B10-169.4. ....$30-$40
- *A Glimmering Dream*, 1995. 8⅛"; plate 5 in the Reflections of Marilyn Collection; limited numbered edition; limited to 95 firing days; artwork by Chris Notarile; Bradex No. 84-B10-169.5. ....$30-$40
- *Sparkling Cherie*, 1995. 8⅛"; plate 6 in the Reflections of Marilyn Collection; limited numbered edition; limited to 95 firing days; artwork by Chris Notarile; Bradex No. 84-B10-169.6. ...$30-$40
- *Luminous Lorelei*, 1995. 8⅛"; plate 7 in the Reflections of Marilyn Collection; limited numbered edition; limited to 95 firing days; artwork by Chris Notarile; Bradex No. 84-B10-169.7. ...$30-$40
- *Dazzling Dreamgirl*, 1995. 8⅛"; plate 8 and final plate in the Reflections of Marilyn Collection; limited numbered edition; limited to 95 firing days; artwork by Chris Notarile; Bradex No. 84-B10-169.8. ....$30-$40

The tremendous ten of Bradford Series IV: The Gold Collection, $30-$40 each.

The enselmble of eight plates in the Bradford Series V: Silver Screen Collection, each $30-$40.

Two Bradford sculptural plates below from the Diamonds and Pearls Collection, $60-$75 each.

Series IV

- *Sultry Yet Regal*, 1995. 8½"; plate 1 in Marilyn—The Gold Collection; limited numbered edition; limited to 95 firing days; artwork by Michael Dias; reproduces U.S. postage stamp of MM; Bradex No. 84-B10-339.1 .... $30-$40
- *Graceful Beauty*, 1995. 8½"; plate 2 in Marilyn—The Gold Collection; limited numbered edition; limited to 95 firing days; artwork by Chris Notarile; Bradex No. 84-B10-339.2. ...$30-$40
- *Essence of Glamour*, 1995. 8½"; plate 3 in Marilyn—The Gold Collection; limited numbered edition; limited to 95 firing days; artwork by Chris Notarile; Bradex No. 84-B10-339.3. ...$30-$40
- *Sweet Sizzle*, 1996. 8½"; plate 4 in Marilyn—The Gold Collection; limited numbered edition; limited to 95 firing days; artwork by Chris Notarile; Bradex No. 84-B10-339.4. ....$30-$40
- *Fire and Ice*, 1996. 8½"; plate 5 in Marilyn—The Gold Collection; limited numbered edition; limited to 95 firing days; artwork by Chris Notarile; Bradex No. 84-B10-339.5. ....$30-$40
- *Satin and Cream*, 1996. 8½"; plate 6 in Marilyn—The Gold Collection; limited numbered edition; limited to 95 firing days; artwork by Chris Notarile; Bradex No. 84-B10-339.6. ...$30-$40
- *Shimmer and Chiffon*, 1996. 8½"; plate 7 in Marilyn—The Gold Collection; limited numbered edition; limited to 95 firing days; artwork by Chris Notarile; Bradex No. 84-B10-339.7. ...$30-$40
- *Frankly Feminine*, 1997. 8½"; plate 8 in Marilyn—The Gold Collection; limited numbered edition; limited to 95 firing days; artwork by Chris Notarile; Bradex No. 84-B10-339.8. ...$30-$40
- *Forever Radiant*, 1997. 8½"; plate 9 in Marilyn—The Gold Collection; limited numbered edition; limited to 95 firing days; artwork by Chris Notarile; Bradex No. 84-B10-339.9. ...$30-$40
- *Radiant in Red*, 1997. 8½"; plate 10 in Marilyn—The Gold Collection; limited numbered edition; limited to 95 firing days; artwork by Chris Notarile; Bradex No. 84-B10-339.10. .$30-$40

Series V

- *Isn't It Delicious*, 1997. 8⅛"; plate 1 in the Silver Screen Marilyn Collection; limited numbered edition; limited to 95 firing days; artwork by Victor Gadino; banded in platinum; Bradex No. 84-B10-550.1. ....$30-$40
- *I Don't Mean Rhinestones*, 1997. 8⅛"; plate 2 in the Silver Screen Marilyn Collection; limited numbered edition; limited to 95 firing days; artwork by Victor Gadino; Bradex No. 84-B10-550.2. ....$30-$40
- *Everything About it is Appealing*, 1997. 8⅛"; plate 3 in the Silver Screen Marilyn Collection; limited numbered edition; limited to 95 firing days; artwork by Victor Gadino; Bradex No. 84-B10-550.3. ....$30-$40
- *Looking Like a Million*, 1997. 8⅛"; plate 4 in the Silver Screen Marilyn Collection; limited numbered edition; limited to 95 firing days; artwork by Victor Gadino; Bradex No. 84-B10-550.4. ....$30-$40
- *Quite a Strudel*, 1998. 8⅛"; plate 5 in the Silver Screen Marilyn Collection; limited numbered edition; limited to 95 firing days; artwork by Victor Gadino; Bradex No. 84-B10-550.5. ...$30-$40
- *Get Out the Fire Hose*, 1998. 8⅛"; plate 6 in the Silver Screen Marilyn Collection; limited numbered edition; limited to 95 firing days; artwork by Victor Gadino; Bradex No. 84-B10-550.6. ....$30-$40
- *Cherie, the Chanteuse*, 1998. 8⅛"; plate 7 in the Silver Screen Marilyn Collection; limited numbered edition; limited to 95 firing days; artwork by Victor Gadino; Bradex No. 84-B10-550.7. ....$30-$40

- *Lazy*, 1999. 8⅛"; plate 8 in the Silver Screen Marilyn Collection; limited numbered edition; limited to 95 firing days; artwork by Victor Gadino; Bradex No. 84-B10-550.8. ....$30-$40

Series VI

- *Forever, Marilyn*, 1997. 8⅛"; plate 1 in the Marilyn by Milton H. Greene: Up Close and Personal Collection; limited numbered edition; limited to 95 firing days; features actual Greene photo; Bradex No. 84-B10-809.1. Originally $34.95................$30-$40
- *Body and Soul*, 1997. 8⅛"; plate 2 in the Marilyn by Milton H. Greene: Up Close and Personal Collection; limited numbered edition; limited to 95 firing days; features actual Greene photo; Bradex No. 84-B10-809.2..$30-$40
- *Lady in Red*, 1997. 8⅛"; plate 3 in the Marilyn by Milton H. Greene: Up Close and Personal Collection; limited numbered edition; limited to 95 firing days; features actual Greene photo; Bradex No. 84-B10-809.3..$30-$40
- *Sophisticated Lady*, 1997. 8⅛"; plate 4 in the Marilyn by Milton H. Greene: Up Close and Personal Collection; limited numbered edition; limited to 95 firing days; features actual Greene photo; Bradex No. 84-B10-809.4..$30-$40
- *Relaxed Elegance*, 1998. 8⅛"; plate 5 in the Marilyn by Milton H. Greene: Up Close and Personal Collection; limited numbered edition; limited to 95 firing days; features actual Greene photo; Bradex No. 84-B10-809.5..$30-$40
- *Bewitching in Black*, 1998. 8⅛"; plate 6 in the Marilyn by Milton H. Greene: Up Close and Personal Collection; limited numbered edition; limited to 95 firing days; features actual Greene photo; Bradex No. 84-B10-809.6..$30-$40
- *Golden Glamour*, 1998. 8⅛"; plate 7 in the Marilyn by Milton H. Greene: Up Close and Personal Collection; limited numbered edition; limited to 95 firing days; features actual Greene photo; Bradex No. 84-B10-809.7..$30-$40
- *Satin and Lace*, 1998. 8⅛"; plate 8 in the Marilyn by Milton H. Greene: Up Close and Personal Collection; limited numbered edition; limited to 95 firing days; features actual Greene photo; Bradex No. 84-B10-809.8..$30-$40

Series VII

- *Blonde Passion*, 1998. 8⅛"; plate 1 in the Love, Marilyn Collection; limited numbered edition; limited to 95 firing days; artwork by Joanie Schwarz; Bradex No. 84-B10-917.1..................$30-$40
- *Bewitching in Black*, circa 1998. 8⅛"; plate 2 in the Love, Marilyn Collection; limited numbered edition; limited to 95 firing days; art by Joanie Schwarz; Bradex No. 84-B10-917.2.........$30-$40
- *Tempting in Terrycloth*, circa 1998. 8⅛"; plate 3 in the Love, Marilyn Collection; limited numbered edition; limited to 95 firing days; artwork by Joanie Schwarz; Bradex No. 84-B10-917.3. ....$30-$40
- *Golden Glow*, circa 1999. 8⅛"; plate 4 in the Love, Marilyn Collection; limited to 95 firing days; artwork by Joanie Schwarz; Bradex No. 84-B10-917.4..$30-$40
- *Luscious in Lace*, circa 1999. 8⅛"; plate 5 in the Love, Marilyn Collection; limited to 95 firing days; artwork by Joanie Schwarz; Bradex No. 84-B10-917.5..$30-$40
- *Irresistible in Red*, circa 1999. 8⅛"; plate 6 in the Love, Marilyn Collection; limited to 95 firing days; artwork by Joanie Schwarz; Bradex No. 84-B10-917.6..$30-$40

Eight intimate shots by Milton H. Greene captured on plates in Bradford Series VI: Up Close and Personal, $30-$40 each.

Two R.J. Ernst plates painted by Susie Morton below; 10" (left) worth $90-$130 and 8¼" is $65-$95.

Ten beautiful Hamilton plates, $30-$45 each.

Sculptural Plates

- *Satin Sensation*, 1996. 7½ x 5½; plate 1 in the Showstoppers: The Glamour of Marilyn Monroe Collection; limited numbered edition of 9,000; designed by Chris Notarile; Bradex No. 84-B10-266.1. Originally $64.84. ....$60-$75
- *Happy Birthday Mr. President*, 2000. Plate 1 in the Diamonds and Pearls: The Fashions of Marilyn Monroe Collection; limited to 295 casting days; designed by Chris Notarile; Bradex No. 84-B10-875.1. ....$60-$75
- *A Girl's Best Friend*, 2000. Plate 2 in Diamonds and Pearls: The Fashions of Marilyn Monroe Collection; limited to 295 casting days; designed by Chris Notarile; Bradex No. 84-B10-875.2. ....$60-$75

Connecting Plates

- *Hollywood Venus*, 1999. Plate 1 in the Marilyn Every Inch a Star Collection; designed by Keith Birdsong; Bradex No. 84-B11-509.1. ....$60-$70
- *Dressed to Thrill*, 1999. Plate 2 in the Marilyn Every Inch a Star Collection; designed by Keith Birdsong; Bradex No. 84-B11-509.2. ....$60-$70

Hamilton Plates

- *The Girl Next Door*, 1994. 8¼"; 23-karat gold border; limited to 28 firing days; artwork by FRANCO based on photos by Andre de Dienes; came with COA. ....$30-$45
- *A Star Is Born*, 1994. 8¼"; 23-karat gold border; limited to 28 firing days; artwork by FRANCO based on photos by Andre de Dienes; came with COA. ....$30-$45
- *Her Day In The Sun*, 1994. 8¼"; 23-karat gold border; limited to 28 firing days; artwork by FRANCO based on photos by Andre de Dienes; came with COA. ....$30-$45
- *In The Spotlight*, 1994. 8¼"; 23-karat gold border; limited to 28 firing days; artwork by FRANCO based on photos by Andre de Dienes; came with COA. ....$30-$45
- *Beauty Secrets*, 1994. 8¼"; 23-karat gold border; limited to 28 firing days; artwork by FRANCO based on photos by Andre de Dienes; came with COA. ....$30-$45
- *Bathing Beauty*, 1995. 8¼"; 23-karat gold border; limited to 28 firing days; artwork by FRANCO based on photos by Andre de Dienes; came with COA. ....$30-$45
- *Young And Carefree*, 1995. 8¼"; 23-karat gold border; limited to 28 firing days; artwork by FRANCO based on photos by Andre de Dienes; came with COA. ....$30-$45
- *Free Spirit*, 1995. 8¼"; 23-karat gold border; limited to 28 firing days; artwork by FRANCO based on photos by Andre de Dienes; came with COA. ....$30-$45
- *A Country Girl At Heart*, 1995. 8¼"; 23-karat gold border; limited to 28 firing days; artwork by FRANCO based on photos by Andre de Dienes; came with COA. ....$30-$45
- *Home Town Girl*, 1995. 8¼"; 23-karat gold border; limited to 28 firing days; artwork by FRANCO based on photos by Andre de Dienes; came with COA. ....$30-$45

D.J. Ernst Plates

- *A Commemorative to Marilyn Monroe*, 1980s. 10"; with two images of Marilyn painted by Susie Morton; painted in blue, pink and purple hues; limited to 30 firing days, then closed forever. ....$90-$130
- *Tribute Series—The One and Only Marilyn Monroe*, 1980s. 8 1/4"; MM in black dress; painted by Susie Morton; limited to 10 firing days, then closed forever. ....$65-$95

An array of Royal Orleans plates, $25-$40 each.

Royal Orleans Plates

- *The Seven Year Itch*, 1982. 8 5/16"; plate 1 in the Marilyn—An American Classic Series; limited numbered edition of 20,000; came with COA. Originally $25. ....$25-$40
- *Gentlemen Prefer Blondes*, 1982. 8 5/16"; plate 2 in the Marilyn—An American Classic Series; limited numbered edition of 20,000; came with COA. ....$25-$40
- *Niagara*, 1982. 8 5/16"; plate 3 in the Marilyn—An American Classic Series; limited numbered edition of 20,000; came with COA. ....$25-$40
- *How To Marry A Millionaire*, 1982. 8 5/16"; plate 4 and final plate in the Marilyn—An American Classic Series; limited numbered edition of 20,000; came with COA....................................$25-$40

Miscellaneous Plates

- Unidentified 10" hard plastic plate featuring Marilyn in the famous white skirt scene from *The Seven Year Itch*; unauthorized by her estate; another variation or two known to exist. ...each $10-$20

Plaques

- Celebrity Plaques by Aardvark Artisans (set of four), June 1, 2001. 12 x 12 and 3/8" thick; solid black granite; hand-numbered limited edition of 2,500; with COA and 1,001-year warranty; complimentary easel included; item numbers LEMonm001, 002, 003, 004. ....(price new) each $249
- *Marilyn*, 1991. 7 x 9 (including white-washed hardwood frame); plaque 1 in Ernst Inc. set by artist Susie Morton; limited numbered edition; limited to 30 firing days; came with COA; MM in glamorous bust pose. ....$40-$60
- *New York, New York*, 1991. 7 x 9 (including frame); plaque 2 in Ernst Inc. set by artist Susie Morton; limited numbered edition; limited to 30 firing days; came with COA; MM standing near a car...$40-$60
- *Lights, Camera, Action!*, 1991. 7 x 9 (including frame); plaque 3 in Ernst Inc. set by artist Susie Morton; limited numbered edition; limited to 30 firing days; came with COA; MM in three different bust poses..$40-$60
- *Manhattan Heat*, 1992. 7 x 9 (including frame); plaque 4 in Ernst Inc. set by artist Susie Morton; limited numbered edition; limited to 30 firing days; came with COA; MM in the famous *Itch* dress. ....$40-$60

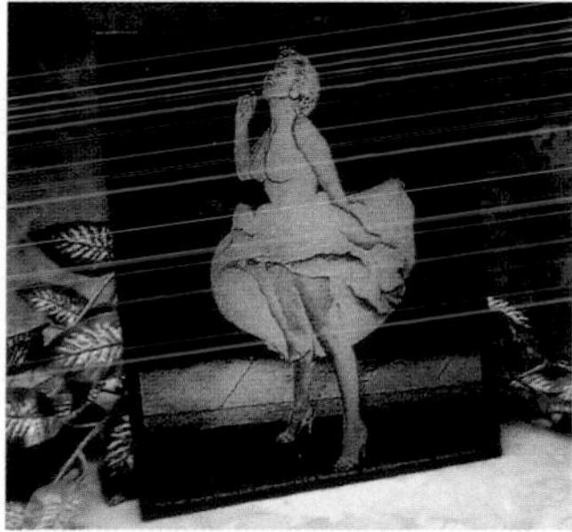

Celebrity Plaques by Aardvark Artisans, each $40-$60.

Chapter 12

Postcards and Related Collectibles

Cards, cards, and more cards: Marilyn Monroe's image has appeared on postcards, greeting cards, cigarette cards, tea cards, arcade cards, gum cards, and a few others.

Beginning in the late-1940s, postcards and arcade cards were produced with Marilyn gracing their surfaces. The earliest card produced seems to be the one commemorating the National Postmaster's Convention in Los Angeles, California, in October of 1947. The next oldest would likely be the arcade card featuring Marilyn in fur mittens and Eskimo boots.

And by the early to mid-1950s, many companies were capitalizing on the public's interest in postcards with Marilyn on them. Some were produced in conjunction with the release of Marilyn's movies, and others were simply produced for her legions of fans, and were part of the publicity blitz created by the Hollywood Studios.

Production of these cards was not limited to the United States. Many countries around the world produced such cards, with fine examples coming from Germany, Italy, and England.

Beginning in the 1970s, companies began producing Marilyn postcards in larger numbers, a practice that continues to this day, with Marilyn remaining as popular as ever, nearly 40 years after her death.

Postcards

Black and White

- Bromofoto, 1950s. No. 1196; 4 x 6; MM lying in the grass in a tight sweater and blowing on a dandelion with one hand behind her head. (ITA) ....$35-$45
- Celebrity Autograph Series, early 1950s. No. 100; MM with her hand to her chin and a big smile; published by L.D. Ltd. (ENG) ....$20-$25
- Celebrity Publishers, 1950s. No. 84; with facsimile autograph. (ENG).........$25-$35
- Celuloide Stars, 1950s. Candid pose from *Some Like It Hot.* (SPA) ....$25-$35
- Celuloide Stars, 1950s. No. 423; shows publicity photo of MM and Richard Widmark from *Don't Bother To Knock*; serrated edges. (SPA) ....$25-$35
- Celuloide Stars, 1950s. No. 48; MM in costume-check pose from *Gentlemen Prefer Blondes*; serrated edges (SPA) ....$25-$35
- Cliche International, mid-1950s. No. 529; full-length pose of MM in one-piece bathing suit with arms outstretched above head. (FRA)............................$20-$30
- Editions P. I., early 1950s. No. 674; vintage bust portrait of MM in sleeveless sweater. (FRA) ....$20-$30
- Editions P. I., 1950s. No number; candid mid-1950s shoulder shot of MM in cotton shirt with collar up (FRA) ....$20-$35
- Film Star Autograph Portrait Series, 1950s. No. 98; early '50s portrait of MM in gold lamé strap dress, with facsimile autograph at bottom of postcard; published by L.D. Ltd. (ENG) ....$20-$30
- Geburtstag, 1950s. No. 54; mid-1950s bust portrait in gold lamé halter gown with mink wrap on one shoulder and facsimile autograph in corner that reads, "Best Always, Marilyn Monroe." (HOL)...$20-$30
- Greetings, 1950s. MM in low-cut gown with pearl-beaded halter and pearl-drop earrings (ENG)..$30-$40
- *Niagara* Promo Postcard, circa 1953. MM in front of Niagara Falls, facsimile autograph, and reads, "Greetings From Niagara, Love Marilyn Monroe." (possibly ENG) ....$25-$35
- Personality Posters, 1960s-early 1970s. No. 25-01; 5 x 8; large heavy cardboard of MM wearing white blouse and standing in a doorway. (USA)...............$20-$30
- Picturegoer Series, 1950s. No. D154; circa 1950 bust portrait of MM holding roses. (ENG) ....$20-$30
- Picturegoer Series, 1950s. No. D333; early '50s bust portrait in gold lamé dress. (ENG)..$20-$30
- Rotalfoto, 1950s. No. 662; MM seated in a black thin-strap gown. (ITA) ....$30-$35
- Santoro, circa 1989. No. GP754; giant 10 x 12 card with an early glamour portrait of MM. (ENG) ....$5-$10
- Santoro, circa 1989. No. GP747; giant 10 x 12 card of MM sitting on rock by Baron Studios. (ENG) ....$5-$10
- Santoro, circa 1989. No. GP704; giant 10 x 12 card with a "white fur" glamour portrait of MM. (ENG) ....$5-$10
- Souvenir Postcard, 1947. From National Postmasters Convention held Oct. 12-16, 1947, in Los Angeles, California; MM one of four people on the card; exceedingly rare. (USA) ....$100-$200
- Soveranas, 1950s. No. 344; *The Seven Year Itch* publicity shot. (SPA) ....$25-$35
- Soveranas, 1950s. No. 321; Early 1950s publicity pose. (SPA) ....$25-$35
- Soveranas, 1950s. No. 440; publicity pose for *Niagara.* (SPA) ....$25-$35
- Turismofoto, 1950s. No. 40; 4 x 6; close-up of MM with chin resting on hand. (ITA) ....$35-$45
- United Artists, 1959. Set of 12; 3½ x 5; came in envelope to promote *Some Like It Hot*; envelope reads, "Hot! Twelve beautiful picture postcards"; colors on envelope are black, white, and red. (USA)............................$100-$200
- Unknown maker, 1950s. No number; early '50s bust portrait of MM with hand to chin and a big smile. (MEX) ....$20-$30
- Unknown maker, 1950s. No. 58; early '50s bust portrait of MM, bare shouldered, with long black gloves and rhinestone bracelet. (MEX)............................$20-$30
- Unknown maker, 1950s. No. 68; early '50s waist shot of MM in gold lamé gown with "Marilyn" printed on the front. (MEX) ....$20-$30

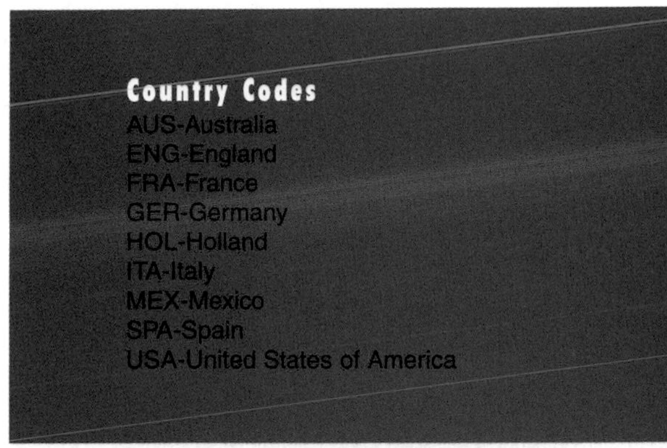

Country Codes

AUS-Australia
ENG-England
FRA-France
GER-Germany
HOL-Holland
ITA-Italy
MEX-Mexico
SPA-Spain
USA-United States of America

Souvenir postcard, 1947, $100-$200.

ISV VI/6, $20-$30.

Cliche International, $20-$30.

ISV A89, $35-$45.

UFA CK-10, $25-$35.

Rotalfoto, $25-$35.

Dexter, $20-$30.

Cliche International, $20-$30.

A selection of vintage postcards.

A selection of 1970s Lusterchrome postcards (L.38-L.40), $5-$10 each.

1950s mutoscope card, $25-$35.

1940s mutoscope card, $25-$35.

Color

- Andy Warhol, circa 1980s-'90s. Set of eight; reproducing different Warhol silk-screened versions of the familiar head shot from *Niagara*; five cards with single images in vivid pop-art colors, and three cards featuring two and four reverse images; published by Nouvelle Images. (USA) .... $6-$8
- Archivo Bermejo, 1950s. No. 8; publicity pose for *The Seven Year Itch.* (SPA) .... $25-$35
- Archivo Bermejo, 1950s. Publicity pose for *River of No Return.* (SPA) .... $25-$35
- CK-10, 1950s. Bust shot of MM in green blouse underneath a tree looking up at the sky. (GER) .... $25-$35
- CK-73, 1950s. Waist shot in gold lamé dress with hands behind her; published by D. Constance Ltd. (ENG) .... $40-$50
- Classico, 1980s-90s. Set of five; featuring French posters for *The Seven Year Itch*, *Niagara*, *Gentlemen Prefer Blondes,* and *Bus Stop*, plus the American poster for *The Seven Year Itch.* (FRA) .... $5-$8
- Editions P. I., 1950s. Shoulder shot of MM in black halter gown with a white collar and red background. (FRA) .... $30-$35
- ISV, 1950s. A89; bust shot of MM in gold lamé gown. (GER) .... $35-$45
- ISV, 1950s. IV/6; full-length shot in yellow one-piece bathing suit, leaning on an upturned metal table, with one hand behind her head. (GER) .... $20-$30
- ISV, 1950s. IV/6; as above, only MM is standing, the background is blue, and one hand on her hip and the other behind her head. (GER) .... $20-$30
- ISV, 1950s. A10; waist shot in gold lamé gown viewed from the side; back of card advertises *How To Marry A Millionaire.* (GER) .... $25-$35
- Lusterchrome, 1950s. L.38; MM in blue-and-white striped bikini kneeling down with hands on knees, red background, and photo captioned, "Beautiful Eyeful." (USA) .... $20-$30
- Lusterchrome, 1950s. L.39; MM lying on side in two-piece yellow bikini with white tie strings, red background, and photo captioned, "Thinking of You." (USA) .... $20-$30
- Lusterchrome, 1950s. L.40; in blue-and-white striped bikini sitting on beach in pair of wedge shoes. (USA) .... $20-$30
- Lusterchrome, circa 1972. JL.13; jumbo 6 x 9 of the same pose as card L.38, "Beautiful Eyeful." (USA) .... $25-$35
- Lusterchrome, circa 1972. JL.14; jumbo 6 x 9 of the same pose as card L.39, "Thinking Of You". (USA) .... $25-$35
- Lusterchrome, circa 1972. JL.15; jumbo 6 x 9 entitled "The Charmer," with same outfit as on card L.38 above, only MM is sitting on beach and wearing wedge shoes. (USA) .... $25-$35
- Lusterchrome, circa 1972. L.38; reproduction of the above card on Marilyn (L.38). (USA) .... $5-$10
- Lusterchrome, circa 1972. L.40; reproduction of the above card on Marilyn (L.40). (USA) .... $5-$10
- Quality Postcards of San Francisco, circa 1980s-90s. Six different cards, No. 360, No. 365, No. 367, No. 374, No. 953, and No. 954; MM in a variety of poses. (USA) .... set $6-$8
- Rotolfoto, 1950s. No. 36; beautiful bust shot of MM in pink dress and gold ring earrings, looking down with her hand up to her head; publicity pose for *Niagara.* (ITA) .... $25-$35
- Rotolfoto, 1950s. No. 109; publicity photo for *How To Marry A Millionaire.* (ITA) .... $25-$35
- Sam Shaw, circa 1993. Uncut sheet of Marilyn postcards measuring 27 x 41. (USA) .... $50-$90
- 20th Century Fox, 1950s. MM standing in white shorts next to a railing; facsimile autograph on front and list of charges for additional photo on back; sent to fans who requested her autograph. (USA) .... $35-$45
- Unknown maker, 1950s. No. 67; shoulder pose of MM in a white fur wrap. (possibly HOL or ENG) .... $25-$35
- Unknown maker, 1950s. No. 23; full-length shot of MM in a potato sack dress and Lucite pumps leaning on a white pillar. (MEX) .... $35-$45

Mutoscope (Arcade) Cards

- Marilyn Mutoscope Card, circa 1954. 3¼ x 5¼; with b&w image of MM in one-piece bathing suit with polka-dot scarf blowing in the wind. ....$25-$35
- Marilyn Mutoscope Card, circa 1949. 3¼ x 5¼; with b&w image of MM in one-piece bathing suit and wearing fur mittens, hands on her hips, and Eskimo-type fur boots on; card is tinted purple. ....$25-$35
- Marilyn Mutoscope Card, circa 1954. 3¼ x 5¼; with color-tinted image of MM in red *Showgirl* outfit (circa 1954) and sitting on the edge of a table. ....$25-$35
- Marilyn Mutoscope Card by artist Earl Moran, circa 1948. 3¼ x 5¼; late-1940s color artwork of MM seated on ottoman with caption that reads, "Now, this is just between you and me." ....$35-$45
- Marilyn Mutoscope Card by artist Earl Moran, circa 1948. 3¼ x 5¼; late-1940s color artwork of MM seated and hand raised in a toast with caption that reads, "The doctor said I needed glasses." ....$35-$45

A selection of contemporary postcards, retail value for each.

Greeting Cards

- Marilyn Greeting Card, 1950s. 5 x 7¼; MM in full-length pose wearing a negligee, with caption that reads, "Marilyn Monroe, Star of 20th Century Fox Productions." (USA) ....$25-$35
- Marilyn Greeting Card, 1950s. 6 x 8¼; MM in waist shot and wearing black strapless gown, long black gloves, and with her hand up to her cheek; caption at bottom reads, "Marilyn Monroe—20th Century Fox." (USA) ....$25-$35
- Marilyn Greeting Card, 1950s. 7 x 9¼; MM in full-length pose, seated, wearing a negligee, with one hand on her thigh and the other on her midriff; similar caption at bottom to those above. (USA) ....$25-$35
- Ambassador Greeting Cards of Marilyn, circa 1995. 5 x 7; set of five—four in color and one b&w; labeled for "Birthday," "Love," "Goodbye," "Inspirational," and blank (for personal note). (USA) ....set $10-$12

Two giant postcards by Santoro, $5-$10 each.

Cigarette, Gum, and Assorted Cards

- Cigarette Card, mid-1950s. No. 95; 1½ x 2; color image of MM in single-strap dress from *How To Marry A Millionaire*; printed on the back is "Marilyn Monroe." (ITA) ....$35-$45
- Cigarette Card, 1953. Cinema and Television Stars No. 24-Barbers Teas; 1¼ x 2¾; color MM photo. (ENG) ....$20-$30
- Marilyn Gum Card, mid-1950s. No. 15; 2¼ x 4; color artwork of MM, with her name at bottom of the card and mentions *The Seven Year Itch*. (ENG) ....$35-$45
- Licorice Card, circa 1957. Film Stars No. 23; 1½ x 2½; color photo of Marilyn. (AUS) ....$35-$45
- Australian Weeties Vita-Brits Crispies Card, circa 1955. Popular Film Stars No. 11; 2¼ x 3¼; color photo of MM. (AUS) ....$35-$45
- Chocolate Card, Geburtstag 1. Juni, circa 1959. No. 30; 2½ x 3¾; heavy stock with color photo of MM from *Some Like It Hot*. (HOL) ....$35-$45
- Topps Flip Book Card, 1950. No. 2 of set R-710-2; 1¼ x 2; MM and Groucho Marx in scene meant for 1949's *Love Happy*, but was never used; MM in one-piece bathing suit; card has indents on each side of one end where a rubber band could be wrapped around after the entire set was completed and the cards could then be flipped with your fingers. (USA) ....$50-$100

A selection of vintage gum, tea, and cigarette cards (above and at left); most are worth $35-$45.

Chapter 13

Records and Related Collectibles

Those fascinated with Marilyn Monroe aren't satisfied with just looking at her—they want to hear about her, too. Enter the wide array of LPs, EPs, 45s, 78s, sound cards, and 8-track tapes.

The earliest sound-inspired Marilyn collectible, to my knowledge, is the 78-RPM record produced by Capitol Records in 1952. The title of the song was "Marilyn," and it was performed by Ray Anthony at a party thrown in honor of Marilyn at his home in California.

A modern-day parallel to that historic song would be Elton John's moving memorial to Marilyn, "Candle in the Wind."

Nearly all of the other records produced about Marilyn were done so in conjunction with the release of one of the films she was starring in, or at a later date, featuring a selection of songs from her films. A great many countries around the world have produced such items.

And Marilyn's splash on the big screen quickly made its way to a series of other media for personal home use, including videocassettes, laser discs, picture discs, CD-ROMs, DVDs, and 8mm movies.

Modern technology has brought about the production of videocassettes, DVDs, and other such media previously mentioned. Now, Marilyn fans have ready access to Marilyn's many movies, with state-of-the-art sound and pictures.

Hollywood Studios has dusted off its old film reels, and has made available even those movies that Marilyn only had bit parts in, realizing the tremendous sales potential created by anything Monroe. Not bad for a gal who hasn't graced the screen in almost 40 years!

LP and EP Records

- *Con Plumas Marilyn Monroe*, 1982. Liberty. ....$40-$60
- *Fabulous Marilyn* (Reissue of *Deux Jolies Blondes*), date not available. Classic Original Productions, Marquis Disque (LP)-1450-50103; personal appearances never before on LP. ....$25-$35
- *Gentlemen Prefer Blondes/Los Caballeros Las Prefieren Rubias*, 1982. Belter serie La Musica en el Cine 2-90.014 (Spain). ....$30-$50
- *Gentlemen Prefer Blondes* (original soundtrack—10"), 1953 and reissued in 1957. MGM Records-E208 (33 RPM); songs: "Bye Bye Baby," "A Little Girl From Little Rock," "Diamonds Are a Girl's Best Friend," "When Love Goes Wrong," plus other musical selections from the movie. ....$60-$75
- *Gentlemen Prefer Blondes/Til The Clouds Roll By* (compilation album), 1957 and reissued in 1972. MGM Records 2353067; songs: "Bye Bye Baby," "A Little Girl From Little Rock," "Diamonds Are a Girl's Best Friend," and "When Love Goes Wrong." ....$30-$50
- *Goodbye, Primadonna*, 1982. German Import, Ultra Phone, LC-0001; includes a poster calendar. ....$20-$30
- *Goodbye Primadonna*, 1980. Ariston AR/LP 12382 (Italy); includes 10 songs. ....$25-$35
- *Goodbye Yellow Brick Road*, 1973. Island Records; includes "Candle In The Wind." ....$20-$30
- *Hear Them Again* (compilation album), 1968. Reader's Digest (RCA-A 10 Album Collection); includes "You'd Be Surprised." ....$20-$30
- *Hi-Fi Story No. 2* (LP), 1980s. Italian Import; compilation featuring Johnny Guitar with color cover of MM and a foldout jacket with more photos. ....$20-$40
- *Hi-Fi Story No. 17* (LP), 1980s. Italian Import; compilation not featuring any Marilyn songs, but she is on cover in color photo, and there's a fold-out jacket with photos. ....$20-$40
- *Hollywood On The Air Presents: The Feminine Touch* (compilation album), date not available. Star-Tone Records; comedy skit featuring MM, Edgar Bergen, and Charlie McCarthy. ....$20-$40
- *Horray For Hollywood* (compilation album), 1972. RCA Victor LSA 3085, produced by Don Schlitter; vintage reissue of original from 1930-1957; 15 other stars singing on album; includes "I'm Going To File My Claim." ....$20-$40
- *Joe Droukes Shadowboxing*, 1984. Southwind Productions by Buddah Records. ....$20-$40
- *La Fantastica (E Indimenticabile) Marilyn*, 1980. Ri-Fi serie Penny Oro RPO/ST 72017 (Italy); includes nine songs. ....$30-$40
- *La Voce, Le Musiche Ei Films—Marilyn Monroe*, 1973. RCA Victor TPL 1 7025 (Italy); songs: "You'd Be Surprised," "My Heart Belongs To Daddy," "Kiss," "A Fine Romance," "Heat Wave," "After You Get What You Want You Don't Want It," "Bye Bye Baby," "River Of No Return," "Diamonds Are A Girl's Best Friend," "I'm Going To File My Claim," "She Acts Like A Woman Should," and "Lazy." ....$50-$60
- *Le Milliardaire*, 1960. French Import, Phillips 6325-150. ....$40-$50
- *Let's Make Love* (original soundtrack), 1960. Columbia CL1527; songs: "My Heart Belongs To Daddy," "Incurably Romantic," "Let's Make Love," "Specialization," plus others from the show. ....$40-$50
- *Let's Make Love* (original soundtrack Collector Series), 1973. Columbia ACS8327 (also available on cassette); as above. ....$25-$35
- *L' Indimenticabile Marilyn Monroe*, 1970. Movietone Records MTL 2603 (Italy); nine songs. ....$40-$60
- *L' Intramontabile Mito Di Marilyn* (LP), 1983. RCA CL89167 (Italy); MM sings 11 songs from her soundtracks; color cover of MM. ....$35-$45
- *Marilyn*, 1952. Capitol 2207, Starlight Songs ASCAP-2:07 10480 (78 RPM); "Marilyn" performed by Ray Anthony and his orchestra, vocal by Tommy Mercer and the Skyliners; MM and Anthony on picture sleeve; record is stamped, "For demonstration purposes only." ....$150-$200

Gentlemen Prefer Blondes (from the original soundtrack), EP, $30-$50.

Hi-Fi Story No. 2 (Italy), $20-$40.

Hi-Fi Story No. 17 (Italy), $20-$40.

Let's Make Love original soundtrack, $25-$35.

Marilyn, 1963 (U.S.), $60-$75.

- *Marilyn*, 1963. 20th Century Fox Records FXG 5000 GEMS; songs: "Heat Wave," "A Little Girl From Little Rock," "One Silver Dollar," "Diamonds Are A Girl's Best Friend," "Lazy," "When Love Goes Wrong," "Bye Bye Baby," "I'm Going To File My Claim," "After You Get What You Want You Don't Want It," and "River Of No Return"; came with b&w ready-to-frame photo of MM; album released in conjunction with the 1963 film *Marilyn*, narrated by Rock Hudson. ....$60-$75
- *Marilyn Monroe/June Hutton*, circa 1953. U.S. government-issued for Armed Forces Radio Service P-3004 SSL-5B48 (16" 33 RPM record); includes "Gentlemen Prefer Blondes," "Bye Bye Baby," "A Little Girl From Little Rock," "Diamonds Are A Girl's Best Friend," and three songs by Hutton. ....$75-$125
- *Marilyn Monroe*, 1973. Japanese Import RA5640; 10 pages of photos and double-page layout. ....$40-$60
- *Marilyn*, 1978. German Import UAS 295601. ....$40-$60
- *Marilyn Monroe*, 1962. Ascot, United Artists ALS 16008; songs: "I Wanna Be Loved By You," "River Of No Return," "I'm Through With Love," "Running Wild," plus other selections from Marilyn's movies; color cover shows MM on stage singing a song in *Some Like It Hot*. ....$80-$90
- *Marilyn Monroe*, 1988. Ricordi serie Orizzonte ORL 8781 (Italy); 17 songs. ....$30-$40
- *Marilyn Monroe Bravo*, 1973. Germany 6370-201. ....$30-$50
- *Marilyn Monroe Chante* (EP), 1960. Philips Medium 432.812 be (France); songs: "My Heart Belongs To Daddy," "Specialization," and "Let's Make Love." ....$50-$70
- *Marilyn Monroe—Diamonds Are A Girl's Best Friend*, 1985. NCB Records (Denmark); songs: "Heat Wave," "Lazy," "After You Get What You Want You Don't Want It," "You'd Be Surprised," "A Fine Romance," "One Silver Dollar," "River Of No Return," "I'm Going To File My Claim," "A Little Girl From Little Rock," "When Love Goes Wrong," "Diamonds Are A Girl's Best Friend," and "Bye Bye Baby." ....$30-$50
- *Marilyn Monroe* (from original soundtrack of *Marilyn* movie), 1963. Great Britain Import, Pleasure MFP mono 1176; five photos of MM on cover. ....$80-$95
- *Marilyn Monroe—Goodbye Primdonna*, 1981. Ariston AR/LP/12382 (Italy); with poster calendar. ....$45-$60
- *Marilyn Monroe—Goodbye Primadonna*, early 1980s. Telefunken 10174 (Mexico); song titles all listed in Spanish. ....$30-$50
- *Marilyn Monroe: Greatest Hits*, 1986. Neon Records (Belgium); songs: "My Heart Belongs To Daddy," "After You Get What You Want You Don't Want It," "Diamonds Are A Girl's Best Friend," "One Silver Dollar," "River Of No Return," "Heat Wave," "I'm Going To File My Claim," "When I Fall In Love," "Bye Bye Baby," and "Specialization." . ...$35-$50
- *Marilyn Monroe: Legends (For The First Time)*, 1974. Legends 1000/1; includes numerous songs, film scenes, and appearances (23 total); has color MM cover and a fold-out jacket. ....$30-$40
- *Marilyn Monroe: Musica Per I Tuoi Sogni*, 1982. Dischi Ricordi SRIC 1005-Ariston (Italy); includes 16-page booklet with a gatefold sleeve. ....$35-$45

Marilyn From the Original Soundtrack, 1963 (U.S.), $60-$75.

Marilyn Monroe (from the original soundtrack), 1963 (England), $80-$95.

Marilyn Monroe—Rare Recordings, $35-$45.

Marilyn Monroe—Never Before and Never Again, $100-$160.

- *Marilyn Monroe—Never Before and Never Again*, 1978. Stet Records DSI5005; songs: "Do It Again," "Diamonds Are A Girl's Best Friend," "Kiss," "A Little Girl From Little Rock," "This Is A Fine Romance," "Bye Bye Baby," "You'd Be Surprised," "A Little Girl From Little Rock—Reprise," "She Acts Like A Woman Should," "When Love Goes Wrong," "Heat Wave," "Happy Birthday, Mr. President." .... $35-$45
- *Marilyn Monroe—Never Before and Never Again*, circa 1996. California Gold; as above, but in 24-karat gold-plated LP; frame measured 18 x 24. .... $100-$160
- *Marilyn Monroe—Rare Recordings 1948-1962*, 1979. Sandy Hook SH2013; includes numerous songs, film scenes, interviews, commercials, etc. .... $35-$45
- *Marilyn Monroe*, date not available. Italy; recorded directly from *Gentlemen Prefer Blondes*. .... $30-$45
- *Marilyn Monroe Sings Her Movie Hits*, 1988. The Entertainers ENT LP 13052 (Italy); 16 songs. .... $30-$40
- *Marilyn Monroe Special (World Star Collection)*, date not available. Unknown label; double album with two full-page b&w photos inside. .... $30-$45
- *Marilyn Monroe—The Best From Her Movies*, 1986. Lotus Records of Italy; songs: "Bye Bye Baby," "Diamonds Are A Girl's Best Friend," "When Love Goes Wrong," "A Fine Romance," "She Acts Like A Woman Should," "Specialization," "When I Fall In Love," "Heat Wave," "River Of No Return," "Lazy," "After You Get What You Want You Don't Want It," "I'm Going To File My Claim," "You'd Be Surprised," "My Heart Belongs To Daddy," "A Little Girl From Little Rock," and "Kiss." .... $35-$45
- *Marilyn Monroe—The Entertainers*, 1988. Sarabandas Ent LP 13.052 (Italy). .... $30-$40
- *Marilyn, Poo Poo Pa Doop*, 1978. United Artists (EP); songs: "I Wanna Be Loved By You," "Running Wild," and "I'm Through With Love." .... $30-$40
- *More Original Soundtracks and Hit Music From Great Motion Picture Themes* (compilation album), 1961. United Artists; includes "I Wanna Be Loved By You." .... $20-$30
- *No Hay Edad Para El Recuerdo*, 1976. RCA Victor AVS 4376 (Argentina); includes "I'm Gonna File My Claim." .... $25-$35
- *Norma Jean*, 1979. RCA; includes song sung by Sammi Smith and nine other songs. .... $20-$30
- *Portrait Of Marilyn Monroe*, 1973. Jamaican Import, United Artists FML-3; songs: "I Wanna Be Loved By You," "Running Wild," and "I'm Thru With Love." .... $30-$50
- *RCA Promo Disc*, 1954. RCA M-146-2 (78 RPM); includes "I'm Gonna File My Claim," and "River of No Return"; released for disc jockey use only and not sold to public; label shows MM photo. .... $80-$120

Marilyn Monroe—The Entertainers (Italy), $30-$40.

Remember Marilyn, 1972 (U.S.), $30-$40.

RCA promo record for River of No Return, 1954, $80-$120.

Remember Marilyn alternate cover, $30-$40.

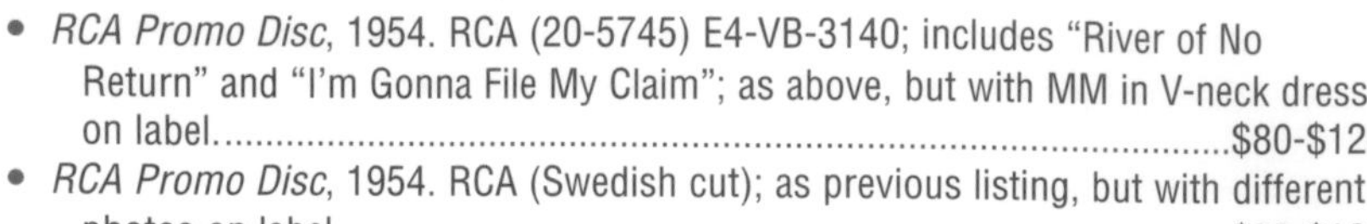

- *RCA Promo Disc*, 1954. RCA (20-5745) E4-VB-3140; includes "River of No Return" and "I'm Gonna File My Claim"; as above, but with MM in V-neck dress on label. ......$80-$120
- *RCA Promo Disc*, 1954. RCA (Swedish cut); as previous listing, but with different photos on label. ......$80-$120
- *Recordando A Marilyn Monroe*, date not available. Diana LPD 201; songs titles all in Spanish. ......$20-$40
- *Remember Marilyn*, 1972 (rerelease of 1963 album *Marilyn*). 20th Century Fox T901; with 12-page booklet of MM from the "Legend and the Truth" photo exhibition; color cover and foldout jacket. ......$30-$40
- *Remember Marilyn*, 1974. Fontana 9286865 (Italy). ......$40-$60
- *Remember Marilyn*, 1970s. Philips 637021 (Germany); color photo of MM on cover and came with 12-page booklet. ......$40-$60
- *Remember Marilyn Monroe*, 1974. Japanese Import V2005; album opens to full cover of MM. ......$50-$70
- *Remember Marilyn*, 1980. Jamaica RPL-6002; includes 10 songs. ......$50-$70
- *Remember Marilyn*, 1989. TVP Records 1022 SLX 02261 (Italy); with album, button, T-shirt, 3-D photo, 10 photos (all 8 x 10), and 20 postcards in a plastic canister. ......$30-$40
- *Some Like It Hot*, 1978. British Import UAC 5097. ......$30-$40
- *Some Like It Hot Cha Cha Cha*, 1959. United Artists UA3029; yellow background. ......$60-$80
- *Some Like It Hot* (original soundtrack),1959 and reissued 1964. Ascot UA 4030; songs: "Running Wild," "Some Like It Hot," "I'm Through With Love," "I Wanna Be Loved By You," plus others from the movie. ......$40-$80
- *Some Like It Hot*, 1960. Philips P 08436 L (Italy); includes "Running Wild," "I Wanna Be Loved By You," and "I'm Thru With Love." ....$50-$80
- *Some Like It Hot*, 1975. UA-LA 272-G; includes "Running Wild," "I Wanna Be Loved By You," and "I'm Thru With Love." ......$25-$35
- *Star Fur Millionen*, 1973. 20th Century Fox Phonogram 6370 201 (Germany); includes nine songs. ......$50-$80

Some Like It Hot, Cha Cha Cha, 1959, $60-$80.

The Ballad of Sweet Marilyn, 1960s, $50-$75.

Some Like It Hot soundtrack, 1975, $25-$35.

Diamond's Are a Girl's Best Friend—Golden Memories, 1984, $40-$50.

- *Super Album: Selections From Original Soundtracks and Scores* (compilation album), 1963. Ascot-United Artists; with "I Wanna Be Loved By You," "I'm Through With Love," and "Running Wild." .... $20-$30
- *The Edgar Bergen Show With Charlie McCarthy: With Special Guest Marilyn Monroe (Comedy Series No. 13)*, 1974. Radiola MR 1034 (CBS Radio Broadcast). .... $25-$35
- *The Marilyn Monroe Collection (20 Golden Greats)*, 1984. Dejavu DVLP 2001 (Italy). .... $30-$40
- *The Marilyn Monroe Story*, 1988. Five FM 14203 (Italy); with 29 songs. .... $35-$45
- *The Misfits* (limited-edition Collector's Series), 1961. UAL A273-G. .... $40-$60
- *The Misfits* (original soundtrack), 1961. UAL 4087. .... $40-$60
- *The Story of Marilyn Monroe*, 1976. Ariston Oxford OX 3039 (Italy); color photo of MM on cover. .... $40-$70
- *The Unforgettable Marilyn Monroe*, 1967. Movietone Records (division of 20th Century Fox Records) S72016; Marilyn sings songs from her soundtracks. .... $40-$70
- *The Very Best of Marilyn Monroe*, date not available. Artisian Import FUN 9001; also on cassette. .... $30-$50
- *The Voice, Songs and Films of Marilyn Monroe*, 1976. RCA; selection of songs from Marilyn's movies. .... $30-$45

Recorded songs from *There's No Business Like Show Business*, $60-$80.

45 RPM Records

- *The Ballad of Sweet Marilyn*, circa early 1960s. Mr. Pisces Productions (BRR-103-A); includes "The Ballad of Sweet Marilyn" and "I'm So Sweet On Sundays"; written and sung by the Lawrences. .... $50-$75
- *Diamonds Are A Girl's Best Friend–Golden Memories*, 1984. GM Production; Yoram Yahana, Transworld, Anabas; printed in England. .... $40-$50
- *Diamonds Are A Girl's Best Friend*, circa 1996. California Gold of Cherry Hill, New Jersey; limited edition of 5,000; included 24-karat gold record with a sheet of stamps depicting MM in the Philippe Halsman photo used on the April 1952 *LIFE* cover. .... $100-$150
- *Elvis and Marilyn*, 1978. PDS 8667; sung by Leon Russell. .... $10-$15
- *Goodbye Yellow Brick Road*, 1973. Island Records; with "Candle In The Wind" by Elton John. .... $10-$15
- *Heat Wave*, circa 1996. California Gold of Cherry Hill, New Jersey; included 12 x 16 framed 24-karat gold record, with photo of MM in the upper right. .... $75-$100
- *Marilyn Monroe Sings*, 1963. 20th Century Fox (promotional for the film *Marilyn*, narrated by Rock Hudson) No. 311; with "One Silver Dollar" and "River of No Return." .... $40-$50
- *Marilyn Monroe Sings*, 1978. United Artists 36484 (England); songs: "I Wanna Be Loved By You," "Running Wild," and "I'm Thru With Love"; has foldout picture sleeve. .... $20-$25
- *Marilyn Monroe Sings*, 1982. Planeta P-181 (Spain); includes "I'm Gonna File My Claim" and "After You Get What You Want You Don't Want It"; has color picture sleeve. .... $20-$25
- *Marilyn Monroe Sings—Some Like It Hot*, 1959. UA 1005; includes "Some Like It Hot," "Running Wild," "I'm Through With Love," "I Wanna Be Loved By You"; in hardcover box with photo jacket. .... $60-$80
- *Marilyn Monroe Sings—Some Like It Hot*, 1959. UA RE-T-1231 (England); as above, but with different cover than the U.S. edition. .... $80-$95
- *Recorded From The Soundtrack of Gentleman Prefer Blondes*, 1953. MGM Records X208 EP; with "Bye Bye Baby" by Marilyn and "Bye Bye Baby" by Jane Russell; two-record set. .... $50-$80
- *Recorded From The Soundtrack of River Of No Return*, 1954. RCA; with "I'm Going To File My Claim" and "River Of No Return"; sold 75,000 copies in the first three weeks of release. .... $50-$80
- *Recorded Songs From There's No Business Like Show Business*, 1954. RCA Records EP-EPA 593; songs: "You'd Be Surprised," "Heat Wave," "Lazy," and "After You Get What You Want You Don't Want It." .... $60-$80

Marilyn Monroe Sings, 1982, $20-$25.

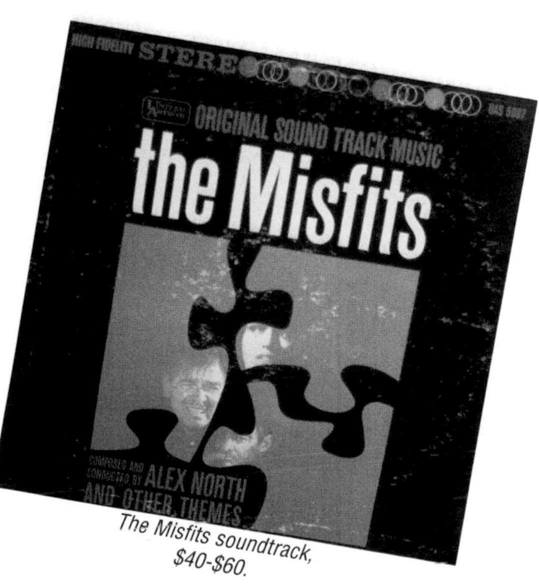

The Misfits soundtrack, $40-$60.

Stemra 830003, circa 1986, $40-$50.

- *River of No Return (il fiume senza ritorno)/I'm Gonna File My Claim (L'uomo che voglio)*, 1954. RCA 45N 0120 (Italy). ....$50-$80
- *There's No Business Like Show Business (Follie Dell' Anno)*, 1954. RCA A72V 0004 (Italy). ....$60-$90
- *There's No Business Like Show Business (Follie Dell' Anno)*, 1954. RCA EPA 593 (Italy). ....$60-$80
- *Some Like It Hot*, 1983. UA-Liberty Serie Dance Forever No. 26 2C 008-83377 (France). ....$20-$30
- *Some Like It Hot Chante*, 1983. French-made. ....$15-$20
- *Some Like It Hot—"I Wanna Be Loved By You/ I'm Through With Love"*, 1959. London 45 HL 8862 (Italy). ....$60-$90
- *Sidney Skolsky Interviews Marilyn Monroe and Marilyn Sings*, June 1954. Dell Publishing Co. MM-SS-1; with "I'm Gonna File My Claim" and "Diamonds Are a Girl's Best Friend." ....$150-$200

A selection of picture disks.

The Legend Lives On, 1986, $40-$55.

Picture Discs

- *Hurray For Hollywood*, 1984. Astan PD 20106 (Germany); Marilyn sings one song. ....$40-$50
- *Marilyn Monroe—The Latest Blonde (Let's Make Love Soundtrack)*, circa 1980s. Unknown label. ....$35-$50
- *Marilyn Monroe*, circa 1986. Stemra-PD 83003 (Denmark); MM in b&w nude pose on one side and b&w pose from *Bus Stop* on the other side. ....$40-$50
- *Marilyn Monroe*, circa 1980s. PD 83006; *Golden Dreams* nude pose and the fishnet stocking pose....$40-$50
- *Marilyn Monroe*, 1984. AR 30031; *Golden Dreams* nude pose and standing with an umbrella; with 12 songs. ....$40-$50
- *Marilyn Monroe, 1987. No. 68, Maybellene; limited edition of 1,000; features "Runnin' Wild" and "I'm Through With Love."* ....$35-$45
- *Marilyn Monroe—Rare Recordings*, 1979. Sandy Hook; *Golden Dreams* nude pose; limited edition of 25,000. ....$40-$50
- *Marilyn Monroe/Runnin' Wild*, 1985. AR 30038 (Denmark); MM in black negligee and in the nude *Golden Dreams* pose; includes an everlasting calendar; features 10 songs. ....$40-$50
- *Marilyn Monroe—When I Fall In Love, circa 1980s. Zuma (Germany); MM sings "When I Fall In Love," "Heat Wave," and "Diamonds Are a Girl's Best Friend."* ....$40-$50
- *Some Like It Hot*, 1979. UASP 30226A; features six small headshots. ....$35-$45
- *The Legend Lives On*, 1986. Sandy Hook Limited Edition 83003-stemra-PD (Denmark); gold lamé pose and white fur pose; features 10 songs. ....$40-$55
- *The Ten*, circa 1980s. PD50-005; MM in an uncommon nude pose on red velvet. ....$35-$45

Marilyn Monroe, 1987, $35-$45.

Some Like It Hot, 1979, $35-$45.

Marilyn Monroe—When I Fall In Love, 1980s, $40-$50.

Hurray For Hollywood, 1984, $40-$50.

Cassettes

- *Ladies Of Burlesque*, 1979. Sandy Hook; MM sings from *Ladies of the Chorus*..........$10-$15
- *Let's Make Love* (original soundtrack Collector Series), 1973. Columbia..........$15-$20
- Marilyn Monroe—Rare Recordings, 1979. Sandy Hook. ....$10-$15
- *1953—Do You Remember?*, 1985. The Great American Gift Co. Inc., New Rochelle, New York; features news of 1953 and says, "Startling new magazine begins publication featuring nude calendar photo of MM."..........$10-$15
- *The Very Best Of Marilyn Monroe*, Artisian Import FUN 9001..........$10-$15

Marilyn Monroe—The Latest Blonde picture disk, $35-$50.

Marilyn Monroe picture disk, 1984, $40-$50.

Compact Discs

- *Ladies of Burlesque*, 1979. Sandy Hook No. 19; songs from *Ladies of the Chorus*..........$15-$30
- Las Canciones Favoritas de Marilyn Monroe, date not available. EMI 2187996782 (Mexico). ....$20-$40
- Legends—Marilyn Monroe, 1994. Wise Pack LECD 067 (England). ....$15-$20
- Legends—Marilyn Monroe, 1995. Wise Pack Vol. 2 LECD 130 (England). ....$15-$20
- Marilyn Monroe, date not available. arc records MEC 949029 (Holland)........$15-$20
- *Marilyn Monroe—Great American Legends Series*, 1992. Delta Music Inc. ....$15-$20
- *Marilyn Monroe—16 Greatest Songs*, 1990. 12012..........$20-$30
- *Marilyn Monroe—24 Great Songs*, 1995. BXCL 284 (Holland)..........$20-$40
- *Marilyn Monroe—Gold*, 1993. Gold 034 (Holland). ....$15-$20
- *Marilyn Monroe—Goodbye Primadonna*, 1984. AZ 339372 ....$20-$30
- *Marilyn Monroe—I Wanna Be Loved By You*, 1986. CD SG 8602. ....$20-$30
- *Marilyn Monroe—Never Before and Never Again*, date not available. DRG CDXP 15005 (Japan) ....$25-$35
- *Marilyn Monroe—The Complete Recordings*, 1988. Rare CD 06/07 (Switzerland). ....$20-$30
- *Marilyn Monroe—The Legend Lives On*, 1986. DARTS CD 180003..........$20-$30
- *Marilyn Monroe—Some Like It Hot*, 1989. CDMX 101 DRG..........$20-$30
- *Presenting Marilyn Monroe—The Essential Collection*, date not available. Wisepack lec dd 621(England); two-pack..........$20-$40
- *Showgirls—Yesterday Gold*, 1989. YDG 2513 (Belgium); set of five, one of which is MM; 21 songs. ....$30-$40
- *Super Stars—Marilyn Monroe*, 1994. Super 027 (Holland). ....$15-$25
- *The Marilyn Monroe Collection*, 1987. Dejavu DVCD 2001 (Switzerland). ...$20-$30
- *The Very Best of Marilyn Monroe*, 1999. Stardust Records (division of Cleopatra); 20 remastered tracks, plus extensive liner notes and rare photos. ....$15-$30
- *The World of Marilyn Monroe—Heatwave*, date not available. Trace 0401092; 10 songs..........$10-$20

Marilyn Monroe—Some Like It Hot CD, $20-$30.

Marilyn Monroe—Never Before and Never Again CD, $25-$35.

Marilyn Monroe—Great American Legends CD, $15-$20.

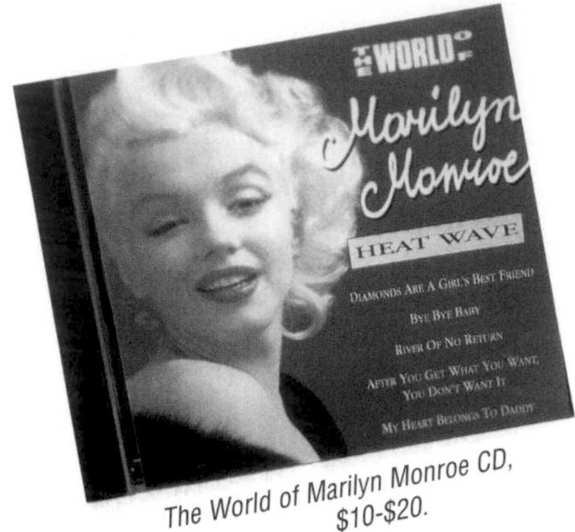

The World of Marilyn Monroe CD, $10-$20.

Marilyn Monroe vs. the Millennium CD, $15-$25.

CD-ROMs

- *Marilyn and André*, 1995. Gazelle Technologies Inc.; available for Mac or MPC; an interactive biography; contains 250 b&w and color photos, various film clips and narration. Originally $54.95. ....$40-$60

DVDs

- *Fox Diamond Collection*, 2001. Set of five movies (*Bus Stop*, *Gentlemen Prefer Blondes*, *The Seven Year Itch*, *How To Marry A Millionaire*, and *There's No Business Like Show Business*) and documentary (*The Final Days*) ....each $12-$15

8-Track Tapes

- *Remember Marilyn*, 1972. TVP Records-8T-TVP-1022; by 20th Century Fox Records; 10 songs. ....$20-$30

Films on Laser Disc

- *All About Eve*, 1987. Fox 1076-80; 138 min., b&w....................$20-$30
- *Asphalt Jungle*, 1987. Voyager CC1126L; 112 min., b&w....................$20-$30
- *Bus Stop*, 1985. Fox 1031-80; 94 min., color....................$20-$30
- *Clash By Night*, 1991. Image 8299TU; 105 min., b&w....................$20-$30
- *Gentlemen Prefer Blondes*, 1988. Fox 1019-80; 92 min., color....................$20-$30
- *How To Marry A Millionaire*, 1988. Fox 1023-80; 96 min., color....................$20-$30

The Diamond Collection DVDs, $12-$15 each.

- *How To Marry A Millionaire*, 1992. Fox 1023-85; 96 min., color. ....$20-$30
- *Love Happy*, 1988. Image 6234RE; 85 min., b&w. ....$20-$30
- *The Misfits*, 1988. Fox; 124 min., b&w. ....$20-$30
- *The Misfits*, 1990. MGM/UA ML101650; 124 min., b&w. ....$20-$30
- *Monkey Business*, 1988. Fox 5140-80; 97 min., b&w. ....$20-$30
- *Niagara*, 1987. Fox 5138-80; 89 min., color. ....$20-$30
- *Remembering Marilyn*, 1989. Image 6526VE (documentary); 60 min., color. ....$20-$30
- *River Of No Return*, 1988. Fox 5139-80; 91 min., color. ....$20-$30
- *Some Like It Hot*, 1988. Fox 4577-80; 121 min., b&w. ....$20-$30
- *Some Like It Hot*, 1989. MGM/UA 103848; 121 min., b&w. ....$20-$30
- *Some Like It Hot*, 1989. Voyager CC1180L; 121 min., b&w.......................$20-$30
- *Some Like It Hot*, 1992. MGM/UA 102699; 121 min., b&w. ....$20-$30
- *Some Like It Hot*, 1992. Voyager CC1180L; 121 min., b&w.......................$20-$30
- *There's No Business Like Show Business*, 1987. Fox 1086-80; 117 min., color. ....$20-$30
- *The Prince and the Showgirl*, 1992. Warner WB11154; 117 min., color. .....$20-$30
- *The Seven Year Itch*, 1987. Fox 1043-80; 105 min., color..........................$20-$30

Remember Marilyn 8-track tape, $20-$30.

Films on Videocassette

- *Home Town Story*, 1994. Diamond Entertainment Corp., No. D-1083; b&w. ....$5-$10
- *Ladies of the Chorus*, 1992. Columbia Tristar Home Video, No. 51013; ISBN-0-8001-1278-4; 61 min., b&w. ....$20-$30
- *Love Happy*, 1988. Republic Pictures Home Video, No. 2467; ISBN-1-55526-025-X; 85 min., b&w. .... $15-$25
- *Marilyn Monroe—Intimate Portrait*, 1996. Lifetime Entertainment Corp., UPX70420; 45 min., color. ....$15-$25
- *Marilyn and the Kennedy's (Say Goodbye To The President)*, 1988. American Video, No. 947; nominated for British Academy Award; 71 min., color. ...$15-$25
- *Marilyn and the Kennedy's (A 30-Year Cover-up Unveiled at Last!)*, 1992. Goodtimes Video, No. 7055; 72 min., color. ....$15-$25
- *The Discovery of Marilyn*, 1991. United American Video, No. 5964; includes David Conover's early photos of Norma Jeane, as well as interviews with Jane Russell, Robert Mitchum, and James Dougherty. ....$10-$20

Home Town Story VHS tape, $5-$10.

A selection of 1987 Fox VHS tapes, $25-$35 each.
(Bus Stop in this series is worth $100-$150.)

- *The Legend of Marilyn Monroe* (narrated by John Houston), 1987. Goodtimes Video, No. 5164; ISBN-1-55510-065-1; 34 min., b&w. .... $15-$25
- *The Legend of Marilyn Monroe* (narrated by John Houston), 1986. Goodtimes Home Video Corp., No. VGT 5164; MM in white fur shot on cover; 34 min., b&w. .... $15-$25
- *The Marilyn Files* (based on Robert Slatzer's book), 1991. Entertainment KVC, No. 11168; ISBN-0-8043-1168-4; 55 min., color. .... $15-$25
- *The Misfits*, 2001. MTSC format - ASIN-6304056877; closed-captioned; Hi-Fi sound; b&w. Originally $9.95. .... $8-$10
- *The Prince and the Showgirl*, 1987. Warner Home Video Inc., No. 11154; 117 min., color. .... $15-$25
- *There's No Business Like Show Business*, 1991. Fox Video Inc., No. 1086; 117 min., color. .... $15-$25

The Discovery of Marilyn VHS tape, $10-$20.

CBS Fox Video Series

- *Bus Stop*, 1987. 20th Century Fox, No. 1031; 94 min., color. (Note: This movie was not licensed for release in the 1992 series of Fox MM movies, because of copyright problems with the writer's family, thus making this a very desirable item. That may change if movie is re-released.) .... $100-$150
- *Gentlemen Prefer Blondes*, 1987. 20th Century Fox, No. 1019; 92 min., color. .... $25-$35
- *How To Marry A Millionaire*, 1987. 20th Century Fox, No. 1023; 96 min., color. .... $25-$35
- *Let's Make Love*, 1987. 20th Century Fox, No. 1141; 118 min., color. .... $25-$35
- *Monkey Business*, 1987. 20th Century Fox, No. 5140; 97 min., b&w. .... $25-$35
- *Niagara*, 1987. 20th Century Fox, No. 5138; 89 min., color. .... $25-$35
- *River of No Return*, 1987. 20th Century Fox, No. 5139; 91 min., color. .... $25-$35
- *Some Like It Hot*, 1987. 20th Century Fox, No. 4577; 122 min., b&w. .... $25-$35
- *The Misfits*, 1987. 20th Century Fox, No. 4584; 125 min., b&w. .... $25-$35
- *The Seven Year Itch*, 1987. 20th Century Fox, No. 1043; 105 min., color. ... $25-$35

Marilyn Monroe 8mm film, 1960s, $80-$120.

Fox Video Series (1992)

- *As Young As You Feel*, 1992. 20th Century Fox, No. 1951; ISBN-0-7939-1951-7; b&w. .... $20-$30
- *Don't Bother To Knock*, 1992. 20th Century Fox, No. 1231; ISBN-0-7939-1231-8; 76 min., b&w. .... $20-$30
- *Gentlemen Prefer Blondes*, 1992. 20th Century Fox, No. 1019; ISBN-0-7939-1019-6; 92 min., color. .... $20-$30
- *How To Marry A Millionaire*, 1992. 20th Century Fox, No. 1023; ISBN-0-7939-1023-4; 96 min., color. .... $20-$30
- *Let's Make It Legal*, 1992. 20th Century Fox, No. 1950; ISBN-0-7939-1950-9; 79 min., b&w. .... $20-$30
- *Let's Make Love*, 1992. 20th Century Fox, No. 1141; ISBN-0-7939-1141-9; 118 min., color. .... $20-$30
- *Love Nest*, 1992. 20th Century Fox, No. 1957; ISBN-0-7939-1957-6; 84 min., b&w. .... $20-$30
- *Monkey Business*, 1992. 20th Century Fox, No.5140; ISBN-0-7939-5140-2; 97 min. , b&w. .... $20-$30
- *Niagara*, 1992. 20th Century Fox, No. 5138; ISBN-0-7939-5138-0; color. ... $20-$30
- *River of No Return*, 1992. 20th Century Fox, No. 5139; ISBN-0-7939-5139-9; 91 min., color. .... $20-$30
- *Something's Got To Give*, 1992. 20th Century Fox, No. 1955; 46 min., color. .... $20-$30

1992 Fox VHS series, $20-$30 each.

Fox "The Marilyn Collection" Series (late-1990s)

- Set of three of Marilyn's movies, including, *The Seven Year Itch*, *Gentlemen Prefer Blondes*, and *Let's Make Love*; total 315 minutes long. ....set $40-$50

Fox Diamond Collection (2001)

- Set of five movies and one documentary. Movies include: *Bus Stop*, *Gentlemen Prefer Blondes*, *The Seven Year Itch*, *How To Marry a Millionaire*, and *There's No Business Like Show Business*. Documentary is titled *The Final Days*." ....each $7-$10

Super-8 film for The Seven Year Itch, $100-$150.

Sound Cards

(All listed are 33 RPM measuring 5½ x 7½ and made in Denmark.)

- *After You Get What You Want*, 1980s. Features photo from *Something's Got To Give*. ....$25-$35
- *Anyone Can See I Love You*, 1980s. Heart-shaped with Marilyn's image on it. ....$25-$35
- *Bye Bye Baby*, 1980s. Features Milton Greene photo of MM. ....$25-$35
- *Diamonds Are A Girl's Best Friend*, 1980s. Features Avedon photo. ....$25-$35
- *My Heart Belongs To Daddy*, 1980s. Features MM in gold lamé dress. ....$25-$35
- *When I Fall In Love*, 1980s. Milton Greene photo on card. ....$25-$35

Super-8 Film Reels

- *Gentleman Prefer Blondes*, 1950s. Boxed; shows selected scenes from the movie in color, with sound. ....$100-$150
- *There's No Business Like Show Business*, 1950s. Boxed ....$100-$150
- *The Seven Year Itch*, 1950s. Boxed ....$100-$150

8mm Movie

- *The Story of Marilyn Monroe by Official Films*, circa 1962. No. A-101; released shortly after MM's death; b&w.. ....$80-$120

Chapter 14

Sheet Music

Although Marilyn Monroe was no Whitney Houston, she was by no means a bad singer. She had received training early on from a half-dozen vocal coaches, most of whom were provided by the studios, and she performed at least one song in 10 of the 29 films she made from 1948 to 1961.

After her 1953 movie, *Gentlemen Prefer Blondes*, some skeptics doubted that it was indeed Marilyn who performed the songs in the film. Fox studio boss Darryl Zanuck promptly offered $10,000 to the first person who could prove that Marilyn did not sing in her own voice in the film. Not a soul ever collected!

Marilyn had a rather soft and sensual singing voice, which matched her soft and sensual persona.

In 1954, while on her honeymoon in Asia with second husband Joe DiMaggio, Marilyn sang to thousands of U.S. troops in Korea. During one of the shows, Marilyn forgot the words to a song. One of the GIs yelled out, "Don't sing and don't talk, just walk!" The crowd roared. Asked later how she held up in the freezing cold of Korea, she replied, "It was the highlight of my life. I swear I didn't feel a thing but good."

Other nonmovie-related Marilyn sheet music has been produced over the years and is very much sought after by collectors. The earliest of these pieces is the song "Marilyn," performed by Ray Anthony and Orchestra for Marilyn at a party thrown by Anthony in her honor pool-side in Brentwood. Mickey Rooney played the drums, and even Lassie attended the party!

Many foreign countries produced sheet music simultaneous with, or within a year or two after, the U.S. releases of her movies. Quite often, the foreign covers used entirely different images of Marilyn. These are equally as sought after by collectors.

As always, condition is a factor in determining the value of sheet music. The most common problems are the occasional pen or pencil signature on the cover by a previous owner. Another common occurence is a rubber stamp stating the store's name and a selling price. Neither of these take a great deal away from the value, unless they are placed on Marilyn's image.

More serious defects are punched holes near the spine from having been bound, significant tears, stains, and badly split or detached spines. These problems have a more drastic impact on the value of the sheet music.

Marilyn performed her very last songs on the evening of May 19, 1962, at Madison Square Garden. The occasion was a birthday party for President John F. Kennedy. The songs were "Happy Birthday" and "Thanks for the Memories."

Movie-Related Sheet Music

(Arranged in order of year of release)

Ladies of the Chorus (1948)
- "Anyone Can See I Love You" ....$100-$200
- "Every Baby Needs a Da Da Daddy" ....$100-$200

A Ticket to Tomahawk (1950)
- "Oh, What a Forward Young Man You Are" ....$100-$200

Niagara (1953)
- "Kiss" ....$30-$50

Gentlemen Prefer Blondes (1953)
- "We're Just Two Little Girls from Little Rock" ....$25-$45
- "Bye Bye Baby" ....$25-$45
- "Diamonds Are a Girl's Best Friend" ....$25-$45
- "When Love Goes Wrong" ....$25-$45
- "Ain't There Anyone Here for Love ....$25-$45

Note: The last two have different cover graphics than the rest of the score.

River of No Return (1954)
- "River of No Return" ....$25-$45
- "I'm Going to File My Claim" ....$25-$45
- "One Silver Dollar" ....$25-$45
- "Down in the Meadow" ....$25-$45

There's No Business Like Show Business (1954)
- "If You Believe" ....$20-$30
- "Let's Have Another Cup of Coffee ....$20-$30
- "After You Get What You Want (You Don't Want It)" ....$20-$30
- "Heat Wave" ....$20-$30
- "Lazy" ....$20-$30
- "There's No Business Like Show Business" ....$20-$30
- "A Man Chases a Girl" ....$20-$30
- "A Sailor's Not a Sailor" ....$20-$30
- "When the Midnight Choo-Choo Leaves" ....$20-$30

Note: The above sheet music features a very small rendition of Marilyn on the cover and is generally worth less to collectors because of this.

The Seven Year Itch (1955)
- "The Girl Upstairs" ....$35-$50

Bus Stop (1956)
- "That Old Black Magic" ....$30-$50
- "The Bus Stop Song" ....$30-$50

The Prince and the Showgirl (1957)
- "I Found a Dream" ....$60-$100

Some Like It Hot (1959)
- "I'm Through with Love" ....$50-$80
- "I Wanna Be Loved By You" ....$50-$80
- "Running Wild" ....$50-$80

Australian sheet music for Niagara, $30-$50.

A selection of U.S. and foreign sheet music for Gentlemen Prefer Blondes, $25-$45 each.

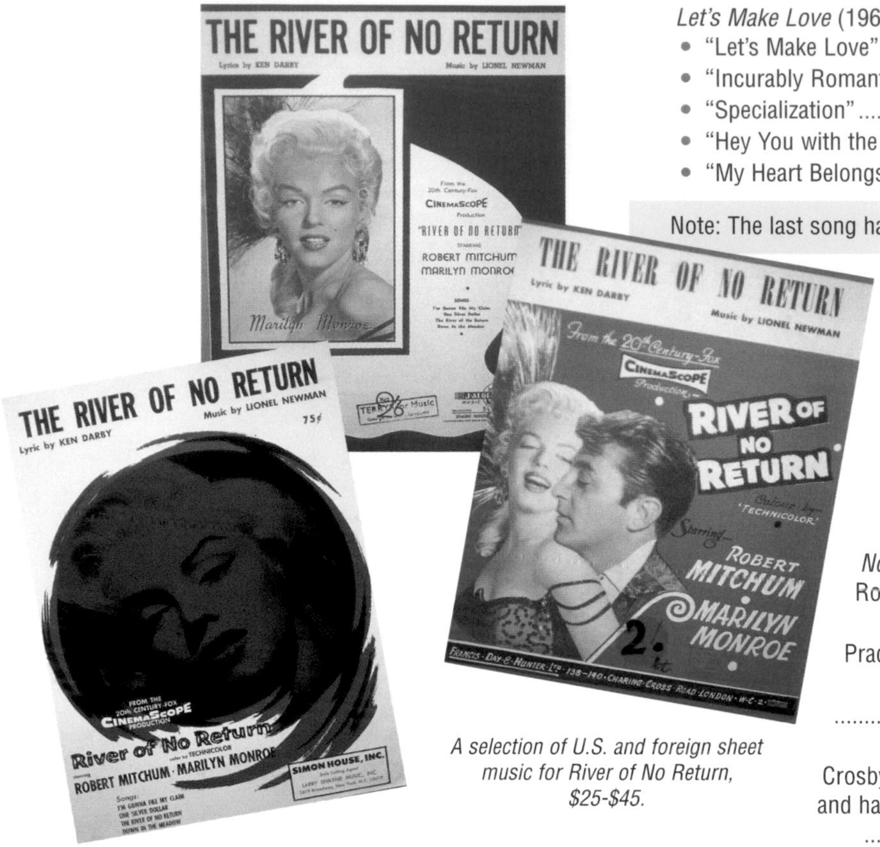

A selection of U.S. and foreign sheet music for River of No Return, $25-$45.

Let's Make Love (1960)

- "Let's Make Love" .... $20-$40
- "Incurably Romantic" .... $20-$40
- "Specialization" .... $20-$40
- "Hey You with the Crazy Eyes" .... $20-$40
- "My Heart Belongs to Daddy" .... $30-$50

Note: The last song has a different cover than the rest, thus the higher price.

The Misfits (1961)

- Theme Song .... $20-$35

Miscellaneous Marilyn Sheet Music

- "Canto Del Niagara," circa 1954. Italian. .... $25-$45
- "Goodbye Norma Jean," 1976. From the movie *Norma Jean Wants to be a Movie Star*, starring Misty Rowe. .... $8-$15
- "Mamba a La Marilyn Monroe," 1954. By Perez Prado. .... $25-$35
- "Marilyn," 1952. By Ervin Drake and Jim Shirl. .... $75-$125
- "Oh Baby Mine I Get So Lonely," 1954. Sung by Bing Crosby and The Four Nights, this is the New Zealand release and has MM pictured prominently on the front of the score. .... $60-$80
- "Old Forgotten Lane," circa 1950. Dedicated to MM; words by Mary Hale Woolsey; music by Neil Moret and George Date; MM's photo on front. .... $75-$125
- "Sentimental Rhapsody," 1950s. From MM's film, *How To Marry A Millionaire*, featuring MM, Betty Grable, and Lauren Bacall on the cover; Italian. .... $80-$100
- "The Rock and Roll Waltz," 1955. British sheet music for a song Kay Starr sang; with a photo cover of various performers, including MM, dancing on stage. .... $60-$80

Note: More modern scores are generally worth $5-$10. The vintage foreign releases are generally worth one-quarter more than the U.S. releases.

Sheet music for There's No Business Like Show Business, $20-$30.

The Seven Year Itch sheet music, $35-$50.

Sheet music for The Prince and the Showgirl, $60-$100.

U.S. and foreign sheet music for Bus Stop (at left), $30-$50.

Marilyn, by Drake and Shirl, 1952, $75-$125.

Oh Baby Mine I Get So Lonely (New Zealand), $60-$80.

Canto Del Niagara (Italy), $25-$45.

U.S. and Italian sheet music for Some Like It Hot (at left), $50-$80.

Chapter 15

Stamps and Related Collectibles

Beginning in the early 1970s, countries in the Caribbean, as well as Africa, began producing stamps in honor of Marilyn. However, production of stamps carrying Marilyn's image really didn't catch on until the early 1990s.

Since then, several countries have gotten on the bandwagon and have produced single stamps, sheetlets, and entire sheets of Marilyn stamps. These have been distributed almost solely by the International Collector's Society, based in the Eastern United States.

In 1995, the U.S. Postal Service decided to produce a stamp in honor of Marilyn Monroe. A painting of Marilyn by Michael Deas was selected to grace the stamp, and featured a side profile of her dressed in the famous gold lamé gown.

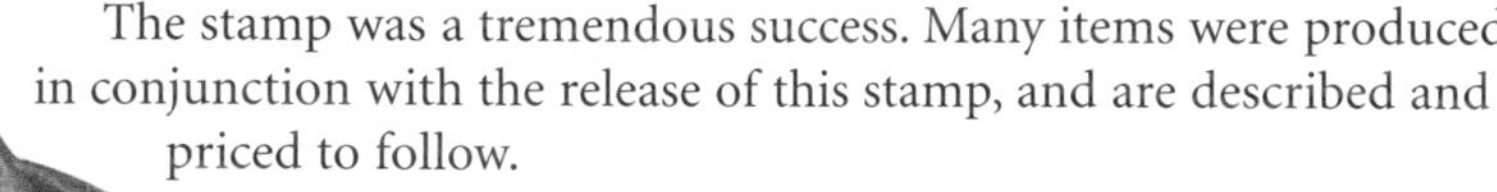

The stamp was a tremendous success. Many items were produced in conjunction with the release of this stamp, and are described and priced to follow.

Stamps

(Arranged alphabetically by country.)

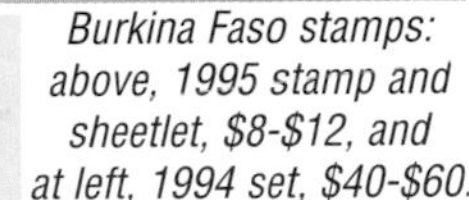

Burkina Faso stamps: above, 1995 stamp and sheetlet, $8-$12, and at left, 1994 set, $40-$60.

- Antigua and Barbuda, May 11, 1987. Single stamp; fourth stamp ever issued featuring MM. Face value of $9. ......$10-12
- Antigua and Barbuda, 1990. Single stamp, which reads, "Marilyn Monroe 1926-1962." Face value of 30¢ ......$8-$10
- Burkina Faso (Africa), 1994. Three single stamp-sheetlets featuring MM on insert and other stars on the sheet and an additional stamp/sheetlet all on Marilyn. Came as a set. ......$40-$60
- Burkina Faso (Africa), 1995. Set of two silver and 23-karat gold foil stamps inserted into two sheets; one shows Dean Martin and space ships and the other shows Frank Sinatra, a rocket, three images of MM and one of John F. Kennedy. Face value of 3000*f*. ......each $15-$20
- Burkina Faso (Africa), Sept. 1995. MM leaning on a car on the sheetlet and is titled, "Entertainment Series." ......$20-$35
- Burkina Faso (Africa), 1995. Single stamp inserted on sheetlet featuring two images of MM and one of a train on the sheetlet, and two images of MM on the stamp; measures 4⅞ x 3¾. Face value of 1500*f*. ......$8-$12
- Burkina Faso (Africa), 1995. Set of two sheetlets featuring numerous stars with a single stamp insert featuring two artists' renditions of MM; each measures 5 5/16 x 3 11/16. Face value of 750*f*. ......each $8-$12
- Batum, 1995. A sheetlet consisting of two stamps, one of Elvis and one of Marilyn, and another sheetlet featuring an additional two stamps of other stars.
  - Two-stamp sheetlet. ......$8-$10
  - Four-stamp sheetlet. ......$10-$15
- Congo Republic, 1971. Single stamp and the second ever issued on MM...$40-$50
- Dominica, Dec. 1994. Nine-stamp sheetlet and two single-stamp sheetlets with the stamps inserted. Face value of 90¢ (single) and $6 (sheet).
  - Singles. ......$7-$9
  - Sheets. ......$12-$15
- Fujaira, 1972. Sheet of 20 movie star postage stamps, including MM, Jean Harlow, Jayne Mansfield, James Dean, Sharon Tate, Vivien Leigh, Clark Gable, Martine Carol (Lola Montes), Rudolph Valentino, etc., each with color art of a star and a b&w scene from one of their films. ......$15-$20
- Gambia, 1992. Nine-stamp sheetlet entitled, "Famous Entertainers"; stamps read, "Marilyn Monroe 1926-1962" and measure 4 7/16 x 6¼. Face value of D3. ......$9-$12
- Gambia, 1995. One nine-stamp sheetlet and two single stamps inserted on each of two different sheetlets. Face value of D4 (single stamp within sheet) and D25 (each single-stamp sheetlet).
  - Sheet of nine......$20-$30
  - Each of two single sheets......$5-$8
- Grenada, 1995. Sheet of 16 stamps with one large image of MM on the right side of the sheet, styled after the U.S. sheet of Marilyn stamps; titled, "Hollywood Legends"; limited and numbered edition of 50,000. Face value of 75¢ each......$15-$20
- Grenada, Sept. 1995. MM on one stamp; also featured are Tom Cruise, Charlie Chaplin, Shirley Temple, Spencer Tracy, Katherine Hepburn, John Wayne, and Marlon Brando; celebrates the 100th birthday of cinema. Face value of $1 each......$15-$20

Two different sheets of Gambia stamps: at left, $9-$12, and above, $20-$30.

1995 nine-stamp sheet from Guyana, $16-$20.

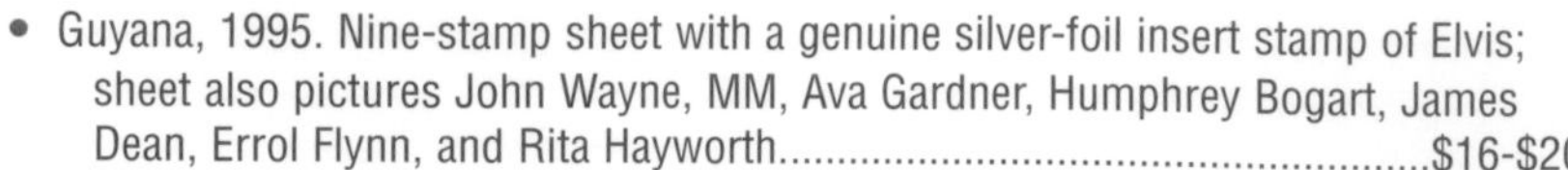

- Guyana, 1995. Nine-stamp sheet with a genuine silver-foil insert stamp of Elvis; sheet also pictures John Wayne, MM, Ava Gardner, Humphrey Bogart, James Dean, Errol Flynn, and Rita Hayworth..$16-$20
- Hungary, 1994. MM's image among two soccer players; Hungary salutes the U.S. Face value of 19Ft...$5-$8
- Madagascar, 1994. Sheet of six stamps, two of which are MM and entitled, "Show Must Go On." Face value of 140 Fmg. ....$10-$15
- Madagascar, 1995. Set of three stamps celebrating the 69th anniversary of Madagascar; represents three of MM's films, *Niagara*, *Some Like It Hot,* and *Gentleman Prefer Blondes*; measure 5⅞ x 3¼. Face values of 100, 550, 5000 Fmg, respectively. ....each $10-$12
- Madagascar, 1995. Sheetlet with a single-stamp insert featuring several well-done artists' renditions of MM; measures 3 x 4. Face value of 10000 Fmg.........$8-$12
- Mali, July 27, 1970. First stamp on Marilyn ever issued; celebrates the discovery of the motion picture machine by the Lamére Brothers; features MM, Jean Harlow, and the brothers. ....$45-$55
- Mali, 1994. Single stamp inserted on a sheet; came perforated or unperforated. Face value of 225*f*. ....$15-$20
- Mongolia, 1995. Sheet of nine color stamps entitled "Cinema"; great artwork and colors; Face value graduates from 60 to 350 in Mongolian currency on nine stamps...$15-$20
- Mongolia, 1995. Sheetlet with single-stamp insert featuring artists' rendition of MM on stamp from *Niagara* and Marilyn's nude image on the sheetlet with flames and Niagara Falls entitled "Marilyn Monroe dans 'Niagara'"; measures 5 11/16 x 4½. Face value of 300..$8-$12
- Mongolia, 1995. Sheetlet with single-stamp insert featuring three artists' renditions of MM and of a cruise ship; measures 5 5/16 x 3½. Face value of 300. ....$8-$12

St. Tome E Principe stamps, $10-$20.

St. Vincent stamps, $10-$15.

Sheet of 20 U.S. stamps issued June 1, 1995, $7-$9.

- Mongolia, 1995. Sheetlet with single-stamp insert entitled, "Marilyn Monroe 'Lifetime'"; features three artists' renditions of MM on sheetlet and one on stamp; shows MM as a baby on the sheetlet; measures $5\frac{1}{4}$ x $4\frac{2}{16}$. Face value of 300. ....$8-$12
- Marshall Islands, 1995. Sheet of 12 stamps. ....$12-$15
- Montserrat, 1995. Sheet of nine stamps featuring various artists' renditions of MM, each stamp says "100 Years of Movies" and "Marilyn Monroe 1926-1962"; measures 5 x $6\frac{1}{2}$. Face value of $1.15. ....$15-$20
- Montserrat, 1995. Sheet featuring artist's rendition of MM and Elvis in embrace; entitled "100 Years of Movies" and gives birth and death dates for both of them; measures 4 x $5\frac{3}{16}$. Face value of $6 ....$15-$20
- Republique Centraficaine, 1995. One stamp inserted on sheet that features three images of MM, one of John Kennedy and several space vehicles. Face value of 2000*f*. ....$16-$20
- Republique Centraficaine, 1995. Single-stamp sheetlet with MM and the new Gyron car; measures 3 x 4.. ....$6-$10
- Republique Centraficaine, 1997. Sheet of nine MM stamps, all different. ....$10-$20
- Republique Du T Chad, date unknown. Sheet of nine stamps, all different. Face value of 500*f* each. ....$10-$20
- Sao Tome e Principe, Jan. 12, 1994. Sheet of eight stamps featuring Elvis, MM, Bette Davis, Humphrey Bogart, James Dean, John Lennon, and Audrey Hepburn; titled "Happy Birthday Elvis." Face value of Db10. ....$16-$20
- Sao Tome e Principe, Jan. 12, 1994. Single stamp of MM inserted in a sheetlet. ....$5-$9
- Sao Tome e Principe, Jan. 12, 1994. Sheet of nine stamps, all of MM with just so-so artistry; measures $4\frac{15}{16}$ x $7\frac{15}{16}$. Face value of Db10. ....$10-$20
- Republique Niger, 1998. MM and the Eiffel Tower on stamp inset and reads Evenements du 20eme siecle 1920-1929. ....$10-$20
- St. Tome E Principe, Jan. 12, 1994. Sheet of eight stamps featuring Elvis, MM, Bette Davis, Bogart, James Dean, John Lennon, and Audrey Hepburn; titled "Happy Birthday Elvis." Face value of Db10. ....$16-$20

1992 nine-stamp sheet from Tanzania, $8-$12.

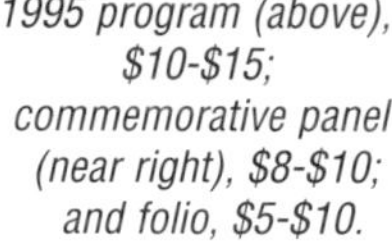
1995 program (above), $10-$15; commemorative panel (near right), $8-$10; and folio, $5-$10.

- St. Tome E Principe, Jan. 12, 1994. Single stamp of MM inserted onto a sheetlet. ....$5-$9
- St. Tome E Principe, Jan. 12, 1994. Sheet of nine stamps, all of MM with just so-so artistry; measures $4\frac{15}{16}$ x $7\frac{15}{16}$. Face value of Db10. ....$10-$20
- St. Vincent, 1994. Sheet of nine Marilyn stamps. Face value of $1. ....$10-$15
- Tanzania, 1991. Single stamp inserted on sheetlet measuring 3 x 4½. Face value of 500/-. ....$10-$15
- Tanzania, 1992. Nine-stamp sheet measuring 5½ x 7. Face value of 75/-. ....$8-$12
- Touva, 1990s. One-sheet of 10 stamps with MM's image occupying 1½. Many different face values.........................$10-$20
- Touva, 1995. Two different two-stamp sheetlets, each featuring one stamp of MM and one of other stars; titled, "Hollywood Stars." Face value of 1800. ....each sheetlet $5-$10
- Touva, May 1996. Sheet of six MM stamps, plus one single stamp of MM.
  - Sheet ....$10-$15
  - Single ....$5-$7
- United States, June 1, 1995. Single or sheet of 20 MM stamps. Face value of 32¢.
  - Single...32¢
  - Sheet ....$7-$9

Stamp-Related Items (1995 Releases)

- Marilyn Stamp Program ....$10-$15
- Marilyn Commemorative Panel with four stamps..........................$8-$10
- Marilyn Stamp Folio...$5-$10
- 22nd Postal Guide with MM on the cover (paperback.) ....$12-$15
- Marilyn Stamp Pin with gold metal edging.....................................$5-$8
- Marilyn Stamp Magnet ....$5-$8
- Marilyn Stamp Key Chain ....$5-$8
- Marilyn Stamp Money Clip ....$9-$12
- Marilyn Stamp Paperweight on a marble base. ....$12-$15

A selection of first day of issue cancellation cachets, 1995, $6-$8.

- Marilyn Stamp T-Shirt .... $15-$30
- Marilyn Stamp Beach Towel .... $20-$30
- Marilyn Stamp First-Day Cover with Universal City postmark. .... $2-$5
- Marilyn Stamp Poster issued in two styles. .... each $20-$40
- Marilyn Stamp Placemat. MM stamp one of several shown; displayed on counter at post office.. $15-$25
- Marilyn Stamp First Day of Issue Cancellation Cachet. Set of five standard-size envelopes with special artwork in color on silk; produced by Colorano Co .... $25-$35
- Marilyn Stamp First Day of Issue Cancellation Cachet. Single standard envelope with special artwork in color on silk, produced by Colorano Co. .... $6-$8
- Marilyn Stamp First Day of Issue Cancellation Cachet. Single standard envelope with special artwork printed in sepia-tone by Washington Press .... $6-$8
- Marilyn Stamp First Day of Issue Cancellation Cachet. Single standard envelope with sepia tone artwork of MM by Artcraft; titled "Legend of Hollywood"; stamped Universal Studios, Hollywood. .... $6-$8
- Marilyn Stamp First Day of Issue Cancellation Cachet. Single standard envelope with four stamps affixed; color painting of MM titled "Diamonds (with a diamond symbol in place of word) are a girl's best friend"; stamped Universal Studios, Hollywood.. $6-$8

Chapter 16

To the Highest Bidder

Christie's Sells Marilyn's Personal Property

When Marilyn Monroe died in 1962, she willed most all of her personal possessions to her friend and famed acting coach, Lee Strassburg, and to his wife, Paula. Marilyn had attended Strassburg's Acting Studio in New York City in the mid-1950s.

All of these items were packed up in Brentwood, California, and shipped to New York City, where they were kept in storage until 1999, when Strassburg's second wife, Anna, decided to sell them at auction. Though it is said that not all of the items were sold, a lion's share of them were. The auction was a veritable time capsule of Marilyn's life. Everything from her costume jewelry to her undergarments was auctioned. The irony of the whole thing was that Marilyn herself was about the furthest thing from a "material girl" that one could get. Indeed, she thought very little of material possessions, simply liking to lounge around the house in a blouse and blue jeans. She preferred to not wear any jewelry at all.

It so happened that just prior to the auction, I had two new books on Marilyn Monroe memorabilia that had just been released. I was asked by the PAX TV network and by MSNBC to fly to New York to be interviewed about the auction. The hotel that my wife and I stayed in was just a few blocks from Christie's. I had the opportunity to view all of the items to be sold on several different occasions. It seemed surreal as I walked along and viewed all of these personal possessions of Marilyn's. Marilyn had seemed almost like a mythical, larger than life figure, previously, but somehow seemed so much more real to me now. My wife and I had tickets to the first day's evening auction, so we witnessed the sale of the famous "Happy Birthday" dress, as well as many more of the highlighted items. When the final hammer dropped, and the auction had ended, more than $13.45 million worth of merchandise was sold.

As a fan and collector of Marilyn Monroe, I could not help but be saddened by the fact that this time capsule of Marilyn's life could not have been kept together and perhaps displayed at a museum in her honor. Marilyn has been called the 20th century's version of Aphrodite, or a modern-day Cleopatra. How wonderful it would be to have such personal memorabilia from the lives of the aforementioned people. We had that chance with Marilyn, but we have lost it.

Perhaps, over time, some of the winning bidders will see to it that some of the more special items will find their way to museums, such as the Smithsonian. That is my hope.

The items listed to follow are the top 100 sellers at Christie's special Marilyn Monroe auction on Oct. 27 and 28, 1999. The auction was titled, "The Personal Property of Marilyn Monroe." The prices listed are prices realized rounded to the nearest dollar and do not include the buyer's premium. There were a total of 576 lots sold in the two-day auction.

Descriptions of the items used herein are with the expressed permission of Christie's New York and are listed from the highest price realized on down.

Author Clark Kidder being interviewed by John Burke for PAX TV on the night of the auction.

Lot No. 55

- The famous flesh-colored silk soufflé gauze dress, which was imported from France and designed by Jean Louis especially for Marilyn for her appearance at Madison Square Garden on May 19, 1962, to sing "Happy Birthday" to President John F. Kennedy. More than 6,000 beads were used, and the process took more than a month. Originally $12,000. ....$1,267,500

Lot No. 10

- Platinum eternity band from Marilyn's 1954 wedding to Joe DiMaggio, set with 35 baguette-cut diamonds (one diamond is missing). $772,500

Lot No. 21

- White lacquered baby grand piano of early 20th century vintage and an unknown American manufacturer that originally belonged to MM's mother, Gladys, and was sold after Gladys was institionalized. Marilyn searched for years to find the piano and buy it back. Her sentimental attachment to the instrument, with its square tapering legs and feet with casters, is well documented in Marilyn's 1974 book, *My Story*, in the first chapter entitled, "How I Rescued A White Piano." $662,500

Lot No. 310

- A five-drawer black traveling case containing the following assortment of makeup: three Max Factor lipsticks; one highlighter and two Elizabeth Arden cream eye shadows in gold tone tubes named "Autumn Smoke" and "Pearly Blue"; two Elizabeth Arden "Eye Stopper" eyeliners, one brown and one black; one cream "Light Green" eye shadow by Leichnr of London; two bottles of Revlon nail polish, one "Cherries a la Mode," the other "Hot Coral," and a bottle of cuticle oil; an eyeliner and a box containing false eyelashes by Glorene of Hollywood; a bottle of black liquid eyeliner; a box of "Hollywood Wings"; two bottles of perfumed lotion from the "Quntess" line by Shisheido, both in their boxes; anita d'Foged "Day Dew" cream makeup and cover-up; two pots of Erno Lazlo makeup; a box of tissue; several matchbooks, including one printed "MMM" and others from restaurants, including Sardi's; two paper fans; three satin purses; two pocket mirrors; and a bottle of smelling salts. $266,500

A view of the outside of the Christie's New York building.

Author Clark Kidder standing next to Marilyn's baby grand piano (Lot No. 21). It sold for $662,500.

Shoes Marilyn wore to a 1956 British film premiere and then while meeting Queen Elizabeth after the screening (Lot No. 19), $33,350.

Lot No. 443

- Six color snapshots taken in Marilyn's home of her dog, "Maf." $222,500

Lot No. 52

- Golden Globe Award with inscription: "Marilyn Monroe World's Favorite Female Star 1961 – Hollywood Foreign Press Association – March 5, 1962." $184,000

Lot No. 41

- A scarlet silk halter dress, featuring full skirts of matching layered scarlet chiffon, worn by MM in a series of photographs to publicize 1957's *The Prince and the Showgirl* and for her well-known sitting for Milton Greene, where she was photographed against a black background. Sold together with a mounted color tearsheet featuring her in the dress. $167,500

Lot No. 51

- A hand-knitted cream wool cardigan with a brown geometric pattern across the center, cuffs, and neck, with matching knitted belt. Worn by MM in 1962 and featured in a series of George Barris photographs taken on the Santa Monica beach in California. $167,500

Lot No. 22

- A 1956 photograph of Marilyn Monroe Miller taken by Cecil Beaton. In one of her most famous sittings, the actress is posed reclining, holding a rose. The photo is signed "Cecil Beaton" on the mat and is accompanied by a two-page signed letter from Beaton in which he details his fascination with and perspective of Marilyn: "Miss Marilyn Monroe calls to mind the bouquet of a fireworks display, eliciting from her awed spectators an open mouthed chorus of ohs and ahs...In her presence, you are startled, then disarmed, by her lack of inhibition. What might at first seem like exhibitionism is yet counterbalanced by a wistful incertitude beneath the surface. If this star is an abandoned spirit, she touchingly looks to her audience for approval. She is strikingly like an overexcited child asked downstairs after tea. The initial shyness over, excitement has now gotten the better of her. She romps, she squeals with delight, she leaps onto the sofa. She puts a flower stem in her mouth, puffing on a daisy as though it were a cigarette. It is an artless, impromptu, high-spirited, infectiously gay performance. It may end in tears. Equally impromptu is her general appearance. This canary blond nymph has been so sufficiently endowed by nature as to pay no attention to the way she looks. Her hair, her nails, her makeup, have a makeshift, spontaneous attractiveness. It is all very contemporary.... Certainly she has no knowledge of the past. Like Giraudoux's Ondine, she is only fifteen years old; and she will never die." Encased in silver, engraved with "To Marilyn Monroe Miller Love Nedda and Joshua Logan." $145,500

Table upon table of Marilyn's clothing filled the auction display areas.

Lot No. 332

- California temporary driver's license, issued Feb. 29, 1956, and signed "Marilyn Monroe." Printed on front and back, on white paper (4 13/16 x 4), and with the following: "Full Name 'Marilyn Monroe'; Address '595 Beverly Glen, Los Angeles 24, Calif.'; Height '5-5¾' Date of Birth '6-1-26'; Weight '120'; Color Eyes 'Blue'; Color Hair 'Blonde'; age '29'; Previous License Number 'W607503'; Year of Expiration '1-9-54'; Married 'No.'" $145,500

Lot No. 29

- Golden Globe Award with inscription, "To Marilyn Monroe *Some Like It Hot* Best Actress in a Comedy 1959 – Hollywood Foreign Press Association – March 8, 1960." $140,000

Lot No. 54

- Program for "Happy Birthday, Mr. President. New York's Birthday Salute to President Kennedy," held at Madison Square Garden, May 19, 1962. Front cover has title between squares of red and blue; to the right, a black and white photograph of President Kennedy. Page 2 lists the "Sponsors," "Committee," and "Patrons" of the event. Page 3 gives the events scheduled for the evening, including appearances by Henry Fonda, Jack Benny, Ella Fitzgerald, Jerome Robbins' Ballet, Jimmy Durante, Bobby Darin, Peter Lawford, and Marilyn Monroe.

  (With): Official invitation to the birthday celebration. Four pages, lightly creased; front with decorative text and page 2 with quote from Mayor Robert F. Wagner.

  (With): Call sheet for the "Salute to the President" (May 19, 1962). Two pages, mimeograph typescript; enumerating 39 events or appearances, Monroe as number 35 "Marilyn Monroe and Stars." Marilyn's copy, with notes in red crayon and pencil on first page, reading "who do you have to be to ask / who do you think you have to be to be disappointment." All three items Marilyn Monroe's personal copies.............$129,000

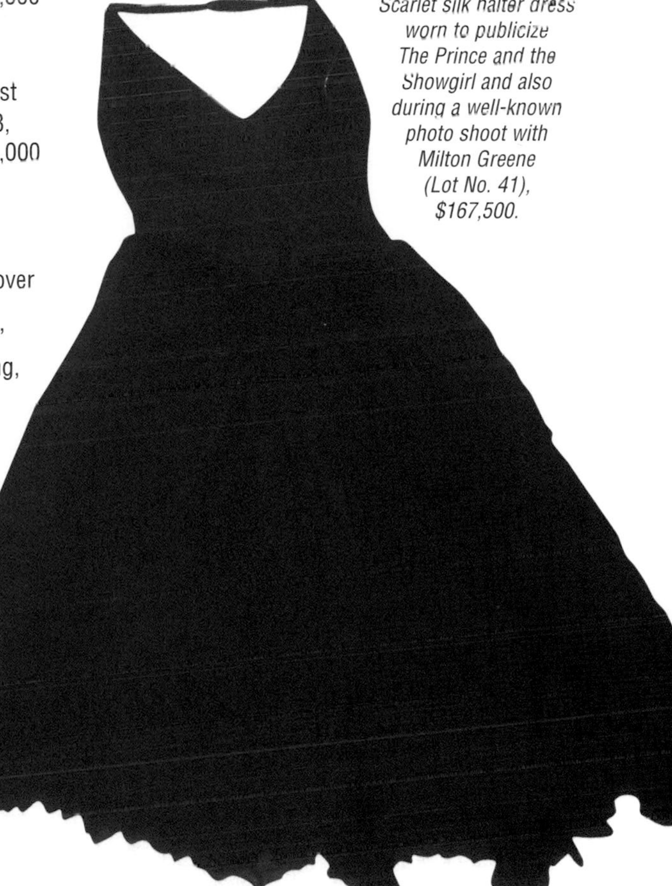

Scarlet silk halter dress worn to publicize The Prince and the Showgirl and also during a well-known photo shoot with Milton Greene (Lot No. 41), $167,500.

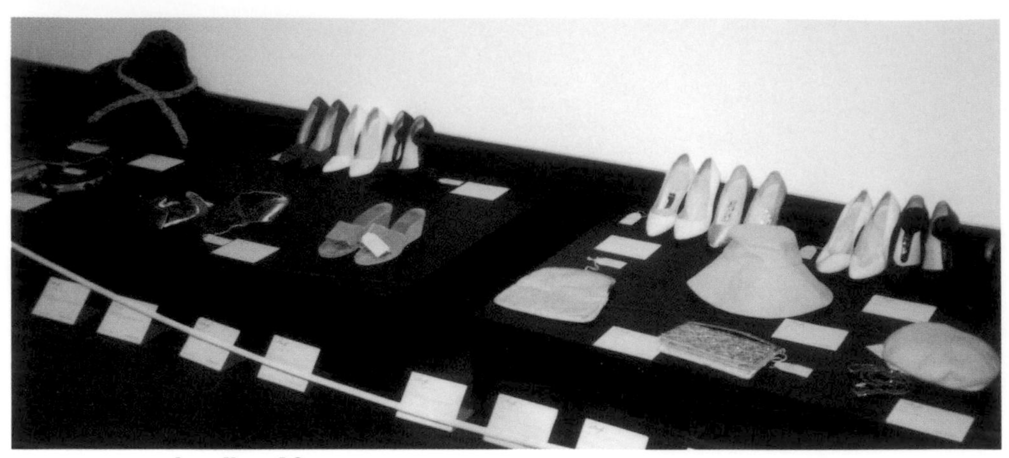

Sometimes accessories really make the outfit work, a rule Marilyn new well judging by the multitude of shoes, bags, hats, jewelry and other accessories displayed during the auction.

Lot No. 12

- Full-length black silk crepe Cecil Chapman evening dress with black bugle beading, believed to have been worn in February 1954 while singing to more than 10,000 soldiers stationed in Korea. Although the dress is floor length, the hem was raised to three-quarter length, held in place with loose stitches and gaffer tape. Not since President Eisenhower's preinaugural visit had there been such a turnout and reception as when Marilyn wowed the troops......................$112,500

Lot No. 38

- Full-length ivory crepe evening sheath with plunging back, halter-neck with shoe-string straps, and embroidery overall with silvered clear bugle beads. Marilyn wore the dress while accompanied by Arthur Miller to the 1959 premiere of *Some Like It Hot*, and to Yves Montand's 1959 one-man-show on Broadway. The dress was also worn in the film, *Let's Make Love*, 1960. Accompanied by a b&w 8 x 10 publicity photo of Marilyn on the set of *Let's Make Love* with Montand. $107,000

Hand-knit cardigan sweater worn by Marilyn in 1962 during a George Barris photo shoot at the Santa Monica beach (Lot No. 51), $167,500.

Lot No. 53

- A backless, full-length emerald green jersey evening dress, embroidered with matching sequins, and decorated with inset waistband. Worn by Marilyn at the Golden Globe ceremonies in Hollywood on March 5, 1962, when accepting her award as 1961's "World's Favorite Female Star." $96,000

Lot No. 355

- Printed 8½ x 11 certificate of conversion to the Jewish faith, signed by Marilyn, Arthur Miller, Rabbi Robert E. Goldburg, and two witnesses. Dated Lewisboro, New York, July 1, 1956. Attractively printed in grey, black, and blue inks, with heading in Hebrew characters ("Hear o Israel The Lord Our God"). Notice in lower right: "Copyright, 1955 by Union of American Hebrew Congregations." With the original printed envelope, which read "Conversion Certificate." The document states that "Marilyn Monroe having sought to join the household of Israel by accepting the religion of Israel and promising to live by its principles and practices was received into the Jewish faith on July 1, 1956, corresponding to the Hebrew date 22nd Tammuz, 5716." $90,500

Lot No. 42

- Pair of tan leather cowgirl boots, worn in 1961's *The Misfits*, Marilyn's last completed film. With embroidered stitching, the boots are stamped with the maker's mark, "Hyer." $85,000

Lot No. 292

- White twilled silk Pucci blouse with Renaissance-inspired jewel pattern in blues, greens, and golds, together with a pair of white leather Ferragamo shoes and a beige beret. $85,000

Lot No. 305

- A pair of transparent Plexiglas shoes with white fox fur straps, labeled "Juel Park, Beverly Hills, California." $85,000

Lot No. 200

- Pair of ear clips, made of five lines of baguette-cut rhinestones, worn by MM to the premiere of *The Seven Year Itch*, June 1, 1955, the premiere of *Rose Tattoo* in 1955, and the Broadway opening of *Middle of the Night*...................... $81,700

Lot No. 24

- A mid-1950s ribbed white ermine coat with deep cape collar, black satin lining, rhinestone cuff button fastener, and "Maximillian, New York" label. Worn Nov. 18, 1957 to the premiere of *Conversation Piece* to see Arthur Miller's sister Joan Copeland perform. $79,500

Lot No. 30

- Sleeveless cocktail dress with coffee-colored chiffon bodice embroidered with black scrolling foliage and matching cropped jacket. Worn by Marilyn opposite Yves Montand in *Let's Make Love*. Also worn to the 1959 presentation of her David Di Donatello Award at the Italian Consulate in New York for her performance in *The Prince and the Showgirl*, 1957. .... $79,500

Lot No. 18

- Black wool crepe Galanos cocktail dress with chiffon overlay of the bare midriff, labeled "Galanos and Bergdorf Goodman, On the Plaza, New York," and tag inscribed, "Miss Monroe, Date: 6/22/56 No Maltide." Worn in July 1956 to a London press call with Laurence Olivier and Arthur Miller to promote *The Prince and the Showgirl*.. $74,000

Lot No. 45

- Sleeveless black silk jersey cocktail dress; elaborately cut, with the irregular neckline threaded with a jersey band. Labeled "Jean Louis" and "No. 4 MARILYN MONROE." Worn in *The Misfits*, 1961. With matching bolero jacket. $72,900

The famous "Happy Birthday, Mr. President" dress (Lot No. 54), $129,000.

Cowgirl boots worn in The Misfits, (Lot No. 42), $85,000.

Lot No. 217

- Full-length sleeveless black silk crepe dress, with slight train (no label)......$68,500

Lot No. 128

- Six dresses: two Ceil Chapman halter-neck dresses, one royal blue, one red; a turquoise sleeveless dress; and three cream dresses...............................$63,000

Lot No. 297

- A group of nightgowns, including: a full-length cream lace negligee appliquéd with rhinestones and pale pink and blue satin leaf motifs; full-length biscuit-colored chiffon nightdress appliquéd with black ribbon flowers and black ribbon ties, decorated with black lace; nightdress of similar style of sheer pink gauze with pale blue nylon ribbon; and a full-length cream silk nightdress with a pattern of appliquéd leaves. $63,000

Lot No. 344

- Four assorted oil portraits of Marilyn done by fans and depicting the actress in various poses and dress...$63,000

Lot No. 478

- Screenplay for *Some Like It Hot* by Billy Wilder. Mimeograph typescript, 156 pages, one page on blue paper representing changes to the script (dated 10/20/58 at top). Bound in black three-ring binder, handwritten label "MM's Script of *Some Like It Hot*" on upper cover. Marilyn's copy, with the name of her character ("Sugar") circled in orange or red crayon on 46 pages, and her notes on six pages in pencil and ink. On page 41, where Sugar is supposed to down a cupful of bourbon, she writes "using drink / censor." On page 43, where the stage directions describe the bass player "Jerry" (Jack Lemmon) leaning forward as Sugar sings her solo, the words "view of Sugar's backfield in motion" is underlined in orange. On page 94, she pencils in new lines for "Joe" (Tony Curtis) and Sugar: "Oh, I'm not going to let this one get away. He's so cute! He collects shells." Carbon typescript synopsis of Act 3 (three pages) and carbon typescript revised shooting schedule, Oct. 7, 1958 (two pages) following the script...$63,000

Lot No. 487

- Two original licenses and the brass tag for Marilyn's dog, "Mafia": New York City, July 18, 1961, and Los Angeles, July 9, 1962, with certificate of rabies vaccination (in all, three pages). With metal dog tag, issued by ASPCA, embossed with tag number, "M40513." Original tag and envelope included with New York license. $63,000

Lot No. 13

- A late-1950s sleeveless ivory satin gown designed by and labeled "Jeanne Lanvin and Castillo"; with front band in a classic leaf pattern, continuing in cascading three-quarter rows...$61,900

Lot No. 365

- Circa 1950s set of gym equipment, including red vinyl weight bench and about 25 exercise weights ranging from 1¼ to 10 pounds.................................$59,700

Lot No. 27

- A group of five 8 x 10 b&w contact sheets from *Some Like It Hot*, co-starring Jack Lemmon and Tony Curtis. With more than 45 images, the shots depict the actors, cast, and crew in various scenes, including on the beach and yacht – both on camera and relaxing between takes...$57,500

Black cocktail dress worn in 1960 film, Let's Make Love, and before that in 1959 for Marilyn's receipt of the David Di Donatello Award at the Italian Consulate in New York (Lot No. 30), $79,500.

Just like peeking into the closet of the legend.

Lot No. 31

- MM's copy of the promptbook for *Let's Make Love*, 1960, evidently used in the filming, with her lines circled in red crayon on many pages, and with many notes in pencil and ink on inside wrappers and throughout. Typescript, 33 pages (of 35, without pages 23 and 25). Bound in yellow wrappers; several pages detached and loosely inserted; some pages with creases and other signs of use; covers worn. Random notes on the front cover include: "The situation," "enjoy," "just work for the situation," and "dream sequence: everything you do – do more / Amanda in a dream." On the inside front cover are a number of interesting inscriptions, including: "using my intelligence / am not a baby any longer," "she's a person / I am playing her," and (possibly referring to her character, Amanda) "For the theatre / She'll do anything." On the inside back cover: "Accept it, summon all strength needed – save myself for other things / don't fight / enjoy when I can," and "Not intense / leads to only tension / relax." Every page of the promptbook is marked up, with Marilyn's lines underlined or bracketed in bright red ink. There are numerous changes in the lines and cues noted, and the margins of each page contain notes in ink and in pencil, evidently made at different times during the filming. At the bottom of page 3, she writes "what a small world / only in theatre"; on page 4, where she is describing the attitudes towards women in the theater, she writes "types like J. Gould," and reminds herself to say certain lines "like a child." National politics are the subject on a note on page 9, where she has written: "What's wrong with the Democratic party letting Nixon win" (the filming took place during the presidential contest between Nixon and Kennedy). At page 8, she writes "Joan of Arc" at the top, and in the margin: "Joan of Arc hears voices – sound the wind makes in Roxbury around the corner of the house – like a human whistle." At the top of page 33 appear several provocative inscriptions: "If I have to kill myself I must do it," and "acting must / occur not be made / use something to make / this possible." On the inside back wrapper, she wrote several telephone numbers, including that of Dr. Greenson, her Beverly Hills psychiatrist. $55,200

Lot No. 324

- Crystal Star (France) – "A Marilyn Monroe L'Academie du Cinema, Paris 31 Mars 1958." $55,200

Faux fur coat with leather trim (Lot No. 168), $27,600.

Set of gym equipment (Lot No. 365), $59,700.

Three-quarter-length ivory silk jersey evening dress with silver bugle beads and low-dipping open back (Lot No. 251), $14,950.

Lot No. 40

- A grey silk halter-style "JAX" jersey dress worn in *Let's Make Love*............$52,900

Lot No. 26

- Marilyn's copy of the script for *Some Like It Hot*, July 18, 1958. Mimeographed typescript, title page, list of characters and the actors playing them, 122 pages. Bound in bright green paper wrappers, stamped "56" on the cover and first page (very slight wear). A number of pages preceding Marilyn's character's first entrance are folded diagonally. With her initials "MMM" in large letters in red crayon on upper cover and repeated on first page; with the name of her character, "Sugar," circled in red crayon on 54 pages. A note on page 91 – "to a child" – written by someone other than Marilyn.......................................$51,750

Lot No. 133

- Pair of unlabled sleeveless boat neck-style lace dresses: one white lace with blue underdress and the other white lace dress with white underdress............$51,750

Lot No. 479

- MM's copy of promptbook for Some Like It Hot, evidently used in the filming, with her lines circled in red crayon on many pages, and with extensive notes in pencil and ink on inside wrappers and throughout. Typescript, 39 pages. Bound in tan wrappers, with ink label on front wrapper: "Marilyn Monroe/Goldwyn Studios/ N.Formosa." Several pages detached and loosely inserted, pages with creases; folds and other signs of use; several with yellowed cellophane tape repairs; covers worn. On the inside front cover Monroe wrote, "What am I doing, not how," "Don't take their tone!" and "The 'save it' method." On the inside back wrapper: "Acting: being private in public / to be brave." On the first page, she wrote a phonetic spelling for the pronunciation of her character's last name, Kowalczyk: "col vol chick." In many places, she has added notes on the action taking place on camera: on one page she adds the direction "going into his berth," on another the instruction "freeze like a bunny," and later, "watching like a cat." A large penciled note at the bottom of scene 35 reads "Soak in a hot tub / on a day like this its lovely." On one page in scene 55, on the yacht, she writes, "all I have to do is to play that moment"; beneath are the notes: "seduction scene," "trust it, enjoy it, be brave," and "champagne." On the following page: "watching him (she's caught up)"; "getting drunk on kisses," and "she kisses him again." $51,750

Lot No. 2

- A pair of scarlet satin stiletto-heeled Ferragamo shoes encrusted with matching rhinestones. $48,300

Lot No. 39

- A black silk jersey cocktail dress worn by Marilyn in the 1960 film *Let's Make Love*. Labeled "JAX" and the paper wardrobe tag inscribed "ENOLA." $48,300

Lot No. 47

- An early 1960s set of two lighters in a fitted velvet case. Signed "Wellington-Thin," the lighters are engraved "Frank Sinatra's Calneva Lodge," the Lake Tahoe resort Sinatra owned. $48,300

Lot No. 138

- An ivory silk jersey dress printed with a pattern of peacock eyes, pleated onto center waistband, labeled "Jean Louis" and inscribed "2MM." Worn to the 1961 celebration party at the start of *The Misfits* filming. $48,300

Lot No. 154

- A blue jersey and a brown striped bikini, a pair of black cotton shorts, and a leopard-skin print bikini bottom...$48,300

Lot No. 373

- Terra cotta bust of Carl Sandberg. $48,300

Galanos cocktail dress worn in London while promoting The Prince and the Showgirl (Lot No. 18), $74,000.

Lot No. 9A

- MM's copy of *The Union Prayerbook For Jewish Worship, Part I* with gilt-lettered "Marilyn Monroe Miller" on front cover and presentation inscription on front free endpaper. "For Marilyn – with all my best wishes and deepest respect. Fondly – Bob". $46,000

Lot No. 25

- Harem costume from December 1958 Richard Avedon photo shoot for *LIFE Magazine*. Besides posing as Jean Harlow, Marlene Dietrich, Lillian Russell, and Clara Bow, Marilyn donned an exotic harem girl's outfit to imitate Theda Bara in *Cleopatra*, with the hope of winning the role that ultimately went to Elizabeth Taylor. The skirt of orange and yellow chiffon scarves is attached to a gold lamé bikini bottom with an ornate belt of embossed gold leather encrusted with amber-colored imitation jewels; gold lamé top designed with snake motif cups. With matching headdress and three imitation gold slave bracelets and four copies of *LIFE*, including the 1962 issue that reprinted the photos...$46,000

Lot No. 156

- Black knitted wool bikini, together with a b&w leaf-pattern cotton bikini. $46,000

Lot No. 209

- A black silk jersey evening stole, trimmed with white fox fur. $46,000

Lot No. 287

- A long-sleeved boat neck-style Pucci dress of printed silk jersey, geometric patterns in greens and pinks, together with matching belt. $46,000

Lot No. 306

- A group of bustiers: black lace with pink underlay, trimmed with a rosebud, padded, labeled "Jantzen, original Curvallue, 36B" with a white lace Basque and padded cups, labeled "Jantzen, original Curvallue, 36B"; black lace Basque, with deep plunge trimmed with black satin bows, with stocking suspenders, and labeled "Warner Original, Merry Widow"; and a strapless black lace over pink underwired zip-front bustier labeled "Lady Marlene, 36C." $46,000

A handmade birthday card by Joseph Krutak that includes the signatures of the cast and crew of Let's Make Love, including Yves Montand (Lot No. 362), $13,800.

Lot No. 320

- Trophy that reads, "World Film Favorite, 1953. The International Press of Hollywood." $46,000

Lot No. 187

- A three-quarter length black silk cocktail dress with bodice and straps of ivory organza, trimmed with an oversized organza bow at the front center, and labeled "Talmack, John Moore, New York." $43,700

Lot No. 221

- Pair of scarlet red satin stiletto heels labeled "Marilyn Miller," together with a pair of Ferragamo red leather stiletto heels. $43,700

Lot No. 334

- Two framed photographs of Marilyn in a black feather boa and black top hat from her famous 1956 "Black Sitting" with photographer Milton Greene. $43,700

Handmade 1962 birthday card by Joseph Krutak with signatures of Wally Cox, Les Berry, and Mickey Shirrard, among many others (Lot No. 363), $14,950.

Lot No. 484

- MM's copy of the script for *The Misfits* by Arthur Miller with the name of her character ("Roslyn") circled on six pages, and with pencil notes on four pages. Mimeograph typescript, title page, and 146 pages; 80 pages on blue paper representing changes to the script (each dated at top). Punched and bound with three brass rivets (title page loose, minor coffee stains to edges of some pages at back). On page 24 is the note: "take it from him"; page 28, "2 Drink," as Roslyn and Isabelle have cocktails in the kitchen, and at the top of page 32, "inner ear music." Next to Roslyn's line, "I suddenly miss my mother" on page 15, she wrote "personalization." With typescript sheets with revisions to script (17 pages). Five pages with Marilyn's notes like: "freedom leaves emptiness" and "I can't answer him." As Roslyn falls asleep she writes, "like lulibay (lullaby)," and at the bottom: "Nothing human is going to help her. She has to find it in herself." $43,700

Lot No. 7

- Three pairs of denim blue jeans, worn by Marilyn as "Kay Weston.". $42,550

Lot No. 37

- A white stole with center panel of white chiffon, trimmed with white fox fur, and labeled "Frederica." Worn to the premiere of *Some Like It Hot*, held at Loew's State Theater on Broadway on March 28, 1959............................ $41,400

Lot No. 206

- A three-quarter-length black velvet "JAX" dress with spaghetti straps......... $40,250

Lot No. 252

- A group of necklaces – one single-row pearl necklace and three imitation pearl necklaces, designed as one graduated necklace of four rows; one uniform bead necklace of two rows; and two single-row necklaces. $40,250

Lot No. 300

- Cream cotton nightshirt embroidered "Marilyn" at the neck in beige silk..... $40,250

Silk jersey dress worn in *Let's Make Love* (Lot No. 40), $52,900.

Lot No. 313

- Plaque that reads, "Photoplay Magazine Presents The New Star Award to Marilyn Monroe For Her Rapid Rise to Stardom In 1952."................................... $40,250

Lot No. 473

- MM's copy of the *Bus Stop* script, with her initials ("MM") in red ink on first page, and with the name of her character ("Cherie") circled in red on each page in which it appears, from her first entrance to the Blue Dragon Café (on page 14). Screenplay by George Axelrod. Final Script. Feb. 27, 1956. Mimeograph title page, 123 pages script, with 27 pages on blue paper representing changes to the script (each dated at top). Bound in medium blue paper wrappers with 20th Century Fox logo, title on spine, stamped with "109" on front wrapper and first page. With Marilyn's line changes, cross-outs, and notes in pencil and ink on 23 pages. $40,250

Lot No. 36

- Rhinestone ear clips, worn to the 1959 *Some Like It Hot* premiere party. $39,100

Lot No. 121

- Two prescription cat-eye style eyeglasses in fabric cases, labeled "Evonaire." $39,100

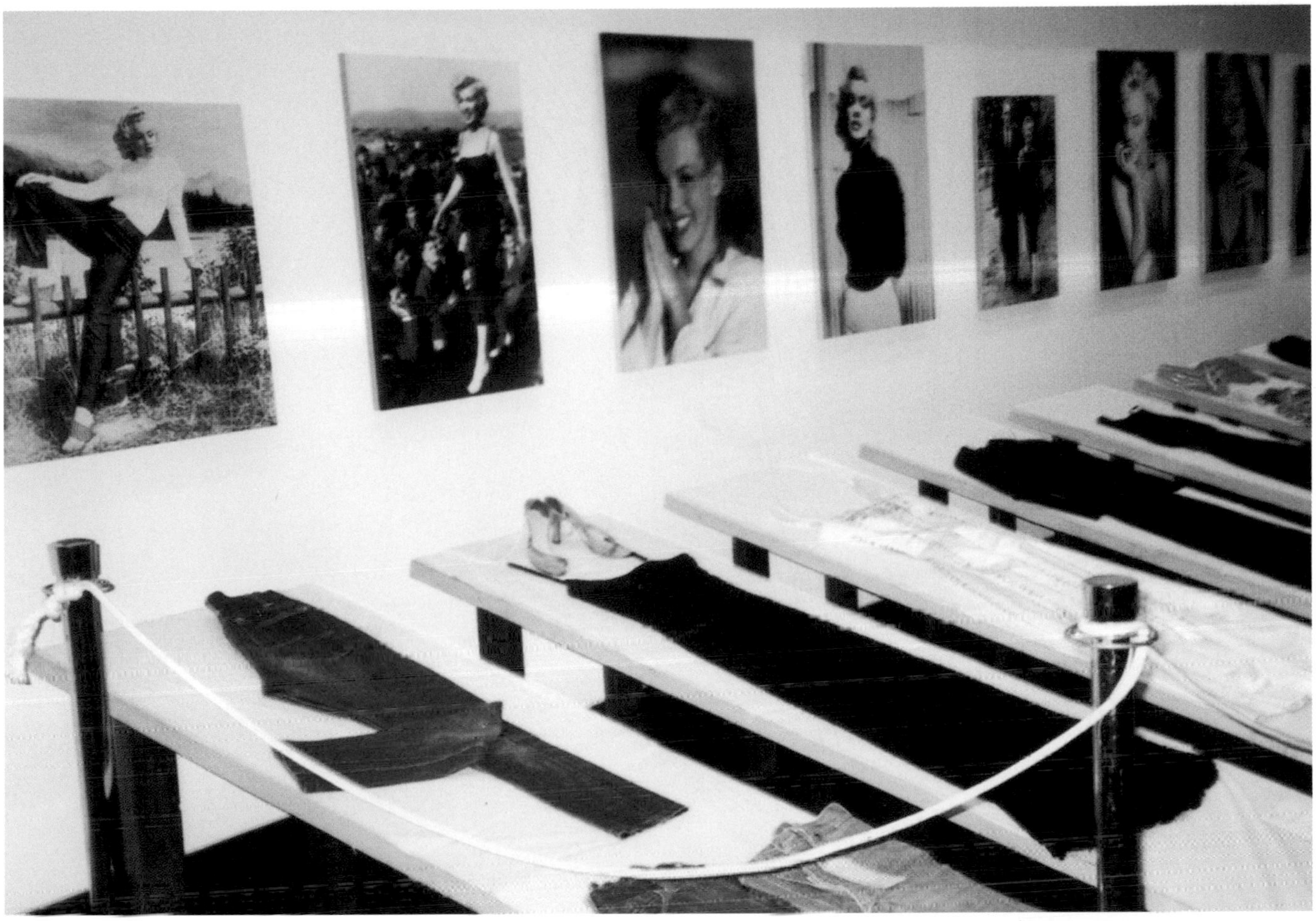

Another angle of the display of clothing sold during the auction.

Lot No. 155

- Summer clothing, including a turquoise printed cotton bikini, shorts and blue polka dot string bikini top, a pair of yellow polka-dot cotton shorts, and a pair of lime green shorts and lime green silk chiffon scarf. $39,100

Lot No. 9

- Marilyn's copy of *The Holy Bible*, with a few pencil markings inside; authorized King James Version; original red leather. $37,950

Lot No. 49

- MM's copy of *Something's Got To Give* script, with numerous markings and notes in pencil on 39 pages. Screenplay by Arnold Schulman. Nov. 22, 1961. Confidentiality notice, mimeographed title page, and 138 pages script. Bound in light green paper wrapper with 20th Century Fox logo, title on spine (one tear front cover). On the blank page facing the title, MM wrote: "she maneuvers, she gets him to chase her – he resents her leaving her husband." On the title page appear several notes and page references to the script and the observation "at one point in the story two women like each other but hate the man." Below, she writes, emphatically, "not a story for MM," and adds, "it's for a man and just any two girls except the first 45 pages." On the same page, she apparently records her reactions to the change of screenwriter: "why was the writer who wrote it let go?" and queries "New Producer, How come?" On page 57, where the stage directions call for Richard and Priscilla to "embrace and kiss passionately," she added: "but mechanically." On page 58, she likens the towering rage of the forsaken Ellen to the emotions expressed in a song from Lerner and Loew's *My Fair Lady*, "I can do without you, or just you wait, Henry Higgins, just you wait." $36,800

Sleeveless cocktail dress and matching jacket worn in The Misfits, 1961 (Lot No. 45), $72,900.

A selection of Marilyn's jewelry.

Late-1950s Lanvin and Castillo ivory satin evening gown (Lot No. 13), $61,900.

Lot No. 164

- A blue and white jersey diamond-pattern coat, silk-lined, and labeled "Women's Haberdashers." $36,800

Lot No. 214

- Two black wool, high-neck, close-fitting three-quarter-length dresses; one possibly worn on the announcement of Marilyn's divorce from Joe DiMaggio on Oct. 6, 1954. .... $36,800

Lot No. 248

- A group of 18 crystal necklaces of various colors, including pink, blue-purple, clear, yellow, and black, of various lengths. $36,800

Lot No. 303

- A group of baby doll nightgowns: one of black chiffon, trimmed with lace and decorated with appliquéd bows, labeled "Juel Park, Beverly Hills, California"; another of pale pink gauze decorated with peach lace and trimmed with pink silk ribbon; and a third of pale pink gauze with frilled hem and sleeves. $36,800

Lot No. 321

- A trophy base that reads, "Presented to Marilyn Monroe In Commemoration of Her Unselfish Service Rendered to the Armed Forces in Korea June 19, 1954, Morningside Park, Post No. 398, Inglewood, Calif." $36,800

Lot No. 326

- Cecil Beaton 9¾ x 9¾ photograph of Marilyn holding a rose. $36,800

Lot No. 499

- Autographed manuscript poem, "A Sorry Song," no date. Two pages, boldly written in pencil on a sheet of paper (discovered folded into a book from Monroe's library). A melancholy lament: "I've got a tear hanging over / my beer that I can't let go. / it(s) too bad / I feel sad / When I got all my life behind me / If I had a little relief / From this grief / Then I could find a drowning / straw to hold on to / its great to be alive / They say I'm lucky to be alive / it's hard to figure out – / when everything I feel – hurts!" $36,800

Lot No. 6

- A pair of earrings, with three varying links of rhinestones, fastened to a rhinestone scroll; worn on March 14, 1954, as Marilyn accepted her *Photoplay Magazine* Award for "Most Popular Film Actress of 1953." $35,650

Lot No. 28
- Hollywood Foreign Press Association "Certificate of Nomination for Golden Globe Award of Merit For Outstanding Achievement Best performance by an Actress in a Musical or Comedy Marilyn Monroe *Some Like It Hot*, 1959." $34,500

Lot No. 189
- Black suede polka-dot Ferragamo shoes; with a small black feather boa.....$34,500

Lot No. 203
- Two pairs Ferragamo stiletto shoes: one pair gold, the other black suede ...$34,500

Lot No. 213
- Two pairs Ferragamo stiletto shoes: one pair black satin with a cluster of circular rhinestones, the other black leather. $34,500

The colors and variety of styles in Marilyn's wardrobe were quite diverse.

Lot No. 235
- Two pair Ferragamo shoes: one pair cutout black suede with mauve lining, the other black suede stilettos. $34,500

Lot No. 307
- A square black-lacquer compact with mirror and a square typed 11-line speech inside, possibly written as Marilyn's acceptance speech for winning the 1961 Golden Globe for "World's Favorite Female Star." Reads: "I'd like to thank you. But, what am I doing here? I would have been here sooner, but I was down in Florida. Fungos (whatever they are) this is a wonderful surprise for me being named most popular in the world. Up until last week I never left Redlands... I'm moved – thrilled." $34,500

Lot No. 347
- Three 20½ x 16¼ framed Jack Cardiff photographs of Marilyn taken in London during the filming of *The Prince and the Showgirl*, 1957. ....$34,500

Lot No. 349
- Seven 6¼ x 9½ b&w photographs (taken on and off-camera) of Marilyn on the set of *The Misfits* with director John Huston, Arthur Miller, and co stars Clark Gable and Montgomery Clift. $34,500

Lot No. 383
- Carved grey stone 20½" female torso on white marble base. $34,500

Lot No. 19
- Gold patina lamé stiletto-heeled mules, labeled "Anello Et Davide, London WC2" and worn Oct. 29, 1956 to premiere the British film, *The Battle of the River Plate*. After the screening, Marilyn met Queen Elizabeth II..............................$33,350

Lot No. 46
- A book by John Huston, Frankie and Johnny, New York: Albert and Charles Boni, 1930. First edition, inscribed by Huston on the title page: "Marilyn dear / all those years ago when you were hardly born I wrote this for you – the perfect Frankie – Johnny (himself) Huston." $33,350

Shoes worn in Korea (Lot No. 11), along with a dress believed to have been worn in Korea (Lot No. 12). The shoes sold for $32,200, and the dress brought $112,500.

Lot No. 11
- Pair of gold leather high-heeled shoes with curved front and ankle straps labeled "The French Room" and worn in February 1954 while entertaining the troops in Korea. $32,200

Lot No. 178
- A black cashmere cardigan, trimmed with a natural Russian sable collar, labeled "Jay Thorpe, New York." $32,200

Marilyn certainly had more than one "little black dress." Above, a selection of black dresses.

Lot No. 191

- A black silk jersey three-quarter-length dress with empire waist and spaghetti straps. $32,200

Lot No. 273

- Two pairs of Ferragamo stilletto heels: one of flesh-colored silk, the other in ivory/beige leather; together with an ivory canvas clutch purse. $32,200

Lot No. 310

- Circa 1950s black leatherette-covered traveling case. $32,200

Lot No. 338

- A circa 1956 brass key with "W.B." emblem on one side and "Welcome to Warner Bros. Studio, the Largest in the World" on the other. $32,200

A 1940s mahogany foot locker Marilyn used in her home (Lot No. 440), $6,900.

Lot No. 414

- A pair of 8¾" "Gorham" sterling silver candlesticks, each with a trumpet-form stem and flaring foot. Together with a pair of three-light 13½" candelabra extension and two companions; two urn form nozzle extensions, filled. $32,200

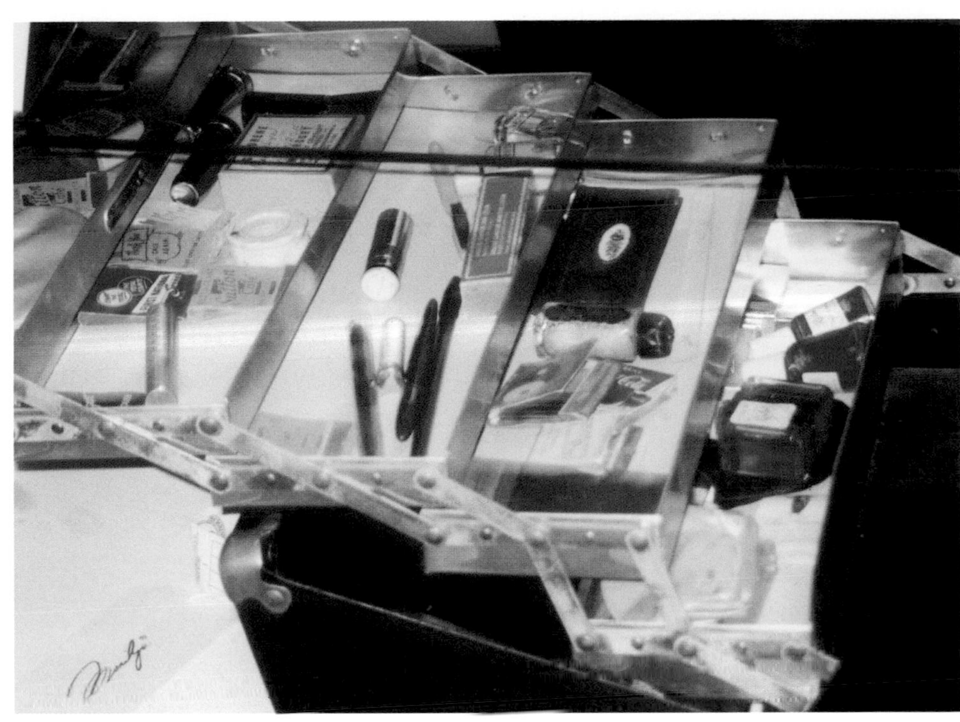

Traveling case and makeup (Lot No. 310), $32,200.

Lot No. 43

- Marilyn's copy of the script for *The Misfits*, 1961, by Arthur Miller with Marilyn's penciled notes on 46 pages of script and on facing blank pages. Revision – March 1960. Mimeographed typescript, title page and 147 pages. Punched and bound with three brass rivets, the different settings ("Ranch House," "Car," "Bar," "Mustanging") marked with alternating white or pink index tabs affixed to certain pages (title page soiled, some margins frayed). With "M.M." on title page and large note "Paula's script" deleted in pencil, the lines of her character "Roslyn" underlined in pink ink and her character's name circled in the same color throughout. At the top of the title, Marilyn wrote: "The effort is made by one's will." On page 6 are several notes, including: "play the situation / don't push it," "when she listens she smiles, when she talks, she doesn't," and "talk differently to him than to her!" On page 8, "plead for understanding," "try to smile a little," and "not to worry how I say it." On page 14, "look straight at Gable – just look don't say anything don't do anything." At the bottom of page 16, "lean back, stretch, unconcerned feminine sex." On page 20, where Isabelle cautions Roslyn about cowboys, "men that are men can't be trusted." On page 37, Roslyn has the line "I didn't want children. Not with him," and on the facing blank, connected by a pencil line, she wrote: "Like with J.D." (possibly a reference to Joe DiMaggio). On page 44, commenting on Roslyn's kissing Gay: "she kisses him because she could say that she's lonely – then when he doesn't seem to respond she's hurt then glad for the interruption."......................$31,050

Lot No. 162

- An fawn silk overcoat with black velvet collar worn in June 1956...............$29,900

Lot No. 194

- A three-quarter-length black silk crepe Ceil Chapman dress with a pattern of black bugle beads and front slit pockets...$29,900

Lot No. 265

- A shocking pink silk jersey dress with jewel-neck and long sleeves, together with a shocking pink Pucci rope belt with beaded tassels...................................$29,900

Lot No. 350

- A blonde wig and hairpiece for *The Misfits* in a marked box.......................$29,900

About the Author

As a specialist in the appraisal of Marilyn Monroe items, Clark Kidder receives calls, letters, and faxes on a daily basis from Marilyn Monroe collectors around the world wanting to purchase, trade, and sell Marilyn memorabilia, or query the value of such items. He is constantly amazed at the number of new and previously unknown items that continue to surface on Marilyn.

Drawing upon his expertise, Kidder is the author of the following Monroe-related books: *Marilyn Monroe UnCovers* (Quon Editions, 1994), *Marilyn Monroe - Cover To Cover* (Krause Publications, 1999), and *Marilyn Monroe Collectibles* (HarperCollins, 1999).

And when he's not immersed in Marilyn, Clark farms 200 acres of land in rural Wisconsin, along with his wife, Linda, and their two sons, Robby and Nathan. He also enjoys genealogy, having traced his Kidder roots back to 1320 in Maresfield, Sussex, England.

Kidder is always open to suggestions on how he can improve his work. If anyone would like to assist with any additions or corrections to the material contained in this book, or for information regarding Marilyn memorabilia, contact Kidder via e-mail at: ckidder@jvlnet.com.

Fan Clubs and Collector Sources

International Fan Clubs

America
None active at the present time, except online.

Australia
Glamour Preferred
c/o Jane Guy
P.O. Box 539
Camberwell, Victoria 3124
(Founded in 1989.)

England
Marilyn Lives Society
c/o Michelle Finn
14 Clifton Square
Corby, Northants NN17 2DB

France
c/o Miss Mary Belzunce
5 Avenue B
Hakeim, 06110 Le Cannet

Germany
Some Like It Hot Fan Club
c/o Marina Muller
Link St. 2
31134 Hildesheim

Fan Clubs and Collector Sources

Collectible-Related Publications

Antiques & Collecting Hobbies Magazine
1006 S. Michigan Ave.
Chicago, IL 60650
Phone: (312) 939-4767
Fax: (312) 939-0053
Features all types of collectibles and has very nice articles. Lots of color.

Antique Trader Weekly
100 Bryant St.
Dubuque, IA 52003
Phone: (319) 588-2073
Fax: (800) 531-0880
Canada/Foreign Fax: (319) 588-0888
Lists auctions by region and features great articles, along with classified ads. Newspaper format.

Collectible Madness
483 Federal Road
Brookfield, CT 06804
Phone: (203) 740-9472 or (800) 784-7796
Catalog issued on TV and movie collectibles.

Collecting Hollywood
2401 Broad St.
Chattanooga, TN 37408
Fax: (423) 265-5506
Features poster- and film-related items for sale and has very nice articles. Items are consignable.

Country Accents *COLLECTIBLES Magazine*
P.O. Box 336
Mount Morris, IL 61054-7535
Published quarterly. Features lots of color and very nice articles on a wide variety of collectibles.

eBay Auction Online
This is an Internet auction where you can buy and sell any number of MM items and anything else you can imagine!

Manion's International Auction House
P.O. Box 12214
Kansas City, MO 66112
Phone: (913) 299-6692
Fax: (913) 299-6792
E-mail: collecting@manions.com
Catalogs priced reasonably and cover a wide variety of collectible items in both U.S. and foreign categories.

Movie Collector's World
Box 309-P
Fraser, MI 48026
Phone: (800) 273-6883 for VISA/MasterCard orders
Web site: www.mcwonline.com
Features nice articles and movie-related collectibles wanted and/or for sale. Classifieds as well.

Paper Collector's Marketplace
470 Main St.
P.O. Box 128
Scandinavia, WI 54977
Phone: (715) 467-2379
Fax: (715) 467-2243
Wide variety of paper and related items wanted and for sale. Classifieds.

Paper Pile Enterprises
P.O. Box 337
San Anselmo, CA 94979-0337
Phone: (415) 454-5552
Fax: (415) 454-2947
Various collectibles offered in categories.

Postcard Collector
P.O. Box 1050
Dubuque, IA 52004-1050
Phone: (800) 482-7151
Fax: (800) 531 0000
E-mail: traderpubs@aol.com
Various collectibles offered with an emphasis on postcards.

Profiles In History
345 N. Maple Drive
Suite 202
Beverly Hills, CA 90210
Phone: (800) 942-8856
Fax: (310) 859-3842
Periodic Hollywood memorabilia auctions.

Southern Antiques
P.O. Drawer 1107
Decatur, GA 30031-1107
Published monthly and covers various collectibles.

Startifacts
3101 E. Hennepin Ave.
Minneapolis, MN 55413
Phone: (612) 331-6454
Fax: (612) 331-8083
E-mail: startifacts@earthlink.net
Feature authentic costumes and Hollywood memorabilia.

The Paper and Advertising Collector
P.O. Box 500
Mount Joy, PA 17552
Phone: (717) 653-4300
Published monthly and features a wide variety of collectible items.

Trap Door Spider
531 S. Prescott
Memphis, TN 38111

Warman's Today's Collector
Krause Publications
700 E. State St.
Iola, WI 54990-0001
Phone: (800) 258-0929 (Subscription Services)
Covers the gamut of collectibles items in all categories. Has great articles and classifieds.

Index

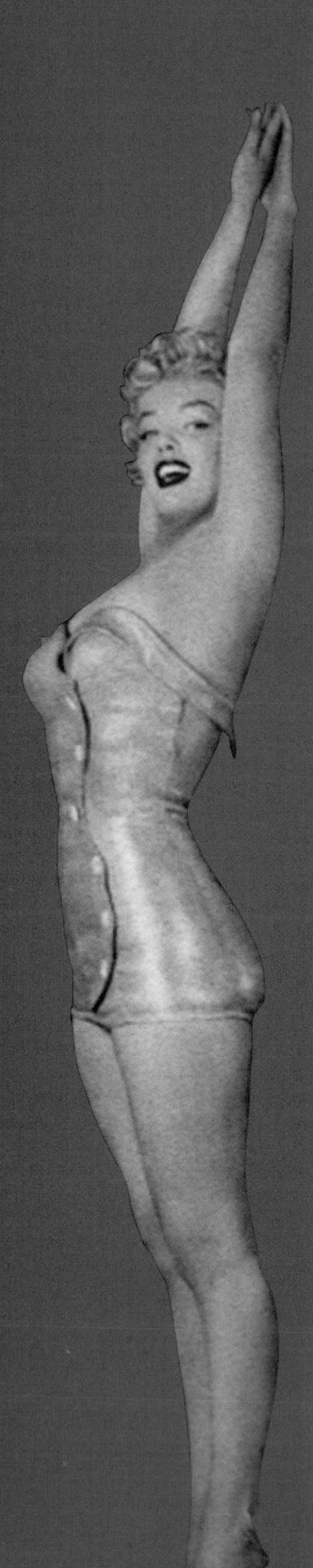